Berserkiley Farms Inc Ltd et Cie 1/81
RO Rev. Kilroy Zukas, Eq.
Memorial Bequest

POLITICAL POWER
AND PERSONAL FREEDOM

BOOKS BY SIDNEY HOOK

Metaphysics of Pragmatism

Towards the Understanding of Karl Marx

From Hegel to Marx

John Dewey: an Intellectual Portrait

Reason, Social Myths and Democracy

The Hero in History: a Study in Limitation and Possibility

Education for Modern Man

Heresy, Yes—Conspiracy, No!

Marx and the Marxists: the Ambiguous Legacy

Common Sense and the Fifth Amendment

Political Power and Personal Freedom

Editor—John Dewey: Philosopher of Science and Freedom

Editor (With H. M. Kallen)—American Philosophy Today and Tomorrow

Editor (with M. Konvitz)—Freedom and Experience

Editor—American Philosophers at Work: the Philosophic Scene in the United States

Editor—Science and Freedom in the Age of Modern Science

Editor—Philosophy, Psychoanalysis and Scientific Method

Political Power and Personal Freedom

CRITICAL STUDIES IN DEMOCRACY, COMMUNISM, AND CIVIL RIGHTS

By Sidney Hook

CRITERION BOOKS———*NEW YORK*

To S. F. AND S. M. L. WHO HAVE STOOD FIRM
AND ENCOURAGED ME IN MY BELIEF THAT:
IT IS BETTER TO BE A LIVE JACKAL THAN A DEAD LION—
FOR JACKALS, NOT MEN; AND THAT
THOSE WHO ARE PREPARED TO LIVE LIKE MEN AND,
IF NECESSARY, DIE LIKE MEN, HAVE THE BEST
PROSPECT OF SURVIVING AS FREE MEN AND ESCAPING
THE FATE OF BOTH JACKALS AND LIONS

Contents

POLITICAL POWER
AND PERSONAL FREEDOM

Introduction

THESE ESSAYS, written for the most part during the last decade and here partly integrated, are concerned with themes that will be topical for a long time to come. Directly or indirectly, they involve the basic beliefs central to the free world in its struggle for survival. In the long run, what Abraham Lincoln said of the United States is true of the entire world—it will be either all slave or all free. But the long run is an indeterminate run; its length depends on many factors, not the least of which are ideas and ideals.

Within the larger context of freedom, this book sets out to explore four key ideas: democracy, coexistence, tolerance, and socialism. I should like to say a brief word about each here.

There are some thinkers who believe that there is an opposition between democracy and freedom, that democracy levels all eminences into a uniform plain and imposes the tyranny of the majority upon the individual. They overlook the massive fact that historically democracy, as understood and practiced in the West, is the process by which freedoms are institutionalized. The conflict is not between democracy and freedom, but between freedom and freedom. Since democracy is the process by which freedoms are reconciled and maximized, some freedoms in some areas of life must of necessity be abridged. This leads to the concept of strategic or preferred freedoms, on whose functioning the very processes of democracy depend. Those who subordinate the processes and strategic freedoms of democracy to particular programs, no matter how desirable and progressive, tend to become fanatical. Sometimes in their impatience they complain that the faith that moves mountains seems more in evidence during our century among the fanatical opponents of democracy, obsessed with a specific program, than among those who enjoy the benefits and achievements of democracy, limited though these be. Critics have asserted that our youth stands morally disarmed and intellectually unprepared before the enemies of our culture, bewildered about or indifferent to its basic values. The air is thick with proposals to remedy the situation by reviving faith in democracy or religion or the gospel of hard work, in school and out.

I have never been impressed by reports about what American youth allegedly thinks or feels. Checked against my own not inconsiderable experience with youth, these reports reflect mainly what the reporters think or feel. American youth does not constitute a separate sector of the population in terms of belief or value-attitudes; it honors and esteems what its elders do, even in its exuberant moments of revolt—which are usually expressions of vital animal spirits and hardly ever of considered judgment. Defects of knowledge, intellectual discipline, and wisdom are real enough, but these are rather community afflictions than peculiar to youth. In any case they are not remediable by appeals to faith.

For there are faiths and faiths. No faith has truth value or even a high survival value unless it is based on a prior faith in intelligence. Faith in intelligence excludes fanaticism, for it is expressed in a willingness to examine all relevant alternatives to our beliefs and practices. That is why it can lead to conclusions which are firm without being dogmatic, and to actions which are resolute and yet flexible enough to deal with the inescapably contingent.

Since democracy is challenged by communism in theory and practice, we must understand it or perish as a free culture. Blind fear and hatred are obstacles to understanding. Understanding, by removing blindness, tends to dissolve fear and hatred. But there are also occasions when understanding is, and by right should be, followed by intelligent fear and justified hatred of evil. Would that the West had understood Hitlerism before it achieved power. Our task is to understand Russian Communism even as we coexist with it.

Like many other expressions with positive emotive overtones, the term "coexistence" has been kidnaped by the Communists for political exploitation. The ethics of words as well as the wisdom of political strategy dictate that, instead of yielding up the term to them, we must wrest it away from partisan political use. By "competitive coexistence" I mean the presence of peaceful relations between the free and the Communist world which permit each to preserve its own system and to strive by all means, short of war, to make its ideals prevail. I believe that competitive coexistence between the free and the Communist areas of the world is certainly *possible*. Whether it is *probable* or feasible depends more upon the Communist world than upon us. To those who doubt whether it is *desirable,* we must make clear how these terms are to be understood. There are various forms of coexistence and competition. In a sense, Rome coexisted with all its colonies, but the relationship was one of exploitation, even if by comparison with, say, Soviet practices in Hungary the exploitation was mild. In another sense, a shepherd coexists with his flock of sheep at the cost of their fleece and spring lamb for market. But if the only alternative to the rule of the shepherd is the rule of the wolves, who are always hungry or consumed by blood lust, wise sheep may prefer coexistence.

But men are not sheep and can live without wolves or shepherds or shepherds-in-wolves'-clothing. The only coexistence acceptable to us should be one which does not diminish the area in which free institutions exist. The Soviet concept of coexistence is that of a breather, or truce from armed struggle, which will enable the Communists by propaganda or subversion to expand their empire until it absorbs the entire globe. In this sense coexistence has always been conceived of as competitive by the Communists. It is the height of naiveté to imagine that they will ever cease considering it in this way. And if their leaders are convinced of the validity of their ideals, why not? On what grounds can we object? My view is that for us, too, coexistence, which we have faithfully practiced, should be competitive, which until now we have failed to make it. The goal of *our* competition should be, by all means short of war and with the explosive bombs of truth, to expand the world sector of freedom. This we have failed to do despite the manifold opportunities afforded by Communist aggression outside the Soviet Union and by its system of terror within the Communist world.

One of the glories of the tradition of the free world is our open house and tolerance in the life of the mind. This tradition is misapplied by two groups. One group interprets this as tolerance only for ideas which agree with its own. Since very few ideas agree completely with one another, this puts the group in a position of permanent intolerance, unhappy and suspicious of all deviation in thought and practice, unaware of how much we owe to our critics and heretics. The second group, mistakenly believing it to be possible to be liberal without being intelligent, maintains that tolerance requires that we be tolerant, not only of the tolerant, but of the intolerant as well. Now it is one thing to be tolerant of different ideas, to be tolerant of different ways of playing the game, no matter how extreme, *within* the rules of the game. But to be tolerant of those who cheat, or of those who are convinced that it is permissible to cheat, in the same way as we are tolerant of those who play differently under the accepted rules, is something else again. Here, of course, certain necessary distinctions are in order.

A liberal should be tolerant of the expression of any idea under the strategic freedoms of the Bill of Rights; but he cannot be tolerant in the same way of those who wish to destroy the strategic freedoms and who organize for that purpose. He may extend the protection of the Bill of Rights even to those who wish to destroy it, in the same way that he might protect a man from being lynched for having defended the practice of lynching, or protest a judicial injustice against a man who condoned the Moscow Frame-Up Trials. But he would not permit a man who "in a good cause" justified lynch law or judicial frame-ups to be a member or officer of an organization devoted to the defence of civil liberties or allow him to hold or retain judicial office. The plea that a man merely advocated lynching but did not practice it, or incite it in a specific case where it constituted a clear and present danger to life and limb, would keep him out of jail and safeguard him against criminal penalties. But if the law is to meet certain minimum standards of justice and professional integrity, it would not permit such a man to occupy a judicial post. It would be better after a judicial hearing to retire him from the bench, if need be even on a pension, than permit him to arbitrate the destinies of others. The ideas a man professes may *sometimes* be relevant to his fitness in holding a certain post. In such cases it is not inconsistent legally to protect him in the expression of his ideas and yet rule him ineligible for the post because of his ideas.

Similarly there are other strategic positions in a society where professional qualifications require certain standards of integrity, the absence of which may be indicated by certain beliefs and associations. A man who believes that there is nothing wrong in the sale of habit-forming drugs to children and who associates with narcotics peddlers, is not fit to be a narcotics-enforcement officer. A teacher who believes that there is nothing morally objectionable in cheating, or voluntarily is a member of an organization which instructs him to take advantage of his position to indoctrinate for some line laid down by an outside organization, is unfit to teach. The notion that a man is being deprived of his civil rights if he is denied employment when he lacks the moral qualifications for his position, or that he is being victimized if action is taken against him until he is caught in the act of carrying out his dishonorable instructions, is one of the pernicious myths of ritualistic liberalism. It is held by that faction of the United States Supreme Court which has been described as consisting of "bleeding hearts with hemophilia." The ailment, it seems to me, is not a disease of the heart, but a defect of intelligence. Where the question is one of national security the issues are both graver and more complex. The reader is asked to suspend judgment on them until he has had an opportunity to read the essays in Part III.

My interest in this particular problem arose many years ago as a result of experience with the attitudes of ritualistic liberals in the German Weimar regime. They argued that, so long as the Nazis did not overtly break any law, they would be acting as intolerantly as the Nazis themselves if they cleared out the nests of Nazi infiltrators in the schools, the government, and the military forces. Hitler had proclaimed that he intended to come to power legally; the National Socialist Workers' Party was a legal political party just like any other party; one must wait until the hand that holds the knife actually strikes or makes an attempt to strike before taking preventive measures; words were cheap and Hitler would be tamed by the responsibility of power, if his minuscule group ever did come to power—these were some of the arguments I heard in Berlin in 1929 when I recounted to responsible leaders in public life what I had observed as an interested spectator during my first Guggenheim Fellowship year in Germany. The causes of the downfall of the Weimar regime were many: one of them undoubtedly was the existence of ritualistic liberalism which believed that genuine democracy demanded tolerance of the intolerant.

Felix Cohen and Kurt Lewin were among the few writers on social affairs who recognized that belief in a democracy, with a Bill of Rights which gave protection to all citizens, did not entail tolerance for the intolerant, and that there is a profound difference between keeping a man in jail because he is a pledged enemy or conspirator or opponent of democracy, and keeping him from a position in which he could betray his trust and country. "It has been one of the tragedies of the German Republic," wrote Kurt Lewin, "that the democratically minded people who were in power immediately after [the First World War] . . . did not know that 'intolerance against the intolerant' is as essential for maintaining, and particularly for establishing a democracy, as 'tolerance for the tolerant.' " Some writers who in the light of the tragic German experience adopted this position toward Fascism refused to do the same with respect to members of the Communist Party or those under its discipline.

A few words in conclusion about what the term "socialism" means to me. The first Socialist candidate I voted for was Allen Benson, candidate for the Presidency on the Socialist Party ticket, in a straw vote in a public-school classroom at the age of thirteen. The time was 1916. My classmates, and I fear most other people, had never heard of him. Since then I have always considered myself a Socialist. The concept and the movement were rich enough to justify several interpretations of its meaning, and I have often thought that the term was too ambiguous to be used as a criterion of differentiation. Today one must explicate rather than succinctly define the meaning of "socialism" to do justice to one's belief in it. Before answering any question as to whether I believe in "socialism" I always try to find out first what the questioner takes it to mean.

Socialism as we understood it when the world was young was not only a program for the economic reorganization of society, but faith in a moral ideal. We became socialists in a time of relative prosperity, not depression. The economic program—socialization—was conceived of as the instrument of achieving the moral ideal of social equality in the most comprehensive sense of that phrase. We were socialists, not because we wanted wealth, but because we hated poverty; and we hated poverty because it degraded human beings, and because we took it, in an oversimplified way, as a symbol of the arbitrary power of man over man, of the irrationality of social existence in an age of science and potential plenty. In consequence, as economic and political changes removed the more conspicuous illustrations of human waste and tragedy, it did not mitigate in our eyes the validity and relevance of the socialist ideal. We were still socialists even after starvation and permanent unemployment had apparently been abolished under capitalism, because glaring social inequalities were still there. Although the welfare state has raised the standards of living of the masses, reduced their hours of employment, and may even give them a guaranteed annual wage, thus abolishing in effect some of the major evils of unemployment, those socialists who wedded their economic beliefs to a moral ideal are still socialists pressing for still greater social equality to the end that no child will suffer material deprivation or any *social* penalties because he happened to be born in one family rather than another.

The same considerations will explain why even when socialization of the means of production is introduced, socialists are not satisfied that this is sufficient, or that it is even necessary for all sectors of the economy. For it is painfully clear that inequitable differences in living conditions and rewards are just as compatible wth social ownership as with private ownership of property. Even in the unlikely event that all workers in a particular industry, or in the still more unlikely event that all workers in all industries, receive equal monetary rewards, socialism would not forthwith or necessarily be realized. For what is essential to the concept of social equality is a sense of *genuine participation* among individuals, of meaningful, uncoerced contribution to the world's work, a sense of counting for something in the concerns and decisions of the community. Totalitarian movements seek by propaganda to supply synthetic substitutes for this sense of genuine participation. They succeed only with some of their elite membership groups. But they fail and must fail with the population at large because they are intolerant of dissent, rule by the whip, and never practice the equality they originally preach.

Reference to a sense of participation may sound vague and rhetorical, but it is based on hard psychological fact easily observable in both the public and private sectors of employment. These facts are part of an order of phenomena which will loom larger in the social landscape as the clouds of economic want and insecurity are dissipated by scientific technology. Everyone knows that, as a rule, the happiest individuals in any enterprise are those who get a feeling of personal fulfillment in their activities, who are aware, and know others are aware, that in some way, however modest, their initiative, their skill and know how, their alertness and spirit and judgment contribute to getting the day's work done. There is a certain reward of appreciation for what is well done, or even well attempted, which when consistently denied makes men listless and indifferent, and sometimes envious and bitter. Resentment does not take root only when there is injustice in the distribution of material rewards. Particularly under our ideological traditions, it flowers most luxuriously when an imposed sustained inequality of status generates marked differences in social esteem. Higher pay is always a solid consolation; but not everything can be cured by it. Most human beings I have known, when offered a choice between higher pay and promotion, have chosen promotion even when they weren't assured subsequent pay increases. When they can't have both, they take the social credit and let the cash go.

With respect to some things in this world, like variations in beauty and intelligence and natural skill, nothing can be done except to shed and enjoy the radiance of natural grace wherever possible. Whether it is genetic accident or divine design, as far as the lot of the individual is concerned it is a matter of luck. But with respect to social status, there is always something that can be done, especially as to where and how one spends most of his working day. This is not a matter of luck. It is a matter of justice. Ideally what is required for the good society is the development of a mutuality of esteem for the contributions all individuals make to the work of society, not as an empty propaganda gesture to increase production, but as a genuine recognition of the specific way in which the specific person helps in creating the objects and services that are the products and conditions of a good society.

Where such esteem is missing, a positive hunger for it seems to develop. Modern industry with its conveyor belts and assembly lines, its tendency toward specialization and excessive division of labor, makes the development of this mutuality of esteem difficult; but it does not make the need for it illusory. Sometimes the need to count and be counted takes pathetic forms, as in the vicarious identification of the worker with the achievements of his factory, industry, class, race, or nation, past or present. Men seek to relate themselves even to glory beyond their reach. There is an anecdote about an applicant for admission to a famous graduate school who, when asked by the Dean of Admissions whether he had graduated in the upper half of his college class, drew himself up and proudly replied: "Sir, I belong to that section of the class which makes the upper half possible."

Occasionally we hear it said, by those who believe that social inequality is an inescapable corollary of natural inequality, that where everybody is somebody nobody is anybody. This is a particularly deceptive half-truth whose implausibility is apparent in any normal family. It is false even where the blood tie is absent. A good team, whether in athletics, chess, or music, a circle of friends, a research laboratory, a social club, a faculty of scholars, and many other forms of association show that it is possible to combine recognition of uniqueness without imposing invidious distinctions. Mankind owes something to the valet of a genius, even if some geniuses may be forgiven for being oblivious to debts of this kind.

It will be easy for some malicious critic to caricature this ideal of socialism, and to represent it as the absurd belief that men are not and should not be different, or that all men are geniuses or should be treated as geniuses. It would be more accurate to say that, according to the moral ideal of socialism, no man should be a spiritual valet to another, that irrespective of the way any man earns an honorable living he should be treated with the same dignity accorded any other, and that his material conditions of life should be such as to enable him to achieve his full growth as a human being. This, together with the specific programs necessary to realize it, is what I mean by socialism.

In conclusion I should like to ask the reader's indulgence for occasional overlapping of themes and arguments, unavoidable in the treatment of questions so intimately interrelated. In an age of indifference and confusion a certain emphasis and repetition may be excusable.

SIDNEY HOOK

South Wardsboro, Vermont

PART ONE . . . Studies

in

Democracy

1 The Philosophical Heritage of

the Atlantic Democracies

INCREASINGLY in recent years I have been struck by the frequency with which practitioners of the arts and sciences have turned to philosophy to supply some basic formula or comprehensive scheme of values to solve the world's ills. This faith in the role of philosophy, whether well founded or not, is a sign of cultural quickening, testifying to a belief in the power of ideas even among those who are always talking about *the concrete*—which has been called the most deceptive abstraction in our language. It is a faith that should recall philosophy to its perennial mission. For modern professional philosophers have not been overmuch concerned with the great questions of value and value conflict, whose critical study constitutes the distinctive subject matter of philosophy in the grand tradition.

Nonetheless many of the tasks assigned to philosophers already predetermine the issues which we rely on philosophers to illuminate with clarity and wisdom. They are asked to develop a philosophy that will make for peace among nations, safeguard democracy, preserve the classical tradition, reinforce religious belief and practice, diminish the divorce rate, justify free enterprise, or strengthen the United Nations. Any philosopher today can find an audience if his book is advertised as a contribution to world unity. All he need do is to tack a chapter of inspirational platitudes on to his pet epistemology or metaphysic. But he has not proceeded in a philosophical way unless among other things he has asked whether world unity is desirable if it involves the existence of a totalitarian police state on a world scale. After all, if peace is the be-all and end-all of human life we should have surrendered to Hitler long

3

ago or, in the light of the development of nuclear weapons, capitulated to the Kremlin. The philosopher is distinguished from the ideologist in that he is not the hired man of some national or party interest, in that his primary allegiance is to the truth—hard as it may be to come by and unwelcome though it be when found. He has no special gifts for discovering or discerning values; but his critical training should equip him to see the implications of the values to which we commit ourselves, their alternatives, their relation to our needs, and to see the kind of evidence relevant to making those rational choices without which self-understanding is impossible.

Among the most fruitful subject matters for philosophical analysis are value conflicts both within our own tradition and between our tradition and other traditions. But a successful approach to them requires a degree of knowledge of social, political, and economic fact which few philosophers, as I have observed them, show. This explains in part why philosophers avoid such themes, and why, when they do not, they say such extraordinary things—such as the pronouncement of one American philosopher that the conflict between democracy and communism is essentially a conflict between pre-Kantian British epistemology and post-Kantian German epistemology, and that the future of world peace depends upon teaching the true theory (which happens to be his own) of the relation between perception, sense data, and scientific objects.

In any case the crisis of our time, of which the Communist crusade against the Western democracies, particularly the United States and England, is a part, challenges us to engage in a process of self-understanding. Let us explore the question of what remains valid in the heritage of the English speaking peoples without necessarily assuming that such validity is universal, or that its forms are either the sole or superior expression of the values they embody. The original language and inspiration of democracy was Greek, not English. And today other countries besides English speaking ones have as good a right to be considered democratic as their older sisters. There is no gene which determines political allegiance or behavior. The influence of democratic Anglo-American institutions on other countries is a consequence of historical rather than biological diffusion.

In the order of exposition rather than logic, an analysis of the Anglo-American heritage may seem more helpful to begin with than a discussion of the definition of democracy. But such an analysis is extremely difficult if this heritage is conceived in exclusively historical terms. I shall treat its historical aspects very briefly because it seems to me apparent that whenever we invoke tradition, especially to settle or recommend matters of policy, *we are not merely describing what the tradition is, but also prescribing what it should be.* Traditions are multiple, so much so that every departure from tradition is justified in terms of something selected from that same tradition. William of Ockham insisted he was only returning to Aristotle, Luther to basic Christianity, and Lenin to Marx. Few would deny that Hamilton and Jefferson are both part of the American tradition, as are Lincoln and Jefferson Davis, Huey Long and Roosevelt. In England the divergence is no less evident, whether we consider thinkers such as Hobbes and Locke, Carlyle and Mill, or such political figures as Cobden and Disraeli, Churchill and Morrison.

The histories of all peoples show sharp vicissitudes and great overturns. Traditions have resulted in part from civil wars, conquests, and revolutions. This indicates that no one can predict from a current tradition what its future will be. We are therefore rightly suspicious of anyone who speaks of *the* tradition of a country as if it gave a final patent of legitimacy. Finding a tradition is like finding an ancestor on a genealogical tree—we pass over the sinners as an alien strain and stop with someone who seems to us exemplary, the fount of our tradition.

In discussing what I regard as most valid in the tradition of the English speaking peoples, I am quite aware that other things besides those selected here are part of it. But beneath all the diversity, there is, it seems to me, a dominant tendency.

Three facets of the Anglo-American cultural tradition stand out as of prime significance. These are (1) the institutionalization of the principle of freely given consent; (2) the development of the experimental, empirical attitude—which, were it not for the inevitable misunderstandings that attend the phrase, I should like to call "the pragmatic temper"; and (3) the recognition of the worth of diversity, and the appreciation of the possibility of many different varieties of "excellence." All of these are obviously imperfectly realized, but I think it can be established that our culture has developed in these directions, and that they count for more than they do in other traditional cultures, such as, for example, the Chinese or Russian.

I have selected them for discussion because, among other reasons, they are under a heavy ordeal of fire from other—I will not say peoples, but governments; and because, although they are an indigenous part of our tradition, they can be broadened to become an integral part of human culture—of a world culture in which various national cultures may preserve their differences and still unite in coping with problems of common concern.

Of these three features obviously the most important is the experimental, empirical attitude. It is an attitude that assesses the truth of assertions and claims, both of fact and value, in terms of relevant results and consequences. It judges profession by performance. It looks upon principles as rules of action. Without eschewing abstractions—for no one can think without abstractions—it relates them to what is observed or observable in public experience. It does not denigrate appearances in behalf of a reality with a higher claim to truth; the appearances are always part of reality and the real is rational only to the extent that the appearances are, while a reality that makes no difference to appearances is a chimera. This attitude is tentative in its judgments but, because it makes judgments, it is not irresolute. It is initially skeptical of all large claims but, by admitting that some are better guides to conduct than others, it is not cynical. It is profane, common-sensical, open-minded about possibilities, but tough-minded about evidence.

This attitude seems to me to represent the dominant philosophic genius of the English speaking peoples—often misunderstood and scorned from without and attacked from within. The fanaticisms of political and social creeds emotionally based on *Weltanschauungen* are foreign to it—so foreign that it has difficulty in understanding them, for which it has sometimes paid heavily.

The wisdom of this attitude is most clearly apparent in the fact that it has developed a consensus of agreement on its basic political institutions without an *official* metaphysics or theology. Within the Anglo-American community are to be found groups and individuals who subscribe to mutually incompatible views on the nature of God, the universe, the origin of life, and its destiny. Yet all of them accept the values and mechanisms of the democratic way of life even when their respective theoretical justifications are unacceptable to each other. This is a fact of enormous significance on which is shattered the arrogant claim that no one can be a principled and consistent democrat unless he accepts some particular metaphysical or theological dogma.

That this working agreement can be achieved despite the multitudinous presuppositions from which the pattern of democratic living is allegedly derived, suggests two conclusions. First, that logically no metaphysical or theological doctrine entails any specific form of social or political life. Accept any such doctrine you please! I believe it is demonstrable that it is not a necessary condition of democracy, that individuals and groups can be and actually have been good democrats without subscribing to it. Nor is any such doctrine a sufficient condition because individuals and groups can be found who sincerely believe it and disbelieve in democracy. I think it can be established that even in countries where official metaphysical or theological views—as distinct from false scientific theories—are prescribed, these do not by themselves logically justify the dictatorial political and social practices which prevail. Such practices are only imposed to further the material interests of whatever power groups are in control or to jibe with the obsession of some dictator.

Why, then, do Protestants and Catholics, Jews, Gentiles and Mohammedans, theists and atheists, absolute idealists, solipsists and materialists for all their differences accept the democratic procedures and institutions characteristic of Anglo-American culture? I suggest that when they consciously and rationally do so it is because they reach their political judgments by following the lead of empirical evidence, by observing the consequences of these practices for weal and woe in their own lives and that of the community, by adopting in principle, however inadequately, the same generic approach by which they attempt to reach reliable conclusions about everyday problems of experience. That they do not often consciously and rationally evaluate political and social affairs is another matter; I am speaking of the way they proceed when they do. We may not agree with their judgments. We may be impatient with their slovenliness or unwillingness to evaluate what the empirical consequences of proposals are, and in determining what is responsible for what. But our argument with the community—if we are socialists, single taxers, free-money men, New Dealers, or anti-New Dealers—doesn't turn on metaphysical considerations but on empirical fact. Such-and-such a proposal—we say—will have these determinate observable consequences. No political principle is so sacred that, when it leads to unendurable practical consequences, it will not be overthrown. And there is much less difference among men as to what is endurable or not endurable than there is about the first principles of metaphysics or theology.

The quest for a philosophical theory of man is irrelevant to the quest for peace and a just social order—so long as it does not deny those empirical traits of man we take note of in our everyday transactions. When it fails to take note of these traits it is worse than irrelevant—it becomes misleading, an obstacle to further inquiry. Man may be conceived of as a soul inhabiting a tenement of clay—so long as it is admitted that the activity of the soul is a function of the organization of a body in a society. Man may be conceived of as a machine—so long as it is granted that he is a thinking, feeling machine. He may be considered a complex of sense data, just so long as the order of connection between different complexes of sense data is not reduced to a sense datum. He may be thought of as a complex of electrons or as a handful of salts in a solution of water—so long as he is also recognized as a creature who makes choices. No matter what our view here, the decisive question still remains to be settled, viz., whether these visiting souls or thinking machines or colonies of sense data or electro-chemical systems should or should not organize themselves democratically. And the considerations that bear on this question are usually of an entirely different order from those that incline us to one or another philosophy of man.

Second, we may note that the empirical temper of the Anglo-American tradition is perhaps most focally in evidence in its refusal to be bound by, or even to believe in, *all* the logical implications of its theoretical propositions about social and political life. The purely logical implications of any assertion are always greater than those we draw, and especially more complex than those we intend. The context of any proposition is a situation, a problem, a difficulty which cannot be expressed in that proposition. In consequence there is almost always some disparity between the formal meaning of propositions considered independently of the situation they are formulated to resolve and what we really mean by them. This makes us particularly attentive to what is done in the name of principles rather than to what is said or written, to the public behavior to which they lead rather than to the personal emotional overtones they arouse. What is sometimes referred to as English and American indifference to principle is not really indifference but rather a realization that more than one principle usually applies, and that principles are to be interpreted as operating guides to actions. Depending on the case, now one, now another of the principles receives the greater weight—a process often called bungling or blundering through. If the British wanted socialism only, in the conventional sense, they could easily achieve it by a series of neatly planned and ruthlessly executed Draconian decrees. If they wanted freedom at any price, they could slip back to the economy of rust and rot of the thirties. Since they want both socialism *and* freedom, they must make compromises that for various reasons offend doctrinaires in different camps.

By and large our tendency is to judge our politicians, not by their party programs, but by the concrete actions taken in their names. And when we look abroad at the "new democracies" in Russia and Eastern Europe, at the "organic democracies" of Spain and, until yesterday, Argentina we naturally, to their great irritation, pay more attention to their reigns of terror and bloodshed than to the propagandistic documents and speeches with which their apologists regale us.

There are, to be sure, intellectual circles in both England and America who believe that the proper approach to political fact in *other* countries is through ideological analysis. A few American philosophers —whom one would expect to be watchdogs of our critical tradition— have publicly detected a family likeness between Anglo-American democracy and Soviet Communism, on the ground that the slogans and official documents of Soviet ideology sound very much like our own. What is especially mystifying about this particular piece of political innocence is that these philosophers would rightfully repudiate the notion that, because the dictatorships of Spain and Portugal profess to base themselves upon a belief in "the brotherhood of man under the fatherhood of God" and in "the infinite worth and dignity of the individual soul," this makes them members of the same political family as the Anglo-American democracies where the same phrases are also current. Franco is judged by what he does, but the man in the Kremlin by what he says—and even this is carefully picked over to reinforce the impression that he is a democrat merely speaking with a Russian accent. When it is pointed out that there is all the difference in the world between the formal implications of these propaganda statements and the tragic facts in the case, the inevitable retort is, "Perhaps so, but we aren't perfect either—there is a discrepancy between *our* ideals and practices, too." That such discrepancies if we disapprove of them can be, and have been, progressively reduced by the exercise of our rights of criticism and opposition under our functioning Bill of Rights—which is conspicuously not true in Soviet Russia in which absolutely no opposition is permitted—is dismissed as a trivial consideration, although it is surely the essence of the matter. Apparently, both countries are democracies, differing only in degree.

It was not so long ago that Hitler accused English and American public opinion of hypocrisy for protesting against the extermination of the Jews while discriminating against colored people. Did that silence us? Those who protested against Hitler's practices were certainly not those who defended or practiced discrimination in their own country. The status of the colored people has been slowly but steadily improving since their emancipation—even though they have far to go to achieve political and social equality. But the fact is that the number of individuals destroyed or sentenced to living deaths in the concentration camps of the Communist countries of the world is greater than the whole Negro population of the United States. We are morally responsible for our own imperfections, but they do not extenuate others' crimes. Even sentimentalists understand that, although we are not free of blame when crime is rampant in our community, this does not put us on the same plane as those who commit murder or militate against our moral right—no, our moral duty—to denounce and restrain those guilty of murder. And a state—at least in the Anglo-American moral tradition—can be just as guilty of murder as an individual.

To claim that the Atlantic democracies and Soviet Russia are equally democracies, differing only in degree, is to debauch our language—unless when we hear the claim we remind ourselves that the difference between life and death is also in a sense a matter of degree. The situation reminds me of the plea of a notorious thief and confidence man who cheerfully admitted his guilt in passing himself off as an ordained minister. He argued, however, that since no man is morally perfect—the very claim would betoken immodesty and lack of perfection—there was after all only a difference in degree of virtue between himself and the honest pastor whom he had defrauded. When official apologists of the Russian regime talk this way, it is noteworthy that they forget one of their favorite Hegelian dicta: a difference in degree may make a difference in kind.

In truth, without an empirical approach to meaning and truth there is a great danger of our never arriving at a common denotative reference to what we are talking about—of debasing our whole intellectual currency, of so confusing rational discourse about freedom of the press, economic democracy, national self-determination, free and unfettered elections, that nothing will appear clear but the logic of the iron fist. The best defence against this kind of semantic corruption is the experimental, empirical temper of mind which historically, although far from exclusively, has been associated with Anglo-American culture from Yorkshire to Missouri.

The institutionalization of freely given consent is the second notable facet in the culture of the English speaking peoples. Critics within and without our culture (with the exception of lineal descendants of Plato and Thrasymachus) do not question the validity of the ideal of freely given consent, but dispute the extent to which it pervades our political and social institutions. But since our task is to examine our uncriticized assumptions we may ask: why is freely given consent better than coercion? Where rules, laws, and plans rest upon freely given consent there is less friction, less fear, and more abundant opportunity for a more abundant life for more people. It is not necessary to labor the point. In almost every area of human relationships where decisions affecting others must be taken, freely given consent enhances the quality of the goals for which the decisions are made, as well as facilitating the execution of these same decisions.

It is obvious that freely given consent is no guarantee of just or wise decisions. But so long as that consent can be granted, withheld, or periodically renewed, there is a greater likelihood that the consequences of our policies will be considered. That is why it is better to accept a foolish decision of a democratic community—provided we are able to agitate against it—than to insist on our dose of wisdom, about which we may be wrong anyhow. The risks in accepting decisions that rest, directly or indirectly, upon freely given consent are far fewer than the risks involved in the only alternatives—anarchy and despotism.

The acceptance of the principle of freely given consent as a binding rule of social life entails certain beliefs about the empirical nature of man. The two most important are: first, that men are responsible; and second, that they are sufficiently rational to know when and where the shoe pinches and when and where not. No one would advocate democracy in an insane asylum or in an institution for the feeble-minded, except possibly an inmate.

Are these empirical beliefs true? I believe they are. But because the evidence is difficult to assess, a certain element of faith—of reasonable faith, since it is not arbitrary—enters into our allegiance to the ways of democracy.

The best way to test this faith, if the historical evidence seems uncertain, is to state the conditions under which freely given consent is most widely achieved. What are these conditions? When is consent free —when is it not? It is not enough that I have a choice. The man who pokes a pistol in my ribs and says, "Your money or your life," may argue that I have a choice, but he cannot decently claim that it was a free one. The presence of physical constraint, the threat of concentration camps for dissenters and their families, which attend elections and plebiscites in totalitarian countries, makes a grotesque mockery of the claims of such governments to be based on consent.

Coercion, of course, may take other than physical forms. There are few things to which a starving man will not consent. Even in the absence of physical and economic coercion, consent is not free if it is bound or blinded by ignorance. I am not speaking now of our inevitable ignorance, of the absence of knowledge because there is no knowledge, which is part of the human estate; such coercion is an aspect of the coercion of the natural scene—it can be mitigated but never entirely removed. I am speaking of the ignorance of what *is* or *could be* known, of the ignorance of other points of view and policies and the reasons therefor, which is engendered when all sources of information and inquiry are controlled by the state.

These considerations are elementary but decisive. From them we can derive the justification of the freedoms of the Bill of Rights—political democracy—of "economic democracy," and above all, because it is an infallible index of the presence of others, the legal right of opposition. Whatever limits are set to such opposition must depend on rules or laws which are themselves derived through the self-corrective procedures of democracy. The more nearly we approach these conditions, the more reliable becomes the test of our assumption that men are sufficiently reasonable and responsible to achieve their purposes better, and to compose their differences more peacefully, by the method of free consent than by any other method.

The acceptance of the principle of consent does *not* imply that the individuals from whom consent is derived are isolated, atomic centers of interest whose existence as fully developed persons is prior to the social order or state which arises out of contract or agreement. The social relationships into which all human beings are born are as essential to their natures as their biological endowments. Personality is a cultural achievement, not a precondition of culture. But from this it does not follow that we can draw an equation between the individual and the social, and legitimately speak of the social good or public welfare as if it were more than the good and welfare of you, of me, and our neighbors. The origin of social and political institutions is logically and morally irrelevant to their present functions. And in evaluating this function individuals are primary, and their judgment, imperfect as it is, must be regarded as supreme. Whoever denies this still speaks as an individual for other individual interests, no matter whether he speaks in the name of the general will, the state, the nation, a class, or a party. The state as an instrument, if it is to serve human interests adequately, has positive functions to perform, and not merely the negative ones of preserving domestic order. But insofar as the state rests upon consent, individual persons morally and collectively are just as much its master as they are of any other instrumentality of their will. This, it seems to me, represents the abiding insight of John Locke, who had more to do with formulating the principles that express the political traditions of Anglo-American culture than any other thinker. None of the strictures by his current detractors affect his wisdom on this point.

Consent is rarely if ever unanimous. There are losers as well as victors in every legislative battle, and the dissent of the former is usually more vehement than the assent of the latter. This raises the difficult problem of minority rights and majority rule in governments that profess to be based on freely given consent. Minorities can be and have been oppressed by majorities as well as by despots. The traditional doctrine, according to which all human beings possess absolute and inalienable rights which can never be abridged by any agency of government, is more coherent as an emotion than as a doctrine. Its meaning is ambiguous: and when not ambiguous, false. It is a very uncertain guide to action. For in most political situations a claim to one alleged absolute right conflicts with a claim to another alleged absolute right. There is no method by which we can measure degrees of absoluteness or establish the priority of absolutes in relation to each other. More important, it is doubtful whether anyone really believes in absolute rights that are unqualifiedly valid no matter what the consequences of their exercise upon social life. Every right in the Bill of Rights is subject to qualification and abridgment if its practice results in widespread misery and public danger.

Sometimes it is argued that, because democracies cannot guarantee absolute rights in all circumstances, and because totalitarian governments do not recognize them at all, that there is in principle no difference between the two kinds of states. This overlooks an all-important distinction. In a democracy, the abridgment of the Bill of Rights, whether for good or bad, is a crisis phenomenon of limited duration, and depends on the processes of consent, if not for its initiation then for its continuation. In a dictatorship the abridgment of any bill of rights is systematic, rather than episodic, and depends upon the arbitrary decree of a small minority. The dictatorship of the proletariat in the Soviet Union which, according to Stalin, is "substantially the dictatorship of the Communist Party" is supposed to be transitional; but who determines when the transition is over—the Russian people or their rulers? Officially, Soviet Russia boasts of being a classless society; but the state instead of withering away has become stronger.

How then does a minority have redress for its grievances in a democracy? If it is given a hearing according to the rules and conditions that truly permit freely given consent, the majority may override what the minority believes to be its just claims. There is always the possibility of resort to revolution. This may have moral sanction but it entails abandonment of the theory of democratic consent according to which no minority is justified in using force to impose on the majority its conception of the true, the good, and the honorable. Such revolutionists may be good men, even saints, but they cannot be called democrats.

Short of this, however, there is the possibility of compromise, or integration of conflicting interests. In order to avoid the greater evil of civil war, we yield to the lesser evil of enduring what seems to us an unjust majority decision, in the hope that continued political education will lead to a reversal of majority judgment. This is the wisdom of Socrates rather than of John Brown: in a dictatorship the only appeal from Philip drunk is to Philip sober; in a democracy the appeal from an unenlightened majority is to an enlightened one. Justice Felix Frankfurter has put this admirably in one of his opinions: "Where all the effective means of inducing political changes are left free from interference, education in the abandonment of foolish legislation is itself a training in liberty." The English speaking peoples have learned this at a great cost, but they have learned it and it is now part of their tradition. The one great exception to this in the United States (but *not* in England) is "government by judiciary" which resides in the power of the U. S. Supreme Court Justices to nullify Congressional legislation.

No democracy can long survive in which majority decisions are consistently foolish or aimed at destroying minorities as well as defeating them. A majority is made up of individuals whose differences are not canceled out by their unity on certain questions. In virtue of these differences some may find themselves in a minority in respect to other questions when the wheel of history makes its next turn. The precedents established by unjust majority decisions may ultimately affect members of the leading group as well as those of the minority.

The causes of injustice are many. Among them two seem to me the most insidious—the interpretation of rules of equality as if they applied only to individuals in identical positions, and an insensitiveness and unimaginativeness to the experiences of others. We may conclude from this that the survival of democracy depends not only upon a faith in human educability, not only on commitment to continuous programs of public education for its citizens, but on the development of an attitude which appreciates and encourages differences instead of merely tolerating them. This brings us to the third and final facet of the heritage of the English speaking world.

That diversity of experience, direct or vicarious, is immediately enjoyable, few will be inclined to deny. It safeguards us against provincialism, and against the tyranny of the familiar whose hold may sometimes be so strong as to incapacitate us from making the new responses necessary for survival. Diversity in modes of experience freshens and refreshens the human spirit. Every new discovery is a triumph of variation over repetition.

Natural as human joy in diversity may be, so is human fear and dislike of diversity—and we know enough about ourselves to realize that both these emotions can be experienced together. There are plausible reasons for believing that our fears prove most stubborn in the presence of differences which we suspect threaten in some way our existence, our uniqueness, our *conatus sui persevare*. Most of the time these suspicions are false; most differences are compatible with, not exclusive of, each other. Growth toward maturity consists largely in learning to appreciate differences, learning to understand them when we cannot appreciate them, and at the very least learning to live with them when we cannot understand them. Whenever we are challenged by the presence of differences, the task of intelligence is to find a way by which those differences that can enrich our lives may be distinguished from those that would destroy them. It is hard to tell which is the more foolish belief—that all differences threaten our life or that none of them do.

In the field of culture and politics, the traditions and present tendencies of the English speaking countries come closer to achieving a reasonable, practical solution of the problem of cultural unity and difference than any other dominant tradition. We have heard a good deal in recent years about the necessity for a basically unified culture to produce that community of taste, judgment, and ideals without which, so it is asserted, social life is in a state of potential civil war. Most of the discussion has been *a priori* and disregards patent fact. That a common religion or language or origin is not a *sufficient* condition for peace is evidenced by the Spanish insurrection—and our own Civil War which occurred at a time when the States of the Union were in many respects much more homogeneous culturally than they are today. That it is not a *necessary* condition is revealed in the histories of Switzerland and of Canada, and in the greater part of the period of American national existence.

Whatever cultural differences exist in the community, and whatever our feeling toward them, they do not constitute a threat to a common life in society unless these differences are accompanied by *practices* which deny the right of differences to others, which fail to recognize the equality of all attitudes that accept a *common method* of negotiating differences. It seems to me that it is this emphasis upon method as more important than any specific result, as a way of insuring progress without anarchy, which underlies all three facets of our heritage—the empirical temper, the democratic attitude, and our cultural pluralism.

Ignazio Silone, the Italian novelist, has said that men must agree on a certain number of fundamental positions—on what is good or evil, true or false—in order not to massacre each other. I believe it is more accurate to say that they must agree on a basic method of reaching the truth or testing the good, rather than upon any *particular* truth or good. For so long as they agree on this method, all other differences about specific truths or goods are in principle resolvable.

There is an exact analogue to this in our political life. In a democracy, no matter what our political faith or beliefs may be, so long as we sincerely accept the basic rules of the game, so long as we are willing to abide by the consequences of the free give-and-take of critical debate, we may legitimately hold and practice any notion or doctrine we please. Our differences may reveal valuable insights and truths which we have missed, and would continue to miss, if no one were permitted to play under the rules unless he accepted our version of the true and desirable to begin with.

The same analogue holds for the even vaster region of cultural differences. We permit—or should permit—each group to preserve and develop its own cultural ways provided it does not attempt to impose its specific, exclusive pattern upon others, provided it leaves its individual members free to choose among the diversities of tradition which compete with each other.

It should be obvious that what is called cultural or ethnic democracy is no more possible without political democracy than is "economic democracy." This has been denied by those who point to Soviet Russia as a model of cultural and ethnic democracy. The principle and practice of Soviet Russia decrees that "culture must be socialist in content and national in form"; but the only national differences that are recognized are primarily those of language. The separation of content from form is a myth. No opportunity for the free development of the culture of the constituent Republics exists, precisely because what is called the socialist *content* of their culture, from art and music to astronomy and zoology, is prescribed for them by the Kremlin. Without the right to develop responses that are critical or even hostile to the reigning cultural dogmas (and this involves the freedom of the press together with other political freedoms) "ethnic democracy" is another deceptive phrase. What we have is ethnic equality, which in the Soviet Union turns out to be little more than the freedom to praise Stalin or any of his successors and the party line in many different languages (including the Scandinavian but not Hebrew).

The upshot of all this is that what is required to live prosperously and peacefully together is not a fixed common doctrine or a fixed body of truths, but a common method or set of rules under which we can live with our differences—mitigate, integrate, transcend them if we wish, or let them alone if *that* is our wish. We cannot make absolutes of doctrines, tastes, or principles without inviting the evils of fanaticism.

Nonetheless, there must be one working absolute on which there can be no compromise, about which we must be fanatical: the rules of the game, by which we settle differences. Whoever plays outside the rules, whoever tries to write his own rules, has given a clear declaration in advance that he proposes to interpret differences as *ipso facto* evidence of hostility. He has in effect declared war which can be avoided only if we knuckle under to any arbitrary demand. There is no inconsistency whatsoever in being intolerant of those who show intolerance. In fact, tolerance of the actively intolerant is not only intellectually stultifying, but is practical complicity in the crimes of intolerance.

The method of the empirical temper, of the democratic process, of cultural pluralism is open-minded but not tender-minded. It is a perpetual invitation to sit down in the face of differences and reason together, to consider the evidence, explore alternative proposals, assess the consequences, and let the decision rest—when matters of human concern are at stake—with the consent of those affected by the proposals.

This method does not guarantee results, not even the results of agreement. Values are relative to human interests and, although objective, may genuinely conflict. The conflict *may* be so deep that resolution is impossible *even* if we agree to negotiate. The assumption that in any particular case agreement on conflicting interests and values can be won rests upon the faith (or bet) that men are sufficiently alike to work out ways of becoming *more* alike, or sufficiently alike to agree on the permissible limits of being different.

We must not confuse an objective morality with a universal morality. Between a human being and a tiger on the prowl, there is no ground for agreement. But it does not follow that human values are not objective because they cannot be shared in this situation. The error of those who would forego the use of a critical method to reach ethical truths is the assumption *in advance* that in every conflict between two men or two groups one is human and another merely a tiger in disguise.

The qualities I have selected have not always been characteristic of the tradition of the English speaking peoples: they have become so. Some aspects already have, and more of them may become, part of the traditions of other peoples and cultures. It was on its way to becoming the settled tradition of Western Europe until the First World War (which should never have been fought) prepared the ground for Lenin, Trotsky, and Stalin, and Mussolini, Hitler, and Franco. If the democratic tradition were to be combined with the welfare economy of democratic socialism, it might establish itself elsewhere, not only in Europe, but in the East. We undoubtedly have much to learn from Indian and Chinese wisdom, but the Sikhs, Moslems, and Hindus can also learn a little from us about religious freedom and toleration, and the Chinese about the processes of representative government.

Democracy is a way of life that outside of its own territories challenges no other way of life except in the urgencies of self-defense. Unfortunately, its existence has been threatened all along the line, first by Hitlerism and now by Soviet Communism. Whoever believed that Nazi expansionism constituted a threat to the survival of democratic institutions must conclude by the same logic and the same type of evidence that Soviet Communism represents today an even greater threat to our survival, because the potential opposition to totalitarianism is now much weaker in consequence of World War II, and because the Soviet government commands a fifth column in democratic countries stronger than anything Hitler or Franco ever imagined possible.

Here is not the place to outline in detail how this formidable crusade against what is permanently valid in the tradition of the English speaking peoples is to be met. Subsequent chapters will treat of this theme. Suffice it to say that, necessary as it is to build a decent social order and remedy injustices in our own countries to prevent totalitarianism from spreading for internal reasons, this would no more be sufficient to stop the march of Communism than social reforms in England and France were sufficient to stop Hitler.

The immediate desideratum is to conduct our foreign and domestic affairs so that more and more peoples of the world *voluntarily* associate themselves in a world union in which, on the basis of primary allegiance to democratic processes, the widest development of cultural diversity is encouraged.

The first step toward such a world union of democracies would be Federal Union among the Atlantic democracies. But this would be only a first step, and it raises the question of what nations are to be regarded as democratic. Here we must go beyond the heritage of the Anglo-American community. What are we to understand by democracy—what are its definition and presuppositions?

To these questions we now turn.

2 Democracy or Republic?

IN NO COUNTRY in the world is more deference paid to "public opinion" than in the United States. Legislators claim to follow it; special organizations exist to measure it; newspapers, radio networks, and other media of mass communication seek to reflect and influence it. The underlying assumption behind the appeal to public opinion is that, whatever else good government may be, it is better when it is an expression of public opinion. Every group affected by a major piece of legislation mobilizes public opinion on its behalf. The passage of any legislative act is sure to call forth from some quarter the outcry that it really doesn't represent public opinion—or what might be an entirely different thing, enlightened public opinion.

This emphasis on public opinion raises one of the perennial issues of representative government. Should elected officials always vote as they believe the majority of their constitutents wish them to vote, or should they be guided only by their own sense of responsibility? The question is complex: simple answers are not likely to be adequate.

To deny that elected officials in a popular government are in a sense morally bound by the mandate given them on the strength of their program and promises, is to call into doubt the validity of popular rule. Systematic denial of public opinion is a mark of autocracy, and is rarely avowed openly even under such rule. Autocrats usually profess to be following public opinion and pretend that they can determine more accurately than legislative majorities the public wish. In making such a claim, even when not true, those who defend autocracy admit, despite themselves, the validity of the principle of self-determination which is essential to the theory of popular sovereignty. On the other hand, the elected official pledges himself to represent, not only those who voted for him, but his entire constituency—both majority and minority. His majority is not seldom composed of different groups voting for him for different reasons. He has an obligation also to the minority which opposed him, to strive for political justice and to protect their human rights—an obligation that transcends narrow political lines. Further, because of the pace of historical events, the specific questions on which he must take a stand are likely to be far different from those on which he campaigned and won the approval of public opinion. Where not tested by the trial of an election, "public opinion" is a vague concept, ill defined and mechanically measured, and hard to make out in the synthetic din of pressure groups. Finally, much as he may wish to follow public opinion, he knows that it is not always in possession of the relevant facts, and that some sort of leadership is expected of him. To serve the public interest is not the same as being a servant of public opinion.

One of the recurrent controversies in American political thought concerns the extent to which the principles of popular sovereignty and responsible leadership characterize the American system of government. For historical reasons, this usually takes the form of a discussion of whether we live under a democracy or a republic. The implied contrast is not a happy one because it obscures the central issues at stake.

A hundred and fifty years ago, if anyone had asked whether the United States was a republic or a democracy, he would have received the almost universal answer that our form of government was republican. The term "democracy" was not then a word in good standing. It connoted the rule of the mob and the tyranny of the demagogue who steps to power on its shoulders. Madison's observation that democracies "have ever been spectacles of turbulence and contention . . . and in general as short in their lives as violent in their deaths" was a representative judgment of the time. It was only slowly that the term "democracy" came to be accepted as a designation of the political system under which we live. Not until the era of Theodore Roosevelt and Woodrow Wilson did it become widely popular, both as a slogan and a principle.

Nonetheless this shift in our semantic habits has not gone uncontested. Voices have been periodically raised in protest against the notion that we live in a democracy. It has been asserted that such a conception is a grave error fraught with evil consequences, that the United States was designed to be, and still is, a republic whose constitutional traditions of freedom cannot endure if we mistake it for a democracy. More than one organization, armed with quotations from the writings of the Founding Fathers, has devoted itself to re-educating the American people to an understanding of the nation's true republican form.

The ardor with which the distinction between the terms "republic" and "democracy" is pressed suggests that we are not dealing with a matter of academic terminology, but with issues of considerable moment to our political way of life. But what these issues are cannot be clarified if the question is considered merely in relation to the text of the Constitution. What the Constitution meant to those who wrote it is certainly an interesting theme; what it was *interpreted* to mean by those who came after has been far more important in influencing our political history.

Nor is the text of the Constitution decisive on the question. It is sometimes asserted that the United States is not a democracy because the word "democracy" is nowhere to be found in the Constitution. But neither is the word "republic" although Article IV, Section Four, guarantees to every *state* in the Union "a republican form of government." The meaning of this phrase is not further explained, but at the time it was inserted it probably meant no more than opposition to the institution of monarchy. Having rejected the monarchical form of government for the Federal Union, the early American statesmen could not countenance any rule of hereditary succession for the chief executives of the constituent states.

This suggests that the proper opposite of the term "republic" is not "democracy" but "monarchy," which conforms to widespread usage today. We recognize that England and Sweden are not republics but they are certainly democracies. The King of England has notoriously much less power in political affairs than the President of the United States, not to speak of the presidents of some South American Republics. On the other hand, Russia refers to itself as a Union of Socialist Soviet Republics, but neither the Union nor its member republics can be called democratic without a violent abuse of language. For essential to the meaning of democracy is the rule of government by virtue of the *freely* given consent of the governed—a consent which presupposes the legal right of opposition and the existence, not on paper but in fact, of the freedoms of the Bill of Rights. That is why, although Germany under Hitler was a republic and Italy under Mussolini a monarchy, neither was a democracy.

The definition appropriate to this distinction is: a republic is a form of government in which the chief executive is elected, regardless of whether he is elected by a few, as in the Athenian and Venetian republics, or by the many, as in our own; while a monarchy is a form of government in which the chief executive is hereditary, regardless of how much actual power he possesses.

Since there is no problem about this simple definition, it is obvious that those who counterpose the terms "republic" and "democracy," as if they were opposite, rather than distinct, are giving some special significance to these words. And it is at this point that the underlying issues begin to emerge. Writers who maintain that the United States is a republic mean to call attention to the fact that our government is not an absolute or direct democracy, but a limited or indirect one. An absolute or direct democracy is "government of the whole people by the whole people." The nearest approximation to it is the town meeting in which all adults possess the franchise and transact together the business of the community. Where a community exceeds a certain size, a direct democracy is technically impossible and the rule of the whole people is exercised through freely chosen representatives. A republic would then be a representative government, and in one of the Federalist papers Madison indeed speaks of "the republican or representative form of government." Jefferson, on the other hand, in his private papers and letters uses the terms "republicanism" and "democracy" as if they were practically synonymous, and judges governments republican in proportion "as they embody the will of their people and execute it."

Were we today to use the term "republic" strictly in Madison's sense we should have to call England a republic or a "republican monarchy"—a phrase actually employed by Mably, a French social philosopher of the eighteenth century, in urging a reform of the French absolute monarchy.

By this reasoning those who distinguish themselves as believers in a "republic" rather than in a "democracy" support the extension of indirect, representative forms of government. They urge that individuals to whom power is delegated should assume a greater personal responsibility in initiating and determining policy under fixed constitutional provisions. This power is to be subject to ultimate correction by the people at periodic intervals through elections and constitutional amendment. Legislators are duty bound to follow their own judgment and not to trail behind the polls of opinion which indicate the way the fickle mind of the public is veering at any moment.

According to this same distinction, those who believe in "democracy" are loath to delegate power and, when they do, regard representatives and officials merely as spokesmen for the people whose feelings and judgments they should at all times express. They strive to increase, wherever possible, the degree of direct participation in the processes of government through the mechanisms of plebiscite, initiative, referendum, recall, and associated forms of public agitation. Their ideal of a democratic community is one in which every citizen plays an active role in some sphere of political life.

Even here, however, we are not confronted by a clear, major issue, although it is adumbrated in the distrust of popular judgment and passion displayed by partisans of "the republic," and the faith in the common sense and decency of the masses expressed by "democrats." For, after all, not even in a direct democracy can all the people rule themselves all the time. With the multiplication of the functions of government, popular participation can hardly catch up with the growth in administrative complexity. The delegation of power to representative authorities is therefore inevitable. This is recognized even by those who are aware that such power may easily be abused and consequently seek to hedge it in with safeguards that are admittedly not infallible.

The basic issue, around which all the significant differences between these two schools of belief polarize, is not the desirability of representative government but the extent to which the principle of *majority rule* should be decisive in settling questions. Those who speak for a republic profess the same opposition to despotism as those who speak for a democracy. But their argument is that a majority can no more be entrusted with absolute power than can nonelective officials. Since a majority may abridge the fundamental rights of individuals and minorities as ruthlessly as any despot, curbs and checks must be placed upon its power by the same logic that justifies imposing them on the power of officials. "One hundred and seventy three despots would surely be as oppressive as one" was a warning penned by Thomas Jefferson, who nonetheless placed his ultimate faith in the growth of popular enlightenment and love of freedom as the most powerful restraint on "elective despotism."

Most criticisms of the tyranny of the majority have been voiced by conservatives who feared that property rights would be imperiled by the majority vote of the representatives of unpropertied citizens. But it would be a fundamental error to assume that all who oppose the rule of the majority are conservatives or foes of social progress. Liberals concerned with the preservation of the political and human rights of the individual have often denounced the arbitrariness and blindness of majority decisions. They have pointed to the ease with which majorities can be seduced into voting away their liberties and even their democratic form of government, as under the plebiscites of the two Napoleons. The rule of the mob, Plato warned long ago, is always a prelude to the rule of the tyrant. And although liberals refuse to accept government by a benevolent philosophic despot, which Plato proposed as the solution, many of them have shared his distrust of the bias and ignorance of an uninformed majority.

As is well known, the compromise worked out by the authors of the United States Constitution, to forestall elective despotism and a monopoly of political power, balanced the various branches of government against each other without producing the state of paralysis that some of its critics had predicted. In addition, in order to preserve "the blessings of liberty to ourselves and our descendants" the Bill of Rights amendments were written into the Constitution as brakes upon the power of legislative majorities to destroy the rights of individuals at their pleasure. That is why a great American liberal, Charles A. Beard, describes the United States government not as a democracy. whose decisions rest upon mechanical majorities, but as a constitutional republic.

Nonetheless even a constitutional republic which guarantees the right of individuals against legislative oppression recognizes the legitimacy of majority power, through the process of amendment. This means not the abandonment of the principle of majority rule but reliance upon the safeguard of a *large* or extraordinary majority wherever fundamental changes are proposed. The moral issue, however, remains the same. For it may be asked: what is sacred about a seventy-five percent majority? Cannot the extraordinary majority required to amend the constitution be just as tyrannical to a minority as an ordinary majority? A constitutional republic is one in which fundamental rights are reserved to the individual. But who is to determine which rights are fundamental, and which are to receive precedence when rights conflict, as they often do? Unless it is ultimately the majority, or those who are elected by and responsible to the majority, that makes this decision, constitutional government is not fully democratic.

We are now in a position to determine whether the United States is a democracy or a republic in the special sense considered above.

If we judge the form of government under which we live by the history and direction of its political practices, it is correct to say that it has moved steadily toward a constitutional *democratic* republic in which the will of popular majorities has had increasing weight. The growth of the Constitution illustrates the process and shows how far we have come from the old Federalist view that the Constitution should serve primarily as a check on popular majorities. But the description of our government as a constitutional democratic republic is subject to two important qualifications that explain the ebb and flow in the movement toward democracy. The first arises from the constitutional power of any minority to thwart the will of the majority whenever, as in the case of a constitutional amendment, a large or extraordinary majority is required. The representatives of thirteen sparsely settled states can theoretically block any fundamental reform. The second stems from the power of the Supreme Court to nullify Congressional legislation and, through judicial interpretation of amendments to the constitution, to impose the will of a majority of Supreme Court justices upon the majority of the electorate and its representatives.

Let us consider them in reverse order. The composition of the Supreme Court, to be sure, shifts from time to time and the justices are neither immortal nor immune to waves of popular influence. Nonetheless, the court on the whole changes much more slowly than Congress, and its decisions do not, contrary to Mr. Dooley, simply follow the election returns. (It requires several sets of election returns to register an effect. In crucial cases this must sometimes be coupled with a threat by Congress or the President to increase or reduce the number of Supreme Court justices.) The observation that Mr. Justice Stone once addressed to his colleagues remains substantially true: "While unconstitutional exercise by the executive and legislative branch of the government is subject to judicial restraint, the only check upon our own exercise of power is our own sense of self-restraint."

Many liberals refuse to recognize the fact, implicit in Justice Stone's statement, that the Supreme Court is the supreme law-*making* because law-*interpreting* body in the land, and that its power to nullify the legislation of the representatives of the people is a patent restriction of democracy or, put more provocatively, is an undemocratic feature of American public life which at any time can override the democratic features. With his characteristic honesty, Justice Frankfurther makes explicit what is implicit in Justice Stone's reminder: "Judicial review is a deliberate check upon democracy through an organ of government not subject to popular control."

Nor is the theoretical power of a minority to hold up the actions of a majority necessarily fatal to the democratic process, provided it is exercised in a spirit of reasonableness. There is a difference between an absolute veto on majority rule by a nonelective agency and temporary checks upon majority decisions that may be gradually overcome in the course of political education and action. A wise democracy knows that fruits which are forced or plucked too hastily in the legislative process are likely to be bitter. The majority in such a democracy, therefore, lays down for itself rules by which to proceed cautiously where great issues are in dispute. Generally caution is a good rule, but there are times when a democracy must act quickly to preserve itself. To repent at leisure it must at least survive. It is in such critical situations that the power of a small minority to frustrate the will of the majority may imperil the very existence of democracy. The prospect of democratic survival in a crisis may depend just as much upon the minority's sense of responsibility as upon that of the majority.

No intelligent democrat can deny the possibility that a majority may run wild and trample upon individual rights. But if the rights of individuals are not safe in the hands of a majority, are they any safer in the hands of a minority? Who is to select the minority, and how are the rights of the majority to be safeguarded against the minority? The appeal to absolute and inalienable natural rights is no help here, because in practice even those who invoke them are not prepared to assert that an individual can justifiably make any claim against society independently of the *consequences* of that claim upon others. And if a claim can be limited because of its consequences, it cannot be regarded as absolute. Since, then, all natural rights must be interpreted in respect to their meaning and limits of application, the problem arises once more: who is to be given the ultimate authority in interpreting rights—the majority or the minority? Put this way the question may be misleading unless the answer indicates *how* such authority develops and expresses itself.

The answer the democrat makes involves certain principles that are the philosophical bedrock of his belief. First, it is not the bare fact of a majority which is significant but of a majority reached through the democratic process. This process is characterized by a whole set of conditions that explain why a majority vote has no legitimacy in the eyes of a democrat if it is cast in an atmosphere of terror, or when legal opposition is impossible.

Second, even a majority formed in and through the democratic process may be tragically mistaken in what it approves or condemns. The voice of the people is not the voice of God or necessarily the voice of reason. The reasonableness of the democratic process does not lie in any specific piece of legislation, but in the rationale of the *method* by which majority decisions are reached. The essence of the democratic faith is that through the continuing process of political education men can become sufficiently reasonable to discover, through evidence and the give-and-take of free discussion, a better way of solving common problems than by anarchy or despotism, which Lincoln properly regarded as the only alternatives to democratic majority rule.

Third, part of the faith in the democratic process maintains that errors resulting from its operation may be corrected by deepening, extending, and improving that process. By educating the majority to deplore foolish legislation, a better process may be achieved.

Fourth, from this it follows that the processes of education in a democracy must be so conceived as to bring democracy's underlying spirit in juxtaposition with its processes. The philosophy of democracy rests not on the belief in the natural goodness of man but in his educability, not in the inevitability of social progress but in the potentialities of human nature and intelligence.

The history of the two largest democracies in the world, Great Britain and the United States, serves to show that the most reliable check upon what De Tocqueville called the "legitimate tyranny and holy injustice" of majorities is, not any absolute veto by a minority, but the development of appreciation of the constructive function of minority dissent in a world where we cannot achieve final truth. When to this is added the realization that the members of today's majority may be part of tomorrow's minority, the majority may be more likely to recognize that self-restraint in the exercise of power sets a precedent for which it may some day be grateful. The record of the past reveals that minorities have suffered much more at the hands of undemocratic minorities than of democratic majorities. Nor is it without significance that the state of personal and civil liberty in England, where legislative majorities are subject to no executive or judicial check, is at least as healthy as it is in our own country. Those who maintain that a Supreme Court, in addition to ruling on the constitutionality of local and state legislation, must be entrusted with the power to nullify Congressional legislation in order to safeguard the liberties of the people are demonstrably mistaken, as the English experience shows.

The moral that may be drawn from this is that where majority rule prevails its decisions will reflect the degree of enlightenment, the ways of thought, and habits of action which are characteristic of the community. Governments may sink to depths lower than their source; they cannot rise higher.

But if the majoritarian principle is not a sufficient condition for a justly ordered democratic community, it is a necessary one. Before a people can be declared unfit to be the custodian of its own conscience, it must be trusted and given the opportunity to learn from its own mistakes.

Not all who declare themselves friends of the people are prepared to trust it. In the eighteenth century, many impassioned liberals looked to benevolent despots as the necessary instruments of reform rather than to the uncertainties of democratic assemblies. In the twentieth century we observe "totalitarian liberals," all hot for progress, supporting without qualms minority-party dictatorships in many countries, which promise to surrender their dictatorship only when *they* have judged that progressive aims have been achieved. Although they often speak in the name of the people, such groups are at heart extremely contemptuous of the people's capacities for self-government and self-education.

History has shown, of course, that conflicts between majorities and minorities may involve interests some of which will not submit to the arbitration and compromise of the democratic process. A functioning democracy presupposes that it is possible to find in any community a degree of common interest among all groups sufficient to make resort to civil war unnecessary. Intelligent democratic programs of action, therefore, will aim, among other things, at introducing those institutional changes that will permit even those who lose in the peaceful processes of democratic struggle to lead lives of usefulness and dignity. Whoever rejects the democratic process must risk the fortunes of war and the total loss of what he has refused to compromise in part. The ultimate hope of peace and freedom, nationally and internationally, rests on the belief that in time loyalty to the democratic method of reaching decisions may take priority over loyalties to any one of the things we hope to win by it.

3 Are There Two Kinds of Democracy?

HENRY WALLACE was wont to contrast what he called the "political democracy" of the United States with "the economic democracy" of the Soviet Union, definitely implying that it is possible to have the latter without the former. In a famous speech at Madison Square Garden (November 8, 1942) he said, referring to those who hold this view: "Some in the United States believe that we have overemphasized what might be called political or Bill of Rights democracy." From a man who might have been through death or election the President of the United States, this should give us pause. The claim that "political democracy" and "economic democracy" can exist independently of each other was asserted with extraordinary emphasis by Harold J. Laski in the last decade or so of his life. Laski was the mentor of American ritualistic liberalism and similar movements in intellectually under-developed countries. Admitting that the Soviet Union was a one-party police state, he added, "in my judgment it has gone further towards an effective democracy in economic life than any other country" (*The Nation,* March 1, 1947).

What is the basis of such claims, and what are they worth? Is it legitimate to speak of two *kinds* of democracy? These questions are not academic. Our future depends in part upon how we answer them.

In its primary *historical* significance, democracy refers to a form of government and only to government. A government is democratic to the extent that those who are affected by its decisions—leaving aside children—have a share, direct or more often indirect, through election of its agents or representatives, in determining the nature of the decisions. Its fundamental assumption in the eyes of those who offer rea-

29

sonable justification for preferring it to other systems of electing rulers is that by and large human beings are themselves the best judges of their own interests, or at the very least, better judges as a rule than any one man or group of men. This assumption is denied by all despotisms including benevolent ones.

This must not be misunderstood as asserting that in a democracy the voters always know what their best interests are. Sometimes they do not. But if they *never* did, what reasonable ground could be offered to let them decide on what their interests were? If men are like sheep, as some neo-Machiavellians would have us believe, they need shepherds to protect them as much from the consequences of their own stupidity as from wolves. But although men are not altogether rational animals, they are far from accepting like sheep the false doctrine that other individuals can be better trusted to discover and administer to their needs than their own imperfect selves.

In this connection something should be said of the short and easy way some critics take to dispose of the definition of democracy which makes it rest upon the consent of the governed, loosely referred to as "control by the people." They usually ask: what laws do Tom, Dick, or Harry who are ordinary citizens and not legislators pass? But the real question is whether those to whom the legislative mandates have been delegated can be removed; this is power enough. Its importance can be gauged from the fact that some individuals and sometimes whole groups and classes would die rather than permit the people to exercise this power.

It is not hard to see that the primary meaning of democracy involves two other basic notions—political equality and political freedom. Governments are more or less democratic depending upon whether political power or influence on political power is shared equally. If we arrange governments in a series in which their electorates are composed of the following groups: wealthy white men, white men, Christian men, men and women, it would be universally admitted that the order of arrangement was one of increasing democracy. It is interesting to observe what happens when those who profess themselves democrats oppose extending to groups other than their own a share in political power or influence—whether to religious or racial minorities or to women. Sooner or later, they are compelled to maintain, if they are consistent, that those whom they would exclude from the democratic process are not sufficiently mature persons, and that in political matters they must be treated as wards of those who are. Whatever we think of their anthropology, even such people admit, therefore, that the logic of democracy requires complete political equality—an equality unaffected by differences in station, race, religion, and sex. If Negroes, Jews,

Catholics, women, or redheads are excluded from the political process those who do so in the end tend to deny that they are "people" or "human" in some way presumably relevant to the performance of the political function. Since they have no evidence for their claim the base of democracy tends to widen as the history of Western democracy shows.

But the concept of political equality in a democracy also entails the concept of political freedom. Since not all can govern, power must be delegated. Government must rest upon consent. Unless this consent is *freely* given it is not a genuine consent. How do we know when consent is freely given? When it is voluntary—not subject to coercion. An election or plebiscite held in the shadow of bayonets, or in which one can vote only "Yes," or in which no opposition candidates are permitted, is obviously one which does not register freely given consent.

There are subtler ways of frustrating the expression of free consent. If one is kept ignorant of alternatives, denied access to information, deprived of the opportunity to influence and be influenced by the opinions of others, consent is not free. Wherever, therefore, a monopoly of the instruments of education and propaganda exists, we cannot speak of a democratic decision. Even when elections or plebiscites are held without overt terror or the constraining presence of the military and police, they cannot be accepted as evidence that they reflect the judgment of the elctorate if there is no freedom of speech, press, assembly, and especially the *rights of opposition*. That is why the specific freedoms of the Bill of Rights are of such strategic importance in every democratic community. Without them there is no political freedom, and consequently no political equality—since those who are denied them are placed in an unequal position over against those who have them. Absence of political equality is therefore a measure of the absence of political democracy.

All this is straightforward enough, and rather elementary. But elementary truths bear reaffirmation when they are ignored or denied. Matters become more complex when, because of inequalities in social status and economic power, political equality before the law is in effect undermined. This is an insight that goes back not to Marx but to Aristotle and Madison, although Marx made the most of it. Differences in economic power make it possible for the more powerful economic group to exercise a much greater influence upon decisions that affect public welfare than their numbers or deserts warrant.

This they do in two ways. Insofar as large areas of social existence, particularly daily economic life, are outside the sphere of political control, those who command the greater economic resources command the greater economic power. The effects of that power may render nugatory even legislative action. Secondly, even when these areas become subject to political control, large disproportions in economic power will allow one group to enjoy greater advantages in mobilizing resources to influence public opinion and consent.

It is linguistically possible to restrict the term democracy *entirely* to government so that the very expression "political democracy" is a redundancy, and such expressions as "economic democracy," "industrial democracy," "educational democracy," "social democracy" are all meaningless. Little would be gained by such a narrow restriction of the term. For even outside the realm of government, we regard it desirable to evaluate institutions from the point of view of the degree to which controlling decisions are determined by the consent of the participants. We know perfectly well what we mean when we say that one school, a family, or factory, functions more democratically than another school, family or factory: we mean that the individuals are consulted more frequently, invited to express an opinion, and empowered to decide direction of policy. There are some situations in which democratic processes may be inappropriate to the proper performance of function, e.g., in an army. Yet even here we know what we mean to impart by the term when we say that one army is or could be more democratic than another. The connotation of democracy can finally be broadened so that it represents a way of life, an ethic contrasted with the ethics of aristocracy.

It is at the point where great disparities in economic power affect the expression of political power that the demand for economic democracy arises. And insofar as the logic of democracy is concerned, a good case can be made for the claim that where political life is influenced by economic, legal, or even religious power political democracy by itself is *incomplete*. It is incomplete until its rationale of participation and uncoerced agreement, reached through the process of free discussion and criticism, has been extended to economic life as well, and until a true welfare economy has been instituted which will reduce the great differences between economic classes and make them more nearly equal in economic power. The two provisions designed to achieve this are collective bargaining by free trade unions and a guarantee of the right to work. (The question of whether the right to work can best be guaranteed in an economy of free enterprise, a mixed economy, or a predominantly planned economy need not be pursued here.)

It follows at once that "economic democracy" cannot be contrasted with political democracy because without the latter the former is impossible. For if the workers are to exercise the right to bargain freely, to help determine the conditions and rewards of their work, to participate as equals in the process of discussion—how can they do this unless they enjoy the freedoms of speech, press, assembly, and opposition that define political democracy? If the government recognizes its responsibility to undertake measures that will provide opportunities for employment, what guarantee have workers that these opportunities will be nothing better than an industrial draft for work in forced-labor factories and slave-labor camps unless they share in the political decisions through a democratic political process?

Those who speak of two *kinds* of democracy make the fundamental mistake of separating what cannot be separated. Democracy is a matter of degree, not of kind. Political democracy without economic democracy is incomplete: but economic democracy without political democracy is impossible. As well as say that there are two kinds of life: life with oxygen, and life with any quality you please but without oxygen. *Political* democracy is the oxygen of the democratic body politic.

What, then, do those who contrast economic democracy with political democracy mean by the phrase "economic democracy"? If we examine the social systems which they regard as exemplifications of it, we will find that by "economic democracy" they really mean *economic security,* a radically different concept. That it cannot legitimately be regarded as a species of democracy is apparent when we realize that one may be secure without having any control over the conditions of security. Children may be economically secure in a family without sharing responsibility. Soldiers have economic security but not democracy. Perhaps the most economically secure groups in our midst are the inhabitants of our jails who are provided with food, clothing, shelter, and medical care to the end of their terms and sometimes to the end of their lives, and with an almost unrestricted freedom to criticize their jailors. Economic security is not economic democracy although a genuine economic democracy includes a large measure of economic security.

When it is admitted that economic security must be distinguished from economic democracy, the argument again shifts and we are told that our choice lies between political democracy or freedom and economic security. But reflection will show that this, too, is an overfacile disjunction, and a *dangerous* one because the absence of freedom in many parts of the world, especially in some underdeveloped areas, is defended on the ground that security has thereby been achieved. What does it mean to say that a person has economic security in a social system in which he has no political freedom? A sober evaluation of the practices in such systems shows that a man is secure in his job—*provided* he does not criticize the government, *provided* he does not run foul of arbitrary administrative decrees which regulate his work, *pro-*

vided he does not try to publish an independent newspaper, listen to a foreign radio, hold an unauthorized meeting, publicly express a dangerous thought, and *provided* the system to which he is loyal does not become overthrown by another. It means in actuality that there is no economic security except for those who are prepared to exchange their status as free men for that of subjects or slaves. (Were this exchange *freely* made after deliberation about its consequences, something could be said for it, if the decision were not forever binding and could some day be reversed after a taste of the fruits of bondage.)

Even under outright slavery, unless certain laws protect the slave against the whims of his master, we can speak of economic security only in a Pickwickian sense. Similarly, when we speak of economic security in a totalitarian state which cannot be controlled by the political actions of its members and which can deny to any recalcitrants access to the instruments of production, we are also using Pickwickian language. Without specific political freedoms and a system of justice which defines rights and duties that *limit* the power of one group of men over others, there is no basic security in economic life.

How complete is democracy in the United States? Very far from complete. The political mechanism of registering consent in some states is faulty, and in others lies in the hands of a minority of bigots. The processes of economic democracy in some industries are primitive, and in many quarters even these are under attack. And, most disgraceful of all, large sections of our Negro population are practically disfranchised in some communities and suffer from one or another variety of segregation and discrimination almost everywhere else. In far lesser measure, other minority groups are occasionally victims of undemocratic practices.

When all this is granted it still remains true that American democracy, with all its imperfections, possesses the instruments by which it can move towards the realization of the promise of equality and freedom it contains. So long as it retains its Bill of Rights democracy—so long as the conditions for opposition and change remain—every remediable social evil can yield to courage, organization, and hard work. It is difficult to see on what grounds it can be reasonably maintained, as Mr. Wallace did, that we have "overemphasized" political or Bill of Rights democracy. For it is the *sine qua non* of every expression of democracy wherever we use that word properly. It is the one thing that cannot be overemphasized, save possibly in war, or when confronted by a clear and present danger to the basic structure of our freedoms. Primary loyalty to its processes rather than to any specific thing we hope to win through them marks the principled democrat from the opportunistic one.

The basic issue therefore is not between two kinds of democracy. It is, I suggest, between two ways of life. One aspires toward ever greater freedom and equality, solving its difficulties by struggles within the rules of the game which recognize the legitimacy of opposition. The other has no place for opposition nor for freely given consent but concentrates all power, political, economic, and educational, in the hands of a minority convinced that it is a better judge of the interests of the vast majority of men and women than they themselves. The issue in short, and this transcends all other differences today, is between democracy and totalitarianism.

4 The Justifications of Democracy

THE SUCCESSFUL DEFENSE of democracy does not rest primarily upon the analysis of its nature and presuppositions. Nonetheless, some clarification of the meaning of democracy, of the ground upon which we hold our beliefs, and of the procedure by which we arrive at conclusions for the class of problems and decisions of this kind is necessary if our choice to defend democracy is to be an intelligent one. Insofar as intelligent choice makes a difference to events, analysis is not without ultimate bearing upon conduct. Particularly today, when the allegiances of large numbers of people have become unhinged, and when even larger numbers are more certain of what they want to believe than of the reasons for their belief, the answers to our questions may be of some practical moment. It is noteworthy that, in an age not conspicuous for its appeal to reason, few will give assent to doctrines which they admit to be demonstrably false or out of line with verifiable fact.

Perhaps more dangerous to democracy than arguments against it is the feeling that analysis or reflection is irrelevant to those "beliefs" for which we are prepared to suffer, to fight, and sometimes to die. They are then regarded either as automatic consequences of conditioning—social or biological—or as sacred commands from a divine source or as the irresistible cry of conscience. Once the rational nerve of belief is paralyzed, action in behalf of expressed goals may still be vigorous, but it cannot be intelligent. For whatever else intelligence is, it is sensitiveness to, and awareness of, the presence of *alternate means* which in fact determine the realized content of the goals we profess. Belief without reasons blinds us to the presence of alternate means. That is why the action it inspires is so often self-defeating. There are many causes in history of which we can say that they have been betrayed by their own successes.

It is hard to separate a discussion of democracy from a discussion of its alleged philosophical presuppositions, for the nature of democracy is itself often in dispute. In addition, the meaning of the word "presuppositions" is not unequivocal. Its customary usage includes "consequences" and "implications" as well as "assumptions." What I propose to do, therefore, in order to facilitate the joining of issues, is to ask and answer three generic questions. The first is: What is democracy? The second: What are the grounds on or reasons by which we can justify our belief in democracy? The third: Are there any facts of a cosmic, historical, or psychological kind which stand in the way of our acceptance of democracy, i.e., which make democracy an impracticable ideal? It is apparent that these last two questions are related, since if any ideal is demonstrably impracticable, in a sense other than completely realizable (for no ideal can be completely realized) this would have some bearing on its desirability or on the grounds of our choice.

I

Any adequate description of the nature of democracy must at the very least do justice to customary usage, which distinguishes between democratic and nondemocratic societies and among historic phases within any one society, regarded as more or less democratic in relation to each other. Although for propaganda purposes even totalitarian states claim to be democratic "in a higher sense," their canonic writings recognize the differences between the structure of these states and those considered democratic in a less esoteric sense. This is often betrayed in such adjectives prefixed to the latter as "so-called," "alleged," "parliamentary," or "bourgeois." Historically, Spain and Russia and China are not democratic states; England and the United States are. And when historians examine the development of English and American society they unanimously acknowledge (although they evaluate the fact differently) that these societies were less democratic when property, racial, or religious qualifications were set for citizenship than they are today when these qualifications have been eliminated or reduced.

What principle is expressed in these customary distinctions? The principle may be stated in various ways, but for our purposes we may say that a democratic state is one in which the basic decisions of government rest upon the freely given consent of the governed. This obviously is only a beginning. For just as soon as we begin to investigate the conditions which must be present before we grant that a state lives up to this principle, we are carried beyond the sphere of political considerations into the domain of ethics. Thus, if information has been withheld or withdrawn before consent is assessed; if the opposition is muzzled or suppressed so that consent is as unanimous as a totalitarian plebiscite; or if economic sanctions are threatened against a section of the community in the event that consent takes one form or another, we declare that the "spirit" or "logic" or "rationale" of democracy is absent from its political forms. If birth does not give divine right, neither do numbers. We are all acquainted with situations in which we say that a political democracy has traduced its own ideals. Whenever we criticize existing states which conform to the political definition of democracy on the ground that they are not democratic enough; whenever we point out that Athenian democracy was limited only to free men, or that in some parts of the American South it is limited only to white men, or in some countries it is limited only to men—we are invoking a broader principle of democracy as a controlling reference in our judgments of comparison. This principle is an ethical one.

What is this principle of ethical democracy? It is a principle of equality—an equality not of status or origin but of opportunity, relevant functions, and social participation. The enormous literature and bitter controversy which center around the concept of equality indicate that it is only a little less ambiguous than the concept of democracy. It is necessary, therefore, to block it off from some current notions before developing the argument.

(*A*) The principle of equality is not a *description* of fact about men's physical or intellectual natures. It is a *prescription* or policy of treating men.

(*B*) It is not a prescription to treat in identical ways men who are unequal in their physical or intellectual nature. It is a policy of equality of concern or consideration for men whose different needs may require differential treatment.

(*C*) It is not a mechanical policy of equal opportunity for everyone at *any* time and in *all* respects. A musical genius is entitled to greater opportunities for developing his musical talents than someone who is tone deaf. It is equality of opportunity for all individuals to develop whatever personal and socially desirable talents they possess and to make whatever unique contributions their capacities permit.

(*D*) It is not a demand for absolute uniformity of living conditions or even for arithmetically equal compensation for socially useful work. It demands that, when the productive forces of a society make possible the gratification of basic human needs (which are, of course, historical variables), no one should be deprived of necessities in order to provide others with luxuries.

(*E*) It is not a policy of restricting the freedom of being different or becoming different. It is a policy of *encouraging* the freedom to be different, restricting only that exercise of freedom which converts talents or possessions into a monopoly that frustrates the emergence of other free personalities.

(*F*) It is not a demand that all people be leaders or that none should be. It does demand that the career of leadership, like all other careers, be open to all whose natural or acquired talents qualify them; that everyone have a say in the process of selecting leaders; that the initiative of leaders operate within a framework of basic laws; and that these laws in turn ultimately rest upon the freely given consent of the persons who constitute the community.

(*G*) It does not make the assumption of sentimental humanitarianism that all men are naturally good. It does assume that men, treated as equals in a community of persons, may become better. The emphasis upon respect for the personality of all individuals, the attitude which treats the personality not as something fixed but as a growing, developing pattern, is unique to the philosophy of democracy.

What I have been trying to show is that the logic of the democrat's position compels him to go beyond the limited conception of political democracy—the equality of freedom—to a broader attitude extending to those other phases of social existence that bear upon the effective exercise of equality of freedom. This in fact has been the historical tendency observable wherever democratic principles and programs are permitted to operate. Perhaps the synoptic phrase "social equality," whose connotations encompass political, educational, and economic democracy, may be taken as the most appropriate expression of the meaning of democracy in the broadest sense.

It is clear that the principle of equality, like any principle of justice, cannot by itself determine what is specifically right or good in each concrete case. But whatever the right is discovered to be, from the point of view of democracy it is the result of an analysis which considers equally the needs of all the persons involved in the situation; and, further, whatever the good is, it becomes better to the extent that it is shared among other members of the community. It is also clear that in concrete situations there will be conflicts among various demands for equality, and that in negotiating these conflicts the methods of intelligence are indispensable to a functioning democracy. If empiricism is a generic term for the philosophic attitude which submits *all* claims of fact and value to test by experience, then empiricism as a philosophy is more congenial to a democratic than to an antidemocratic community, for it brings into the open light of criticism the interests in which moral values and social institutions are rooted. Empiricism so conceived is commitment to a procedure, not to a theory of metaphysics.

In this brief account of the nature of democracy as a way of life I have not aimed at an exhaustive analysis of the *forms* in which it may be expressed, but have tried to indicate the basic ideals which are involved in the customary usage of the term and in the implications of that usage.

Before proceeding to the question of the justification of democracy I wish to discuss briefly two points of possible criticism. The first takes issue with the conception of democracy as equality of concern, concretized above; the second believes that if democracy is not defined as the rule of law, at least the recognition of the primacy of law must be given a high order of priority in the democratic community.

From the point of view of democracy as purely and only a form of government, reference to equality of concern is indeed irrelevant. Theoretically, and sometimes even historically, democratic governments have shown less equality of concern for all members of the community than have some benevolent, or even feudal, despots. But if we broaden the term to speak of democracy as an ethical way of life then we would deny that equality of concern can be manifested by a master or ruler or despot without equality of power. A master who has no more power than a slave is not a master, and a ruler or despot whose interest counts for one and no more than one is not likely to hold on to his power without being forced to share it. Whatever designation we give the term, its meaning is the one intended when we charge that a democratic state, government, or community has acted undemocratically. If anyone bogs at the expression "democracy," let him substitute for it the phrase "social justice."

It is sometimes said that the distinguishing feature of democratic government is that it represents the rule of laws, not of men. This emphasis upon laws, unless qualified by reference to the kind of laws and how they are adopted, seems to me to miss the essential point. It describes not what is distinctive of democratic society but of *any stable society,* with definite laws, traditions, and procedures, whether democratic or not. The rule of law holds for slave societies and feudal societies as well as for democratic societies—perhaps more so in virtue of the complexity of the social relationships involved. In slave and feudal societies differences of interest are usually settled by an appeal to principles and customs which define rights and duties. Even tyrants to the extent that they are rational creatures lay down rules, so that their subjects will know what to do or avoid, and try to follow them. Even in abandoning them, they enunciate new rules. At most the rule of law differentiates between societies in a state of anarchy and societies in a state of stability. But there are many different ways of being stable, and many different types of law regulating stability.

A democratic society is one ordered by laws; but the laws in such a society must be made or interpreted by individuals who, ultimately, are responsible to (and removable by) the community. The community must be one in which equality of civic status obtains, in which the laws ultimately rest upon the freely given consent of the adult population. For certain purposes the contrast between the rule of laws and the rule of men is legitimate, but very often it has deceptive connotations. For laws do not rule by themselves; they must always be interpreted and administered by men. And these men, no matter how august their robes or presence, are fallible human beings who read their different, and often conflicting, meanings into the same set of laws. The diverse meanings judges can torture out of apparently plain texts constitute a large part of the history of Anglo-American law, as precedent is stretched to meet new cases never even envisaged by legislatures and courts. The arbitrary nature of judicial interpretation of law finds its most notorious illustration perhaps in some of the decisions of the United States Supreme Court. In the light of the history of that court, its reversals of judgment as the composition of the court changes, its interpretations of the meaning of words by thought processes compared to which the derivation of the name of Middletown from the name of Moses is a straightforward inference, the belief that the United States is ruled by laws rather than by men is untenable. In many areas, it is easier to predict what the decision of the Supreme Court will be from the composition of the Court than from the existence of the basic law which presumably guides its decision.

II

We now come to the problem which is of primary concern to philosophers, and not only to philosophers. What are the grounds on which we can justify our acceptance of democracy in contradistinction to other modes of social life? So far as I can see there are five generic types of justification which have been or can be offered. And by justification here I do not mean "proof," but the offering of valid reasons.

The first asserts that the rational foundation of democratic belief consists in a set of supernatural religious truths, in the sense that there can be no intelligent ground for choosing between democracy and other forms of society which does not logically commit us to some kind of theology.

The second asserts the same thing about metaphysics understood as a theory of "reality." Usually these two approaches go hand in hand.

The third attempts to derive democracy from natural law, leaving aside the origin of this law. It is a cross between metaphysics and theology, but important enough to consider by itself.

The fourth maintains that the choice of democracy is a nonrational preference rooted in the constitution of our natures and brought to flower by nurture and education.

The fifth affirms that the belief in democracy is a hypothesis controlled by the same general pattern of inquiry which we apply to any scientific hypothesis but referring to different subject matter, i.e., our evaluations.

(1) *Democracy and religion.* Does democracy as a way of life rest upon belief in supernatural religious truths in the sense that, if the latter are denied, the former must necessarily be denied? It is becoming increasingly fashionable to maintain this. Were historical considerations relevant here, I think it could be conclusively established that the great institutional religions, with the possible exception of some forms of Protestantism, have tended in fact to support theocratic forms of government. Nor is this surprising if the Kingdom of Heaven be taken as a model or inspiration for the Kingdom of Earth. Whoever heard of a democratically organized Paradise? Walt Whitman in heaven would meet with the same fate as Lucifer, but for different reasons. Not only is the notion of a democratically organized heaven blasphemous, but the proposal to reform along democratic lines a hierarchically organized church would lead to excommunication. If we examine the actual behavior which has been sanctified by the maxim, "Render unto Caesar what is Caesar's and to God what is God's," we will discover that historically institutional religion has always been able to adapt itself to any form of government or society that will tolerate its existence.

But our concern is not with historical questions, fascinating as they are, but with the logic of the position. We must consequently rephrase the question to read: Does belief in democracy logically rest upon any theological propositions in the sense that the denial of the second entails the denial of the first? And for this discussion I shall take as illustrative of theological propositions the two cardinal propositions of natural theology, viz., "God exists" and "Man has an immortal soul." To assert that whoever has no grounds for affirming the existence of God and immortality has no ground for affirming the validity of democracy is to claim that the former are at least necessary conditions of the latter. I shall argue that they constitute neither necessary nor sufficient conditions.

(*a*) Before examining this claim, let us note the tremendous risk it involves. Were those who advance it ever compelled to admit that these theological propositions are undemonstrable or false, they would have to surrender their belief in democracy. But this, I submit, very few of them are prepared to do. They would search for other reasons and grounds. Like those who would make the validity of moral judgments dependent upon the existence of God and immortality, the theological defenders of democracy shift from a problem in which, although difficult, it is possible to reach an agreement on the basis of some empirical evidence to one in which the nature of the terms and sphere of discourse makes such agreement much more difficult. Confirmed democrats, it seems to me, are much more convinced of the validity of the democratic ideal than they are of the theological propositions upon which it presumably depends. They would no more exonerate an atheist or agnostic who pleaded that he had no reason to believe in God and the hereafter from the obligation of accepting the democratic ideal than they would from the obligation of living honestly.

(*b*) Aside from the difficulties of establishing God's existence, how can we get from the fact of his existence to the desirability of the democratic way of life? None of the attributes of God, save the moral attributes, can serve as a premise justifying one way of life rather than another. And if the moral attributes of God can serve as premises, necessary or sufficient, for the democratic way of life, it is only because *we* regard them as worthy, i.e. as truly moral. Obviously any theology which makes God's power the justification or source of his goodness is worse than useless for purposes of deriving democracy. The attribution of moral qualities to God is an expression of what we think his qualities ought to be. And this is a problem of precisely the same order as we are called upon to answer when we ask for the grounds of our democratic allegiance.

(*c*) The situation is the same if we grant that human beings have immortal souls. In what way is this a necessary or sufficient presupposition of democracy? The brotherhood of man may be a theological fact as it is a biological fact, but that which makes it wrong for Cain to kill his brother Abel and right, under certain circumstances, for us to kill Cain, and noble for Jonathan to lay down his life for David who was *not* his brother, is a moral principle which can no more be derived from theology than from biology—unless, of course, the moral principle is one of the premises of our theological (or biological) system. In which case we are no further along than we were when we raised the question about the democratic way of life. In passing it should be observed that belief in the immortality of the soul can be, and has been, used (in the Hindu doctrines of *Samsara* and *Karma*) to sanctify the tightest system of antidemocratic social stratification the world has even seen.[1]

(2) *Democracy and metaphysics.* The problem of the metaphysical foundations of democracy is more difficult because of the varying conceptions of metaphysics. By metaphysics I shall understand the discipline designated by the term "ontology" or any theory of "being *überhaupt.*" The evidence seems to me to be overwhelming that there is a definite historical connection between the social movements of any period and its dominant metaphysical teachings; further, I am prepared to defend as historically true the proposition that systems of idealistic metaphysics, because of the semi-official roles they have played in their respective cultures, have been more generally employed to bolster antidemocratic social movements than have systems of empirical or materialistic metaphysics. Whether there is always an intrinsic personal or psychological relation between a philosopher's metaphysics and his ethics or politics is a more difficult question, but one which seems to me to require an answer in the negative. But more germane to our present concern is my contention that there is no necessary logical connection between a theory of being or becoming and any particular theory of ethics or politics. Stated more accurately, it seems to me demonstrable that no system of metaphysics unequivocally determines a system of ethics or politics. There may be certain facts about man and nature which might have a bearing upon our judgment about what social system is of the highest worth, but these are facts concerning which the empirical sciences are qualified to report without benefit of metaphysics.

Two species of metaphysics are most often invoked on behalf of democracy. One asserts that the value of democracy or the values from which it may be derived are "grounded in reality," a phrase which is interpreted to mean that the universe "justifies" or "guarantees" both the validity and the ultimate supremacy of basic human ideals. I must confess that it is difficult for me to understand this view except as a shamefaced kind of theology. But however that may be, there is no agreed-upon denotation of *the* universe; there are many universes. Nor is there any one basic human ideal, but many human ideals which are often in conflict with one another, even though they all invoke the universe as a ground of their validity and as a guarantee of their

---

[1] Cf. Max Weber, *Religionssoziologie,* II, 119–20. The lot of the Hindu in this life is a consequence of his sins or virtues in a previous life. Therefore, he cannot complain about the injustice of any "accident of birth" or station. But, no matter how unclean his caste, he has the hope that, by exemplary observance of the caste rituals and cheerful acceptance of his present lot, he may improve his social position in the next cycle of rebirth.

triumph. Finally, and most important, no matter what character the universe is alleged to have, no matter what the nature of the far-off event toward which it is moving, no matter who wins or loses, nothing logically compelling in the way of judgment follows unless *we* have already morally evaluated the character of events. For most metaphysicians the very word "reality" is an implicit value term. To be sure, history may be conceived as a struggle between the Prince of Darkness and the Prince of Light, but the latter is so named because he carries *our* moral flag.

The second metaphysical view to which resort is often made is at the same time a kind of rejoinder to our position. It distinguishes between a metaphysical realm of being and a metaphysical realm of values, and grounds the democratic way of life in the latter. Just as the spectrum of colors is there to be beheld by all who are not color blind and would still be there even if man's ancestors had climbed no higher than the mole in the tree of evolution, so the spectrum of values is there to be beheld by all who are not value blind and would still be there even if human beings had never existed at all. The view that colors would still be there even if human beings had no eyes is not without its difficulties. But they do not begin to compare in difficulty with the view that values are essentially unrelated to an evaluator and his interests. Santayana has quite aptly remarked of this doctrine that there is as much sense in saying that whiskey "is pervaded as it were, by an inherent intoxication, and stands dead drunk in its bottle."

The subject is vast, but it is enough to show that this view begs the question in precisely the same way as do other theological and metaphysical derivations. The existence of these absolute norms is presumably certified or authenticated at some point by an act of immediate intuition. If the testimony of the intuition is construed not merely from what individuals *say* they intuit but from the conduct that flows from their intuition—and in any moral scheme conduct counts for more than mere words—then it is clear that individuals intuit or "see" *different* values. The "great" visions are not at all compatible with one another in what they command, not to mention the visions which we do not call great. Which visions are the authentic ones? Prior to every conclusion that these are the objective values of all eternity, or even of all time and existence, is the assumption that *this* is the trustworthy seer. In a dispute between two men, one of whom asserts that the other is color blind and the other that the first is "just seeing things," there are definite ways of determining who is right. In a dispute between two seers whose immediate intuitions report conflicting news about the nature and hierarchy of absolute values, there is no rational way of reaching a consensus. The true prophet cannot be distinguished from the false by invoking absolute values whose validity depends upon a prior assumption of the reliability of prophetic testimony. The complacency with which some writers have cut the Gordian knot by introducing reference to the intuitions of "the best people" or "the most cultured people" or "the saving remnant" is evidence either of parochialism or of snobbery.

The record of human error and cruelty shows what ghastly consequences often result from the conviction that one's moral insight cannot possibly be wrong and that it needs no further justification than its own incandescent purity. No more than a solipsist can make plausible on his own assumptions the existence of another solipsist, can an absolutist find a rightful place for another absolutist who disagrees with him. Absolutists face each other over an abyss which cannot be bridged even by their weapons of war.

(3) *Democracy and natural law*. The attempt to justify democracy on the basis of "natural law" suffers from root ambiguities in the conception of natural law. There is a threefold confusion between the physical conception of law, the legal conception of law, and the conception of moral laws as laws of what should be.

The physical or scientific conception of law is descriptive, not prescriptive. It tells us how events of different kinds are in fact related. It cannot serve as a basis for an unequivocal judgment of what we should do. It is the nature of chickens to lay eggs and of fertilized eggs to become chickens. But this law of nature does not tell us whether we should permit chickens to lay eggs or put them in the pot, or whether we should permit eggs to hatch instead of making omelets of them. Further confusion is produced by the ambiguity of the term "natural." Sometimes it is taken to mean "normal"; sometimes merely "existent." The confusion is confounded when "normal" is given the connotation of "good" or "desirable" and "abnormal" is given the connotation of "bad" or "undesirable." Obviously "the abnormal" is just as natural as the normal though less frequent, and the "unnatural" unfortunately exists just as much as the natural, as when we speak of "the unnatural vices." This does not mean that the natural vices are desirable because they may be normal. And great courage and unselfishness are also abnormal without being undesirable.

Whatever the natural laws of physics or biology, they cannot by themselves serve as legitimate justifying premises of democracy. At most one can argue that the order a democratic society seeks to build is rendered impossible by such natural laws. But even if laws of nature make certain social arrangements impossible, this would not make the attempt to achieve them impossible, only foolish. It is obvious that the

laws of physics are irrelevant to, or equally compatible with, any proposal to organize government or society on democratic or undemocratic
lines. The same is true of the laws of biology. Even if it were a biological law that all animals love one another and live at peace with each
other, it would not follow that men should do so. And if the opposite
view were held that "nature is red in tooth and claw," it would not
follow that because dog eats dog, man should eat man.

Natural law, in ordinary contexts, refers to connections or relations
which cannot be violated. A violation of a natural law is an exception
to a natural law and by definition an exception to a natural law is
evidence that it is not a law and that the statement asserting that it
holds is false. If the natural law of gravitation or cell division is violated
there is no law. But the natural law upon which democracy presumably
rests is violable. We are told that we "should" follow it and are condemned for not following it. This indicates that the natural law is
neither "natural" nor "a law" in the ordinary sense of these terms.

Those who speak of a conception of immutable, universal, and rational order which should serve as a model for human behavior cannot
sensibly mean that it is a legal order, for all sorts of legal systems
exist—some just, some unjust, some rational, some unrational. The
problem is to make the legal order a moral one and, in part, to develop
legal sanctions for some of our moral values.

This indicates that those who speak of natural law as a basis for
democracy really have in mind some transcendent metaphysical or
theological principle as a basis for human institutions, to which they
misleadingly refer as natural law. They should claim either that it is a
law of God or that it is a metaphysical law of being which even God,
if he exists, cannot alter. In either case, however, the difficulties in
connection with these themes remain.

For purposes of summary let us examine a recent and eloquent
claim to derive democracy from natural law.

> The human person possesses rights because of the very fact that
> it is a person, a whole, master of itself and of its acts, and which
> consequently is not merely a means to an end, but an end, an end
> which must be treated as such. The dignity of the human person?
> The expression means nothing if it does not signify that by virtue
> of natural law, the human person has the right to be respected, is
> the subject of rights, possesses rights. There are things which are
> owed to man because of the very fact that he is man. The notion
> of right and the notion of moral obligation are correlative. They
> are both founded on the freedom proper to spiritual agents. If
> man is morally bound to the things which are necessary to the

fulfillment of his destiny; and if he has the right to fulfill his destiny he has the right to the things necessary for this purpose.[2]

To begin with, we note that those who have held this view in the past have not been outstanding for their defense of democracy. On the contrary, they have defended on the basis of natural law undemocratic systems. Secondly, although we are told that the human being possesses rights and that things are owed him "because of the very fact that he is a man" we are not told specifically what those rights and what those things are. Is there any specific right that an individual human has which is absolute and inalienable? Is it the right to life? If an individual has an absolute and inalienable right to life, he has a right to what makes that life possible. But suppose he can only survive, as sometimes happens, by taking the life of another? Do both have an absolute right to live when the destruction of one is a condition for the survival of the other? Has an individual criminal a right to life independently of the character and frequency of his crimes? Had Hitler or Stalin, moral monsters both, more of a natural right to life than some innocent animal who never harmed anyone? Has any man a natural and absolute right to refuse to bear arms in the service of his country on the ground that he has a natural right to life—a right which is owed him merely because he is a man? M. Maritain and his ideological forebears would hardly grant this.

Is there, then, a natural, absolute, and inalienable right to liberty? Of speech? But what of the laws which punish criminal libel and the treason of betraying the secrets of national defence to an enemy? A right of action? But what of the laws which define the conditions under which our behavior is a nuisance, if not worse? Right of assembly? Surely not when traffic is obstructed or an emergency conveyance must have the right of way?

Is there, then, a natural, absolute, and inalienable right to property, as Locke believed? But what if the things I make as a result of "mixing" my own labor with it are necessary for the safety and security of the community whose traditions and schools provided me with the skills and knowledge required to produce the "property"? What of "property" in land to which the community claims the right of eminent domain?

Is there, then, a natural, absolute, and inalienable right to happiness, as Jefferson claimed? What, then, shall we answer the young man who claimed the right to kidnap his beloved on the ground that she was absolutely necessary to his happiness? If we took seriously this asser-

---

[2] Jacques Maritain, *The Rights of Man and Natural Law* (New York, Charles Scribner's Sons, 1943), p. 65. Used with permission.

tion of the absolute right to the pursuit of happiness the world would be a much more unhappy place than it is.

And finally, what of the conflicts between these natural rights? Every difficult moral situation can be construed in terms of such a conflict. Our own time has spawned a whole series of moral problems in which the right to security conflicts with the right to liberty and which challenges us to fruitful and creative devices that aim at giving us as much as possible of both but must on occasion risk our security or curb our freedom. The theory of natural law does not take us an inch forward in negotiating such conflicts.

Even if all of these difficulties were met it would still be necessary to show in what way this theory of natural law, which some of its devotees call integral humanism or integral liberalism, justifies democracy rather than benevolent despotism. One modern exponent of natural law who attributes the decline of liberalism to a point of view which rejects metaphysical premises accepted on faith explicitly cites the following lines from Goethe, that consummate dabbler in politics, as "capturing the essential spirit of integral liberalism."

> *Es ist kein schoen'rer Anblich in der Welt,*
> *Als einen Fuersten seh'n, der klug regieret,*
> *Das Reich zu seh'n, wo jeder stolz gehorcht,*
> *Wo jeder sich nur selbst zu diene glaubt,*
> *Weil ihm das Rechte nur befohlen wird.*[3]

The failure of the theory of natural law and natural rights to further the solution of any specific problem suggests that in the past it served as a rhetorical expression of man's sense of injustice against the *status quo*. Taken literally it was not credible. Taken with the saving grace of intellectual sophistication it was an appeal to reason, to the arts of intelligence, to make social life more humane and just. This made it often a linguistic preface to a more empirical approach.

(4) Democracy and preferences. The view that an acceptance of democracy is an expression of a preference does not carry us far until the kind of preference is indicated. A preference may express a passing whim or a deep natural bent; it may be impulsive or reflective. Preferences are rooted in our natures. Their forms, occasions, and objects are supplied by education, i.e., broadly speaking, by social habits and

---

[3] Hallowel, "The Decline of Liberalism," *Ethics* (1942), p. 336. Freely translated the passage runs: "There is no more beautiful sight in the world than to observe a Prince who rules wisely and to see a country where everyone proudly obeys, and where everyone believes that he is serving his own interest because he is commanded to do only what is just."

intelligence. But either our natures can be changed or the educators re-educated. If neither is possible, then the fact of moral choice becomes unintelligible. If we can offer no justification of a preference except that it is ours, obviously no point of intellectual or moral issue is raised, nor, *a fortiori,* can any be settled by the trial of arms. If we offer a justification of a preference, it will take one of the other four generic forms.

(5) *Democracy as a hypothesis.* When democracy is taken strictly as a form of political government, its superiority over other forms of government can be established to the extent that it achieves more security, freedom, and cooperative diversity than any of its alternatives. If we test the workings of political democracy by Paul's scheme of virtues or by Nietzsche's, we may perhaps reach another conclusion. So long as there is no dispute about observable effects and so long as we raise no question about the moral ideals by which we evaluate these effects, we have clear sailing.

But, as has already been made plain, by democracy as a way of life we mean a way of organizing human relationships which embodies a certain complex of moral ideals. Can these ideals be treated as hypotheses? The conventional reply has always been that no moral principle can be regarded as a hypothesis, for we must already have certain knowledge of what is good before we can evaluate the consequences of acting upon it. If any position is question-begging, surely this seems to be!

Were this a symposium on value theory, I would devote all my time to developing the general theory of moral ideals as hypotheses. But here I can only barely indicate that the notion is not viciously circular. A moral ideal is a prescription to act in a certain situation or class of situations in determinate ways that will organize the human needs and wants involved so as to fulfil a set of *other* values which are *postulated* as binding in relation to the problem in hand. No more than in other cases of inquiry do we start with an empty head. The cluster of values we bring to the situation is the result of prior experience and reflection. They are not arbitrarily postulated. The consequences of acting upon the hypothesis may lead us to challenge a postulated or assumed value. This in turn can become the subject of a similar investigation. Terminal values are always related to specific contexts; there is no absolute terminal value which is either self-evident or beyond the necessity of justifying itself if its credentials are challenged. There is no vicious infinite regress involved if we take our problems concretely and one at a time. Nor is the procedure narrowly circular. For if, in a long history of raising and solving moral problems, we postulate as a value in solving a later problem a value which had itself to be certified in an earlier problem, this would testify to the presence of a fruitful set of systematically related values in the structure of our moral behavior. New values would emerge, or be discovered, in the course of our attempt to act upon our ideals and from the necessity of mediating the conflict between the postulated values as they bear on concrete human needs in specific situations.

I should like, however, to make the general position take form out of the discussion of the theme before us. That theme is: Why should we treat individuals of unequal talents and endowments as persons who are equally entitled to relevant consideration and care? Short of a treatise I can state only the reasons, without amplification of the concrete needs of the social situation which democracy seeks to meet and the institutional practices by which it must meet them.

(*a*) This method of treating human beings is more successful than any other in evoking a maximum of creative, voluntary effort from all members of the community. Properly implemented it gives all persons a stake in the community and elicits a maximum of intelligent loyalty.

(*b*) It enlarges the scope of our experience by enabling us to acquire insight into the needs, drives, and aspirations of others. Learning to understand how life is organized by other centers of experience is both a challenge and a discipline for our imagination. In aiding the growth of others, we aid our own growth.

(*c*) The willingness to understand another man's point of view without necessarily surrendering to it makes it more likely that different points of view may negotiate their differences and learn to live peacefully with one another. A democratic community cannot be free from strife in a world where inequalities will always exist, but its ethics when intelligently acted upon make more likely the diminution of strife or its transference to socially harmless forms than is the case when the principle of equality is denied. In consequence there is less toadying, less fear, and less duplicity in the equalitarian community than in the non-equalitarian society.

(*d*) In nurturing the capacities of each individual so that they may come to their greatest fulfillment, we can best share our existing stores of truth and beauty and uncover new dimensions in these realms. How can anyone dedicated to the values of science and art consistently oppose a policy which maximizes the possibility of the discovery and widest dispersion of scientific truths and artistic meanings?

(*e*) Regard for the potentialities of all individuals makes for less cruelty of man toward man, especially where cruelty is the result of blindness to, or ignorance of, others' needs. A community organized along democratic lines is guilty of cruelty only at those points where it has failed to live up to its own ideals. A totalitarian community is systematically insensitive to the personal needs not only of members of the outlawed scapegoat group but of the majority of its subjects who are excluded from policy-making discussions. At best, there is no way of determining these personal needs except by the interpretation of the dictator and his experts who operate with the dogma that they know the true interests of their subjects better than the subjects themselves. At worst, the dictator assumes not only that he speaks for his subjects but that in some mystic way he feels and thinks for them too. Despite the great limitations—limitations from the point of view of their own ideals —under which the nineteenth- and twentieth-century democracies of the Western world suffered, I think it is indisputable, on the evidence, that by and large their social life, in so far as this was the consequence of policy, displayed less cruelty than the social life of any other historical period.

(*f*) Reasonableness of conclusions, where attitudes and interests conflict, depends upon the degree of mutual consultation and free intellectual communication between the principals involved. The democratic way of life makes possible the widest forms of mutual consultation and communication. Conclusions reached by these processes have a quality that can never be found where conclusions are imposed by force or authority—even if they are our own. Who among us would forego the methods of public discussion, criticism, argument, and rejoinder for a philosophical consensus imposed by a Gestapo or a G.P.U., even if by a strange quirk of affairs it was *our* philosophic position that the goon squads of orthodoxy sought to make the way of salvation? Who among us, knowing that outside the door stood an individual of a strange country, color, or faith, capable of making a contribution to our lives, would not open the door to him? These are not rhetorical questions framed to discover philosophical fifth columnists. They are designed to show that the procedures of critical discussion and discovery, which are pre-eminently exhibited in the work of a scientific community, take for granted that national, racial, or religious origins are irrelevant to the logic of the method by which reasonable conclusions are reached. Democracy as a way of life differs from its alternatives in that it makes possible the extension of these methods of reaching reasonable conclusions from the fields of professional science and philosophy to all areas of human experience in which genuine problems arise.

There are other grounds that may be offered in justification of democracy as the most adequate social philosophy for our times. Every one of them postulates implicitly or explicitly values or desiderata. But I repeat: these postulates are ultimate only for the problem in hand. They may require justification. When we undertake such justification, we have undertaken a new inquiry into a new problem.

There are two important consequences of approaching democracy in this way. The first is that we avoid the temptation, which is rapidly gaining vogue, of making democracy absolutely valid in and for itself. There are many today who write as if they believe that democracy should prevail even though the heavens fall, and who say in so many words that "to question the validity of democracy is to disbelieve in it" and that we can meet the blind fanatical faith of fascism only with a faith in democracy which is at least just as fanatical. This temptation, it seems to me, must be avoided because, by counterposing subrational dogma to subrational dogma, it prepares the ground for an acceptance of a might-makes-right morality. Second, those who make of democracy an absolute value, which requires no justification but its inherent rightness, tend to identify this absolute democracy with whatever particular democratic *status quo* exists. On the other hand, among those who cannot distinguish between social philosophies on the ground of their inherent rightness the natural tendency is to test a social philosophy by the social institutions in which it is embodied. They are, therefore, more attentive to the actual workings and effects of democracy, more historically minded, and less likely to gloss over existing imperfections.

To those who say that human beings will not fight wholeheartedly except for certainties, and emphatically not for a hypothesis which is only probable, the reply must be made that this empirical proposition is highly dubious. Men have fought and do fight vigorously for causes on the basis of preponderant evidence. Vigorous action, indeed, is only desirable when we have first decided what is intelligent action. And intelligent action does not result when we assume that our ideas or ideals simply cannot be wrong. That both intelligence and resoluteness are compatible is clear in fields as far apart as military science and medicine. Once it is decided that the chances of one action are relatively better than another, once it is decided that an operation gives a patient a better chance of surviving than no operation, wisdom demands that the best-warranted alternative be pursued with all our hearts and souls. Let us remember that when we fight for democracy we are not fighting for an ideal which has just been proposed as a merely possible valid ideal for our times; we already have considerable evidence in its behalf, the weight of which, unfortunately too often, is properly evaluated only when democracy is lost or imperiled.

III

We now turn to the question of the feasibility of democracy. We can imagine someone, who has accepted the tentative ends by which we evaluate ways of life, criticizing us as follows: "If only the assertions made in the previous section could be established as true, the case for democracy would be convincing. But the nature of man as we know him, of history as scientifically understood, and of the larger world we live in precludes the possibility of ever achieving democracy. It runs counter to the facts. Although you may still choose to live or die for democracy, the attempt to realize it, like any attempt to realize an ideal which has no natural basis, will be a ghastly failure. Its natural consequences will be worse than the evils it sets out to cure, and it will subvert the very ideals to which you have appealed in your argument. Democracy is an infirmity of noble but innocent minds who have never understood the world. It is not an intelligent option."

I will consider briefly three types of objection to the feasibility of the democratic ideal.

(1) The first is based upon its alleged psychological impossibility. It maintains that democracy is too good for men who are essentially evil, fallen creatures, dominated by lust for power, property, and self. In less theological form it asserts that democracy makes too high a call upon human intelligence and disinterestedness.

It is true that the psychological nature of man is quite relevant to our problem. If most human beings were idiots or infantile or permanently incapable of self-development, the democratic ideal could hardly be defended on plausible grounds. But there is no evidence that most human beings are such, and an intelligent attempt to find out whether they are would require that equalization of social opportunity which is of the essence of democracy. Even without such an experiment, if we surrender the utopian expectation of the complete realization of the democratic ideal and bear in mind that the forms of democracy may be direct as well as indirect and that democracy is compatible with the delegation of powers and responsibilities, the evidence at hand could hardly justify the belief either in universal cretinism or in man's permanent ineducability. Nor do we have to counter with the assertion that men are *infinitely* perfectible to make our option for democracy reasonable. We require merely that they be sufficiently plastic, sufficiently capable of learning, criticism, and improvement, to choose responsibly between alternatives of action whenever—and here lies the crux—they have alternatives of choice. It is only the democratic community which will systematically give them the alternatives of choice on basic decisions. It is not without significance that no free people has ever voluntarily relinquished its democratic forms for a government which openly proclaimed as its aim the establishment of a permanent dictatorship. Principled dictatorships, as distinct from those that come in through the unguarded doors of democracy, always triumph by usurpation. As low as the human estate is today, there is no reason to believe that human beings belong to a psychological species inferior to that of their ancestors. Although history is rich in human stupidities and lost opportunities, in the face of men's achievements in the arts and sciences it would be simply foolish to read history as nothing but the record of human error.

The theological doctrine of man's essentially evil nature metaphorically expresses the truth that he is always limited, always tempted, and never free of his animal origins. But, taken literally, it makes any kind of moral virtue inconceivable except by interposition of divine grace or mystery. Here, too, we do not have to counter with a contrary theological proposition that man is essentially good. He is neither one or the other but becomes good or evil depending upon his society, his habits, and his intelligence.

(2) The most powerful arguments against the feasibility of democracy, strangely enough, have been neglected by most social philosophers. These are developed in the writings of Gaetano Mosca, Vilfredo Pareto, and Roberto Michels. Their common thesis, formulated on the basis of vast, detailed studies of political and social history, is that all historical change, whether reform or revolution, consists of the substitution of one ruling minority for another. This rule rests upon three pillars: vital myths which cement human relationships and conceal differences of interests; fraud or chicanery which prevent conflicting interests from becoming articulate when myths lose their vitality; and force which ultimately settles differences of interest. The nature of social organization, they claim, is such that democrats may be victorious but democracy never. So it has been, so it is, and so it will be.

Here I content myself with one consideration which points to the self-confessed inadequacy of their position. Despite this alleged law, every one of them admits, explicitly or implicitly, that some forms of society are better than others—and in every case it is the society which has a greater degree of democracy than the others. Thus Mosca, after maintaining the inescapability of minority rule, pays strong tribute to the superiority of parliamentary democracy over all other alternatives.[4]

Three basic errors, it seems to me, vitiate their conclusion. The first is that the amount of freedom and democracy in a society is determined

---

[4] *The Ruling Classes* (Eng. trans.), p. 256.

by a law *already known* or, as some would say today, by a historical wave. The truth is that the amount of freedom and democracy in the present and future depends as much upon human willingness to fight for them as upon anything else. The second error is the belief, common not only to these thinkers but to countless others, that human nature is unchangeable. Insofar as this is neither a proposition of biology or of theology nor a logical tautology, but refers to psychological and social traits, it can be shown to be false. The third is their confusion between an organizing principle and the individual members of the series organized. Since no identification is possible between the principle of democracy and any one member of the series, they go from the true conclusion that the principle is incompletely realized in any one case to the false conclusion that there are no degrees of realization in the series of cases.

(3) The third class of objections to the feasibility of the democratic ideal is derived from alleged cosmic or physicochemical laws which contain the equations of doom for man and all his works. Even granting the validity of such laws, they would hold no matter what society exists, and, therefore, they establish nothing about the relative superiority of one form of society over another. Such laws, as William James already pointed out in a definitive refutation of all views of this type, tell us about the *size* of "energy-rills," not their *significance*.[5]

That the cosmic home of man limits his power, if not his dreams, is of course true. It is a perennial source of his humility before the intractabilities of things and the transient character of what he builds. But it is also true that this limitation is the source of his opportunities and a necessary condition for all achievement. From these truths we cannot infer that nature is the guarantor of man's ideals, certainly not of the democratic ideal. But neither is it the enemy of human ideals. Man's friends and enemies are other men. To forget this is to go from natural piety to superstition. The cosmic scene against which men live out their lives will not be affected by the victory or defeat of a Hitler or Napoleon. Democracy needs no cosmic support other than the *chance* to make good. That chance it has, because man is part of nature. To ask for more is unreasonable as well as unworthy. The way in which man acts upon his chances is additional evidence of the objective possibilities and novelties of existence. In so far as he is caught in the flux of things, the intelligent democratic man honestly confronts the potentialities of existence, its futurities, its openness, its indeterminate-

---

[5] See his reply to Henry Adams, who tried to draw social and historical implications from the second law of thermodynamics (*The Letters of William James,* II, 344–47).

ness. He is free of the romantic madness which would seek to outlaw the truths of science and of the quaint conceit, permissible only as poetry, that nature is a democratic republic. He takes the world as science describes it. He employs his knowledge of the world to achieve a more just and happier society.

5 Bread, Freedom, and Free Enterprise

LIKE EVERY OTHER group in the American community, business professes a highly vocal concern for freedom. It seems to me that the expression of this concern is frequently open to criticism on two important counts. There is, for one thing, a tendency to blur the extremely complicated problem of bread and freedom; this tendency is manifested notably in the too-easy identification of freedom with free enterprise. And, secondly, there is a tendency to grapple inadequately with the relationship between free enterprise and other freedoms.

Freedoms, like rights, may limit as well as reinforce each other. Despite various doctrines of absolute and inalienable rights, no one can reasonably hold that any specific right or freedom should be gratified regardless of its consequences on the community and its bearings on other rights and freedoms. Some order of priority among freedoms must be recognized, and some method of determining that priority must be found. Freedoms may be ordered in relation to each other in the light of some encompassing value or ideal although the precise emphasis is a matter of degree dependent upon specific historical situations. In one sense of John Dewey's much misunderstood phrase that "each situation has its own unique good," we can also say that each situation has its own unique combination of freedoms which only intelligence can determine.

Perhaps the nearest we can come to a justifying principle for that complex of freedoms which we select as preferred in any situation is its tendency to maximize the amount of freedom for the individual. We want a world in which all individuals are as free as possible to develop their personalities in a peaceful community. Among the cultures of the West, different philosophical schools interpret and ground this value in the light of conflicting assumptions about the nature of man and the universe. But whatever else they would say about man, they would agree that to be human is to be capable of intelligence and moral choice, and that all freedoms are justified which enhance the capacity of intelligent moral choice.

Democracy is the fairest and most peaceful method that has been found to resolve the conflicts of interests underlying the conflicts of freedoms. Its central concept of freely given consent rests on the operation of a whole cluster of freedoms, here called political, not all of which are explicitly formulated in the Bill of Rights. The exercise of these political freedoms is what we should primarily mean by the American way of life. For these are the *strategic* freedoms; they enable us to win new freedoms and check the excesses of the old. So long as they prevail, modifications of and restrictions on other freedoms are reversible. Where they are undermined, no other freedom can be anything but an assertion of power by a privileged group. That is why every group that wishes to see conflicting interests resolved reasonably, or is wise about the conditions under which it enjoys its own freedom, must be profoundly concerned with the state of freedom of speech and assembly, freedom of inquiry and teaching, freedom of press and other forms of communication, freedom of cultural opportunity and development. For in large measure intelligent moral choice depends upon them.

Like other groups in American life, business has seldom given any indication that it is aware of the connection between these strategic freedoms. There has been a tendency to ignore them except when a direct relationship of a most immediate kind with the narrow group interest could be demonstrated. Until recently, this was largely true of the labor movement; many American unions fought for civil rights only in the limited sector of labor organization, and they tolerated or condoned discriminatory practices against Negroes. But today organized labor usually combines the struggle for economic betterment with a lively appreciation of the importance of the strategic freedoms for the entire community. The churches have also shown an increasing awareness of this. There are, of course, some churches which spring into immediate action with indignant protests when their communicants are interfered with in freedom of worship but are strangely quiescent when the freedoms of other religious groups are violated. But by and large, and granting some notable exceptions, both labor and the churches are furnishing increasing evidence that they realize the struggle for freedom is morally indivisible.

The statement cannot be made of the American businessman, who continues to represent the largest group in the community which is yet to be drawn into the continuing struggle to preserve the heritage of freedom all along the line. There is no record of any large business having evinced a concern for freedom of speech and press until some NLRB decisions limited the right of companies to distribute literature to workers on the eve of representation elections. Indeed, efforts by some companies to prevent the distribution of literature by unions outside plant doors have not been unknown. Although many businessmen are quite concerned with threats to free enterprise—especially where the threat takes the shape of government controls in a rising economy—they have not displayed anywhere near the same zeal about improving the state of cultural and political freedom in their communities. Why is it that the fight for civil liberties, for academic freedom, for minority rights, is left largely to bishops, lawyers, and professors? There is no need to exaggerate. There have been notable exceptions, especially if we include publishers of newspapers and magazines among business groups. We must also recognize that in opposing the practices of discrimination and segregation against Negroes and other minorities, business has sometimes performed valiant and distinguished service—in International Harvester, for example. But on the whole it is incontestable that American businessmen have not accepted the challenge and opportunity to take or share leadership in rallying the community when outright violations of cultural and political freedoms occur. They have contented themselves largely with renewed affirmations of faith in free enterprise—despite certain difficulties entailed by their acceptance of tariffs and in some cases government loans and subsidies—as if this constituted the alpha and omega of the American faith in freedom. And by a strange paradox the few businessmen who have become interested in the defense of freedom are as likely as not to follow with touching naiveté the leadership of such ritualistic liberals as Mr. Robert Hutchins.

This comparative inactivity of the American businessman in the strengthening of the culture complex of freedom is surprising from the point of view of his own ideology. Although in theory he often interprets the American way of life as if it were identical with free enterprise, if not an outgrowth of it, in practice he has until recently left the actual defense of the specific freedoms which constitute the American way of life as it is actually lived and experienced largely to socialists and liberals who are vigorous critics of free enterprise. What businessman has fought as hard for civil liberties all along the line as the socialist, Norman Thomas?

If we judge the American businessman not by what he says but by what he does and fails to do, then it sometimes seems as if he shared a common premise with his bitterest enemy, the doctrinaire, orthodox communist. Although they differ about what constitutes an economically sound basis of society, and in their conception of economic freedom, they both believe that once an economically sound system is established, cultural and political freedoms will take care of themselves. Both regard freedoms as by-products of, or superstructural additions to, the economic foundations. Both are caught in a kind of historical automatism from whose implications the businessman releases himself only by abandoning, rather inconsistently, the causal monism which rules out the role of ideas and ideals in redetermining the direction of history.

The orthodox communist is more consistent than any other believer in economic determinism, but he pays a terrible price for his consistency. He identifies freedom with the acceptance of historical necessity and its inevitabilities. What seem to be genuine alternatives of diminishing or increasing the amount of freedom in society appear to him to be nothing but ripples on an irresistible undertow carrying us to a more "progressive" economy which through the terror regime of a self-selected political elite guarantees freedom for all and luxuries for everyone.

In orthodox communist ideology, this fetishism of the historical process, and unscientific belief in the inevitability of a future kingdom of heavenly freedom, have fateful consequences. They tend to paralyze the nerve of intelligence in social activity; the historical goal is destined to be achieved anyhow, independently of the particular means employed. They lead to an extreme moral insensitivity, since the moral costs of any action become part of the necessary historical process, a demand of a personified History for which we are not responsible. Finally, since someone must make decisions in concrete circumstances, political power must be entrusted to a handful of ideological initiates into the mysteries of the historical dialectic. Because they presumably know best what is to everyone's real interests, they can explain the ways of History to man.

This is, indeed, a far cry from the conscious ideology of the American businessman (to the extent that he has any). He assumes that the operation of natural laws in a free-enterprise system, provided that the government does not attempt to interfere with them, *necessarily* carries with it the structure of all our other freedoms. If we make explicit what follows from that assumption, a world view not dissimilar to that of dialectical materialism results.

If our argument is sound, then no matter what the character of the economic system, political and cultural freedom can never be taken for granted. They must always be fought for. A particular economic system may make certain political and cultural freedoms unlikely, but there is an entire spectrum of possibilities compatible with it whose realization

involves moral choices and commitments. Belief in a free-market economy is not the same as belief in a free society. Conversely, it is clear that
in England and the Scandinavian countries a faith in a free society does
not entail a belief in a free economy (although it is compatible with
such a belief). In economics, as in every other aspect of human behavior, fundamental decisions are moral decisions—informed or uninformed, wise or foolish. The probability that they will be informed and
wise is largely dependent on the extent to which the strategic freedoms
pervade the social structure.

The businessman's commonly expressed conviction that freedom is
rooted in free enterprise tends to paralyze him into inaction, or at least
hopelessness, when he is confronted with the problem of strengthening
freedom in depressed areas of the world. Because he so frequently believes that freedom (i.e., democracy) is impossible without an economic base similar to America's, he tends to have little confidence in
any program for keeping Asia, for example, noncommunist. His opinion although grounded differently is not dissimilar to one expressed by
certain delegates to the Indian Congress for Cultural Freedom. The
delegates, who were generally quite sympathetic to the purposes of the
Congress, asked: "What is the use of talking about cultural freedom to
a starving man? Is there any point in discussing threats to intellectual
and cultural life where poverty is so widespread that many people cannot begin to enjoy the freedoms of such life?"

The issues posed by these questions are relevant to the struggle for
freedom, not merely in Asia, but everywhere in the world where economic hardships and misery abound. They are focused most sharply
wherever Communist propaganda seizes upon existing economic conditions to dismiss democratic concern for freedom as a desire merely to
perpetuate the cultural privileges of a leisured class. The fact is that
Communist performance with respect to living conditions falls far
short not only of Communist promises but also of democratic performance. But this, unfortunately, is usually discovered by those who have
been seduced only after their freedoms have been destroyed. It therefore becomes important to clarify the issues, particularly since there is
evidence that many Europeans and even more Asians have found the
argument persuasive.

Is the antithesis between bread and freedom a legitimate one? Can
more bread be produced and distributed by sacrificing cultural and
intellectual freedom, by dismissing the latter as spiritual goods that will
automatically be added to the human estate *after* first things have been
provided for?

Let us begin with starving men. It is certainly futile to talk about cultural freedom to those who are starving. By the same token, it is just as futile to talk to them about education, hygiene, cruelty to women and children, social reform, or even love of God. The one thing to do about starving men is to feed them. But it is noteworthy to observe that those who protest against talking about freedom to men who are starving do not themselves feed them. Nor do they content themselves with advocating that they be fed by others. Instead they *talk* about other things, offer panaceas, and seek support for programs involving an apparent concern for many excellent matters except freedom. To be blunt, the argument against discussing freedom with starving men is usually not much more than an apology for some form of cultural tyranny.

Except where we are confronted with a situation of actual or near-starvation, as in some parts of Asia and Africa, the relation between bread (in the generic sense of standards of living) and freedom is not so simple. Particularly in Western Europe and the Americas, the problem is one of poverty, not starvation, and "poverty" is a relative term. It is relative to two things: variations in existing standards of living, and degrees of freedom and power to change the economic status.

Oddly enough, it was Karl Marx himself who stressed the relative nature of poverty and the irreducible psychological element it involved.

> A house may be large or small, but as long as the surrounding houses are equally small, it satisfies all social requirements of a dwelling place. But let a palace arise by the side of this small house, and it shrinks from a house to a hut. . . . And however high it may shoot up with the progress of civilization, if the neighboring palace shoots up also in the same or greater proportion, the occupant of the comparatively small house will always find himself more uncomfortable, more discontented, confined within his four walls. . . .

What Marx did not see is that from this it follows that socialism without equality could not solve the problem of poverty, and he himself was very dubious about the possibility of equality. At any rate, it has been argued that in a socialist economy like that of the Soviet Union, where in some sectors the differences in living conditions and earned income are greater than in our own country, there is far greater poverty than in the United States.

The basic problem consists of understanding the relationships between bread and freedom. But before discussing them a number of preliminary questions must be considered.

First, even if it were granted that bread is a necessary condition of freedom, this by itself would not be sufficient to justify any particular social program, or to justify indifference to the defense of freedom. For believers in free enterprise, collectivism, a welfare state, and a mixed economy are all equally convinced that only through the systems they espouse can bread be most effectively produced and distributed. Unless one is to make a claim to infallibility, the right of the people *freely to choose* which economic system is to minister to their material needs cannot be abridged. And this right freely to choose carries with it, as we have seen, a cluster of other rights which, if embodied in practice, constitute a considerable part of what we mean by cultural and intellectual freedom.

Second, in our complex world it is undoubtedly true that most social problems are interrelated. However, it does not follow that they can all be tackled at once or that there is no point in addressing ourselves to one particular problem at a time. Years ago when associations were organized to abolish child labor, some writers criticized these efforts on the ground that it was fruitless to agitate for abolition until the whole complex of conditions that produced child labor was removed. Yet, although it is far from certain that the causes of child labor have been eliminated, child labor has in large measure been abolished by efforts directed to that specific end. The social causes of illiteracy, violation of civil liberties, and cruelty to children are many and complex, but it would be downright foolish to criticize efforts to extend literacy, protect civil liberties, and prevent inhumanity to children on the ground that until their fundamental causes are removed—causes about whose nature there is no universal agreement—nothing or little can be done.

Similarly, whatever the social conditions which bear upon cultural and intellectual life, whenever intelligent men value the specific freedoms which define that life they can always do something to preserve or enlarge the area of freedom in historical situations where they are confronted by concrete problems of choice. It will take a long time to remove the restrictions against Negroes in the South and elsewhere, but right now, instead of lamenting the situation or waiting for public opinion to change, an immense educational program can be launched in northern schools to bring home to millions of students—tomorrow's citizens—their moral co-responsibility for the conditions under which their Negro brethren live. Laws and judicial decisions are often necessary to crystallize and give additional sanctions to the declarations of conscience, but in the end to be truly effective they must be accepted by re-educated public opinion.

Our final preliminary point is necessary as a caution to those who naively believe that social reforms by themselves are sufficient to prevent cultural freedom from being destroyed by the aggressive expansion of Communist totalitarianism in its crusade for world domination. No one can deny the contributing role economic conditions played in bringing Hitler to power. But once he achieved power, not all the Point Four programs in the world would have prevented him from embarking upon his program of world conquest. If anything, they would have whetted his appetite. Social conditions in Denmark, Belgium, Norway, and other Western countries were definitely superior to those of Germany. Conditions in Finland and Poland and the Baltic countries were superior to those in the Soviet Union. But this did not deter Hitler or Stalin.

In the present state of international affairs, social reforms are certainly necessary whenever acute need and poverty exist. But those who say that freedom can take care of itself once the slums of London or Bombay are razed are ignorant of the nature of modern totalitarianism. The model housing projects of Socialist Vienna were no deterrent either to Dollfuss' Heimwehr or Hitler's S.S. troops.

It is not without significance that, except in certain situations of natural disaster such as drought and flood, higher standards of living seem to prevail in countries with greater cultural and intellectual freedom. This is of course a rough judgment, for standards of living may be a function of the presence or absence of natural resources, and comparisons, to be instructive, must be drawn between nations whose physical potentials are not too diverse. What is sometimes attributed to politics may be due to geography in the comprehensive sense of the term. Yet that geography explains little is apparent from the history of countries almost devoid of natural resources, such as Holland and Switzerland. But when all allowance is made, it seems clear that there is a very impressive correlation between freedom and bread. There may be dearth for some even in nations whose average is high. But the impressive fact is that the voluntary movement of populations in quest for a better material life is always towards countries in which a freer cultural and intellectual climate obtains.

When people suffer from want, immediate relief from suffering becomes focal in their minds. They may identify this relief with social progress somewhat in the same way that a man who suffers from toothache identifies health with sound teeth. In such circumstances they may not look too closely at the means proposed to bring them relief and may give credence to the exhortations of the demagogue and to the typical rhetorical questions; "When you are hungry can you eat freedom? Can you feed it to your children? Can it keep you warm?" It becomes relevant to inquire, therefore, whether, in fact, the economic conditions of the masses have ever actually been improved as a consequence of the destruction of their cultural and political freedoms. Concretely, are the Russian worker and peasant better off today than say in 1914?

That in a number of respects social conditions in the Soviet Union have improved over the past, for example in literacy, availability of electric power, and so forth, is undeniable, just as it is true that the railroads ran more punctually in Italy after Mussolini's march on Rome. But these gains could certainly have been achieved by democratic means, even if at a slower pace, and at a lesser cost in human life, liberty, and happiness. Any comparison between the forty-year gains of large democratic countries with respect to the increase of the real wages of the workers as well as productivity, and the forty-year gains of the U.S.S.R. will show that the workers have benefited more in the former than in the latter. Further we must also inquire what the likely increases of real wages and production would be if the pre-revolutionary curve of rising productivity and increase in real wages had been extrapolated after making allowances for setbacks, wars, and depressions.

A more difficult question is whether the lot of the German workers and lower middle classes was improved after Hitler destroyed the Weimar Republic. Only if one disregards the fact that Hitler's war economy suffered disastrous defeat can it be asserted that the conditions of the German masses were improved by nondemocratic means. I have never met a German worker who, comparing the state of Germany in 1933 and 1945, after twelve years of Hitler's rule, did not infinitely prefer the former.

Sometimes those who counterpose bread and freedom suggest that it is entirely possible to surrender freedom for the security of a job and living quarters and the privileges of education and health insurance. But again a little reflection indicates the absurdity of such a separation of freedom and security. How can there be genuine security so long as arbitrary power, whether it be of an employer or a group, or especially of the *state as employer,* is not subject to the restraints of a freely operating democratic process?

The profoundest lesson of our era is the fact that without political freedom there can be no other freedoms, but only an uncertain and uneasy exercise of privileges which may be terminated abruptly without anybody's having to account to those who are affected by these decisions.

The notion that *first* one must strive to improve working conditions and *then* begin to be concerned with freedom is really foreign to the workers themselves whenever they are able to make voluntary choices. For they have learned from their own experience that without *free* trade unions, so-called improvements in their conditions can be snatched from them by arbitrary decrees. Without free trade unions, without the right to speak, assemble, and publish freely in opposition to their employers, whether the latter be private individuals or public officials, participation in determining the conditions and rewards of work is at best a farce, and usually nothing more than a legal device for imposing a system of forced labor. In all countries where political freedoms do not exist, the function of trade unions is not to protect the worker or to fight for his material interests but to increase his production—in the distribution of which, incidentally, he has no voice. The worker without political freedom, far from enjoying his security, becomes enslaved to the machinery of production regardless of the legal forms of ownership.

This suggests that it is a grave error to assume that freedom is a concern only of the cultured or professional groups whose task is the creation and dissemination of ideas. Even more mistaken is the view that freedom is something to be won only after sufficient leisure has been acquired in which to enjoy it. The truth is, even as the advertisements proclaim, that everyone has a stake in freedom in his every-day life and work. Although Marx is still one of the inconvenient minor deities in the Communist pantheon, his own writings deny in the most emphatic way the validity of the antithesis between bread and freedom. "The proletariat," he writes, "which will not allow itself to be treated as canaille, regards its courage, self-confidence, independence and sense of personal dignity as more necessary than its daily bread."[1]

Whatever may be the historical facts, it is certainly conceivable that human beings may surrender their freedom for the comforts of a well-appointed jail including the right (not possessed by the citizens of Iron Curtain countries) to denounce their jailors. It is conceivable but psychologically extremely unlikely when they understand what they are committing themselves to. Who, indeed, would exchange the uncertainties of a life outside a jail and the right to work and fight as a free man for all the food, clothing, shelter, medical service, and even congenial occupational therapy that the most enlightened penal institution can provide? And to be offered this kind of security for life would hardly enhance its attractiveness.

It is not necessary to claim that there is a freedom reflex in the human psyche in order to recognize that the desire for freedom is not reducible *merely* to a desire for material goods and services, important as these are. There is an irreducible quality in the experience of uncoerced choice which leads men to risk their very lives in its behalf. Whether our choices are good or bad, wise or foolish, we feel diminished as human beings if we are prevented from making them. Denied freedom to make

---

[1] *Gesamtausgabe*, I, 6, p. 278.

choices, we are denied responsibiliy, and to deny our responsibility is to deny our humanity. It is the unique glory of man that although he hopes and works for an abundant life, he is prepared to die in order to prove that he is human.

A peculiar aspect of situations in which the removal of poverty or great want is cited, however reluctantly, by the liberal as a justification of the absence or deprivation of political and cultural freedom, is that these situations are almost always ones in which the Communists exercise dictatorship. No liberal has ever been impressed in the least by the improvement made by Peron for Argentinian labor, by increase in the real wages of German workers under Hitler, in the benefits introduced by Mussolini. In 1957 a huge advertisement appeared in *The New York Times,* published by the government of Venezuela which is headed by the dictator, General Jiminez. It set forth in great and incontrovertible detail the social improvements, the public-works program, housing projects, schools, hospitals, popular cafeterias, superhighways, railroads, flood-control irrigation, and power plants initiated by the Venezuelan dictator. It asserts that "first things come first," these being health, standard of living, and education of the masses. It tells what is being done to improve them. And even if we accepted the claims of the Venezuelan dictator at only half their face value, they would still represent more than the Soviet dictatorship has done.

Nonetheless, no liberal would ever dream of accepting this as a justification of General Jiminez's rule or of that of any other South American dictator. Even though the cultural and political terror of these dictatorships does not begin to compare in severity with that of Communist regimes, liberals scorn to accept an apology of "more bread for less freedom." A score of arguments always come to hand to scuttle the claims of these benevolent dictators, all designed to prove that in those countries "more bread and more freedom" are both possible, and if there were a choice it would be, short of actual starvation, "more freedom and less bread"—for more freedom would enable the community to have more bread.

The great mystery is why this position, so clear and forthright when applied to Fascist and authoritarian dictatorships, is repudiated by some eminent liberals when the issue of bread and freedom arises in Communist dictatorships.

6 Democracy as a Philosophy of History

THE PHRASE "philosophy of history" is an ambiguous expression used to designate many different kinds of subject matter and types of inquiry. Every sense of the phrase, however, connotes reference to human culture. Whatever else a philosophy of history is, it is also a theory of the nature and development of culture. What explains history, explains culture and conversely, except when historical events have physical causes.

The most interesting questions about human culture concern the causes of the differences among cultures and their subsequent development. This quest for causes despite difficulties in finding the proper analysis of the *concept* of causation, cannot be called into question without impugning the very possibility of genuine knowledge of historical and social affairs, and without making unintelligible our efforts to control the conditions of our historical existence.

Certain methodological objections have been raised against the empirical validity of any large scale interpretation of history and culture. Provided we do not seek more accuracy than our subject permits, I do not believe they are fatal.

First of all, it has been denied that it is permissible to speak empirically of an explanation of culture or civilization as a whole any more than we can intelligibly explain the world as a whole. The situation, however, is not comparable. It is true that we cannot empirically explain the world as a whole because all the factors in such an explanation must be part of the whole. But theoretically cultures and civilizations can be explained as wholes if we believe, as I do *not,* that all social phenomena can be accounted for in non-cultural terms, physical or biological. The difficulty has point *only* for those who regard cultural phenomena as relatively autonomous in respect to natural processes and *only* if by the phrase cultures or civilizations "as a whole" is meant, *all* of a culture, or everything within it. But we do not need to equate the meaning of "culture as a whole" with "everything about the whole," any more than when we speak of something true about "the organism as a whole" we mean everything about the organism. So long as we remember that explanations are always selective, that no explanation of anything is or can be an explanation of everything about it, the point of the difficulty is turned.

Any theory or explanation of the nature and development of a culture as a whole is then reduced to a series of hypotheses about determinate connections between changes in some of its institutions and changes in other institutions. Similarly any theory or explanation of an historical pattern of events as a whole like the rise of capitalism, the decline of the Greek city states, the French Revolution is reducible to a series of hypotheses about the relation between certain events, natural and/or social, and other social events.

This gives rise to a second difficulty, the character of the relationship within any culture between the system of ideas or value-norms which prevail and the material institutions present. It is sometimes argued, particularly by Spengler, Sorokin, and others, that it is futile to try to assign any order of causal dependence among ideal and material factors, or even to distinguish the relative weight of different material factors in explaining changes within any culture complex. The economic system, the architecture, the legal system, educational curriculum, and technology—so it is said—are given together in such organic inextricability that it makes no sense to distinguish between causally dependent and independent factors. But cultures are not organisms, and even if they were, it would be possible in relation to some *specific problem* to isolate elements that are relevant from those that are not, and among the former those whose relevance is stronger from those whose relevance is weaker. For example, the necessity of insuring grain for Rome as well as the shape of Cleopatra's nose are both more relevant in explaining the presence of the Roman legions in fertile Egypt than the character of Roman religion; but no informed historian, Pascal to the contrary notwithstanding, would regard both the cosmetic fact and the economic fact in this case as of equal weight.

Without some such set of working distinctions we could neither affirm nor deny any statement that goes beyond chronicle. All historiography which distinguishes itself from fiction must employ them. And not only historiography, all intelligent behavior must do so as well. Once we define a specific problem for inquiry—e.g., why slavery which was in a state of gradual atrophy at the close of the eighteenth century in the United States took on a new lease of life, we can often find the factor of decisive causal significance, in this case the invention of the cotton-gin. To justify this causal attribution, if it is challenged, we construct a class of similar instances and show by certain techniques I have described elsewhere[1] that the other factors which are operating in the situation exercise no great importance. Our procedure here is no different in principle from the causal analysis we make in a field like medicine in which the multiplicity and reciprocity of factors that enter into the functioning of the organism in no way prevents the physician from reasonably attributing, say, to a certain diet deficiency, the most decisive cause of a certain disease, or from saying that diseases of the kidney in a certain class of cases are caused more often by one thing than another.

It has become fashionable partly because of the influence of Toynbee and lesser writers to explain the character of a culture by reference to a pervasive belief in some meta-cultural value grounded in a meta-physical reality. The notion that social institutions and historical changes within a culture are *logically* dependent upon some philosophical conception of reality is as demonstrably false as anything can be in human affairs. First of all, any general proposition about the meta-physical character of the world is *logically* compatible with the most diverse, and even contradictory, beliefs about the nature of the social world and the direction historical affairs should take. Whether a man believes that reality consists of a Great Self or a Great Material Atom, the question whether that Great Self or Atom should organize itself hierarchically or democratically is a completely independent question which in fact is always settled by considerations of an entirely different order from those that lead to belief in the metaphysical Great Self or Atom.

Secondly, if we examine any specific historical event or institutional change which has had profound cultural effects like the industrial revolution, we observe that it has spread into cultures as diverse as those of England, Germany, Russia, Japan, and Turkey whose alleged philosophical presuppositions are at variance with each other. And it is safe to predict if the world lasts another generation that the industrial revolution will come of age in China and India long before their regnant philosophical and theological dogmas are eclipsed by others.

Thirdly, philosophical traditions in many cultures have remained comparatively invariant despite striking changes in social and economic

---

[1] Cf. my discussion of "cause" in *Theory and Practice in Historical Study: A Report of the Committee on Historiography.* Bulletin 54, Social Science Research Council (1946), pp. 110–115.

institutions, like the transition in England from capitalism to socialism. On purely historical evidence a much better case can be made for the view that the dominant metaphysical ideas of an age have been in the main *ex post facto* rationalizations of social changes rather than causative factors in such changes. If by philosophy we mean metaphysical theories of reality from Plato to Whitehead, then Frederick Engels, despite his crude and oversimple formulations, is a thousand times right in his contention that the causes of basic social and political changes are to be sought not in the philosophy of any particular epoch but in the way in which human beings make their living and the consequences that flow therefrom.

Finally, when we infer from this false theory concerning the metaphysical determination of culture, the conclusion that the only durable road to world peace is through a common acceptance of some kind of metaphysical synthesis, confusion runs out into utter futility. For what could be clearer than the perception that it is notoriously much more difficult to win agreement for a set of metaphysical or theological premises than for a pattern of institutional behavior which because it is neutral to any kind of transcendental notions can let them all flourish? A common metaphysics or religion is neither a necessary nor sufficient condition of peace.

Sometimes when it is alleged that metaphysical beliefs are of decisive significance in a culture no more is meant than that the *moral* values prevalent within it to some extent may redetermine the movement of events—a situation illustrated by the different effects of the spirit of London after Dunkirk and the spirit of Vichy. On a pluralistic theory of historical causation it is perfectly intelligible that under certain circumstances moral values should play a great role in social life. Chesterton's famous *bon mot* about landladies and their boarders has its analogues in some social situations, to be considered subsequently. But at the moment, I wish to indicate how completely arbitrary it is to assume that the different moral values which move us to action rest upon different metaphysical assumptions from which they presumably are logically derived. I have never seen anything resembling a cogent argument to prove that moral values like honesty or kindness or democracy owe their validity to the acceptance or denial of any metaphysical statement whatsoever—except where that metaphysical statement turns out to be merely a value judgment in disguise. To assert as one philosopher has recently done that "we need a metaphysical synthesis as an underpinning for the common values on which our society depends" is to shatter whatever community exists and to prevent the rifts which divide men from being bridged over by intelligent social engineering. Common values rest upon consequences in experience, not upon presuppositions of theory and dialectic.

Relevant to values in their behavior-determining function are concrete interests of men, and the nature of the physical and social and personal world out of which these interests develop. But even in respect to the propositions of natural and social science about any state of affairs, I should deny that *by themselves* they uniquely determine one set of values rather than another. At most they exclude certain combinations of values as irrelevant, narrow the field of feasible alternatives, reveal the costs of integrity. They still leave open the possibility of moral affirmation or denial and the creative action which confirms or disproves the wisdom of our choice.

Were it not for the revival of mystical and metaphysical views of history, it would be unnecessary to stress their irrelevance to understanding any concrete problem of historical or cultural inquiry. But equally unsatisfactory, and more deceptive because of their claim to empirical validity, are the pretensions of monistic philosophies of history to account for the pattern and development of cultures—whether the causal factor be the physical environment, the race, the hero, the mode of economic production, or the spirit of nationalism. All of these theories, in a desperate effort to save the appearances, stretch the meaning of their basic terms until it encompasses everything including their opposites. Here, as elsewhere, a maxim of Peirce is useful in helping us to determine whether we are dealing with an empirical theory or not. He reminds us that one way of grasping the meaning of an assertion is to state the proposition which it must deny if the assertion is true, for unless we know what we are denying we don't know what we are asserting. We then ask under what circumstances and in the light of what evidence would one who makes an assertion admit that its denial was true. The inability to give a determinate answer indicates the inability of the proponent of the original assertion even to imagine or conceive it false.

I offer one illustration which may be taken as paradigmatic for all. Although I believe that properly formulated and qualified, the theory of historical materialism is more fruitful than any other theory in explaining the developments of modern history up to the rise of totalitarianism, in some of its customary formulations and applications it sins against the caution Peirce laid down. For example, the proposition is deduced from it that the state is always an instrument of the ruling class where the latter is defined in terms of its relation to the economy of the period. If it is now asked, how would the state have to behave in any conflict between capital and labor to prove that it was *not* being used as an instrument of the ruling economic class, no answer has ever been given by those who are certain about its essential nature. If one points to the Wagner Labor Relations Act as evidence that the state *sometimes* acts against the interests of the dominant economic class, the invariable response is that such acts are concessions granted to ward off worse evils. One would imagine that the power to exact concessions from the state is actually a power of control over the state and that this would constitute a precise illustration of the falsity of the above proposition if it is taken as a universal, necessary proposition about the behavior of states in class societies. But the apologetic literature of orthodox Marxism insists that any use of state power *in behalf* of a workingclass interest proves the proposition about the class character of the state just as much as the use of state power *against* the workingclass interest. This obviously converts the thesis into a non-empirical statement. It is true no matter what.

A similar difficulty faces other monistic theories. Whenever a thinker persists in holding such a theory—and he holds such a theory if he cannot indicate the conditions which would have to be fulfilled to make the theory false—it is almost invariably a sign that he is attaching to his fundamental category some arbitrary value predicate. It is easier to make history in behalf of some cause or ideal if faith is buttressed by the belief—logically irrelevant but emotionally comforting—that all history establishes as an inescapable fact what the historical protagonist affirms as desirable.

If we examine the historical period from the rise of capitalism to, and including, the first World War, it is hard to escape the conclusion that the economic structure of society, and the class antagonisms and conflicts to which it gave rise, exercised a more pervasive and decisive role in determining the direction of events, domestic and international, and in fashioning the basic values by which people lived, than any other factor or conjunction of factors within Western culture. This empirical proposition cannot be established here but it can be supported by a study of the approaches of most contemporary historians to the past.

With the rise, however, of the modern totalitarian state, economic considerations have become secondary and political ones primary. The state no longer functions as an instrument which permits the process of economic expansion and consolidation to run its course according to the laws of a free market. On the contrary, the state (defined empirically) uses the economic process as an instrument to further its political purpose. A great deal of evidence can be cited of which, perhaps, the most dramatic is the second World War in which not economic but political factors were decisive. On the traditional scheme of orthodox Marxism one would have expected that since the mode of economic production of the Atlantic democracies and Germany were more similar to each other than to that of the Soviet Union, they would either have made common cause against her or at least remained neutral when Hitler's legions marched East. But this was not the case. The struggle against Fascism was *not* waged for the survival or extension of capitalism. Organized capitalist interests were not very ardent about combating totalitarianism anywhere. Nor was the war fought for brute survival which could have been achieved through appeasement and at a lesser cost. Although it is false to say that it was a war for the *extension* of democracy, it is not false to say that on the part of the West it was fought in *defence* of its democratic institutions.

The existence of totalitarian states whose objectives threaten the survival of democratic institutions imposes upon democratic nations recognition of the primacy of the political factor. No longer are we able to explain political events plausibly in terms of economic changes as significant as these still are. More and more we are witnessing how the domestic economy of democratic countries is being subject to controls in behalf of political purposes—and inescapably so.

The trend from the primacy of the economic to the primacy of the political factor in history is probably irreversible in view of the technological revolution of our time. The nature of modern weapons is such that if democratic institutions are once overthrown and a totalitarian order is clamped upon the entire world comparable to what exists in Eastern Europe and Russia, it is extremely unlikely that any democratic movement of opposition can ever succeed.

If this is true the fundamental conflict of our age is not between capitalism and collectivism but between democracy and totalitarianism, and upon its outcome the culture of the planet depends in its every phase from works of art to theories of zoology. This is denied by many who maintain that any kind of planned economy must inevitably destroy democracy, and who, despite their opposition to Marxism, assert the most fundamental dogma of orthodox Marxism, *viz.*, that a given economic system determines one, and only one, political system. What is overlooked is first, the existence of different varieties and degrees of planned economies, and second, that not a single one of them uniquely determines only one type of political control.

There is a more striking paradox involved in the logic of the historical situation today. Marx and Engels looked forward to the future when after the fetishism of commodities had been abolished, mankind would make its history in the light of freely chosen ideals limited only by the knowledge of natural necessities. The processes of technology, however, have run far ahead of the processes of socialization, and we do not have to wait for some hypothetical *future* to win a position in which *our* decision, *our* choice, *our* assumption of responsibility significantly determines history. Scientific advance has thrust us in this position, and that future is now.

The recognition that our own lives and those of our descendants depend mainly upon the political decisions we take in *this* generation makes political ideas today causal factors of the first rank. It reinforces the necessity for an analysis of the democratic ideals that are invoked as principles of justification. It is at this point particularly that philosophers can do a much needed job of clarification making the central issues emerge and struggling against what I have called "the degradation of the word." As we have seen, all totalitarian governments have sought to pass themselves off as species of democracy. It is intellectually scandalous that even some American philosophers have lent themselves to this campaign of semantic corruption which judges a culture not by its practices and institutions but by the holiday rhetoric with which its public documents and officials gloss them over. Such stupendous naiveté which would make every ruthless despot a brother democrat provided he talks about the classless society, or about the brotherhood of man under the fatherhood of God, is a preface to political folly.

The conflict between democracy and expanding Soviet totalitarianism may be solved peacefully or it may not. That depends on the fate of an intelligent, fool-proof plan for international control and inspection of all sources of nuclear energy—a plan which recognizes that it requires all nations to keep the peace but only one to break it. This problem at the moment is not my concern, for independently of whether it is adopted, we cannot blink the fact that there is a struggle going on for men's souls all over the world, and that the democratic philosophy, which makes the values of *political* democracy central, is everywhere on the defensive, partly because of inner confusion, partly because of the strategy of audacity and mendacity, and ever renewed audacity and mendacity, common to all expanding totalitarianisms.

Even if the overt aggressions of totalitarianism are contained, the battle to win men's minds and souls for the values of democracy will remain. Today because several cardinal truths have been overlooked, that battle is in doubt. First, no greater boon can be made to the totalitarians than to identify the defence of democratic values with the defence of the democratic *status quo*. The *status quo*, if it could be immobilized, is still many times better than the best totalitarianism that has ever flourished. But it cannot be immobilized. There is no *status quo*. It must grow better or worse, and worse if not better, until a point is reached when the despairs of want and insecurity generate a fever which sees in the fantasies of Utopian rhetoric a substantial deposit on happiness. Democracy must progressively institutionalize the processes of consent even as it girds for defence and takes the measures proper for its security.

Second, to make the justification for democracy rest upon any metaphysical or theological premise is an invitation to disaster. It substitutes for the quest of a common way of life that will reconcile all differences that are reconciliable the quest of a common metaphysics—the intellectual will o' the wisp of the ages. It leaves the plane of differences that may be resolved for the plane of differences that cannot be resolved. It makes the agreements which democrats of the most varied metaphysical persuasions have actually built into the fabric of community life, impossible to explain except as opportunistic evasion or philosophic inconsistency. It leads to such preposterous notions as the belief that the difference between democracy and totalitarian communism rests upon the difference between the pre-Kantian empirical epistemology on the one hand, and post-Kantian metaphysical idealism on the other, and that these differences can be solved by a proper metaphysical synthesis. As if one could not equally well be a Tory, or Whig, or plain Machiavellian on the basis of Locke's theory of mental substance, and as if one could not equally well be a *laissez-faire* liberal, a democratic socialist, or a totalitarian Fascist or Bolshevik on the basis of either dialectical idealism or dialectical materialism.

The philosophy of democracy can best function as a philosophy of history today not by excogitating formulae of salvation or equations of doom for our society but by finding the operational equivalent of ideals, by suggesting specific institutional devices, specific mechanisms and instrumentalities governmental and nongovernmental for increasing the area of uncoerced agreement among men. It doesn't presuppose a method—it *is* a method which starts from what men have in common and explores the possibilities of meeting common needs while preserving all human differences compatible with a peaceful and prosperous issue of their conflicts. It requires neither an official metaphysics nor an official epistemology but a set of working rules *analogous* to the rules we recognize in determining issues of truth in any empirical inquiry. It does not identify unity with uniformity. It welcomes all differences except those differences which in *practice* deny the right of difference to others, and except those differences which deny the equality of all differences that accept a common method of negotiating differences. So long as we sincerely accept these rules of the game, so long as we pledge ourselves to abide by the consequences of the free give-and-take of critical debate, we may legitimately hold and practice in a democratic community any doctrine on any subject whatsoever. But we cannot make absolutes of doctrines, tastes, or principles as *preconditions* of the democratic process without unloosing the furies of fanaticism. The only things we can be fanatical about are the processes of democratic consensus within nations and among nations.

This is to stake a great deal on the reasonableness of the empirical temper, on the potentialities of democratic process, and the viability of cultural pluralism. But if we find ourselves compelled to defend them—as we must when they are attacked—we will at least know what we are defending, and safeguard ourselves from the twin evils of Utopianism and cynicism.

7 The Degradation of the Word

IN ONE OF THE EARLY DIALOGUES, *The Phaedrus,* Plato relates a charming myth about the Egyptian God, Thamus, who sat in judgment upon the creations of Theuth, polymath and inventor of the art of writing. Theuth pleads for the dissemination of letters among the Egyptians on the ground that they are a kind of medicine for memory and wisdom. But Thamus sternly rejects the plea. "For this invention of yours," Plato makes him say, "will produce forgetfulness in the minds of those who learn it, by causing them to neglect their memory, inasmuch as, from their confidence in writing, they will recollect by the external aid of foreign symbols, and not by the internal use of their own faculties."

Plato's myths are often expressions of dramatic irony suggesting different meanings hard to reconcile by those who forget the poet in the system maker. Classical scholars may dispute concerning which meaning is the one Plato really intended, but we may enjoy them all.

One of the simple yet profound truths suggested by this Platonic myth is the danger of mechanical literacy to the life of intelligence. We all know that the ability to read is not the same as the ability to think. But can it ever be that an ability to read is an obstacle to thinking? To suggest that it can be and, at the same time, to admit that the ability to read is a natural good, sounds like a paradox. And yet we are all familiar with situations in which goods and values seem, in a manner of speaking, to turn into bads and disvalues. Goods and values in our experience come in clusters, not separately. Whatever may be the immediate quality of a specific good or value, its validity or worth depends upon its relations to other goods and values. One of the ways by which we check the worth of a good or value in a concrete situation is by its effects on the family of goods and values to which it belongs. Friendship without generosity, justice without sympathy, strength without sensitivity, courage without intelligence, do not lose their meanings but their validity as desirable ends. Moral insight consists in knowledge of the way in which goods and values are related to each other. Sometimes the relationships are obvious and at hand; sometimes they are obscure and surprising.

One of the interesting aspects of literacy as a natural good—and we are beginning to see that this is true for a great many other natural goods—is that its "goodness" is organically related to *human freedoms.* By human freedom we mean here rights found in a libertarian society where democratic institutions make it possible for individuals to criticize their governing agencies. Where there is no human freedom in this sense, literacy may not be a blessing but what the Egyptian God, Thamus, feared it would be.

The reason for this is not hard to see. In a totalitarian society, whose tyranny as distinct from the past requires a mass base, literacy can and has been used as an instrument of consolidating the power of the minority. Through universal literacy under a monopoly of power, words and slogans reach into the mind of every man. There is no escaping them. They root out the very recalcitrance of silence. They supply a continual and unvarying stimulus to all who cannot keep their eyes shut. "Thinking" becomes a conditioned response to words, and "thought" is completed by providing the appropriate words to the opening cue. The unconscious processes are "educated." This education reaches its triumph when the right response from the point of view of those who control the propaganda seems to their victims to be an expression of uncoerced first nature. Without the challenge and the stimulus provoked by open criticism of word by word, to read means to acquire the habit of credulity. It is to rely on external symbols, not "on the internal use of their own faculties."

An unfailing argument in the arsenal of defenders of totalitarianism is the increase in literacy which has taken place under dictatorial rule. The argument has been made for Japan, Germany, most frequently for Russia, and least frequently for Italy—and most recently for Venezuela. Those who argue about the percentages of increase to indicate that they are not as great as claimed miss the main point. Grant the apologists of totalitarianism all their claims; it still remains true that where only what the government approves can be read, literacy may become an effective means for the mental enslavement of the people.

The skepticism and shrewdness of the illiterate European peasant has probably been exaggerated. Tolstoy and other novelists idealized their portraits of the peasant type. But the kernel of truth behind the legend is the reliance the peasant placed upon the deliverances of his own experience as evidential signs of what he was told. His data were crude, limited, but strictly verifiable. He was ignorant and could easily be misled. But when he counted his bruises and pains he could recognize that he had been misled. It is said that some Russian peasants were so illiterate that they disbelieved the existence of remotely distant countries and suspected that wars against them were government inventions designed to increase taxes and recruit their sons for forced labor. But such deep distrust was really a demand for evidence. The range of evidence was limited by the horizon of his interest and feelings. Even his superstitions testify to his "vulgar" empiricism. He knew exactly what to expect in the hereafter. (One is tempted to describe him as living according to the faith of the popular semanticists who lump together all abstractions as untrustworthy, without distinguishing between those that can lead us at some point to definite observation tests and those that cannot.) The result was that the peasant was often fooled. *But he didn't fool himself.*

In a free society, where words do not come from one center and men are exposed to the clash of conflicting doctrines, it is *possible* for the individual to employ abstractions of high order and relate them to experience as a test. *But in an unfree society there is a tendency for literacy to corrupt the natural pragmatism of the human mind.* The illiterate peasant knew when he was hungry; he knew when and where his boots—when he had any—pinched. He knew that the knout which lashed him was not wielded by his hand, and that it was not *his* will which moved the officials of the state to imprison and deport him. Teach him to read, but let him read nothing except what the dictatorship approves; give him schooling, but only according to the party line; subject him to a sustained barrage of slogans—and lo and behold! he can be led to deny the evidence of his own senses. His hunger is now a subjective illusion. The boots he hasn't got are on order for when the nth five-year plan is finished. And as for the boots he has: they don't really pinch, nothing wrong with them—it is merely that his *feet* are defective, and therefore not properly molded to the perfect shoe the factory has sold him. His feet are the real saboteurs. He himself is the state which deprives him of freedom, because, forsooth, he is a worker and the state is a worker's state. And if the secret police find it necessary to shoot him, they are merely carrying out the sentence of his own judgment—which Rousseau, Hegel, and the commissarphilosopher Mitin all teach.

Totalitarian countries are not the only breeding grounds of metaphysical syntheses which wipe out empirical differences. But by imposing literacy, they can see to it that no one escapes their influence. And by monopolizing the use of words, they prevent the conflict of metaphysical systems with each other, and the conflict between all of them and scientific philosophy, which safeguards the intelligence in democratic culture.

I am not, of course, making a plea for illiteracy. I am on the side of Theuth, not of Thamus. But even in a democracy, literacy is not enough for the intelligent performance of the duties of citizenship unless it is accompanied by the critical training in the use and analysis of language which our schools only too often fail to give. A few years ago there was an outcry against the few educators who called for a vigorous program of critical analysis in our educational institutions. They were taxed with being skeptics who robbed youth of its faith, philosophical fifth columnists who subverted the simple pieties toward God and a decent foreign policy: all because they maintained that literacy which was not the gateway to intellectual sophistication, an ability to read without a developed sense of what constitutes evidence, a failure to distinguish between a definition and a hypothesis and the consequent inability to apply the proper criteria in considering them—that these softened the minds of Americans for the onslaught of domestic and foreign propaganda.

One of the most popular techniques of undermining free society is the *degradation of the word*. Intellectually, this marks our era just as much as the "new failure of nerve." The comparatively recent spectacle of the head of a large American news service seriously accepting the claim of a Russian propaganda sheet that Russia enjoys a free press, the instance a few years ago of a Town Hall audience leaving unchallenged the plea by a professional propagandist that Russia is entitled to a third of Poland because the London Polish government was undemocratic, is some evidence of how far the degradation of the word went during and just after the end of World War II.

Or consider the argument that no state is completely democratic! The United States is in some respects undemocratic: the U.S.S.R. is in some respects democratic: therefore they are both democracies, differing merely in degree. The same line of argument would also have proved Germany and the United States both democracies, differing merely in degree—a conclusion violently opposed by those who at the same time accepted the sequence in the first sentence. The same line of argument would prove that the United States and the U.S.S.R. are both dictatorships; this might be accepted by some muddled apologists because it would remove the odium of totalitarianism from Russia. This same line of argument would prove that since no one can be perfectly good, and since Hitler was kind to animals, there was only a mere difference in degree of goodness between Hitler and Eugene Debs. This argument would be indignantly repudiated, by those who would applaud its analogue, were Stalin's name or that of his successor to be substituted for Debs.

There is no quick remedy for uneducated literacy. The schools by themselves cannot solve the problem, for at bottom it is an aspect of deeper social and political problems. But the schools can do something—how much cannot be known until they reorganize their curriculums on every level to educate for critical intelligence. The very least we can expect from them in a society still democratic is that they recognize the problem. Everybody wants the schools to educate students so that they will not be ensnared by the other fellow's illusions. At this point perhaps the schools can attempt to implement what everybody agrees on, and then press on to the conclusions that follow from an illusionless method.

But in the last decade the degradation of the word has sunk to even lower depths. The use of the slogan of "peace" by the Kremlin regime at the very time it inspired the Korean invasion seemed to indicate that the Communist chieftains were intent upon substantiating the actuality of Orwell's account of intellectual life in *1984*. The mystery is not that the Communist "peace partisans" could regard a war initiated by their ideological fellows-in-arms as a method of waging peace, but that this was also believed by some on this side of the Iron Curtain. And these believers included not only those who had given no evidence of intellectual sophistication, but also eminent men in the arts and sciences who in their own field have a keen sense for the unproved and falsely inferred. Something more is at work than the "degradation of the word"—there is a receptivity, a need, a positive willingness to believe, despite the apparent evidence which destroys illusions.

I wish to safeguard myself against the charge made by an editorial writer on *The Washington Post* that these ironical observations are an argument against literacy and that in effect I am rewriting Marx's revolutionary manifesto to conclude with the warning: "Workers of the World, don't read or write, you will lose your brains!" The simple point is not that these reflections are an argument against literacy, but merely that literacy is not an argument *for* totalitarianism even if in the end totalitarianism cannot succeed in reconditioning the human mind to wipe out the difference between the true and false.

A closer examination of the record of totalitarian countries reveals that it is difficult to condition the human mind to ignore completely the evidence of experience and the senses. Much indeed can be accomplished, but after a few Barmecidean feasts the clamor of the senses, physical and mental, makes itself heard. This is especially true if knowledge of the different thoughtways of free countries can percolate the barriers totalitarian countries throw up around themselves.

We have additional evidence that a generation of students brought up under the severe ideological indoctrination of Marxist-Leninism can challenge much that it has been taught to repeat without question. Although this critical post-revolutionary generation has expressed itself most openly in satellite countries where the unquenchable fires of nationalism burn through ideological pretense, there is even in the Soviet Union some critical questioning which increases in volume as the pitch of terror is slightly lessened. There is a tendency to magnify human intellectual resistance to totalitarian conditioning when we are confronted with heroic cases of those who cling to their own integrity. There is also a tendency to magnify human suggestibility and ability to believe what is false when we see or hear crowds acclaiming the executioner of their own liberties. Undoubtedly there is a genetic factor at work which accounts in part for the diverse reactions of individuals similarly situated socially to the techniques of unintellectual persuasion. Each one can recall some incident which renews his faith in what seems the natural curiosity, perversity, or cantankerousness of man. The question one must ask, however, is how general and sustained such a reaction can be. An unforgettable experience during the Communist blockade of Berlin in August, 1948, illustrates the point.

I met a young Red Army lieutenant, born and nurtured under the Stalin regime, who had deserted to our side. Naturally I was eager to find out why he had broken. He told me that his hostility to the Soviet regime had anteceded the war and that he had seized the first opportunity to escape. It appeared from his account that he had been a student in a technical institute and was taking the prescribed course in Marxist-Leninism. His instructor was laying down the orthodox line on historical materialism, and had asserted that the mode of economic production in any culture uniquely determines the political system in that culture. In the most innocent way, this young man asked why different political forms of government weren't compatible with the same economic base. He pointed to the capitalist system in Italy which existed first with democratic then dictatorial forms. The instructor, unable to give him a satisfactory answer, then tried to talk the student down, to ridicule him, and finally to charge him with revisionism, mechanism, formalism, Menshevik idealism, and other heresies the young man didn't understand. That young man in his own way had discovered for himself the distinction between necessary and sufficient conditions, and he clung to it even when he was expelled from the Young Communist League for refusing to yield. He narrowly escaped the charge of counter-revolutionary Trotskyism, but he was always under suspicion, and his hatred of the regime grew apace.

I expressed wonder that a purely intellectual difficulty should have had such fateful consequences. Men are rational animals, but not that rational. But his answer was very revealing (even though it sounded as if he had been reading Karl Jaspers).

"If I had been asked," he replied, "to say that two plus two is five I would not have cared—everyone knows it's four and this truth did not particularly concern me. But if I had denied my notion about the relation between economics and politics, it would have been like renouncing a piece of myself. *You see, I had thought this out for myself.*"

He uttered this last sentence with emphasis. What he was telling me was that he had risked his life for the sake of his creative and critical integrity. It was not the abstract truth he was struggling for, but his dignity and self-respect as a person.

Can we rely altogether upon the indestructibility of this natural impulse to speak truth, to distinguish, to argue, to contradict, to find out, to do things alone, or differently, or privately? Perhaps in the long run. But the opposite is also true in the long run: terror is a great persuader even though it is not omnipotent. And a terror which can use modern technology to change the mind and self is more often successful than unsuccessful in persuading the subjects to be changed. That is why it seems to me that, honor the heroes of intellectual resistance as we should, we cannot expect, independently of what the free peoples themselves do, that their example will necessarily inspire their fellow subjects. For one thing the "example" is rarely known, and totalitarian dictators sometimes organize their own opposition in order to be able to deal effectively with it in good time.

We cannot rely only upon the rare chance of a distinguished spirit to see through and resist the degradation of the word. We must find ways of reaching the citizens of totalitarian countries so that at the very least the knowledge of the examples is not lost.

8 Democracy and Desegregation

IT IS COMMONLY AGREED that the United States Supreme Court's decision on integration in education is one of the most important rulings in its long and controversial history. Since its promulgation the decision has been subjected to a steadily mounting barrage of criticism on all sorts of grounds and from almost all points of the ideological compass. What has been most surprising is the absence of a principled defense of desegregation and the program of school integration from the point of view of the ethics of democracy. Most defenses of the decision, particularly since Little Rock, have consisted in shifting the issue by insisting that the supreme law of the land, whatever we may think of its wisdom, should be obeyed. Although this is a justifiable position with respect to the laws of a democracy, which, if unwise and unjust, are modifiable and reversible, it evades the basic moral issues that in the last analysis underlie every fundamental conflict of values and social policy.

The opposition to desegregation comes from various groups. The oldline Southerners, who represent the majority of the opposition, hardly deign to offer reasons for their opposition except that laws against desegregation destroy their traditional "way of life." They are more convinced of the validity of their way of life than of the abstract rights of man and of citizens in whose name such ways of life may be condemned. That their way of life has a history; that it involves the use and abuse of other human beings who are bitterly opposed to this way of life; and that, unless they have some other justification for the *status quo* than that it is a *status quo,* a new *status quo* may be imposed upon them with the same warrant—all this they are content to ignore. For they hope to reverse the decision or transform it into a dead letter not by argument or reason but by delaying tactics and sporadic outbursts of recalcitrance.

A second group opposes desegregation on constitutional grounds. Some regard this area of human relations as one in which the Supreme Court is really legislating and therefore usurping the functions of Congress and state legislatures. Others believe that education is exclusively a matter for state jurisdiction and no concern of the Federal Government. A third group protests against the clear violation of previous controlling precedents—especially *Plessy vs. Ferguson*—which established the "separate but equal" doctrine. These constitutional questions are not really germane to the basic argument. It is true that the Supreme Court "legislates." It always has. The ultimate question is the character, grounds and wisdom of its legislation. Education may be exclusively a matter for state jurisdiction. Yet the effects of some state actions may have consequences affecting the rights and privileges of citizens. Aside from this, the moral issue of segregation in education still remains, whether it is a question for the states or the Federal Government. That the Supreme Court decision overturns earlier precedents is true. This is not unusual. The real question is: Should the precedents be retained or overturned? I shall, therefore, avoid the strictly legalistic aspects of the question.

Finally, I come to the criticism made by some conservative liberals and liberal conservatives who see in the legal prohibition of segregation in educational facilities (as in employment and in housing) a violation of one's personal freedom or private right to choose one's associations, companions, neighbors and fellow workers. There is some written criticism of desegregation along these lines, but the volume of spoken criticism is much greater. Even before the Supreme Court decision, some exponents of discrimination as a personal right related it to the defense of free enterprise. Natural law as well as Judeo-Christian ideals have been invoked to prove that man is essentially a discriminatory creature because he is capable of choice. The greater his knowledge, the greater his range of discrimination. According to this argument, many of our difficulties arise from attempts to curb by law the exercise of a discrimination which is ours by natural right and which is justified in addition by the greater power it gives us to advance the arts of civilization. Thus, F. A. Harper, in a pamphlet on *Blessings of Discrimination* published a few years ago by the Foundation for Economic Education, asserts: "Many of the leading problems of our day stem from a thought-disease about discrimination. It is well known that discrimination has come to be widely scorned. And politicians have teamed up with those who scorn it, to pass laws against it—as though morals can be manufactured by the pen of a legislator and the gun of a policeman."

Since the desegregation decision, this note has been struck with increasing frequency by critics who believe that discrimination in education lies in the field of private morals and is thus beyond the reach of law. They are prepared to defend the human rights, they tell us, of all minorities, but they insist that the right to discriminate in education, even if this results in segregated schools, is one of the basic human rights. The more liberal among these critics make a distinction between the public and private domain according to which it would be wrong to *permit* segregation on buses and railroads because these lie in the public domain but wrong to *prevent* segregation, on the ground of personal freedom, in private life. Education, they say, is one of those areas of personal life that are by their very nature outside the purview of law in a democratic society.

The case against Negro segregation in any area of public life, whether enforced by law or by custom, rests upon simple ethical principles which are implicit in the Declaration of Independence and which later guided the adoption of the Thirteenth and Fourteenth Amendments. These principles of equality and freedom are expressed in the language of natural rights, but they are best defended in terms of their empirical consequences: The Negroes are part of the human race and as such should enjoy the same human rights of freedom and the same protection of our laws as any other group of human beings in the United States. The Thirteenth Amendment abolished their slavery and involuntary servitude generally. In so doing, we sought to redress a crime—one perhaps even greater than those committed in some settlements against the Indians. If slavery is abolished, then all the institutional restraints and indignities which constituted servitude must be abolished, too. There can be no justification for first- and second-class citizens derivative from a previous condition of servitude. Morally, Negroes are entitled to life, liberty, property, and equal protection of laws on the same terms as the rest of us. This is independent of vicissitudes in the Supreme Court's interpretations of these rights we enjoy as citizens of our individual states or as citizens of the Federal Republic.

Atoning in part for the long history of moral evasion by previous Courts, the Supreme Court in *Brown vs. Board of Education of Topeka* declared that segregated public educational facilities are "inherently unequal." Despite the obscurity of the Court's language, this was not based on a discovery of a new fact or on recovery of an old law, but on the reaffirmation of a moral principle that led to a new law in the land. The moral principle is the same one which justified the abolition of slavery. In the light of the *historical* situation which has developed since the abolition of slavery, segregated educational facilities are "inherently unequal," not because of the actual differences in facilities, great as they are, but because they are inherently cruel, unjust and degrading to the group discriminated against. They are degrading in the same way that the yellow patch or badge of inferiority, the mark of the pariah, the stigma of the outcast, are degrading. Even if the physical facilities of Negro schools (or buses) were physically better than those set aside for the whites, segregation would still be degrading for the same reason that we regard a well-fed slave as still a slave.

Prejudice is sometimes distinguished by psychologists and sociologists from discrimination. Prejudice is an antipathetic feeling or attitude against some person or group not rationally justified by objective evidence. Discrimination is a pattern of behavior in which one acts against others by excluding them from opportunities commonly enjoyed. At the moment it is experienced, one can't help feeling prejudiced. But one *can* help discriminating unless under some compulsion. No one chooses to be prejudiced. But one chooses to discriminate. And because one does, one's choice can be inhibited or influenced by many things besides his prejudice. In a sense, everyone has a right to his thoughts or feelings. But not everyone has a right to discriminate. Neither the state by law nor society by custom has a moral right to discriminate prejudicially against individuals and groups in public life. Such a pattern of discrimination is segregation.

Has the individual ever a right to discriminate, and if so, where?

In 1947, in a review of *To Secure These Rights,* the report of the President's Committee on Civil Rights, I pointed to the necessity of establishing a principle which would guide us in drawing a line between "justifiable" and "unjustifiable" discrimination: "The presence of a justifying principle with respect to legitimate and illegitimate discrimination is necessary in order to allay fears that, under the cover of social welfare, individual freedom and the rights of privacy may be abridged." I no longer believe that the principle I then too briefly formulated in terms of the needs of *personal growth* is adequate. But it seemed to me that it enabled us to condemn all types of community segregation and at the same time permit a man to choose his friends and control the pattern of his personal and family life. I mention this merely to indicate that critics of laws against segregation are not alone in their concern for personal freedom and the right to privacy. But the unfortunate thing is that their argument so interprets the right of privacy that it embraces the entire realm of the social or public, if not the narrowly political. It is as if someone were to define personal property, without which there could be no privacy or personal freedom, in such a way that ownership of a steel mill, which gives power over the lives of those who live by it, is a piece of personal property, necessary for the owner's sense of privacy and freedom. The fact is that extreme Southern segregationists have defined *their* right of privacy, their right to live according to customs and folkways they call the Southern way of life, so as to deny the equal protection of laws to all but native whites.

Opponents of integration do not contest the right of every child, Negro or white, to receive an education in the public schools. They know that the public schools are supported by tax money levied directly or indirectly upon all citizens irrespective of race. They contend, however, that it is wrong to force parents to send their children to an integrated school. For this deprives them of rights which clearly belong to them in all free societies—the private right over their children and the social right to free association. At most, these spokesmen hold, the state may prescribe some of the content of education but not the context of association and social life which invariably develops out of attendance at school.

It is instructive to explore some of the implications of this position and observe to what it commits anyone holding it. If it is wrong to force white parents to send their children to an integrated school because of *their* private right over their children, it is wrong to force Negro parents to send *their* children to segregated schools, and wrong to force white parents who do not object to *their* children associating with Negro children to do the same. The same principle obviously obtains with respect to the feelings of parents toward the children of *any* minority. It is wrong to force parents to send their children to legally unsegregated public schools if they do not wish *their* children to associate with the children of religious, racial or ethnic minorities. Since most of these critics do not propose to abolish our compulsory education laws, and rule out private education as economically unfeasible, they must require the state or community to build separate schools for any group of parents who wish to safeguard their children from any kind of context and association they regard as seriously undesirable.

Educational context and association, however, extend far beyond the classroom into school buses, lunchrooms, playgrounds, pools, gymnasiums. If desegregated schools violate the personal and social rights of parents to discriminate against undesirable associates and contexts for their children, so do desegregated buses and all other public educational facilities where context and association are prolonged for hours. Since these are normally incidental to public education, special facilities would have to be provided for the entire gamut of parental fastidiousness. What holds for public education must by these principles also hold for public health and medical facilities. Parents may object to having Negro physicians or nurses treat their children in public hospitals to which Negro children are admitted. And it is surely obvious that public housing projects which legally bar segregation also violate the private rights of white parents not to have their children associate with undesirables.

Actually, parents are *not* forced to send their children to an integrated school. Parents may choose to send their children to private schools which are not integrated. Or, in most states, they may provide education at home. This the law permits (*Pierce vs. Society of Sisters*). To be sure, they have to pay a certain economic price for it, even though in its tradition of tolerance the community subsidizes these private schools by giving them remission from taxes and allowing those who contribute to their support to deduct contributions from their income tax. One would think that this was a generous, even over-generous attitude toward individuals whose prejudice against permitting their children to associate with Negroes was so overwhelming. But—the objection runs—it will not do to tell parents they can educate their children at home or send them to private schools. This involves another kind of discrimination. Since private education requires the possession of means, it would make the safeguarding of certain private rights dependent upon economic status and consequently underprivilege those who are forced to send their children to public school.

In other words, unless we can guarantee the equal economic status of the prejudiced, segregation would be a privilege of the rich! But why should we be concerned with economic equality here? Why not make the segregationists pay the costs of their prejudices? If the cost is sufficiently high, they may give up their opposition to integration if not their prejudices. In time even their prejudices may wither.

What a strange state of affairs! These opponents of school integration tell us they really are not opposed to equality. But equality can be legislated only in the political sphere; all we can enforce is the right to vote, *political* equality. The numerous ways in which economic inequalities affect the political realm, especially in the winning of consent, bother this school of thought not at all. But with respect to the exercise of the private right of sending children to segregated schools, they become economic equalitarians. Is it not more humane to fortify the principle of political equality by equality of educational opportunity, which is negated by segregated schools, than by invoking the principle of economic equality to justify perpetuating such schools?

Consider the meaning of this concern for economically underprivileged bigots in another sphere in which we recognize private rights. One has a right to have his wife and children treated by a physician of his choice. If he regards membership in a certain race or religion as a *sine qua non* of professional suitability, no one can morally or legally compel him to believe or act otherwise (barring emergencies). The public hospitals are unsegregated and therefore objectionable to him. His neighbor, similarly prejudiced, can afford the services of a private physician or segregated hospital, but he himself cannot. Is there not here, too, a manifest injustice on the basis of the above principle? Are not his private rights to see that his wife and offspring get tender and loving care from racially or ideologically qualified physicians and nurses, and to insure the proper contexts and associations for his children, likewise dependent upon his economically underprivileged status? Should we therefore, reasoning *pari passu,* insist that public hospitals and facilities not be legally integrated or desegregated? I can see no reason why the community should be concerned about this man's prejudices unless he could show that his wife and children were going to suffer unjust discriminatory treatment. But the situation we are discussing presupposes hospitals (and schools) in which irrelevant and therefore unjust discrimination is legally forbidden. To be sure, there are great differences between public schools and public health facilities, even when the latter have mainly preventive and remedial functions. They are not relevant, however, to the principle invoked by anti-integrationists in discussing a possible injustice to the economically underprivileged segregationist.

So far I have not been criticizing the argument against legal desegregation so much as exploring the consequences of some of the principles and distinctions on which it rests in order to see where they lead. It seems to me that they would lead not only to the abolition of laws which *compel* segregation in about twenty states but to the abolition of laws which *prohibit* discrimination in public education and allied fields in about as many states. It would take us back to the days, with respect to education at least, of *Plessy vs. Ferguson* and the Civil Rights Cases of 1883 when the Supreme Court nullified Congressional legislation of which Professor Milton Konvitz has said that "it was probably the first attempt in the history of mankind to destroy the branches of slavery after its root had been destroyed."[1]

I regard this as a *reductio ad absurdum* of their argument. The difficulty with this kind of analysis, however, is that it cannot convince those who are prepared to swallow one absurdity to defend another. I therefore focus directly on some of the basic premises of their position.

One of the main premises is contained in the explicit acceptance of William Faulkner's declaration that "enforced integration is no better than enforced segregation." This is a very curious statement. Leaving aside the strictly legal questions created by the most recent interpretations of Section I of the Fourteenth Amendment, particularly the pro-

---

[1] *The Constitution and Civil Rights* (New York, 1947)—an invaluable book!

vision extending the equal protection of laws to all citizens, this equation in condemnation seems to me completely inadmissible morally. It assumes either that integration and segregation are, morally, on all fours, or that the evils of enforcement *always* outweigh any alternative good to be derived therefrom. This is not necessarily true and in the case in hand—the historical situation of the Negro in the United States —patently false. To deny children equal public educational opportunities and possibilities of proper vocational fulfilment merely because of the color of their skin or their religion or national origin, whether enforced by law or by social custom, is manifestly unjust. On the other hand, to require students, if they wish a public school education supported by tax monies levied upon all alike, to attend unsegregated schools is not unjust.

There are situations in which legally to compel certain practices is as bad as legally to prohibit them. This is so when the practices in question are equally evil, or when they are morally indifferent. Legally to compel us to consume bananas is as bad as legally to prohibit us from doing so. But what is true for bananas would not be true for habit-forming drugs, or for smoking in a powder plant. To enforce vaccination or the medical segregation of children with contagious diseases is certainly not as bad as preventing it even if we admit it is always deplorable to compel parents to comply with school and health laws.

Some anti-integrationists make a distinction between segregation as a "social custom" and segregation as "discrimination enforced by law." They oppose the latter—but then, just as resolutely, oppose the legal prohibition of such discrimination as a social custom. They do so on the ground that this violates the personal freedom of those who discriminate to act as they please "within the four walls" of their own home.

There are social customs and social customs. A social custom which violates human rights, and imposes unfair and cruel penalties upon individuals, hurts no less even if it is not enforced by law. It is enough that it is enforced by habit, custom, use and wont. Suttee was a social custom, too—as was child marriage, infanticide, dueling, and quite a number of other quaint practices described in anthropological texts. If there is any relation between morality and law, the existence of certain evil social practices *may* (not must) justify us in taking legal action to prevent them. And if this is of necessity an abridgment of some human freedom, as is true of every law, it is taken in behalf of other human freedoms. The human freedoms we safeguard by legal action against segregation and unfair discrimination are more important than those we restrict. Some Southern moderates see this in the case of certain public facilities, such as transportation. But surely the social discrimination which prevents a Negro student from attending a medical or engineering school, which bars him from certain vocations even after he has spent years of his adult life in preparing himself for it, which denies him housing in restricted communities without even providing him with the separate and equal facilities of the segregated bus, is a much crasser violation of his rights as a human being. The classification which puts transportation in the field of the political, and education and employment in the field of the personal, is completely arbitrary as well as irrelevant. For the moral question is primary and it cuts across all categories.

It is on moral grounds that we are justified in adopting a Fair Education Practices Act prohibiting certain discriminatory practices not only in public schools but sometimes even in private schools which are dependent upon the public largesse in various ways. It is on moral grounds that we are justified in adopting a Fair Employment Practices Act. If it is morally wrong for a trade union to exclude from membership individuals of certain racial or religious groups, when such membership is essential to continued employment, it is just as morally wrong for an employer, except in some highly special circumstances of personal service, to deny people work on the same grounds. Finally, it is on moral grounds that we are justified in adopting a Fair Housing Law the exact provisions of which we need not specify here. I believe I am as much concerned with preserving the rights of privacy as any segregationist, but I cannot see how the right of every person to do as he pleases within the four walls of his own house is undermined by legislation designed to make it possible for our colored neighbor to live within *his* four walls. For make no mistake about it: Social discrimination in housing in effect confines Negroes and other minority groups to ghettos where they must share their four walls with multiple families and are in consequence denied their own sacred rights of privacy. Actually there are both moral and legal limits to what a person can do in the privacy of his own home; but, even if the right of privacy were absolute, it would not carry with it the right to push out one's walls until they encompassed the public neighborhood, school and factory.

Many inconsistencies and confusions in this position flow from vague distinctions between the political, the public, the social, and the personal or private. According to this view, only the political sphere is the sphere of equality. Focal to it is the right to vote. The social sphere is the sphere in which discrimination is legitimate even if unwise. The public sphere includes both. The private sphere is one of exclusion. But to what sphere, then, belong the inalienable human rights "to life, liberty, and the pursuit of happiness"?

A moment's reflection will show that they have mixed everything up. Equality "exists" *first* in the field of human rights. It is the premise from which we derive the most powerful argument against slavery. Political equality, especially equality in voting, is only one form of equality. Negroes desire political equality in order to enforce recognition of their human rights, which they believe they have even when they lack political equality. They were liberated and admitted to citizenship even before the Fifteenth Amendment specifically forbade abridgment of the right to vote on account of race, color or previous condition of servitude. Under certain historical conditions, restrictions on the right to vote—age, literacy, residence—provided they are *equitably* applied to all, may actually lead to inequality in the exercise of the vote. It is manifestly improper to confuse the political realm with one very special form of political life—a democracy of universal suffrage. It is clear that sometimes we may wonder whether a people is ready for universal suffrage but never whether they have human or social rights, no matter how primitive they are.

The social realm, the locus of most of our associations with other human beings, is the sphere in which the questions of justice arise in their most complex as well as most acute form. The social realm is emphatically not in the first instance the realm of discrimination and inequality, although they are found there. That would automatically and necessarily make it one of injustice. It is precisely here that, as moral creatures, reflecting upon the consequences of our actions on others, we are called upon to apply appropriate rules of equality and, where differences are relevant, rules of equitable inequality in the light of some shared ideal, even if it be no more than the ideal of peace or mutual sufferance. The nub of many an error here is the confusion, where social relationships and membership in social groups are involved, between "discriminating *against*" and "discriminating *between*" and treating them as synonymous expressions. In identifying the social world with discriminating *against,* one is describing it as it appears to the eyes of the snob with vestigial cultural longings for feudal hierarchy.

One writer of this school of thought, in characterizing the social sphere, asserts flatly that what matters here is not at all personal distinction. He maintains that, in the social sphere, people are identified by their membership in a group and by their differences only insofar as they symbolize group difference. He caps this by proclaiming that their very identifiability as members of a group *demands* that they discriminate against other groups.

Could group snobbery find a more perfect expression? Why, to begin with a trivial matter, must owners of Cadillacs discriminate *against* me, driving a more modest car? Have I not the same human right to use the road as they? I do not feel discriminated against merely because they ride in comfort while I ride in enjoyment and economy. To go on to the discriminations some believe are legitimate within the social sphere, why, if I am a Negro, should I be required by custom to attend segregated schools or to sit in the back of school buses or be fenced in whenever I use educational facilities? Why should differences *not* bound up with personal distinction lead to humiliating discriminations? What these critics declare does not matter—personal distinction—is precisely the only thing that should matter where discriminations operate in the social sphere. If I am to suffer from legitimate discrimination in school, it should be only because I lack certain relevant gifts, knowledge or qualifications, not because of the color of my skin or my religion! In fact, if the discrimination is reasonable and equitably enforced, it does not appear as objectionable discrimination at all. It is discrimination *between* and not discrimination *against;* it marks the degree to which a society has been morally organized into a genuine community.

Finally, there is an ambiguity in the category of the private. In one sense, the opposite of the "private" is the "public," as when we contrast private societies with public ones; in another, the opposite of the "private" is the "social." In the second sense, the "private" means the "personal." The personal realm is not merely the solitary: It involves our friends and families. Because our associations here have no consequences that extend beyond those who are engaged in them, we owe no one an accounting for our choices, however arbitrary, biased, prejudiced or unwise. We may walk, dance, drink, talk philosophy, quarrel or pray with whomever we please. And we *must* not prevent others from doing the same except where, as sometimes is the case in private quarrels, the consequences affect the lives of others. It is evident that since many kinds of private associations, in the first sense of private, have their locus in social space and not in the space within one's four walls, situations may arise which require some kind of public regulation. By arbitrarily extending the realm of the personal and delimiting the realm of the public, the segregationists would give those in possession of power justification to impose their way of life, subtly if possible, brutally if necessary, on any minority and (crowning irony) to do it in the name of personal freedom. Morally, no set of principles will be sufficient to determine by themselves in which cases the law should intervene when private prejudices result in public discrimination. The consequences in each situation must be considered. But we are not without knowledge about the kind of consequences that some types of action have. And at some point, after consultation and negotiation have run their course, the law must be applied.

It is a hateful thing to enforce laws in education, where ideally there should be no coercion except the inescapable cogencies encountered in the quest for truth and beauty. But ideal societies exist only in heaven. It is commonly acknowledged that the state may not only enforce compulsory attendance but prescribe the content or subject matter of instruction in order to insure an education appropriate for the exercise of citizenship. The content of education has some fixed elements, but its variables depend on the *kind* of society in which instruction is given and on its history. The mode of association within a school may have a definite bearing on the content and values of the education it gives. This has always been true of the American public school, which has played a great and unique role in the creation of the modern American nation. It not only provided a ladder of opportunity on which millions climbed out of poverty, but by virtue of its integrated classrooms, in which students studied and played in common, unified the most diverse ethnic groups that elsewhere lived together in snarling hostility. It never even tried to do this in the South, because the pattern of segregation prevailed from the beginning in the schools, which were late in getting founded. The requirements of citizenship in a *democratic* community require the integration of the public classrooms even more than integration in the armed services. Unassailable evidence shows that Negro students, especially in high schools, smart under the restrictions of the segregated school. The more willingly they accept the promised heritage of American ideals, the more they resent their educational conditions. A typical study among Negro high school students in Dade County, Florida shows that, when asked to state the changes they most desired in their way of life, they named most frequently changes in the area of education. Can the democratic state be indifferent to this?

Some assert that the desegregation decision would probably have caused no great furor if it had not been followed by enforced integration. This is really saying that there would have been no trouble at Little Rock if nothing had been done about the matter, if the nine Negro children had not sought to go to the high school. True, there never is any trouble if a law is not enforced, except to those who suffer from its lack of enforcement. One might argue that a more gradual approach might have met with less opposition. This is beside the point to those for whom the issue is not the time and manner of enforcement but the *fact* of enforcement. No matter how gradual, sooner or later the moment comes when the readiness of the community to accept the law of the land is tested by the exercise of the Negro child's right to attend the public high school of his district. Once tested, the law cannot abdicate before the interference of mob violence without making a mockery of the Negro child's constitutional right to the equal protection of the laws.

Is it any different from the situation in which the Negro's right to vote is protected? The state does not actually compel him to vote, any more than it compels parents, black or white, to send their children to a public school. But if he chooses to exercise his right to vote and is prevented from doing so by others, the state would be enforcing his *right* to vote, not actually compelling him to vote against his will.

In reflecting on Little Rock, we must not lose sight of the fact that the people of Little Rock, although opposed to the desegregation decision, voted in effect twice to accept the gradual integration plan, once in election for the city officials, once for a local school board. They were not hard-core segregationists resolved to defy government by force rather than yield to an unpopular court decision. We must note the willingness of the local officials from the Mayor down to comply, as well as the peaceful illustrations of compliance in neighboring states where the Governors did not predict and thereby invite violence. Some Northern liberals have been caustic about the failure of the town's law-abiding citizens, black and white, to enforce the law against the mob and see the Negro children safely to school. I find this attitude explicable only in terms of unfamiliarity with the South. Had the law-abiding citizens of Little Rock, black and white, been as brave as some writers expected them to be, a fracas would have flared into a race riot or small-scale civil war. One does not enforce law by mobs, except in Westerns. Enforcement is the function, first, of the local law officers. If they are on the side of the mobsters and hoodlums, the responsibility rests with the Governor, and, when the Governor is a Faubus, with the Federal authorities.

It is true that law-abiding citizens are rarely heroes. This is so even when they approve the desegregation laws as the people of Little Rock admittedly did not. They desert the streets when the mob takes over, even a small mob. In this respect, law-abiding Southerners are no different from law-abiding Northerners and Europeans. Something else again is the deafening silence of the two Arkansas Senators. No one asked them to fight, but only to open their mouths in safety as widely as they did on vote-risky occasions of lesser moment. Nonetheless, it is false to gauge the true sentiment of a community by the behavior of a hate-crazed minority. One can easily misread the significance of the picture of white students—also a small minority—jeering at Negro children. These children are a product of segregated schools. They reflect the unreasoning authority and hysterical feeling of their homes and parents, which they may come to challenge if only they stay long enough in desegregated schools to test their prejudices against their experiences.

What happened at Little Rock is a national disgrace, but it does not tell the whole story. It does not tell the story of successful integration on a much larger scale in many other communities of the South. It does not tell the story of the great strides that have been made in reducing discrimination all over the country since 1940. It does not tell the story revealed in the most recent and most intensive poll conducted by Professor Tumin and his Princeton associates on "Readiness and Resistance to Desegregation" in Guilford County, North Carolina. This shows that there is considerable variation in the attitude toward segregation among Southern whites. Those who, although opposed to integration, were prepared to live with the Court decision and eschew all violence numbered more than 75 per cent. The hard-core segregationists are found mainly among the poor whites, not among the individuals who have high status and vested interest in a stable community. Together with the better educated and always less prejudiced elements, the latter are more likely to be the opinion-makers in the long haul than the hard-core intransigents. It remains to be seen how representative polls of this character are for the South as a whole, even when their reliability has been tested in local areas. But, together with the record of integration to date, it presents impressive evidence for the belief that a fairly large spread exists in the attitude of Southerners toward desegregation.

Although gradualness and patience are a *sine qua non* of peaceful enforcement, once the law is openly flouted it must be enforced. Worse in such situations than the risks of a firm and rapid enforcement would be the abandonment of the legal position already won or the indefinite postponement of further integration until such time as God softens the hearts of the hard-core segregationists. Beyond a certain point, the longer the delay, the more costly in tears and suffering will be the process of desegregation for everyone concerned, but especially for those who have so far endured the greatest indignities. For a basic human right is violated wherever segregation is practiced, no less in public education, than in public transportation, and the denial of this right to Negroes in education seriously affects the expression of their basic political rights as well.

I conclude as I began. The same argument which opposes slavery opposes the perpetuation of the discrimination that continues in another form some of the practices of slavery. If slavery was a crime, segregation is the still open and unhealed wound it left on the body of the Negro. It bleeds afresh every time the pattern is imposed upon him. Freedom opened the doors not only to citizenship for Negroes but to personhood and brought them into the kingdom of moral ends. In a way, those who oppose legal desegregation in the name of personal freedom were answered a long time ago by Mr. Justice Harlan, grandfather of the present Justice, in his famous dissent in the Civil Rights Cases, with which the present Court is only now catching up. [See appendix for excerpts from his opinion.] Their argument, were it accepted widely, would help pin the badge of servitude upon our Negro fellow citizens in their vocations, their education, their housing, and even their use of public accommodations. Generalized, it is an argument against razing by legal measures the walls of the ghettos by which a local majority arbitrarily and unfairly keeps any minority—racial, religious or ethnic—fenced in and deprived of the benefits of their rights as American citizens and as members of a democratic community.

The history of America has been not only a history of promises made but of promises redeemed. For a long time, American Negroes were excluded from even the promise of American life. After the Civil War, they were cruelly denied the fulfilment of the promise implied in their liberation. For the greater part of the near-century since the Emancipation Proclamation, progress was slow, uncertain and gained through bitter struggle. Since the war against Nazism and its racial ideology, however, enormous gains have been made in integrating Negro citizens into the pattern of democratic life. Little Rock is a severe defeat in a long war which the American people are winning—a war which must be won if we are to survive as a free culture the assaults of Communist totalitarianism. The processes of education work gradually but effectively in eroding the bigotry of fanaticism. That is why the lawful spread of integrated education in South and North is our best hope for making the promises of American life come true. The tide of its advance measures the authentic growth of the democratic idea.

APPENDIX

Justice Harlan's Dissent in the Civil Rights Cases of 1883

After the Civil War, the states ratified the Thirteenth, Fourteenth and Fifteenth Amendments, which abolished slavery, gave the Negro national and state citizenship, and guaranteed his right to vote. Congress also passed numerous anti-bias laws, including the act of March 1, 1875, which outlawed race discrimination by inns, public carriers and places of public amusement. But after the South secured the victory of Republican Rutherford Hayes in the disputed election of 1876, the Washington climate changed. In 1883, the Supreme Court declared the 1875 law unconstitutional. Justice John Marshall Harlan dissented, framing the issues in a manner as appropriate today as it was 75 years ago. Excerpts from his opinion (109 U. S. 26) follow:

The first section of the Thirteenth Amendment provides that "neither slavery nor involuntary servitude, except as a punishment for crime whereof the party shall have been duly convicted, shall exist within the United States, or any place subject to their jurisdiction." . . . The terms of the Thirteenth Amendment are absolute and universal. They embrace every race which

9 The Conflict Between the Communist

and Democratic Philosophies

BY ALL ODDS the central political fact of our time is the existence of Soviet Communism, and its implications for the survival of free institutions everywhere. If one has any doubts about this, the headlines of the world's press would confirm it. The speeches and memoranda of statesmen concern themselves with it. One cannot intelligently discuss many domestic issues without reference to it—whether it be our policy with respect to atomic energy, or our programs of trade, taxation, and education.

Unfortunately our discussions of communism as an international movement are not infrequently unintelligent. Worse, they are not even informed. And worst of all, they sometimes reflect narrow partisan bias that converts the issue of communism into a political football, kicked around for some fancied party advantage, actually profiting no one but the Communists.

The history of relations between the communist and democratic worlds has been marked by large pendular swings between panic and indifference. Naturally enough this has been reflected in democratic public opinion. In influential circles belief in the prospects of peaceful cooperation between the two worlds has veered from blind illusion to equally blind distrust, both rooted in ignorance.

Moral earnestness rather than political sophistication has set the tone of most discussions of Communism in the United States. Moral earnestness or idealism and political sophistication are not incompatible, of course, but the first without the second leads to ineptness and insensitiveness which in foreign affairs especially are the chief ingredients of blunder. On the other hand, political sophistication without some moral idealism leads to cynicism whose practical consequences are either dishonorable appeasement or dishonorable aggression.

In speaking of American public opinion, to the extent that it is articulate, one can take for granted its moral idealism but not its political sophistication. For the latter requires historical understanding. One sign of this lack of understanding, not only in America, but in Western consciousness, of the realities of communism is that it is continually being surprised by the actions of the Soviet regime. It may be pertinent to recall here the number of times the West hailed purely tactical or strategic turns in the policy of the Soviet Union as *basic* reorientations of purpose and goal. After the Treaty of Rapallo was signed, after the Popular Front was initiated, after the Soviet Constitution was proclaimed, after the Soviet Union joined the League of Nations, after the Communist International was formally dissolved, after the Kremlin agreed to initial the Atlantic Charter, after the Geneva meeting had taken place—loud and many were the voices which assured us that the dawn of a new day in the relations between Soviet Communism and the West was in sight. Each time these hopes were soon dashed by Soviet actions.

That changes have taken place and will take place in Soviet tactical policy is undeniable, if only because what democratic powers do—and especially what they fail to do—is sure to provoke some counteraction on the part of the Communist high command. And that conferences at the summit or elsewhere may be useful is undeniable, provided that the representatives of the West enter them without illusions, and with reliable knowledge, among other things, of the thoughtways of those who will face them. We must on occasion confer, and confer with the good faith which has so often been conspicuously lacking in Soviet diplomacy. But good faith without good sense can never achieve good works. And in retrospect it is clear that, at every major conference with the Communists, Western statesmen have been had—with consequences ranging from the surrender to the slaughter chambers of the Communist secret police of hundreds of thousands of innocent refugees from Soviet terror immediately after the war, to the sacrifice of American lives in Berlin and Korea. Those who would draw the lesson from this never to sit down at a conference table with Communists (the cynic is often the disappointed *naif*) overlook the possibility that, properly prepared, one can negotiate with Communists and come away not only with a whole skin but with all one's clothes.

Western statesmen, however, will have to do better, much better, than they have done in the past. They will have to understand that what they are up against is a movement which, whether considered as a mass movement or as a directing influence over the masses, is the greatest movement in human history to date. No religion has had so many converts, has spread so fast and so far in so short a time. They will have to understand that Communism takes Protean and bewildering forms. It speaks in every language and in every idiom—including the Orwellian double-think, double-speak, and double-talk.

How far statesmen will have to go may be measured by their views in the past, which range from bafflement to delusion. In 1940 Winston Churchill, that indomitable figure of British courage and common sense, declared that the policy of the Kremlin was "a riddle wrapped in a mystery inside an enigma." Three years later, after Yalta, he firmly assured the House of Commons that the policy of the Kremlin was "to live in honorable friendship and equality with the West." Three years after that, at Fulton, Missouri, he declared no less firmly that only the American atom bomb prevented the Red Army from marching to the Atlantic. Subsequently he developed another view which culminated in the Geneva Conference. The riddle, mystery, enigma represented a void in Mr. Churchill's understanding of Communism which goes all the way back to the years of its birth, when he thought that by foreign intervention he could "strangle Bolshevism in its cradle."

What is true of Churchill was true of Roosevelt, who was grievously disappointed that, despite his concessions to the Kremlin at Teheran and Yalta, he couldn't charm Stalin with his personality as he could Jim Farley. A master in domestic politics, he was at sea in foreign policy. As for Truman's awareness of the realities of Communism and the world situation, it may be gauged from his firm reply to Senator Capehart's committee which called on him before his trip to Potsdam to express its fear of Soviet expansion. Truman told Senator Capehart that he feared British imperialism much more than Soviet Communism. British imperialism, according to Elliot Roosevelt, was a regnant, if publicly unexpressed, object of suspicion in the Roosevelt family as well. Truman came home from Potsdam with a feeling of triumph—and with one quarter of the City of Berlin, a hundred and fifty *corridorless* miles distant from the American zone. Similar mistaken evaluations, in kind if not degree, were made by Willkie, Eisenhower, and even by Senator McCarthy who had a tendency to interpret everyone's mistakes about Communism, except his own, in Soviet style as treason. Continental statesmen were no wiser than their Anglo-American colleagues. General de Gaulle took the Communist fifth column in France into the government. Others, like Masaryk and Beneš, paid for their illusions with their lives,

My thesis here is that the most important key—the most important, but not the exclusive key—to the phenomenon of the Kremlin's political behavior, apparently so baffling to the statesmen of the West, is to be sought in the one element of the communist movement which despite variations in detail and emphasis has remained relatively constant, and which when applied in different historical situations, has determined the communist line of march, its strategy and tactics. This element is the ideology of communism which it is easier to denounce than to understand, and easiest of all to dismiss, with the bluff common sense of Anglo-American near-sighted empiricism, as irrelevant gobbledegook. (Similarly, since Hitler's rantings made no sense to the British, no one paid them mind.)

The actions of great powers in history are determined by many things, not the least among which are chance and ignorance. Ideological belief and a sense of historical mission rarely motivate political behavior, especially in modern times. But when they do, they play decisive, even if not all powerful, roles. Egoism, jealousy, resentment, love of power, the *idée fixe* in individual life and experience are normally curbed by social pressure and tradition and by the reactions of other individual wills. However, when these traits are sublimated in a fanaticism of nation or party or cause, they acquire a terrifying intensity, and a power made all the more ruthless because the illusion of selflessness dissolves the normal inhibitions to self-assertion. They even take on a touch of grandeur because the energies and ruthlessness which would be suspect as signs of psychotic personality in *ordinary* life acquire a different significance when they appear in the context of a total dedication. That is why even saints are sometimes difficult to live with, and why the best place for an insane or disordered mind to hide is in a fanatical mass movement. This does *not* imply that all fanatics are insane. They are not fanatical about everything—indeed, some of them may be very shrewd and flexible about the means by which they seek to achieve their fixed goals.

I

By an ideology I understand the fundamental beliefs about nature, society, and man which any group offers in justification of the direction and goal of its *political* activity. Not all conflicts are ideological, and not all ideological conflicts threaten peace. Some of the most disastrous wars in history, e.g., wars of royal succession, have been fought among peoples who have shared the same ideology, even the same religious ideology, whereas some ideological oppositions, say as between Czarist Russia (as illustrated in the reactionary mysticism of Pobedonostev), and the United States have not led to armed conflict. It is questionable whether there have ever been great wars that were *purely* ideological.

The nearest to purely ideological wars (for example the Crusades and the Thirty Years War) involved other kinds of opposition as well, revealed in the internecine struggles among the Christian crusaders, and in the alliance of Catholic France and Protestant Sweden against Catholic Austria.

Nonetheless, ideological conflicts are of tremendous importance. For although by themselves they are rarely sufficient to cause armed outbreaks, their presence *may* make the decisive difference in transforming the smouldering frictions which arise from difficulties about trade, frontiers, and natural resources into the raging fires of war. That is why a correct understanding of the ideology of the major powers in the present world struggle—what we may call the geography of their mind —is just as important—no, more important—than a study of their physical geography. For what I propose to show is that the communist ideology, like the Nazi ideology *but for different reasons,* impels those who hold it to embark upon a program of world conquest.

In order to make the significance of communist ideology clear, I shall contrast it to some key points of the American ideology.

One of the central assumptions of the concept of democracy, perhaps its most central assumption, is that by and large human adults are better judges of their own interests, whenever they have free access to information which bears on those interests, than are others. The operating maxim of the democratic ideology is, "Whoever wears the shoe knows best where it pinches." From this most of the other attributes essential to a democracy follow, most notably the legal right of opposition and the power of popular majorities to change political shoes in the light of experience. This certainly does not mean a belief that popular majorities are always right. It does entail a faith that, so long as the processes of free inquiry and critical discussion remain intact, a democratic community is more likely to reach a mutually satisfactory adjustment of the common and conflicting interests of its citizens than is possible either by despotism or anarchy. If this is denied there would be no rational ground for the acceptance of democracy.

It is much more difficult, when writing for an Anglo-American audience, to take for granted familiarity with the communist ideology of the Soviet Union. For one thing, the very term "ideology" is absent from their political linguistic habits. For another, politics based on an explicitly expressed *Weltanschauung* is almost completely alien to their historical experience in which large abstractions are continually being washed in the astringent but cleansing acids of empirical analysis. This very virtue, which gives assurance that the inescapable differences in the domestic political life of a democracy do not take the form of a disguised civil war, has led to certain defects in understanding the political ways of other nations and groups. The proposal to set out to make human history in the large, deliberately according to definite blueprints, somewhat in the same way as one sets out to build a factory or a public monument, would strike most democrats as a form of monomania. The natural tendency is therefore to discount the importance of ideological considerations in assessing the intentions and behavior of others, since such considerations do not explicitly operate in our own intentions and behavior. But such an assumption with respect to totalitarianism has proved to be a ghastly error.

Until we abandon it, and come to grips with the ideology of Communism, I fear that American public opinion on key questions of foreign policy will be misguided, more a matter of nerves than of intelligence.

Before discussing the nature of Communist ideology in detail, a few methodological cautions must be kept in mind. First, how shall we find out what the communist ideology really is? The answer is elementary but too often ignored. We will *not* find out from Soviet diplomatic notes and official letters. In one of his letters Stalin professed his willingness to "insure democracy and defend civil rights in all countries"— which must have been the occasion of Homeric laughter in the Politbureau while at the same time the West debated solemnly what Stalin meant and how far he was prepared to go to democratize the Soviet Union. We shall *not* find out from interviews with, or letters from, foreign correspondents which primarily indicate what Soviet spokesmen would *like us to believe*. We *can* find out by reading carefully what the Communist leaders of the Soviet Union say to their own party members in their basic theoretical documents and which they require them to learn in order to prepare them for action. Special emphasis is placed on theory in Communist doctrine, for theory is regarded as the indispensable guide to practice.

Some of my readers are old enough to recall that a few short years before World War II, Hitler gave an interview to George Lansbury, the great English pacifist. Hitler convinced Lansbury that the Nazi regime and he himself sincerely desired peace. "Peace" was Hitler's unwearying note in all his communications with other governments. Every time he violated a treaty he cried, "Peace! Peace!" But only political cretins took this as evidence of Hitler's actual intentions. What Hitler really believed could be found out much more reliably by analyzing his *Mein Kampf* and his addresses to the Nazi Party at its *Parteitage*. Similarly, what the Soviet regime really believes can be discovered, not so much by reading propagandistic defenses of Soviet policy written for foreign consumption, but by a study of such writings as Stalin's *Problems of Leninism, History of the Communist Party of the Soviet Union,* and other works which have been required study among the Communist Parties of the world. The Soviets themselves have boasted that, with the possible exception of the Bible, these books have had the largest circulation in the world. Where the texts are ambiguous—and on fundamental matters they are not—the acid test of meaning, here as elsewhere, is to be found in Soviet practice. And what was true of Stalin is true of his successors.

Secondly, another gross error and obstacle to understanding the ideology of contemporary communism is to identify it with the principles of Marxism on the strength of the references to Marx as a minor deity in the communist pantheon. This is as uncritical as identifying the clerical fascism of Salazar and Franco with the principles of Christianity on the ground that they often speak of "the brotherhood of man under the fatherhood of God." The Communists, to be sure, make use of Marx's critique of capitalism; but the democratic socialists, their most principled and consistent opponents, do so, too. Consequently, what is *distinctive* about the ideology of contemporary communism cannot be the corpus of Marx's doctrines, which are pervaded by a passion for human freedom and dignity. The greatest of the latter-day Marxists—such men as Kautsky, Plechanov, and Hilferding— regarded the Communists as ideological heirs of Bakunin and Nechayev. Though this is also an oversimplification, it should warn us against a too easy identification of the characteristic principles of Marxism, which taught that socialism could be successfully introduced only in the most highly industrialized and cultured countries of the West, with the Communist doctrine which justified its introduction at any cost and by any means in one of the most backward countries of the world. Marx's thought is essentially a product of West European civilization—a synthesis of German classical philosophy, English economic theory, and French Socialism, fused together by his own genius. His criticism of political democracy is that it is incomplete until its rationale is extended to other spheres of life. He does not seek to *abridge* democracy, but to expand it continuously all along the line. Somewhat too optimistically, he could not conceive of socialism as an economy, except under a democratic political form.

Contemporary communism is not Marxism as much as it is Bolshevik-Leninism. Its ideology is authentically presented in the writings, teachings, and practices of Lenin and Stalin—two of the most event-making men of all times, whose activity, we may note in passing, is difficult to explain in terms of their professed philosophy of history. Although since his death Stalin is no longer coupled with Lenin in every breath drawn by his successors, none of his major political ideas has been repudiated. Only the fury of the internal terror has been somewhat abated.

II

I come now to the fundamental propositions of contemporary Communist ideology.

The first proposition is that the welfare of humanity—its assurance of ultimate peace, continuous prosperity, and final freedom from oppression—rests on the victory of the proletariat, nationally and internationally, in its inevitable class-struggles against the bourgeoisie. This first proposition is a conclusion derived from a number of other premises, among them: (a) that no system of capitalist production, no matter how modified or reformed, can function without periodic crises of increasing intensity, culminating in mass misery and war, and (b) that it is only the proletariat as a class which, because of its strategic place in the processes of production and because it has no vested interest in the legal relations of production, can become the mass base of a movement seeking, not the reform of the existing order, but its revolutionary overthrow. Another key premise in this connection is that the proletariat constitutes the overwhelming majority of the population, so that to the extent that there is an objective and non-negotiable clash of interests between it and other classes, its victory is morally justified besides being historically inevitable. This victory spells the end of all private ownership of instruments of production, and the introduction of complete state ownership and absolute state control of the productive plant and society.

A number of comments are in order here. Strictly speaking, the proletariat is the industrial worker. Nowhere do industrial workers constitute a clear majority of the population, except possibly in England and Germany. The consequence is that in Communist literature the term "proletariat" is indefinitely extensible, a rubber-band term, embracing any category of workers—including clerks, professionals and farm workers—who associate themselves with the political program which the Communist Party presents in the name of the proletariat. Similarly, the term "bourgeoisie," and particularly "petty-bourgeoisie," is used with amazing elasticity. If the groups previously mentioned do not at crucial moments follow the political line of the Communist Party they are thrust into the outer darkness of the category "counter-revolutionary petty-bourgeoisie" even if they earn their living by the sale of their labor power. The importance of the fluidity of the concept of "proletariat" and "worker" in Communist theory becomes increasingly apparent.

The second basic proposition of Communist ideology is that, left to itself, the proletariat or working class, despite its distinctive militancy, cannot find its way to a collectivist society in which all classes and all class-struggles *by definition* disappear. Only by submitting itself to the leadership of professional revolutionists, banded together in the Communist Party, can the existing state power be seized and shattered, and the new society built. In other words, the Communist Party by its superior scientific insight into the processes of history, economics, and politics knows better than the working class what the real interests of the working class are. The working class is the darling child of history, but it is still only a blundering child, not knowing the communist goal by which it can save itself and the rest of humanity until it is put under the tutelage of the Communist Party whose leaders themselves are not necessarily of working-class origin. The writings and practices of Lenin and Stalin both leave no doubt on this score. The working class is never right when it sets itself against the program and strategy which the Communist Party lays down for its liberation. "All Power to the Soviets" is a mandatory slogan when the Soviets agree with the Communist program; but when, without changing their working-class composition in the least, the Soviets disagree with the Communist line, then the slogan "All Power to the Soviets" must be discarded. For such disagreement, if serious enough, is counter-revolutionary and the workers become the enemies of the idealized, even if non-existent, proletariat, whose interest the Communist Party, and the Communist Party alone, knows best. That is why, according to Lenin and Stalin, "the dictatorship of the proletariat is substantially the dictatorship of the Communist Party." Some day, they proclaim, this dictatorship will wither away. The date is not specified but the conditions are: when the last vestiges of capitalism, democratic and nondemocratic, have been destroyed throughout the world, and communism is safe from enemies within and without. Meanwhile the Communist state and dictatorship withers away by growing stronger with every passing year—a fact that cannot be grasped by ordinary logic but only by the logic of dialectic which enables one to swallow objective contradiction. In practice, then, the dictatorship of the proletariat is really a dictatorship *over* the proletariat, and although enforced by the most ruthless system of terror in human history, those who execute it are convinced they are doing the work of (I had almost said God)—but in their language, the work of History.

The view that the Communist Party knows the interests of the working class better than the working class knows them itself is absolutely fundamental to communist ideology. If one knows what someone's real interests are, he can oppose that person's *will* on the ground that it is on behalf of that person's *interests*. The workers' wishes and will may be expressed as democratically as you please; if the Communist Party leadership is convinced that what is wished or willed is against the workers' true interest as the Communist leadership interprets it, it has a justification in principle of opposing and destroying the workers in question. Jan Kadar, the Soviet puppet in Hungary, faced by the necessity of explaining the ruthless suppression of the Hungarian workers by the Communists after the fateful days of the Budapest uprising in 1956, falls back on this distinction between the will and wishes of the workers and their true interest. Addressing the Hungarian National Assembly on May 11, 1957, on the relationship between the Communist leaders and the masses, he declared:

> . . . The task of the leaders is not to put into effect the wishes and will of the masses. . . . The task of the leaders is to realize and accomplish the interest of the masses. Why do I differentiate between the will and the interests of the masses? In the recent past we have encountered the phenomenon of certain categories of workers acting *against* their interests. What is the task of the leader in such a situation? Is it mechanically to implement incorrect ideas? No, it is not. . . . If the will of the masses does not coincide with progress, then one must lead the masses in another direction. . . .[1]

The third main proposition of communist ideology is that no Communist Party can succeed in leading the working class unless it is an hierarchically organized, dedicated group of professional revolutionists, free of factions, bound by military discipline, trained to subordinate itself to the will of its leadership. It was in his conception of the nature of revolutionary organization that Lenin most clearly differentiated himself from Western Marxism. For, according to that conception, "the dictatorship of the Party" (which, remember, has been substantially identified with the dictatorship of the proletariat) is the dictatorship of the Political Bureau of the Party, and at times the dictatorship of one man. Lenin made no secret of how he interpreted "democratic centralism."

> Bureaucracy versus democracy is the same thing as centralism versus autonomism, it is the organizational principle of revolutionary political democracy as opposed to the organizational principle of the opportunists of Social Democracy. The latter want to proceed from the bottom upward. . . . The former proceed from the top, and advocate the extension of the rights and powers of the center in respect of the parts.[2]

---

[1] Reported in *East Europe* (July, 1957), p. 56.
[2] Lenin, *Selected Works,* II, 447–448.

This dictatorial principle of leadership holds not only in politics but in all social and economic organizations.

> Soviet socialist democracy is not contradictory to individual management and dictatorship in any way . . . the will of a class may sometimes be carried out by a dictator, who at times may do more alone and who is frequently more necessary.[3]

The function of the leaders of the Communist Party, among other things, is to see that the monolithic character of its theory and of its organization is preserved against all deviations in thought or practice. The slightest opposition, if persistent, leads to infraction of party discipline. And "whoever in the least weakens the iron discipline of the party of proletariat (especially during its dictatorship) actually aids the bourgeoisie against the proletariat."[4] It must be borne in mind that theory and practice includes the whole field of human knowledge, to which the philosophy of dialectical materialism possesses the seven seals. The key to the seals is entrusted only to the most politically reliable communists. This explains why there is a party line—and a shifting party line—in all subjects from art and astronomy to music and zoology, deviations from which can incur serious penalties. The leadership of the Communist Party is the final authority on what constitutes a deviation in any field and there is no appeal from its judgment either to the membership or to public opinion.

Let us now state these three propositions formally in order to grasp their impact more clearly:

(*1*) The welfare of humanity depends upon the victory of the proletariat.

(*2*) The victory of the proletariat depends on the dictatorship of the Communist Party.

(*3*) The dictatorship of the Communist Party can only function through the dictatorship of the leaders—whether it be the Politbureau, Stalin, or Khrushchev.

It follows with implacable logic—and we are dealing with men who are proud of their logical consistency—that anyone who opposes the program of world change set forth by the Politbureau (as the Communist leadership of the moment) is opposed to the welfare of humanity. He is, to use the favorite Soviet phrase, an enemy of mankind.

There is little reason to doubt the sincerity with which this conclusion is held and the ruthlessness with which it is enforced. Whether it is the workers of Budapest or Barcelona, or the so-called Russian *kulaks* or

---

[3] *Ibid.*, VIII, 222.
[4] *Ibid.*, X, 84.

independent farmers as a class who refuse to enter collective farms; whether it is another working-class or socialist party with a different program, such as the Mensheviks or left Social-Revolutionaries; whether it is a group of workers, soldiers, and sailors such as the Kronstadt Soviet; whether it is a faction within the Communist Party, such as the Worker's Opposition of Shlapniakov; whether it is a galaxy of Lenin's early lieutenants—whoever oppose the decision of the ruling hierarchy of the Communist Party are objectively enemies of mankind. Unless they capitulate, they must be punished as such, the leaders by liquidation, the followers by sentences to slave-labor camps. In principle, even a majority of mankind, whether workers or not, can be regarded as enemies of mankind if it persistently refuses to accept the political salvation offered by the Communist program.

The fact that we are dealing with political thoughtways foreign to the secular political mind of the West should not make us incredulous about their existence. Nor should we imagine that the Communist leaders are unaware of the fantastic discrepancies between their professed ideal and the sad realities of Communism in practice. For them these are the transitional costs of progress, to be redeemed by the felicities of the higher stage of communism in the future.

Marx once observed that no ruling class ever voluntarily surrenders its power. We might apply that maxim to the Communist ruling class, and maintain that unconsciously it seeks a justification in historic necessity for the social privileges it enjoys through political tyranny. Nonetheless, it is important to realize that we are dealing with neither frightened nor unintelligent men but rather with determined men, fortified by an absolute assurance in their program and its messianic significance for the entire world. So much so that they cannot even conceive that anyone who understands their program could reject it except on the three grounds of (a) self-interest, among the bourgeoisie the destruction of whose power and social position is threatened by the state monopoly of production; (b) ignorance or stupidity, among workers who remain insensitive to the Communist message; and (c) dishonesty, among all intellectuals who are critical of Communism, and who are dubbed "the lackeys of Capitalism."

Whether we are dealing here with a fanaticism of virtue or vice is again not so important as to recognize it for what it is, *a fanaticism of program* which subordinates everything to a predetermined end. This end justifies the use of any means in the struggle for power—literally *any* means—and explains why Communist practice is marked by the extremest kind of opportunism and deceit in its slogans, strategy, and tactics. No communist feels bound by any code of honor or principles of morality. Lenin denies that this is tantamount to immorality. "We

say," he declares, "that our morality is *entirely* subordinated to the interest of the class struggle of the proletariat,"[5] which means subordinated to what furthers the victory of the Communist Party. And Lenin's
career—as well as Stalin's, as well as that of their successors—has
clearly shown that Smerdyakov's formula in *The Brothers Karamazov,*
"All things are permissible"—no matter how they outrage our moral
sensibilities—is their own, if only it helps in the conquest of power. That
is why communists throughout the world who are vehement about their
civil rights do not regard it as inconsistent in the slightest to deny all
civil rights to those who disagree with them when they come to power.
That is why those who must negotiate agreements with Soviet representatives, if unacquainted with communist ideology, live a life of continual surprise at what words can be made to mean. And that is why
communists refuse to utilize only the normal processes of democracy,
especially parliamentary institutions, to achieve their goal. If they did
they would have to run the risk of having their program repudiated by
popular majorities or of helping existing society improve conditions to
a point where their own program would have no appeal. "No parliament," writes Lenin, "can in any circumstances be for Communists an
arena of struggle for reforms for betterment of the situation of the
working-class. . . . The only question can be that of utilizing bourgeois state institutions for their own destruction." The behavior of Communist deputies in the Reichstag of the Weimar Republic and in the
French and Italian chambers today illustrates what Lenin meant.
Gromyko, Vishinsky, and other Soviet officials in the U.N. fulfill
Lenin's injunction to the letter. Finally, this explains the Communist
belief that power can only be taken by violent overthrow, and Lenin's
specific and emphatic denial of Marx's contention that in democratic
countries like England and the United States socialism could be
achieved peacefully.[6]

At this juncture we are sure to hear from someone to the effect that
all this is surely not so much the ideology of contemporary international
communism as the ideology only of Russian communism which reflects
the peculiar traits of Russian history. The Czech Communists are different. The French Communists are different. The Italian Communists
are different. The American Communists are different. Now it is undeniable that the ideology of Communism bears the stigmata of centuries of Russian absolutism. It is also true that Communist Parties outside the Soviet Union are sometimes rent by factional division after

[5] *Ibid.,* IX, 475 (my italics).
[6] *Ibid.,* VII, 37.

some particularly gruesome piece of political skullduggery by the Kremlin. In the end, however, the factional dispute dies down and in almost all known cases continued affiliation with the official Communist movement requires capitulation to the line of the Kremlin. The only exception to this, so far, is Poland where former oppositionists returned from jail to power and received support not only from the party but from the noncommunists and even anticommunists. But it is completely false to suppose that there is any essential difference between Soviet Communism, no matter what its origin, and the ideology of official Communist Parties elsewhere. A certain variation in tactics is allowable, but on no fundamental issue of any kind are the Communist Parties of the world permitted to deviate by even a hair'sbreadth, particularly on the strategy laid down for the conquest of power. The case of Tito speaks worlds on this issue. Indeed, affilation with the Communist International, which was rebaptized as the Cominform without ever having really died, depended upon the acceptance of twenty-one conditions which universalized the Russian pattern. If anyone entertains a doubt as to how closely the Communist Parties of the world follow the ideological directives of the Kremlin, let me quote a characteristic passage from William Z. Foster's *Towards Soviet America:*

> Even before the seizure of power, the workers will organize the Red Guard . . . the leader of the revolution in all its stages is the Communist Party. . . . Under the dictatorship, all the Capitalist parties—Republican, Democratic, Progressive, Socialist, etc.—will be liquidated, the Communist Party alone functioning as the Party of the toiling masses. Likewise will be dissolved all other organizations that are political props of all bourgeois rule, including chambers of commerce, employers' associations, Rotary Clubs, American Legion, Y.M.C.A., and such fraternal orders as the Masons, Odd Fellows, Elks, Knights of Columbus, etc.[7]

This is presented as the twentieth-century version of Jeffersonian democracy. On occasions, in accordance with the directives laid down by the center, the Communist Party will profess the most piously democratic sentiments in order to escape detection and criticism. They will even point to the constitutions of their legal parties, but these constitutions are as valid evidence of their belief in democracy as the Soviet's constitution of the presence of democracy in the U.S.S.R.

III

All this is only part of the story. Granted that the foregoing expresses the ideological basis of Soviet communism, what bearing has it on inter-

---

[7] P. 275.

national relations? Each country can solve its own domestic communist problem as it sees fit. Why cannot it then work out a *modus vivendi* with the Soviet Union which, after all, declares itself interested only in building "socialism in one country"? Here, too, we must carefully distinguish between the Soviet goal which remains constant and the diplomatic offensives that are turned on and off to meet some particular situation.

There is a myth currently prevalent that, after Lenin's death, Stalin espoused socialism in one country, and turned his back on international revolutionary communism which Trotsky had sought to continue as part of Lenin's legacy. The truth is that for all their differences, which were largely tactical and personal, both Stalin and Trotsky were out of the same Leninist mold. When Western Europe failed to imitate Russia, Lenin's problem was to build as much socialism as possible in Russia while encouraging revolutionary activities against capitalism in other countries. Stalin emphasized building up the socialist economy but did not neglect revolutionary activity abroad; Trotsky emphasized revolutionary action abroad but also called for the industrialization of the Soviet Union.

What Stalin meant by "socialism in one country" was that *if* the Soviet Union were left alone to work out her own destiny she would achieve socialism out of her own resources. But he never made any bones of the fact that the Soviet Union would not and could not be left alone, and that the final victory of socialism in one country can only be assured when the communist revolution had triumphed in the main countries of the world. Quoting Lenin, Stalin wrote: "We are living not only in a state but in a system of states, and the existence of the Soviet republic side by side with imperialist states for a long time is unthinkable. One or the other must triumph in the end. And before the end comes, a series of frightful clashes between the Soviet republic and the bourgeois states is inevitable."[8] And writing on his own, "It is a Leninist principle that the final victory of socialism . . . is only possible on an international scale. . . . For what else is our country, 'the country that is building up socialism,' but the base of the world revolution?"[9]

There are several reasons why Communist ideologists are convinced that the Soviet Union cannot survive alone in a world of capitalist states, but the chief reason is the nature of the capitalist system. According to their analysis every capitalist system must expand or die, and before it dies it must make an attempt to expand by war unless it is overthrown from within. So fundamental is the belief that capitalism of every variety leads ultimately to economic breakdown and war that even during

---

[8] *Problems of Leninism*, I, 56.
[9] *Ibid.*, pp. 60, 63.

World War II, when some capitalist countries were helping the Soviet Union resist an invasion by another capitalist country, instead of making common cause with the invader, as Communist analysis would have led us to expect, this belief was still being fostered in official Communist text books although absent from government proclamations. To admit that any economy but a completely state-owned economy could possibly stabilize itself under conditions of modern technology, and provide full employment and general prosperity, would pull one of the chief props from under the argument for the Soviet system itself. The Soviet leaders cannot sincerely abandon this belief without having the whole structure of Communist ideology crash to the ground.

Given the dogma, however, that all countries not in the Soviet sphere are impelled to war by the very processes of their economic life, then with characteristic Bolshevik realism the consequences are logically drawn. Until the final conflict is won, the Communist economy must be a war economy and all measures, domestic or in regard to foreign policy, must enhance its military potential as well as its military geographical position. Since the final *dénouement* can be avoided only if Communist regimes are established in other countries, Communist Parties in those countries must function as fifth columns, disorganizing them by propaganda, infiltration, intensification of class struggles, espionage, and striking for power if a favorable revolutionary situation develops. At the very least, once hostilities break out they must sabotage to the death the cause of their own country for the sake of the worker's true fatherland, the Soviet Union.

Unpalatable as it may be to us, the sobering truth is that from the very founding of the Communist International, whose organization was called for by communist ideology even *before* the October Revolution, the Soviet regime has been in a state of undeclared war against the West. This war was launched on the basis of strictly ideological considerations, long before the foolish and fruitless efforts of some Western states to overthrow the Soviet Union by invasion in its early years.

Whether one approves or disapproves, it must be admitted that communist ideology is an impressive body of integrated doctrine. Although sometimes overlaid with transitory slogans and obscured by diplomatic notes, it is always possible to discern its iron features in any serious document issued by the Politbureau. To dismiss this ideology as a kind of quaint ritualism is foolhardy in the face of the unwearying insistence of communist leaders that their theory is a guide to revolutionary practice. And in truth, theory today is the most practical thing in the world.

Of course, one may raise the question of whether communist political *behavior* is in fact determined by ideological considerations, despite the official communist claim that it is, and inquire whether or not it is determined by such simpler factors as geography, control of raw materials, and considerations of balance of power. At the time of the Nazi-Soviet Pact, Mr. Molotov reminded us that ideologies are matters of taste, although he changed his tune about the unimportance of such matters of taste just as soon as Hitler invaded Russia. But as I have previously indicated, it is not necessary to maintain that Soviet political behavior is *exclusively* determined by its professed ideology to recognize how fateful it may be. It is sufficient to maintain only that this ideology explains many things in the expansionist drive of the Soviet Union, and that under certain circumstances it may tip the scales in the direction of overt war, since *any* act of the Soviet Union, no matter how aggressive, can always be justified as a defensive measure against inevitable encirclement. And Stalin made it clear after the war that "encirclement" was not a geographical but a political concept, so that the stronger and more aggressive the Kremlin became the more it could claim that it was politically threatened. In politics it is not only the facts that count, but what makers of policy *believe* those facts to be. A man in the grip of delusions may be cured by knowledge of the facts; but he must first be restrained, for our own sakes if not for his, before he can be cured.

There remains one question: how to explain, then, the Soviet profession of belief in "peaceful coexistence," a slogan which is periodically stressed in propaganda and, sad to say, almost invariably impresses some scientific and cultural figures of the Western world with the sincerity of the Soviet's peaceful aims.

The content if not the actual words of the phrase goes back to February, 1920, when Lenin gave an interview to a correspondent of *The New York Evening Journal* in which he declared: "Let American capitalists not touch us. We will not touch them." This interview remained unpublished in the Soviet Union for more than thirty years, when it was reprinted in *The Bolshevik,* the theoretical and political organ of the Central Committee of the Communist Party, in April, 1950.[10] However, on November 26, 1920, the very year in which the unpublished interview was given, Lenin delivered a speech to the Communist Party functionaries which has been reprinted again and again in innumerable editions in the Soviet Union and studied by party members. In it he said: "As long as capitalism and socialism exist, we cannot live in peace; in the end one or the other will triumph—a funeral dirge will be sung over the Soviet Republic or over world Capitalism."[11]

Which expressed Lenin's real belief and the belief of his disciples? —his remarks made to a visitor for foreign consumption in the camp

---

10 Cf. *The New York Times,* April 21 and 22, 1950.
11 *Selected Works,* VIII, 297.

of his enemies, not published in the Soviet Union, or his remarks to his fellow members published, broadcast, studied, and repeated throughout the land in order to guide behavior? By "peaceful coexistence" the Kremlin now as before understands a noncombatant period of *preparation* for the war which *they* regard as inevitable. This is known as "revolutionary peace policy." And as Stalin once put it in his "Thesis on The Peace Policy of the U.S.S.R." during the days of the Communist International, "Revolutionary war of the proletarian dictatorships is but a continuation of revolutionary peace policy 'by other means.' "

It is deeds, however, not words which are the acid test of meaning and sincerity. And here the plain truth is that the United States, not the Soviet Union, has followed a policy of peaceful coexistence. At the end of World War II, the United States demobilized her troops; the U.S.S.R. kept hers at war strength. Through UNRRA and the Marshall Plan, offered even to Communist countries, the United States fed Europe; the U.S.S.R. bitterly sabotaged these efforts. When the United States had an absolute monopoly of the atomic bomb, she offered to give it up to a world authority on the sole condition that she be protected against an atomic Pearl Harbor. The U.S.S.R. alone vetoed the safeguarding inspection provisions.

Professing a belief in "peaceful coexistence" with other parties, Communists on orders from Moscow strangled democratic Czechoslovakia and plunged Greece into civil war. Pledged to "peaceful coexistence" with her allies, the U.S.S.R. imposed an outrageous blockade of free Berlin. If the test of "peaceful coexistence" is willingness to abide by treaties, then the Soviet Union stands convicted of having violated, not only the Yalta and Potsdam agreements, but more than a score of non-aggression pacts with its neighbors. If it did not openly engineer, it openly approved the invasion of South Korea and the Chinese invasion of North Korea. It not only refused to coexist with a socialist Hungary which sought only to regain its national independence; it butchered tens of thousands who rose to the defence of freedom.

IV

I want to return now for a moment to the ideology of democracy. Its points of conflict with the ideology of communism should have been apparent all along the line. This conflict is epitomized in the opposition between the fanaticism of Communist program and the democratic principle of *process*. No opposition could be more fundamental, since all other oppositions flow from it. The democratic faith in process does not rest on any official theology or metaphysics. It involves the belief that all social institutions must justify themselves by their works, as interpreted not only by an elite of professional revolutionists but by the great masses of the non-elite, here and now. It takes as its point of departure the needs and wishes of persons to lead their own lives, make their own choices, and pursue their own happiness, and not the perfections of social blueprints laid up in heaven or derived from the laws of dialectic. It accepts restrictions upon specific needs and wishes only when in the course of free political process it can be shown that such restrictions are necessary to enrich human experience or to avoid common disaster. Instead of swearing allegiance to a fixed, predetermined end which is used to justify any means, it tests proposed ends by the consequences of the means to achieve them.

The ideology of democracy is not committed to a fixed economic system but only to those processes of freely given consent which enable human beings to determine what kind of economy they want. Those who identify democracy necessarily with free enterprise or capitalism are false to the spirit of democracy and are doing it a great disservice. Democracy is compatible with any economic system, even collectivism, provided only that human beings are free not only to choose it but also to abandon it if they wish, after savoring its fruits. It recognizes that human beings may be exploited not only by private employers but also by the state, and that state exploitation when it takes place is more fearsome because it is backed by total police power. It is experimental in its outlook and sees many more possible economic systems than that given by doctrinaires in the narrow choice between unrestrained *laissez-faire* and complete state monopoly of the instruments of production. That is why it seems to me to be a complete mistake, fraught with the most terrible consequences, to reduce the ideological conflict between communism and democracy today, as many do, to a conflict between free economic enterprise on the one hand and collectivism on the other. After all, it is questionable to what extent the United States really has a free-enterprise system in the classic sense; and certainly democratic England and France have gone pretty far on the road to a planned socialist economy. Yet the ideological opposition between these democracies and the Soviet Union is no less than between the United States and the U.S.S.R. If anything, Communist leaders would rather deal with short-sighted reactionary capitalists, more concerned with the balance sheets of profit and loss, who are convinced that they can do business with the Kremlin as they did with Hitler and the Japanese war lords, than deal with principled democratic socialists who are more concerned with human freedom. No, the basic issue is not economic, but political and moral.

That basic issue, it cannot be repeated too often, is whether human beings are to be entrusted with freedom of choice to determine their own governments, their own cultural outlook, and their own economic system, or whether it is to be chosen *for* them. Despite their campaigns of semantic corruption with such terms as "democracy" and "freedom," the partisans of communist ideology have resolutely denied genuine liberty of choice to the people, first by the methods by which they seize power and even more by the methods by which they keep it. One can openly admit a multitude of evils, some of them shameful, in any existing democratic state, but so long as the processes of criticism, opposition, and education are not monopolized by a minority political party and supervised by a secret police, which is the case in every Communist state in the world, those evils are remediable. It is for this reason that according to the democratic ideology, *political* democracy is at the basis of all other forms of democracy no matter what the sphere of life.

Communism as an ideology cannot sincerely compete under the rules of the game of political democracy without giving up the ghost—but there is no reason to think it will oblige us by competing openly and sincerely. Within a national perspective the problems of coping with communism as a conspiratorial movement are difficult enough. But they are soluble in part by the techniques advocated by the President's Committee on Civil Rights—pitiless exposure and never-ceasing watchfulness, and in part by more effective measures which bar access to strategic posts in government and society to conspirators while taking care to uphold the individual liberties of heretics and dissenters.

Within the international perspective the problem is insoluble by these methods, short of the establishment of a democratic world sovereignty—a remote contingency. Until then, the undeclared cold war will go on between the U.S.S.R. and its satellite states and the Western world. To prevent this cold war whose temperature is daily rising from becoming an open war is the difficult task of Western statesmanship—an extremely difficult task when we reflected that it takes two to keep the peace but only one to violate it. Says a Chinese proverb: "No one can have more peace than his neighbors will allow him."

The danger, I submit, is not equal from both directions. For the existence of representative institutions and a free public opinion in a democratic country acts as a brake upon the power of the executive arm to plunge the nation into war. Under totalitarian regimes, as history has amply evidenced, there is no comparable brake. It requires only the word of the dictator to send armies over the border and give the command for a Pearl Harbor. The problem then reduces itself to this: how can a country like the U.S.S.R., whose regime is fanatically devoted to the communist ideology, be prevented from overrunning, by direct or indirect aggression, one nation after another under the pretext of defensive action against encirclement?

No matter how fanatical the ideology, there is one force which can tame it: fear of failure. The fact that the Communist movement is free of traditional supernaturalism, and is more like a secular Mohammedanism than a Christian heresy (Mr. Toynbee to the contrary) works to a possible advantage if we are realistic enough. This history of the Bolshevik regime shows strategic retreats only when the policy of foreign adventure threatened to provoke a counter-action that might be too strong to withstand. Appeasement of the Soviet regime must fail even if it takes the most generous-hearted form, because according to Communist theory such appeasement always flows from weakness, not strength. So much are the Communist leaders prisoners of their own ideology that they cannot interpret any proposal to them, no matter how magnificent and magnanimous (even the Acheson-Lilienthal plan for the international control of atomic energy) except as maneuvers in the class war, a world civil war. The only remaining alternative, therefore, is the pooling of power by a union of democracies to a point where any major act of aggression by the Soviet regime would be considered too risky to be undertaken.

In this connection, we are sometimes told that it is impossible to prevent the spread of ideas or an ideology by force, or money, or other economic aid, and that the chief defense of the democratic ideology is the construction of a welfare economy with a functioning Bill of Rights. Put this way, two distinct sets of issues are confused which must be kept clear. Before a democratic people can build a better and freer society it must be safeguarded from interference by totalitarian powers. Social reforms in England and France by themselves would no more be sufficient to bring Soviet expansion to a halt than they would have sufficed to prevent Nazi expansion. It was not because Czechoslovakia suffered from economic distress or lack of civil freedom that she lost her democracy in 1948 or that Norway, Holland, and Finland came under the heel of dictatorship in 1941. It is not Soviet ideas that the democratic ideology needs fear, but Soviet paratroopers and illegally operating Communist Action Committees and fifth columnists. A better society by all means, but an iron-clad defence must go with it whenever any powerful nation refuses to submit all issues in dispute to the arbitrament of the democratic process. The adoption of economic measures to remove the whiplash of hunger and want throughout the non-Communist world must go hand in hand with reasonable measures of defence.

The democratic ideology should not fear the competition of communist ideology, it should welcome it. The shoe is really on the other foot: no communist regime will permit its subjects to read the literature of democracy or to hear the broadcasts of the free world. The peoples of totalitarian states are insulated completely from the truth about living and cultural conditions in the West. Because of the absolute monopoly such regimes exercise over all instruments of publication, it is well-nigh impossible to breach this intellectual quarantine. So complete is the control over news and facts about the West that the Russian soldiers who looted the apartment houses in the working-class sections of Vienna and Berlin believed that they were actually the homes of the bourgeoisie. In an official order of the day, the Red Army was even warned against being corrupted by the standard of living observable in—of all countries—Rumania! Far from fearing free and open competition between the democratic and communist ideologies in the market place of world opinion, we should encourage interchanges of ideas and personnel not only in technical fields, which the Soviets are eager to exploit in order to profit from Western technology, but in the fields of economics, and political and social philosophy.

As much as democrats love peace and security, if they understand their own philosophy they know that peace and security are not enough, and that it is possible to pay too high a price for them if they involve the sacrifice of moral and political freedom. Those who surrendered their freedom to Hitler to save their property or their lives discovered often that they lost not only freedom but the self-respect without which man becomes transformed into the cowering victim of a beast of prey. In the last analysis, genuine security and freedom are inseparable, for unless it is possible to curb power the apparent security a man enjoys may be snatched from him at any moment by arbitrary action. For democrats, the matrix of any authority we accord to men, institutions, or laws, is the authority of process, of rational inquiry which alone can increase the areas of public agreement while permitting individual differences to flourish. Democrats aim not at one world with a uniformitarian pattern for all but at one world with compatible diversities, not at the rule of the world by one nation but at a rule of the world by a democratic concert of democratic nations.

10 Historical Determinism and Political Fiat in Soviet Communism

DESPITE THEIR CONCERN about the Soviet Union, the statesmen and generals of the Western world have shown very little interest in its ideology. They have been inclined to regard it as having about as much relevance to Soviet practice as Christian theology to the practices of the West. Few students of Soviet policy, however, would deny that some understanding of Communist (Bolshevik) ideology is relevant to charting, and possibly predicting, the course of conduct followed by the Kremlin. But there is no agreement on how significant that influence is in relation to other considerations, material and ideal.

Some observers seek to explain Soviet practice in terms of the psychology of its leaders or as an expression of the psychology of the Russian Slavic people, naturally or mystically interpreted. Others see it as little different from the traditional policy of national expansion followed by earlier Russian regimes from Peter the Great to Nicholas II. Still others view Soviet policy as a jockeying for a strategic global position in a balance of power the laws of whose equilibrium are invariant for all social systems. Another influential school sees in Communism a kind of Christian heresy embodied in the institutional vestiges of Byzantinism but perverted to a form in which the secular power *openly* declares itself to be the source of all spiritual and temporal authority.

All of these conceptions would be contemptuously dismissed by the Russian Communists themselves as an "ideological" reading of the Russian historical experience since 1917. Strictly speaking the term "ideological" in the vocabulary of the Russian Communists connotes

127

a "false consciousness" which distorts objective historical truth. The truths of history, according to their own account, are specific applications on the level of human affairs of certain fundamental truths embodied in the alleged laws of materialistic dialectics.

These laws, simply summarized, state that all change, including historical change, takes place in virtue of the operation of *internal* and *necessary* causes. The tempo according to which they manifest themselves may be retarded or accelerated by causes *external* to the system under consideration but in no case can they be permanently arrested in their development. Thus in considering the history of any given society, factors like climate, geography, the presence or absence of raw materials, the influence of great men, are assigned at most the role of peripheral factors. They are unable to supply the key to the main movement which always lies in the mode of economic production. The proximity of cultures, the diffusion of cultural forms and practices are relegated to the rank of stimuli which are of themselves never sufficient causes of significant social change. An encounter between civilizations gives rise to a fundamental change only when the internal state of one or both has reached a point of internal readiness or preparedness such that it can confidently be predicted that even without the specific stimulus of contact, the change would have taken place anyhow at a subsequent date. Ideas and ideologies, although not denied some causal influence, are strictly subordinate to the basic immanent economic "contradictions" which constitute the dynamic force in all social evolution.

This conception of an overriding objective historical necessity, triggered by subjective factors and contingent events, is canonic doctrine for all Communists in all countries. It is of course the cardinal tenet of the orthodox Marxism professed by Communists everywhere, especially Lenin,[1] and has remained so down to today. Anyone who has read Mao Tse-Tung will find in his writings the same ideas down to the very illustrations which Stalin took from Lenin who copied them out of Engels.[2]

The uses to which the doctrine of historical determinism has been put are many and profound. Every major policy including the conquest of political power in October, 1917, has been justified in its terms. The Bolsheviks have prided themselves upon being activists,

---

[1] See especially Lenin's comments on historical materialism in the collection of his writings from 1895 to 1923 on Marx and Marxism, issued by the Marx-Engels-Lenin Institute, entitled *Marx-Engels-Marxism* (New York and Moscow, Cooperative Publishing Society of Foreign Workers in the U.S.S.R., 1935).

[2] Mao Tse-Tung, *On Contradictions* (English trans.), (New York, International Publishers, 1953).

unflinching in resolution and prepared for any personal sacrifice. But the more they set themselves to storm the gates of heaven, or achieve the "classless society," the more they felt themselves absolved from ordinary principles of ethical responsibility in virtue of the operation of the economic necessities which they insisted they were helping to fulfill. The establishment of the dictatorship, the programs of industrialization and collectivization, the ironclad control of culture, the major turns in foreign policy—all were defended as, in the last analysis, compelled either by the economic decline of capitalism or by the necessity of building and defending the socialist economy.

This attitude with some variations has been often adopted by Western admirers of the Russian Revolution who have bravely accepted all the hardships and deprivations of the Russian masses on the ground that the Bolsheviks had no real alternatives open to them. Hard and ruthless as Bolshevik actions were, they were not the result of arbitrary decisions, for in a certain sense they were not free decisions at all. The hands of the Kremlin were forced by economic events. They could not have acted differently and succeeded in building socialism. Thus, Harold J. Laski, who towards the end of his life believed that Soviet civilization held up to the Western world an image of its own future, contended that the reduction in the living standards of the Russian people, the liquidation of all democratic institutions including free workers' soviets, the terror and concentration camp regime was the only way in which the socialist economy could have been set up. A democratic course would never have permitted the sacrifice of basic consumption needs for massive investments in capital goods industries. This would have meant inability to stand up against Hitler's war machine.[3] Believing then that capitalist countries must expand or face ruin, and that their expansion could be achieved only by war, the Communists were compelled to follow the logic of the historical situation. Had they pursued instead the gradualist path of democratic socialism or moved towards something like the welfare economies of England and the United States, Hitler would have triumphed. So runs the argument.

I

The question I propose to discuss here is whether in actual fact Communist practice has been guided by its doctrinal justifications, whether Bolshevik historical behavior can be squared with its professed Marxist theory, and, if not, what set of considerations actually determines the fundamental line of Bolshevik policy.

---

[3] Laski, H. J., *Reflections on the Revolution of Our Times*, pp. 55 ff.

The first observation which suggests itself to an unbiased inquiry is that the Communists have inflated the elements of voluntarism in the Marxist system of thought to a point where they have burst out of its framework. From a Communist point of view this is a most heretical and impious charge. To imply that a Communist is not a Marxist is tantamount in the eyes of believers to asserting that one can be Catholic without being Christian. Nonetheless, a sober assessment of Communist practice seems to lead to this conclusion—and this independently of whether one regards Marx's thought as sound or unsound.

One of Marx's central contributions to the study of culture is his theory of historical materialism. It is plagued by all sorts of ambiguities, loose formulations, and difficulties. But its intent is clear. It asserts that politics is a reflex of economics, that the human will does not possess all degrees of historical freedom. Human action is either the mode by which social inevitabilities come to pass or, in a freer and more charitable reading, it is responsible for choices between narrowly limited alternatives in conditions of historical crisis. No Marxist of any persuasion would admit that political action can create a new social order unless the necessary antecedent economic conditions for its successful functioning were already present. Marx, Engels, Kautsky, Plechanov, and the entire Sanhedrin of Social-Democratic expositors of Marx, including Lenin before the First World War,[4] described these economic conditions, and their social and cultural corollaries. A matured capitalist economy with an industrial proletariat schooled by modern processes of production and inspired by an enlightened world view was considered a necessary if not sufficient condition for the great social transformation that would forever end economic class society and the exploitation of man by man. The socialist revolution was expected in advanced industrial countries like England and the United States, not in one of the most economically backward countries of Europe. The Communists, than whom there are none more vehement in their protestations of Marxist orthodoxy, nonetheless seized political power in Russia, destroyed the regime which at one time Lenin declared "the freest" in the world, characterized "by the absence of

---

[4] At the time of the Revolution of 1905, Lenin wrote, "Finally we wish to say that by making it the task of the provisional revolutionary government to achieve the minimum program, the resolution therefore eliminates the absurd, semi-anarchist idea that the maximum program, the conquest of power for a socialist revolution, can be immediately achieved. The present degree of economic development of Russia (an objective condition) and the degree of class consciousness and organization of the broad masses of the proletariat (a subjective condition indissolubly connected with the objective condition), make the immediate, complete emancipation of the working class impossible." Lenin, V. I., *Selected Works*, III, 52.

oppression of the masses,"[5] and built a collectivist economy. Marx had proclaimed in his *Introduction to the Critique of Political Economy* that "no social order ever perishes before all the productive forces for which there is room in it have developed."[6] There was plenty of room for the development of productive forces in the Russia of 1917, certainly not less than in the United States of 1917, which was decades ahead of Russia, and yet more than doubled its productive capacity since then.

At first, Lenin and Trotsky rationalized the Communist conquest of power by considering the world economy as a whole and claiming that on a world scale there was no room for further expansion—again in the teeth of the facts, since world capitalism, measured by increase in productivity, has developed on a tremendous scale. Lenin asserted that capitalism breaks down "at its weakest link" which Russia was supposed to be; Trotsky discovered a "law of combined development" which enables backward countries to telescope their social development so that they can skip a phase of industrial development.[7] These *ad hoc* doctrines could just as well explain a socialist revolution at the time in Spain or Turkey which were still weaker links in the capitalist chain. If valid they would have held even for the time of Marx and Engels, making nonsense of their earlier predictions.

But all this was preliminary to a more far-reaching abandonment of Marxism. The assumption of Lenin and Trotsky was that the world socialist revolution would begin after power was taken in Russia and that the more highly industrialized countries would lead the march to socialism with Russia once more making up the rear. When this did not happen, the Communists set themselves to do what Marxist theory declared economically impossible, *i.e.,* to build a collectivist economy even though the necessary presuppositions were absent. Their very success refuted the theory which presumably guided them. If socialism be defined as collective ownership of the instruments of mass production, then we must regard it as one of history's greatest ironies that Marx has been decisively proved wrong by his most vehement disciples.

To be sure socialism can be defined not merely as a collectivist economy but as one functioning under democratic political controls in which case there can be no talk of socialism under a totalitarian dictatorship. But orthodox Marxism cannot consistently define a culture save

---

[5] Lenin, V. I., *Collected Works,* XX, 107.

[6] Marx-Engels, *Selected Works,* I, 329, Moscow, 1950.

[7] For a discussion of Lenin's and Trotsky's views, *cf.* Trotsky, L., *History of Russian Revolution* III, Appendix 2 (New York, Simon and Schuster, 1932).

on the basis of its economy. After all, it is quite explicit that democracy and dictatorship both are merely superstructural addenda. Just as capitalism still remains capitalism whether it functions under democratic or dictatorial forms so, in accordance with this line of thinking, socialism remains socialism irrespective of whether it is administered under a democracy or dictatorship. At any rate in most contexts socialism is a category of economic, not political, classification.

We are not interested here in the exegetical conflicts between doctrinaire Marxists but in readily verified historical facts which cannot be explained away. A year to the day after the Communists seized power in Russia, Lenin unveiled a memorial to Marx and Engels. In his speech he acclaimed as their great historical merit their "scientific analysis of the inevitability of the collapse of capitalism and its transition to communism."[8] At that very time against great odds, Lenin and his party were trying to make the inevitable come to pass. It was their will to power, together with the ineptitude and disunity of their opponents, which was shaping day by day events and nothing remotely resembling any social or economic necessity.

II

In no aspect of Communist domestic policy is this clearer than in the transformation of the Marxist concept of "the dictatorship of the proletariat" (a phrase infrequently used by Marx as synonymous with a workers' democracy) into a dictatorship of the Communist Party— and its leaders—over the proletariat.

Marx never made any clear distinction between his party and the proletariat and seems to have accepted a kind of "theory of spontaneity" according to which the workers, following the pattern set by the Paris Commune, would democratically control their political and industrial life. He assumed that the socialist revolution when it occurred would have a clear majority of the population in its support. After the February Revolution the Soviets became the special organ of workers, soldiers, and peasants as distinct from the Provisional Government which looked towards the Constituent Assembly for an authoritative democratic mandate. There is no evidence that at any definite time the actual will of the majority of the Russian population was reflected in the Soviets. Representation was uneven, the city Soviets exercised disproportionate influence and there were no direct elections to the Provincial and all Union Soviets. But they did provide a more or less free area of discussion and debate for representatives of the Russian working population and soldiery.

---

[8] Lenin, V. I., *Collected Works*, XXIII, 291.

When Lenin returned to Russia from abroad in April, 1917, he called for the transfer of all political power to the Soviets despite the fact that "we [the Bolsheviks] are in the minority."[9] The Soviets were the political form through which the dictatorship of the proletariat was to be exercised. He made effective capital of the call "All Power to the Soviets" until it appeared that the Soviets, repelled by the premature attempts at the seizure of power by the Bolsheviks in July, showed clearly that they were prepared to defend the Provisional government against further insurrectionary attempts. Then in a revealing and much neglected essay *On Slogans,* Lenin frankly acknowledged that the appeal for all power to the Soviets, hitherto defended as a democratic principle, was nothing but a slogan. He called for its abandonment, despite the fact that the Soviets still represented the largest group of workers and peasants, and for the preparation of an insurrectionary program. "The slogan of the power passing to the Soviets would at present sound quixotic and mocking," he wrote.[10]

The Sixth Congress of the Bolshevik Party formally approved Lenin's new proposal which was a clear declaration that the Bolsheviks would attempt to seize power behind the backs of the Soviet democracy. After the Kornilov affair, Lenin again proposed the slogan "All Power to the Soviets," suspended it when rebuffed by other working class and peasant parties, and returned to it only when the Bolsheviks got a majority in the Petersburg and Moscow Soviets. Trotsky candidly admits that the slogans under which the Bolsheviks carried out their insurrection meant merely "All Power to the *Bolshevik* Soviets."[11]

Although Lenin, and Stalin after him, speak of "the dictatorship of the proletariat" as an "historic necessity"[12] no attempt is ever made to show how the actual nature of such a dictatorship determines any specific *political* institutional form, except that representation shifts from a geographical to an occupational basis. The "dictatorship of the bourgeoisie" is presumed to be present under parliamentary institutions, no matter how democratic, as well as under the rule of a dictator. Yet at no time have the Bolsheviks held that such political dictatorship, or even Fascism as a political system, is *inevitably* bound up with capitalist development. It is always pictured as a consequence of political weakness or betrayal. Why, then, must "the dictatorship of the proletariat" take a *politically* dictatorial form? Neither Lenin nor any other Bolshevik

---

[9] Lenin, V. I., *Collected Works,* XX, 107.
[10] Lenin, V. I., *Collected Works,* XXI, 45.
[11] Trotsky, L., *History of Russian Revolution,* II, 320.
[12] Stalin, J., *Leninism* (New York, International Publishers, 1928), I, 29.

theoretician offers any plausible explanation in terms of their own Marxist doctrines.

The truth seems to be that, confronted with an opportunity to seize power, the Communists abandoned the entire democratic heritage of the Marxist tradition. Despite an elaborate semantic by-play with the terms "democratic" and "leadership," it is clear that neither Lenin nor Stalin regarded majority rule as a necessary element in their conception of democracy. Their idea was first to seize power and then count the votes to determine who won the confidence of the majority. Stalin quotes Lenin with full approval: "If the proletariat is to win over the majority of the population, it *must first of all overthrow the bourgeoisie and seize the powers of the state.*"[13]

The term "proletariat" is a very elastic one and the Communists stretch it to suit their convenience. Strictly speaking it is the class of industrial workers who not only constitute a minority of the population in most countries but a *minority of workers* in industrially backward countries such as Russia was in 1917. In order, therefore, to win over even a majority of the workers, "the victorious proletariat" must seize power. Only *then* will it be in a position "to gain the sympathy and win the support of the majority of the working (though non-proletarian) masses whose wants will be satisfied at the cost of the exploiters."[14]

It remains to ask only, to lift the curtain on the last corner of obscurity: who is the "revolutionary proletariat" which seizes power, overthrows the bourgeoisie, lays down the new rules of suffrage, counts the votes, and determines when the confidence of a majority of workers and, ultimately of the majority of the population, has been won? The actions as well as the writings of the Bolshevik leaders leave no doubt that the answer is the Communist Party.

The relation between the Party and class has always been a very embarrassing one to Communist theoreticians especially since they are well aware that Marx never spoke of the dictatorship of the Party and condemned analogous notions in Bakunin and Blanqui as conspiratorial perversions. Lenin is impatient and scornful of those who counterpose "the dictatorship of the Party" to the "dictatorship of the class." He seeks to conceal the mechanics of political control in which every element is cunningly prearranged in a conceptual maze in which, because the party allegedly knows the interests of the workers better than they do themselves, there is no need for the flummery of freely given consent. When all ambiguities are resolved, the so-called dictatorship of the pro-

---

[13] *Ibid.,* I, 123 (my italics).
[14] *Loc. cit.*

letariat in the Soviet Union and elsewhere is an open dictatorship of a minority Communist Party, or of the leaders of that Party, *over* the proletariat and the population at large. For all of his refusal to face the issues clearly, and his introduction of the dialectic to swallow contradictions, Lenin admits, and Stalin after him, that the dictatorship of the proletariat is *substantially* the "dictatorship of the Party." Long before the Stalin constitution declared it to be the law of the land, Lenin admitted: "In the Soviet Union, the land where the dictatorship of the proletariat is in force, no important political or organizational problem is ever decided by our Soviets and other mass organizations without directives from the Party."[15] The theory and practice of democratic centralism guarantees that the dictatorship of the party sooner or later leads to the outlawry of party factions and to the dictatorship of the Politbureau.

I am not laboring these points to establish what is obvious to anyone who has the slightest acquaintance with the Soviet Union. I cite them to indicate that the theory and practice of Communism, and this is true not only in the Soviet Union but in every country in which Communists have come to power, cannot in essential respects be identified with some of the central doctrines, right, wrong, or confused, of Marxism. The Communists are not the midwives of a social revolution waiting to be born. They are the engineers or professional technicians of revolution at any time and at any place.

Important political corollaries follow from a recognition of what their true ideology is. The Communists are very jealous of their claim to be Marxists; they preen themselves upon their realism, and scornfully distinguish themselves from all varieties of Utopian socialism. But their realism is an entirely different sort of thing from what we should expect from historical materialists. They are not at all realistic about the objective economic presuppositions of socialism, about the problem of finding substitutes for capitalist accumulation, and calculating the costs of enforced technical development. They are realistic only about the problems of conquering political power.[16] Once they have conquered power and can hold on to it by any means, then *by definition* that country is ripe for socialism. The achievement of socialism through the dictatorship of the party is on the agenda of history at any time in any country. Only the prospects of success must be carefully assessed. The Communist Party is, therefore, not only a revolutionary party in virtue of its program but a revolution-making party.

---

[15] Lenin, V. I., *Selected Works,* X, 88.

[16] *Cf.* Plamenatz, J., *German Marxism and Russian Communism* (New York, Longman's, 1954), p. 294.

III

Logically the attempt to build socialism irrespective of the material economic presuppositions can be carried out at a rapid or slow tempo, by partial and piecemeal collectivization or by one fell decree, by the use of pilot plants and force of example or by physical coercion. Similarly, the existence of a political dictatorship does not necessitate a dictatorship in *all* fields of culture as the history of most dictatorships up to the twentieth century shows. The party regime set up by Lenin did not inescapably lead to the cultural totalitarianism of Stalin despite the beginnings already clearly discernible under the former. Decisions were made at each point—decisions which were not merely technical but moral since their consequences had profound bearings on the welfare of others. The evidence is clear that, until Stalin died, every major decision taken, with the exception of the period immediately following War Communism, turned the screws of totalitarian control on Soviet society and culture more tightly. Here, too, the Communists acted *in the name* of the doctrines of Marxism, comforting themselves with the belief that they were recognizing and yielding to the iron necessities of history. In reality they were substituting their own driving wills to consolidate their political power for the driving forces of social development. There is no convincing evidence that the initial decision to seize power in a backward country compelled them to wield that power as they did.

It may be illuminating to discuss from this point of view phenomena as disparate as the enforced total collectivization of agriculture and the straitjacketing of art and science by the state philosophy of dialectical materialism.

Marx predicted that the laws of capitalist production would hold for agriculture as well as for industry. His predictions were so far from becoming true that it led to modifications of the agrarian program of Social-Democrats everywhere. Although according to Marx nationalization of the land was not strictly a socialist measure and could be carried out even under capitalism, most Social Democratic parties soft pedaled this note in rural countries where a strong independent peasantry existed with no feudal background. In Russia nationalization of the land was decreed immediately after the October Revolution but in practice this meant only the expropriation of the landlords without compensation, distribution of their land, and the multiplication and strengthening of millions of independent peasant holdings. In effect the Communists had carried out the agrarian program of the non-Marxist Social Revolutionary Party. The number of collective or government farms established up to 1927 was insignificant. Marxist theory had assumed that the peasants would be put off their lands and proletarianized by the growth of agricutural capitalism. Since this did not happen even in capitalist countries, it could hardly happen in a country in which capitalism had been abolished. The only thing the Bolsheviks could rely on was the force of example, i.e., the greater productivity of the state farms and cooperatives, and the power to supply the technical means to make agriculture viable. Measured by achievement, the force of example turned out to be quite unimpressive. It made no inroads on the peasant's psychology. The state of industry made it impossible to bring economic pressure on the peasants. Wheat, not steel, was king in a socialist economy of scarcity. There was no economic necessity to collectivize the farms in order to guarantee grain deliveries since by relaxing the pace of industrialization the basic technological needs of the peasants could have been gradually met. *A fortiori* there was no economic necessity to collectivize agriculture in a span of four years and in such a fashion that in some respects Soviet agriculture is worse off today than when the program was introduced—aside from the millions of lives destroyed and the ghastly suffering produced in the process. The ruthlessness of the drive defeated the anticipated economic advantages. In a sense, the agricultural revolution undertaken ten years after power had been won had a much more profound effect upon Russian life than the social revolution of the decade which preceded it. Official sources make no secret of the fact that this revolution was commanded and initiated from above. Its effect was to make the Soviet peasant once more a serf —with two differences. He was a serf exclusively of the state and his contributions and rewards were computed by modern bookkeeping methods.

Lenin had placed his hope on the Russian peasant growing into socialism through their village cooperatives aided by Soviet power and electrification. This was a viable procedure. Stalin destroyed the peasant cooperatives, drove the peasants into collective farms which at the time lacked electrification, and launched a program of hypertrophic capital goods construction while the masses lacked adequate food, clothing, and shelter. The "permanent revolution" of Lenin and Trotsky resulted in a permanent shortage of consumption goods and a permanent state of political insecurity. There was nothing inevitable about this development. Once decisions were taken, of course, they limited possible alternatives. But there were always alternatives open which permitted the use of methods more or less democratic, more or less humane.

Some Marxist critics of the Communists who share their professed determinism see in the grim features of Soviet life the unavoidable consequences of the first fall from the state of Marxist virtue and orthodoxy. It is true of course that some decisions and actions entail others. The consequence of taking the first step over the precipice is a further and faster fall. Such criticism if valid would absolve the Communists of any moral responsibility for actions subsequent to their conquest of power. But there is no evidence that the historical concatenation of events in Russia or elsewhere hangs only from one fateful action or that its justification can be derived from one poisoned premise. This may be best seen from an analysis of Soviet controls on culture.

IV

The totalitarianization of Soviet culture has gone so far that it emerges as a culturally unique trait of modern times. Can it be derived from any of the Marxist premises of Bolshevik ideology? Was it required, did it in any way help, the programs of industrialization and collectivization?

Marxist doctrine views the cultural superstructure as a natural outgrowth of the development of the mode of production, not as a hothouse plant that can be made to flourish by forced feeding. Law and political action can have reciprocal effects on the economy but they cannot legislate for literature, art, music, or philosophy. To the extent that they are authentic they are largely "unconscious" expressions of the acceptances and rejections, the moods, the hopes, dreams, and frustrations of the world in which men find themselves. Even science on this oversimplified, monistic view is a derivative response to the needs of production which indirectly influence the basic problems of research. The planned society envisaged by Marx and Engels did not include a planned spiritual life for man but a liberation of the creative spirit from economic and political restraints, and enjoyment of a complete cultural autonomy. The picture is as naive as the prediction of the disappearance of the state but it indicates a perspective of liberation for culture, not one of its coordination by the police power.

Nor, to answer our second question above, has anyone ever presented a particle of evidence that the styles of socialist realism or formalism or any other aesthetic matter on which the Central Executive Committee of the Russian Communist Party has taken a stand possess the slightest practical bearing on productivity in Soviet industry or agriculture. The same is true for moot questions in theoretical science from the Einstein theory of relativity in its cosmic implication to the principle of indeterminacy in atomic physics.

The most that can be argued is that since the philosophy of dialectical materialism asserts that all things are interrelated, different theoretical positions in any field, ranging from art to zoology, must ultimately lead in practice to different political positions. Since by definition the Communist Party has the only true political position, it therefore has the most reliable, if not infallible, criterion on what is sound or unsound in any field whatsoever.

The premise of the argument is false: not all things are interrelated. But even if true, the reasoning is faulty. It would justify scientists claiming a right to a veto on the wisdom of the Politbureau on the presumed ground that its political decisions have scientific implications on which they are the authorities. The patent fact is, however, that the character of any art form or of any specific scientific theory is irrelevant to questions of politics. The attitude towards modern art or to classical and folk music on the part of Truman, Stalin, Churchill, and Hitler was pretty much the same despite their different political faiths. Zhdanov's fulminations against modernism in poetry, music, and literature sound very much like the tirades of philistines everywhere,[17] with the immense difference that the latter would never dream of erecting their private prejudices into public law. The secret of the party line in music is neither the economy of socialist society nor the philosophy of dialectical materialism but simply and solely Stalin's ear—or the ear of whatever tyrants succeed him. This entire episode of cultural degradation was made *possible* by a form of party dictatorship which in turn meant the dictatorship of the leader or leading group. Under other leadership it might not have happened and still have left unaffected the iron clad control of the Party on the political life of Soviet society.

V

There remains to consider the claim that the foreign policy of the Soviet Union was the key to its domestic policy, particularly its prevision of military intervention by its enemies. It is true that the forced pace of Soviet industrialization permitted the Soviet Union to meet Hitler's invasion with weapons and the auxiliary material of war essential to its victory. Without discounting the immense aid received from its allies, the great bulk of the arms and equipment of the Red Army was manufactured in the Soviet Union. Was there not, therefore, an objective logic in the domestic policies and decisions of the Soviet leaders especially in their programs of industrialization and collectivization which provided an arms and grain reserve? If their policies were based upon an analysis of the development of European economy and politics must we not recognize that Marxist doctrine played a role—an intelligent and important one—in the pattern of Soviet events? Can we not say of the

---

[17] Zhdanov, A., *Essays in Literature, Philosophy and Music* (Eng. trans.), (New York, International Publishers, 1950), p. 76. The essay on music is the translation of the text of a speech delivered to a conference of leading Soviet musicians called by the Central Executive Committee of the Russian Communist Party.

Soviet leaders that without being as Talmudic as their Marxist critics in other camps they were not less principled but vastly more creative? Have they not been vindicated by the judgment of history, by their victory over Hitler?

Before an affirmative answer to these questions can be given, we would first have to inquire into the extent to which in foreign affairs the Bolsheviks were the architects of their own isolation and Russia's trial by ordeal; and second, what the likelihood is that they would have been able to withstand the full weight of Nazi ferocity if they had been compelled to face Hitler alone—from which they were saved by no plan or merit of their own.

The first point that requires examination is the responsibility of the Bolshevik leaders for the victory of Fascism in Germany and Italy. A united working-class movement in either one of those countries would have created a political situation in which neither Hitler nor Mussolini might have come to power. But with greater zeal than they attacked capitalism, the Communists set themselves the task of smashing Social Democracy. The organization of the Communist International, the sabotage of the Weimar Republic, including insurrectionary attempts, the promulgation of the doctrine of social-fascism were all parts of an unremitting crusade aimed first at the liquidation of democratic socialism. Even Harold Laski, who inconsistently hailed the Soviet system as the hope of the world, admits it probable "that had Lenin not precipitated the fatal split in the working classes implied in the foundation of the Communist International, certainly not Hitler, and perhaps not Mussolini, would have attained to power."[18]

What Lenin began, Stalin carried to grotesque lengths in his theory of social-fascism, promulgated as early as 1924, faithfully followed by the entire Communist world movement until the Seventh Congress of the Communist International in 1935, never officially abrogated, and periodically revived since then. According to this theory the Social Democrats were "the moderate wing of fascism. These organizations [Fascist and Social-Democratic] do not negate but supplement each other. They are not antipodes, they are twins."[19] This meant it was absurd to expect genuine united action with Social Democrats to combat Fascism since it would be uniting with one group of Fascists to combat another.

The truth is that the rise of Fascism as a social and political movement was never anticipated by the Communists either on the basis of

---

[18] Laski, H. J., *Reflections on the Revolution of Our Times,* p. 84.
[19] Stalin, J., *Collected Works* (Moscow, Foreign Languages Publishing House, 1953), VI, 294.

their professed Marxist faith or of any other. When it appeared on the scene the Communists completely mistook and underestimated its significance. They assumed it would collapse of its own weight shortly after it came to power. They were confident if it did not collapse that they would liquidate it but "only over the corpse of Social Democracy." As late as the May Day pronouncements of the Communist International in 1933, five months after Hitler had been in power, the Kremlin declared that the chief enemy of the German working class was not Hitler but German Social Democracy. On May 2, 1933, Hitler destroyed the Social-Democratic and Communist trade-unions alike.

Having encouraged Fascism to come to power in hopes that the Soviet Union could stand by while the "imperialist Western powers" destroyed each other, the Communist leaders became frightened at the prospects of their isolation and of a concerted world crusade against Bolshevism; they sought to overcome this dangerous isolation by pursuing two radically different approaches—a "popular front" tactic in which Communists dressed themselves in liberal wool and bleated democratic slogans, and by secret overtures to Hitler. The second won out after Munich. By signing a pact with Hitler and guaranteeing him against a second front, Stalin helped precipitate the Second World War. When Hitler turned on Stalin both of them expected an immediate peace among all the capitalist countries, democratic and non-democratic. Although Lenin and Stalin never ceased pointing to "contradictions" among capitalist powers, both had been predicting a world capitalist crusade against the Soviet Union with different countries slated in the lead at different times. And indeed nothing in the Marxist doctrine, which sees in war not only the continuation of politics but a reflex of the clash of economic interests, prepared the Soviet leaders for their grand alliance with one set of capitalist powers *against* another capitalist power which posed as "a savior" of Europe and Christianity from Bolshevism.

It is extremely problematical whether the Soviet Union could have survived, alone and unaided, the full brunt of a German invasion without allies in the West, especially in view of the millions of defections to Hitler's armies by Russian soldiers and peasants at the outset of the war.

In view of all this one is entitled to considerable skepticism concerning the claim that the programs of industrialization and collectivization and total terror were a necessary consequence of a foreign policy of defense against intervention. The threat of intervention worked in two ways. Before, during and after the Civil War, the Bolsheviks never concealed their own program of intervention by revolutionary subversion into the affairs of other countries. This intervention included the possibility of direct military engagement by Sovet military forces beyond their own borders. This is made manifest in many passages. In an edition of Stalin's *Problems of Leninism* published as recently as 1953 in Moscow, the Soviet regime includes Stalin's discussion, fortified by citations from Lenin, of the way in which the first socialist country can render assistance to revolutionary Communist movements in other countries.

In what should this assistance be expressed?

It should be expressed, first, in the victorious country achieving "the utmost possible in one country *for* the development, support and awakening of the revolution *in all* countries." (See Lenin, XXIII, 385.)

Second, it should be expressed in that the "victorious proletariat" of one country, "having expropriated the capitalists and organized socialist production, would stand up *against* the rest of the world, the capitalist world, attracting to its cause the oppressed classes of other countries, raising revolts in those countries against the capitalists, and in the event of necessity coming out even with armed force against the exploiting classes and their states." (See Lenin, XVIII, 232–233.)[20]

In the eyes of the Bolsheviks, all this is dialectically interrelated with "peaceful coexistence." This passage should be pondered together with another important text of Stalin's in which he explains how before the seizure of power every act of planned aggression was represented as a measure of defense.[21]

VI

I close with some considerations by way of summary:

(*1*) The orthodox Marxist theory of social development has received its definitive refutation at the hands of those who flaunt their Marxism to the world.

(*2*) The so-called scientific socialism of Marx and Engels does not guide the Communists in their actions. They are neither historical nor economic determinists. Marxism in the Soviet Union functions strictly in the way Marx defined an ideology, i.e., as a "false consciousness" which masks from the protagonists themselves the causes, grounds, and motives of action.

(*3*) There is no reason to doubt the Communists' belief in their proclaimed goal which is the establishment of a world wide economy

---

[20] *Op. cit.*, p. 147.
[21] Stalin, J., *Collected Works*, VI, 357.

planned from above and functioning under the tightest totalitarian controls which force, ingenuity, and terror can establish. Meanwhile the prediction that the state will some day wither away serves as a consoling myth. Soviet internationalism is Russian nationalism whose actual content has little in common with Russian nationalism of the past.

(4) The actual guiding doctrine of the Communist regime, as distinct from its official ideology of Marxism, is a kind of latter-day Utopianism, a social engineering whose goals recognize no limits except physical or biological impossibility and whose means are of indefinite flexibility. The goals are fixed, pursued with fanaticism, and never tested by the consequences of the means employed to achieve them. If we wish to predict and cope with Communist behavior, much more important than Communist social philosophy is the Communist theory, strategy, and tactics of world revolution.

(5) It is paradoxical but of great significance that the propaganda appeals used by the Communists are more often "ideal" than "material" or "economic." Peace, independence, justice, equality, nationalism, and other psychologically powerful themes are central. When its own existence hung precariously in the balance, the Kremlin rallied support to itself under the slogan of "defence of Mother Russia," not "defence of socialism." Psychological factors are realistically surveyed not from the point of view of what can be achieved but of what human beings can be made to believe.

(6) Although the existence of the Soviet Union refutes the Marxian theory of historical materialism, it may be argued that in a not recondite sense the humanistic aspect of Marxism has been vindicated by the character of Soviet culture. In declaring it impossible to build a socialist economy where the objective preconditions were absent Marx was mistaken. But he assumed that there were certain human needs and moral values which would guide political action and which would limit what human beings are prepared to do to other human beings. That one cannot build a socialist economy in a backward country except at a morally prohibitive cost is the sense of his socialist humanism. If we are completely indifferent to questions of human cost and suffering, only physical and biological necessities limit action. Allowing for comparable starting points, the costs in suffering exacted from the peoples of the Soviet Union as a price for industrialization exceeded by far those endured by the Japanese in the thirty years, by the Germans in the forty years, and the English in the fifty years required to build their large scale industry. Marxists have sometimes implicitly recognized the fact that a moral judgment is involved in every effort to change the course of events. This was realized even by Lenin himself before the Revolution of 1917. He once declared with explicit reference to Russia

that: "Whoever wants to approach socialism by another path, other than by political democracy, will inevitably arrive at absurd and reactionary conclusions in the economic and in the political sense."[22]

This judgment has been confirmed. Lenin and his followers have helped destroy the traditional historical determinisms which set too narrow limits on what human will and action can achieve. But thereby they have brought home to sensitive and reflective men everywhere the centrality of the problem of moral choice and responsibility in historical affairs.

---

[22] Lenin, V. I., *Selected Works,* III, 52.

11   The Individual in a Totalitarian Society

THE ENDURING FAITH of a liberal civilization may be expressed in various ways and in different idioms. Perhaps the most comprehensive characterization of a liberal civilization is that it is one in which institutions fortify freedom of mind and person and contribute to the enrichment of individual experience. The individual, from this point of view, is not a mere biological organism, or an undifferentiated unit of a herd. He is a social creature capable of acquiring a distinctive personality, and of giving rational assent, based on the fruits of his experience, to the kind of institutional world in which he lives. Since to exist is to be an individual, perhaps it would be better to speak of individuality, or personality, which is a matter of degree. Societies would then be appraised, from the liberal criterion, in terms of the degree of variety, freedom, and richness of individuality they exhibit in their institutional life.

I stress the institutional functioning of a society because this is the crucial operational test of the presence of individuality. Words alone are deceptive and may be downright lies. To judge societies by their slogans is to forget that even Hitler proclaimed that what distinguishes the Nazi view of life "is that it not only recognizes the value of the race but by this also the importance of the person, and therefore makes the individual the pillar of its entire edifice."[1]

My theme is the nature of the life of the individual in a totalitarian society. A totalitarian society is one in which there is an absolute and interlocking monopoly of power—economic, juridical, military, educational, and political—in the hands of a minority party which counte-

---

[1] *Mein Kampf* (Eng. trans.), p. 668.

nances no legal opposition and is not removable by the processes of freely given consent. There are, of course, differences among totalitarianisms, not only in ideology but in practice. Tojo's Japan, Mussolini's Italy, Hitler's Germany, and Stalin's Russia were all different from one another. These differences reflect the degree to which the respective countries permit autonomy in spiritual and cultural life. Benedetto Croce survived in Mussolini's Italy, whereas thinkers like him were liquidated in Germany and Russia. But, for all their differences, the historic tendency of all major totalitarian states, particularly when they find themselves in a world of nontotalitarian states, is towards total control. There is no question but that, had the war and Mussolini's dependence on Hitler continued, not only would the anti-Semitic practices of Germany have been extended to Italy, but Croce and other liberals would have been liquidated, with or without staged confessions. Although control may never be absolute in this world, modern technology in communications and weapons makes possible a degree of total repression never approached in antiquity. For this reason alone, historical comparisons are apt to be misleading because too reassuring.

Since the Soviet Union is the most powerful totalitarian state in history, and since all its satellite states, including China,[2] have either faithfully aped its pattern of control or had it imposed upon them, I shall examine the place of the individual in Soviet society today, particularly in the fields in which individuality has traditionally found its prime expression—arts, letters, and science. In this discussion the Soviet Union will be taken as "the ideal type" of totalitarianism in Max Weber's sense of the phrase.*

I shall begin with a brief discussion of the material or social aspects of Soviet society as they bear on the life of the individual, and shall then consider the cultural or intellectual aspects. Two preliminary points should be made by way of preface.

First, the emphasis on what follows will be institutional and ideological, because, for obvious reasons, no one can gather valid psychological data as to how individuals honestly feel or think in a police state—not even the officials of such a state. The cost of indiscretion is so high that public discourse tends to become ritualized, patterned on the stereotypes of the official press and leadership. The only persons who conduct interviews or distribute questionnaires to test public opinion are, so to

---

[2] *Cf.* Edward Hunter, *Brain-Washing in Red China* (1951).

*This essay was written not long before Stalin's death. Although the internal terror in the Soviet Union has somewhat abated, the character of its culture has not fundamentally changed. I have left this essay substantially unaltered so that the development of future cultural trends in the Soviet Union can be checked against it.

speak, the secret police. Even reports of agents of the secret police would be difficult to assess, because suspicion, distrust, and talking for the record become the natural modes of response for individuals who survive in an environment in which remarks critical of the regime, the leadership, or the system may be punishable.

Second, it will be helpful for purposes of objective comparison to check against each other the institutional conditions under which human beings live in free and in totalitarian societies. Such a comparison will enable us to determine precisely how much truth there is in the fashionable hysterical outcries that, as a result of the few faltering efforts the free world is making to resist totalitarian aggression, and of episodic cultural foolishness here and there, it is rapidly assuming the form of a police state.

From the point of view of the material aspects of Soviet society, there is no institutional provision for freedom of choice, without which genuine individuality is impossible. There exists no mechanism in Soviet life which permits citizens—even those who are loyal to the Soviet system—to engage in political opposition to the regime. There is absolutely no opportunity for political criticism and dissent, since no press exists except the censored official press. What is called self-criticism is directed against shortcomings in oneself or others in carrying out decisions made by the leading cadres of the Communist party. Since every means of communication from mimeograph machines to the radio is in the hands of the state, there is no public opinion save that manufactured by the government.

Whatever security the individual worker possesses depends upon his compliance with arbitrary administrative decree. Freedom of movement is controlled by a system of internal passports. There is no freedom to organize independent trade unions and no right to strike; lateness at work is punishable as of a decree of June 26, 1940, and repeated absence may bring a prison sentence or forced labor at one's place of work or in a slave-labor camp.[3] The instruments of production are nationalized, but the distribution of the social product depends upon the arbitrary power of a small group, resulting in enormous inequalities in the living conditions of different strata of the population. Exploitation of labor has not been abolished, but has taken new forms.

A chain of command runs from the apex of the social pyramid to the

---

[3] For relevant literature and documentation on Soviet justice, prison camps, and forced labor, cf. Judah Zelitch, *Administration of the Soviet Law* (Philadelphia, Univ. of Penn. Press, 1931); Harold J. Berman, *Justice in Russia* (Cambridge, Harvard Univ. Press, 1950); Albert K. Herling, *Soviet Slave Empire* (New York, 1951); David Y. Dallin and Boris I. Nicolaevsky, *Forced Labor in the Soviet Union* (New Haven, Yale Univ. Press, 1941).

broad base. In this structure of power, rights and securities are enjoyed subject to the interpretation of one's immediate superiors in the hierarchy, whose own rights and securities in turn depend upon the uncertain sufferance of a higher bureaucratic level up to the very top. No one's position is so high that he cannot be hurled, like a rebellious or suspected archangel, to oblivion, or, if he is permitted to survive, sent to a forced-labor camp. At no point is any genuine democratic control from below permitted, although the use of the word "democracy" is *de rigueur.* Of the celebrated "democratic" Constitution of 1936, which can be considered only as an aspiration, and not as a description, of the Soviet state, Stalin himself blandly claimed as its merit that it did not affect the position of the Communist party, as the only party that can exist in the Soviet Union. There is no independent judiciary, no writ of *habeas-corpus,* or even of *habeas-cadaver.* The courts, industry, agriculture, the army, and the schools are all, in fact, subordinate to the MVD or secret police, whose chief is appointed by the Politbureau.

So much for some representative facts of "material" life in which the Soviet citizen (or subject) moves. Our task is not to offer a complete description but to find the keys to the system considered as a whole. Before proceeding to this phase of our inquiry, we must examine the "mental" or cultural life of this society. For it is in the cultural sphere of any society that we are accustomed to find the pre-eminent exemplars of its conception of the individual.

Soviet culture in every one of its aspects is the most politicalized, the most rigorously controlled and terrorized culture in human history. The facts are not concealed by the Soviet regime. In every field from art and astronomy to music, philology, and philosophy, to relativity and zoology, the party line is laid down by decree of the Central Committee of the party or its representatives,[4] and enforced by a complex system of rewards and punishments ranging from public purge and recantation to exile and liquidation. Nor is the situation any different in the popular or practical arts. Whether it is the circus, the cinema, or pig breeding, the pattern is the same. Laughter is openly declared to be a political weapon. For the first time in the history of modern culture, even the right to be silent has been abolished, for where the Central Committee or its Politbureau has laid down the law, silence is construed as treason. The screw of repression and compulsion is periodically turned to a pitch perhaps unimaginable by any except the victims caught in its vise.

---

[4] The text of some of these decrees will be found in George S. Counts and Nucia Lodge, *The Country of the Blind* (New York, 1949).

Here is not the place to describe the mechanisms of control by which this enforced conformity is achieved. Mr. Crankshaw to the contrary, I do not believe that the Russians are a unique human species, a knout-loving people with a natural craving for despotism.[5] For one thing, the Soviet system is no longer confined to Russia. When bread is used as a weapon of political coercion, when access to housing, press, radio, and every other kind of communication is absolutely dependent upon an all-powerful secret police, the same state of affairs can be developed anywhere.

It used to be fashionable to explain the abject confessions of the old Bolsheviks, kissing the hands of the hangmen who dishonored them before destroying them, by reference to the murky depths of the Dostoyevskian soul. But the hypothesis becomes somewhat unplausible before the spectacle of a Cardinal Mindszenty, a Prince of the Church whose communicants used to face wild animals and crucifixion with equanimity, or before the spectacle of a normal, middle-class American businessman like Vogeler and a sophisticated American newspaperman like Oatis—all performing in similar fashion. It is simpler to begin with less mystical assumptions.

What should interest us is the justification offered in defense of these practices of cultural control. They take many forms, but for purposes of exposition I mention briefly some of the chief doctrines and corresponding heresies often invoked in the bans of cultural excommunication. They are (1) the doctrine of socialist realism, whose alleged violation leads to the heresy of formalism; (2) the principle of *partinost* or partisanship, which when disregarded brings the rebuke of objectivism; (3) Soviet internationalism, which is disregarded by both cosmopolitanism and nationalism.

Socialist realism is not what is called naturalism in the West, but is, rather, a selective representation of experience in words, color, or sound which glorifies the existing regime, edifies the masses, and enhances production directly or indirectly. For example, in painting, portraits of Stalin which win Stalin prizes every year are not photographically or historically accurate in detail, for they cannot reveal his pockmarks or other infirmities, or his modest role in the early history of the revolution; they are idealized portraits. This idealization, because it insinuates the feeling that the leader is wise, kind, and good, is actually more real, according to the doctrine, than the most faithful naturalistic account would be. Music cannot be marked by atonality, but should contain, if possible, tunes that the masses can whistle as they work. The Central Committee decree that condemned Shostako-

---

5 *Cf.* Edward Crankshaw, *Russia by Daylight* (1951).

vitch's *The Great Friendship* for formalism specifically called on composers to write instead works marked by a "wealth of melodies." Literature cannot treat non-political themes in abstract fashion or with esoteric images; it must center on subjects of contemporary and historical life in such a way as to point a moral and instill patriotism and loyalty.

The principle of partisanship affirms that all knowledge must be oriented to a value point of view. Since values conflict, the decisive reference must be to a class point of view and ultimately a party point of view. No truth whatsoever can be considered as neutral. "Science, like all culture in modern society, is national in form and class in content."[6] Objectivism is the belief that supra-class, non-national, universal science and truth exist. Whatever is declared true must be presented in a fashion to show that the Communist party way is always the better way.

Cosmopolitanism is false internationalism. True internationalism however, is not nationalism. It is patriotism, but it differs from every other kind of patriotism. It is a Soviet patriotism, but not Ukrainian Soviet patriotism, for that is Ukrainian nationalism. Neither is it Great Russian patriotism, cultivated during the war. In fact, it is difficult to say what true internationalism is at any moment except what the Politbureau says it is.

Indeed, the odd thing is that even those who profess a fervent belief in socialist realism and ardently condemn formalism, or objectivism, and cosmopolitanism, are no freer from purge and denunciation than those who do not make such profession. For no one can tell before the event of official critical judgment what will or will not fulfill the condition of socialist realism, partisanship, and true internationalism. We are dealing with flexible, even contradictory criteria; so that Fadeyev's *Young Guards,* hailed as a masterpiece of socialist realism in one year, is condemned for lack of partisanship in another. Even a student's doctoral degree is not safe. Certifications of dissertations by academic councils are sometimes revoked four or five years after they have been granted, if the line has changed in the student's field of research.[7] These criteria are invoked so arbitrarily and with such apparent caprice that they cannot serve as principles of explanation. We must look beyond them to more fundamental considerations.

In passing, we can well imagine the state of mind of any creative writer, who cannot remain silent, who cannot rely on any fixed inter-

---

[6] *Problems of Philosophy No. 2,* trans. in *Current Digest of the Soviet Press* (Feb., 1949).

[7] Cf. *CDSP* (Feb. 23, 1952), p. 4.

pretation of socialist realism, and who cannot even be sure that his past triumphs will remain triumphs. It is not surprising, therefore, that some writers ask that the party assign in advance some trusted political figure to work with them lest they unwittingly offend the powers on whom their market, their materials, their housing and subsistence, and their very life absolutely depend. It is not a meaningless gesture when Vavilov, President of the Soviet Academy of Science, hails Stalin as "a scientific giant," as not only "the greatest man of our time" but the "leading light of science"—even though this leading light of science sent the brother of Vavilov, the remarkable Russian geneticist, and other honest scientists to concentration camps for disagreeing with Lysenko. It is not for nothing that the philosophic poet, Leonov, proclaims that Stalin—at least as great as Aristotle, Shakespeare, Galileo, and Newton—gave mankind, for a second time, "its families and freedom" and, despite the theory of historical materialism, affirms the "the history of our planet would have been entirely different had not Stalin led the Soviet regime."[8] No, the ever-increasing chorus of sycophancy which eclipses in servility and degradation the worst manifestation of Byzantinism, is not an expression of the Russian soul but simply a form of life insurance. But why should it be required, and taken as a matter of course by the Soviet regime?

It is necessary to probe deeper into the ideology of Bolshevik Leninism-Stalinism. A cardinal proposition central to Bolshevik ideology, derived from the mystical philosophy of dialectical materialism, which is used to buttress the belief in the validity of total cultural control. According to this proposition, everything in the world is dialectically interrelated. A false proposition in one field therefore leads to implications which are false in every other field, and since there is a unity between theory and practice any false doctrine will sooner or later lead to wrong, if not disastrous, practices in the field of political behavior. Since the Bolshevik leadership possesses superior insight into politics, and since allegedly every field ultimately has political ramifications and consequences, the Politbureau claims not only the power but the intellectual right to pass judgment on the truth or falsity of any doctrine in any field whatsoever, and to lay down the party line in subjects as far removed from each other as art and zoology. This party line is not merely to be endured or suffered, not merely to be regarded as a partisan measure of expediency, but must be believed, or publicly recited, as the truth.

No more sweeping and breath-taking claim has ever been made in the intellectual history of the world. The Pope, to be sure, claims in-

---

8 Cf. *VOKS Bulletin* No. 61 (1950), pp. 39, 49 ff.

fallibility, but only in the realm of faith and morals. The Politbureau does not exactly claim infallibility; it claims to be the most reliable authority in every field of human thought and practice. And this in the name of a science more truculent, more dogmatic, and more sweeping in its knowledge-claims than any revealed religion. Since it is backed by unlimited police power, what can any scientist who wishes to avoid martyrdom do, once the Politbureau of the Central Committee of the Communist party has corrected the findings of scientific method in the light of a higher dialectic method? What can he do except to repeat the words of Professor Zhebrak in the August 15, 1948 issue of *Pravda?*

> As long as our Party recognized both tendencies in Soviet genetics . . . I persistently defended my views, which at some points differed from the views of Academician Lysenko. But now, since it has become clear to me that the basic theories of the Michurin School in Soviet genetics are approved by the Central Committee of the All Union Communist Party, I, as a member of the Party, cannot defend positions which have been declared mistaken by the Central Committee of our Party.[9]

What can Shostakovitch do, if he wishes to avoid the fate of Boris Pilniak, other than say in response to the sharp criticism of his opera *The Great Friendship* by those profound musical critics on the Central Committee of the Communist party, "I know that the Party is right, that the Party wishes me well, and that I must seek and find concrete artistic paths that will bring me to realistic Soviet art of the people."[10]

Let us not imagine that in all or even most cases of such capitulation the explanation is simply craven fear or a desire for the bureaucratic fleshpots. Nor is insincerity always present. Men—even gifted men—have often sought to ease the harshness of external constraint by a willingness to be constrained, by apologies for those who discipline and even torment them. Czeslaw Milosz, the Polish poet, who fled to the West, gives us a very graphic portrait of the mind of the Iron Curtain intellectual who is too sophisticated to take Diamat seriously, yet still tries to find some moral or social justification for his compromises with the inevitable that will give him a *raison d'être* in his own eyes. After all, cynics and opportunists are not trusted by tyrants. The victim must at least be half-willing, half-believing—an accomplice in the compounding of his own subjection. Consequently, we cannot

---

[9] A complete text and translation appears in Counts and Lodge, *op. cit.,* pp. 211–214.

[10] Recalled in *Izvestia* (Dec. 8, 1951), and reprinted in *CDSP* (Jan. 15, 1952), p. 11.

assume that it is hunger or animal fear alone which determines the actions of those who yield to the Central Committee.

But—and here lies the catch—the political line of the Central Committee may change because of the exigencies of world affairs. And when it does, another phase in the alternating cycle of purge and recantation begins. For all their willingness to serve the Central Committee, the victims can enjoy grace only by continuous humbling of the will and mind. This is merely one of many pieces of evidence that could be cited to show that Bolshevik Leninism-Stalinism has no more in common with the Socialist idealism of Marx than Franco's dictatorship has with the ideals of Christianity. Marx, who concludes his preface to *Das Kapital* with a line from Dante which breathes the spirit of creative individualism ("Follow your own course and let people talk"), would have been among the first victims of Stalin's terror. For Marx the dignity of the human being—yes, even of the proletariat, he tells us in one place—is just as important as his daily bread.[11]

In passing, we may observe that, by the ordinary canons of logical and scientific method, no one can establish that everything in the world is interrelated, that the truths of mathematics and science, or even the creative achievements of art, are dependent for their validity on the shifting expediencies of a political policy. Indeed, according to the Bolshevik logic, were everything interrelated, mistakes in politics would reflect themselves as mistakes in science, so that scientists could claim that they were entitled to correct Stalin's blunders in politics, with at least as much authority as he professed to be able to correct their scientific work in physics or linguistics on the basis of his presumed superior political insight. But no scientist is known to have ventured to suggest this.

"The humblest Soviet citizen," said Stalin, "being free from the fetters of capital, stands head and shoulders above any high placed foreign bigwig whose neck wears the yoke of capitalist slavery."[12]

The best comment on the grandeur of the new Soviet man is the complaint of *Pravda,* some years later, that Soviet workers "do not always understand the great heights to which the Soviet state has raised them."[13]

It is characteristic of Soviet totalitarianism that the more its actual practices refute its professions, the more it is compelled to resort to an obscurantism which challenges the validity of normal perception, nor-

---

[11] Karl Marx and Frederick Engels, *Gesamtausgabe,* I, 6, p. 278.
[12] *Report to the Eighteenth Party Congress* (March 10, 1939).
[13] (September 3, 1947.)

mal experience, and judgment. The state, far from disappearing with the advent of a nationalized economy, appears as a naked rule of force responsible only to the Politbureau. The workers, who presumably own the instruments of production, have less control over their economic life, less freedom of movement, even when they manage to keep out of forced labor camps, than in countries where they do not own the instruments of production but belong to free trade unions. Class struggles change their name but not their character, with managerial and political commissars exercising a power more absolute than the rule of employers in democratic states. The governing élite, instead of sharing its power with the cooks and bakers and miners whom Lenin expected to govern, becomes more ruthless and homogeneous, changed not from below but by purge and decree from above. Myths are not replaced by science but by grosser and more vulgar myths. Religion does not atrophy but becomes transformed into the idolatry of a tyrant. All this is officially described by a system of Orwellian double-talk and "double-think," in which peace is war, liberty prostration, equality inequality, and fraternity either bureaucratic rage or fawning servility.

What can one make of a system based presumably on a scientific world view in which its leader is addressed in verse and song in the following language:

Our Stalin:
  As if it were possible in song by a singer to tell how dear thou, beloved, our father, art! Thou, like flint, were tempered in the front line of the crusaders! We hold thee in the cradle of our arms! In the cold of the winter thou art a shelter for us; in the heat of the summer thou art a cooling garden; thou art the wings that raise us to the skies; for the one that goes down under the ground thou art the air. Over our enemies thou art a stormy cloud; over the toilers' people thou art the sun; thou art the guardian who watches over ships in the storm; to all born with an honest heart thou art their glory. . . . Our great father, the son of his country, we bow to thee. . . . As we hold our honor, we swear to thee to safeguard thy life: thy vision is our vision; thy thoughts our thoughts to the last one; thou art the flame of our thoughts and our blood. Thou art the high symbol of our strength.[14]

Imagine anyone talking of the President of the United States that way! Indeed, this is the kind of language we address only to the deity. That those in the ruling hierarchy permit this adulation—even en-

[14] *Ibid.* (August 25, 1936). Original text and translation in H. Stekoll, *Humanity Made to Order,* pp. 189–190.

courage it—suggests that dialectical materialism as a state philosophy may function as an opiate for the people—perhaps as powerful an opiate as any traditional supernaturalism has ever been.

Here, then, we have the image of Soviet individualism or Soviet totalitarianism, which looms over the cultural landscape of the free world. That image has tremendous power not only because of the substance behind it—the massed steel and the massed men—but also because many in the still free countries do not see this image clearly, and they rebuild it out of the gossamer fancy of their longings and wish dreams.

This is not the place to discuss what must be done to restrain or contain or to lift this ever-lengthening shadow of totalitarian culture. Bertrand Russell assures us that no despotisms have proved to be everlasting, and there are some things that the mightiest of tyrants cannot prevent. This is poor consolation. No state of affairs, bad or good, is everlasting. When the British withstood Hitler in 1940, it would have been a sorry wisdom to remind them that even if Hitler won, he wouldn't last a thousand years. Whether a tyranny comes to an end 500 or 600 years after we are dead means little to us, the living. Our problem is not merely to live out our own time in freedom. It is to cherish the freedoms we may lose, not only for our own sake but for the sake of free men everywhere. Only when freedom takes and keeps the psychological offensive can we strengthen its processes and institutions and leave a better heritage to those who will take our place in the unending struggle of the human spirit against despotism, ignorance, and irrational fear.

12 Science and Dialectical Materialism

DIALECTICAL MATERIALISM may be considered as a system of naturalistic or materialistic philosophy, one of a family of doctrines concerning the nature of man and his relation to the world. It may also be considered primarily as the state philosophy of the Soviet Union and its satellite nations.

As a system of naturalistic philosophy the tenets of dialectical materialism have been adumbrated by some forms of evolutionary naturalism in the West which seek to establish certain conclusions about the world, of a generality wider than any to be found in the special sciences. One such conclusion is that wherever values are found they are related to human interest, consciousness or desire, from which the analytic consequence is drawn that truths about the physical world, as a theater of human activity, are politically neutral.

In *this* sense, belief in dialectical materialism is logically compatible with belief in any social philosophy whatsoever—Communism, Democracy or Fascism. In *this* sense, dialectical materialism, although holding that all forms of consciousness, personal and social, arise, develop, and disappear with changes in the material world, which are the subject matter of the physical sciences, is opposed to *reductive* materialism. It recognizes the existence of plural levels of organization, emergent qualities, and the efficacy of human thought and action in redetermining some of the conditions of personal and social life. With *this* sense of dialectical materialism, I shall not be concerned.

Dialectical materialism as the system of Soviet state philosophy differs radically from the above in holding that its doctrines entail the validity of communism as a political, social and economic system, and that the validity of communism entails acceptance of the philosophy of dialectical materialism.[1] This is one of the most fateful assertions ever put forward in the history of ideas, for together with certain vague notions concerning the "dialectical" interrelatedness of things, it serves as a theoretical justification, in the eyes of those who accept dialectical materialism, for such propositions as "science, like all culture in modern society is national in form and class in content." It has often been invoked to defend control of scientific research and publication by political decree. And since similar assertions are being advanced not only in the Soviet Union but in all countries within its political sphere, it is important, even for those who are prone to dismiss this philosophy as a convenient psychological rationalization for the exercise of political power, to understand its claims.

I

According to Lenin, Stalin and other authoritative expositors, the materialistic dialectic is a method "of studying and apprehending" the phenomena of nature: historical materialism is a set of doctrines derived by applying the dialectic method to social phenomena. The dialectic method is therefore central to this philosophy. But just as soon as any authoritative expositor begins to describe the dialectic method, he enunciates statements which are normally found in traditional ontology or metaphysics, e.g., that nature is "a connected and integral whole in which things are organically connected with, dependent on, and determined by, each other"; that nature is in "a state of continuous movement and change," that the movement is from "the lower to the higher"; that "internal contradictions are inherent in all things and phenomena of nature," and so forth.[2] This is just as if someone were to describe the principal features of scientific method merely by reciting the basic laws of dynamics, electromagnetism, genetics, etc., which were discovered by using this method. The whole relation between the dialectical method and scientific method is left in a kind of calculated obscurity. And despite the reiterated statement that the principles of dialectic enter into the development of science no clear and consistent account of the relation can be found.

The relation between the so called objective laws of dialectic and the

---

[1] The best exposition of the doctrine will be found in Wetter's *Der Dialektische Materialismus* and Bochenski, *Der Sowjetrussische Dialektische Materialismus* (1950). The first is slightly marred by special pleading for Thomism. For detailed criticisms of dialectical and historical materialism, cf. my *Reason, Social Myths and Democracy* (1940), and *The Hero in History* (1943).

[2] All references to Stalin are to his section on "Dialectical and Historical Materialism" in chap. iv of his *History of the Communist Party of the Soviet Union* (Bolsheviks) (Short Course, English trans. 1939), pp. 105 ff.

sciences of nature and society are characterized in such a way as to suggest (*a*) sometimes that the first are presuppositions of the second in the sense that they are necessary conditions which if denied would involve the denial of valid scientific knowledge; (*b*) sometimes that the laws and features of dialectic are summaries of the results of scientific inquiry; and most often (*c*) that they are broad hypotheses continually confirmed by the progress of science.

(*a*) One difficulty in evaluating the relationship of presupposition is the vagueness and ambiguity of the statements which express the principles of dialectic. Take the statement that "internal contradictions are inherent in all things and phenomena of nature" (Stalin). Ignore for the moment that the usual and only consistent usage of the term "contradiction" makes it a property of assertions or statements, as Aristotle already pointed out. Like the other principles of dialectic it is assumed to have universal validity. But no matter how it is read, it cannot be regarded as a presupposition or necessary condition of any particular piece of scientific knowledge, e.g., that the passage of an electric current under certain conditions induces a magnetic field. For the truth of this scientific statement, or of any other scientific statement, is compatible with the denial of the alleged dialectical law. Even if there were some way of interpreting a specific scientific statement or law as an illustration of the presence or development of internal contradictions, it would in no way be affected by the falsity of the statement about the alleged *universal* validity of this or any other law of dialectic. For some things and processes of nature could have a certain character even if it were false that *all* things and processes have that character. At most the principles of dialectic would be summaries in peculiar language of some characters exhibited by some classes of things and processes.[3]

(*b*) This would seem to be a reasonable interpretation of what some dialectical materialists mean when they tell us that their philosophy does not stand above the sciences, but that its validity is established step by step within the sciences. From this point of view dialectical materialism would be nothing but a summary, and completely useless, description of the achievements of the sciences at any time. But if this is what is meant, it would be hard to explain why the generalizations of dialectical materialism have remained the same for almost a century, despite the tremendous revolutions in scientific theory and knowledge.

---

[3] *Cf.* A. Pap's interesting and illuminating analysis, "Does Science Have Metaphysical Presuppositions?" (*Elements of Analytic Philosophy* (1949), chap. 16. His general argument applies obviously to dialectical materialism although no specific analysis of doctrine is made. *Cf.* also my chapter "Nature and Dialectic" in *Reason, Social Myths and Democracy*.

It would also make it difficult to understand how at the same time the development of science could be attributed to the fact that scientists were unconsciously following the principles of dialectic in their inquiry. *Any* method that gave correct or fruitful results would be dialectical by definition, and the notion that dialectics is in any way a guide to discovery of new knowledge would be patently false.

(c) "Nature," writes Stalin quoting Engels, "is the test of dialectics, and it must be said for modern natural science that it has furnished extremely rich and daily increasing materials for this test. . . ." It is interesting to observe that nature is characterized as the test of *dialectics* not of materialism. Now a "test," in any usage of the term, is a trial, a question, which theoretically can be answered in more than one way. If nature is a test of dialectics, then the principles or laws of dialectics must be something more than general summaries of results already won in the past. They must assert something testable about the future. They must function as hypotheses no matter how broadly conceived. We are therefore justified in asking: what would the behavior of things have to be, what would we have to discover, what would we in principle have to observe, in order to reach the conclusion that dialectics *fails* to pass the test of nature?

Dialectical materialists have never been able to tell us, because no matter what is observed in nature, no matter what happens, they can square it as easily with the so-called laws of dialectic as a pious believer can square any event that occurs with his belief that everything happens by the will of God, or that it fulfills some Providential cosmic plan. Since no specific conditions are indicated under which the laws of genuine dialectic would be refuted or abandoned there is no test—and illustrations of the law are confused with proof—so that actually they do not function as hypotheses at all. There is no evidence that they have ever even served as aids to scientific discovery. On the contrary like many theological beliefs of the past, they have been invoked to block roads to fresh scientific inquiry and sometimes to contest scientific theories, like the theory of relativity and the biological theory of genes, not on grounds of evidence, but because of all sorts of extra scientific considerations.

It is important to point out that the taboos and prescriptions against *specific* scientific theories, like finitistic conceptions of space and time, or psychoanalytic doctrines, do not follow *logically* from the principles of dialectic, for the latter are either irrelevant to the entire enterprise of scientific inquiry or so indeterminate as to be compatible with any scientific detail. The real explanation, therefore, of the restrictive practices associated with dialectical materialism must come from some other source, usually social or political. This is practically admitted in the doctrine of *partinost* according to which not only is the philosophy of dialectical materialism a partisan, class and party-philosophy, but the findings of science, the alleged applications of the laws of dialectic, have this character, too. It is made explicit not only in the demands imposed on Soviet scientists but in the proclamations of faithful Communists throughout the world. "Dialectical materialism," writes the English Communist, Maurice Cornforth, "asks to be judged and will be judged by whether it serves as an effective instrument to show the way out of capitalist crises and war. . . ."[4] Since the validity of the applications of dialectical materialism are to be judged in the same way, it is clear that the bearings of a doctrine for the conquest and retention of political power replace ordinary scientific evidence as ultimately probative in determining which doctrines are to be accepted.

All this indicates that statements which are *logically* or scientifically irrelevant to practice may nonetheless have a profound influence on practice because of their relation to personal or psychological interests, and social or historical interests. This is sometimes denied. Bertrand Russell, for example, has written that "The belief that metaphysics has any bearing upon practical affairs is a proof of logical incapacity." What he should have written is that the belief that metaphysics has any *logical* bearing upon practical affairs is a proof of logical incapacity. But there are other bearings which metaphysical doctrines may have on practical affairs that do not follow from their logical meaning or cognitive content. The history of dialectical materialism in the Soviet Union is a good illustration of this. From time to time the Central Committee of the Communist Party has intervened in philosophical and scientific debates, to settle by decree which principles are to be emphasized in dialectical materialism, and what doctrines or tendencies are to be taught in fields ranging from art and agronomy to zoology. At one time the role of chance will be played down: at another it will be played up, for, after all, if Lenin or Stalin are truly great men, they cannot be explained *merely* by the mode of production or any other common environmental phenomenon. At one time language will be considered a part of the cultural superstructure, and therefore a field in which the class struggle is reflected. At another, language is decreed to be part of the common social inheritance, and it therefore becomes nonsensical to speak of a "class language" or "grammar." At one time formal logic is driven out of the curriculum as a mode of metaphysical thinking, and therefore an enemy class science; at another it is reinstated as a non-class science with the resolution "to put the science of logic at the service of the Soviet people, to make it a sharply

---

[4] *Dialectical Materialism* (London, 1952), I, 140.

pointed ideological weapon in the struggle against the survivals of the past in the consciousness of people, in the struggle against the bourgeois ideology alien to us."[5]

A variety of causes probably accounts for these different shifts from one doctrine to another. It has been asserted that the rehabilitation of formal logic at the expense of dialectical logic, as well as the fact that Stalin failed even to mention the dialectical law of "the negation of the negation" in his authoritative exposition of "Dialectical and Historical Materialism," can be explained by a desire to use logic as a support of the present status quo in the U.S.S.R. and to dismiss as relatively unimportant the potential dynamism of dialectical thinking with its stress on the mutability of all things and institutions.[6] It is hard to determine how much truth there is in such an interpretation but since Stalin uses language synonymous with the expression of the law of "the negation of the negation" it seems doubtful. It must be admitted, however, that all governments when safely in power tend to be on the side of eternity. But I am confident that if political facts are often decisive, they are not exclusive, causes in the turns and zig-zags of philosophical and scientific doctrine. Nationalism and national pride obviously, even if foolishly, entered. Stalin's own personal tastes and prejudices which in art and music did not differ from the crude, untutored judgments of philistines in the West, were probably an independent factor. His condemnation of Deborin as a "Menshevizing idealist" may have been merely the result of his failure to understand Deborin's philosophical vocabulary. Certainly, the condemnation of the music of Shostakovitch and Prokofiev cannot be explained only in the light of Stalin's politics. His ear had a lot to do with it. After Stalin's death the ban against their "formalist" works was lifted without modifying the principles of dialectic and the right of the Central Committee of the Communist Party to pass upon the political validity of musical works.

Nor is there any convincing evidence that the imposition of the philosophy of dialectical materialism on Soviet scientists is actually justified in the eyes of the Kremlin by the practical results won in consequence. For although the past achievements of Russian scientists in philosophy and psychology in the undialectical days of the Czars are lauded to the skies, the present activities of Soviet scientists in these fields are constantly under attack. The current canonization of Pavlov, and the strictures against Soviet scientists in physiology and psychology for not developing his work, are eloquent testimony on this point. Why

---

[5] V. F. Asmus, quoted in Prof. A. Phillipov, *Logic and Dialectic in the Soviet Union* (New York, 1952), p. 58.

[6] Phillipov, *ibid.*

should Russian scientists who were not dialectical materialists have achieved so much more in the past, in contradistinction to Soviet scientists today, who, although they all profess dialectical materialism, are urged strenuously not only to live up to the achievements of their non-dialectical forbears but even to catch up with, and overtake, the achievements of their non-dialectical contemporaries in the decadent West?

A favorite reply to this is that good scientists anywhere, to the extent that they make valid discoveries, are unconsciously using the dialectical method. A possible corollary of this reply would be that in the interests of fruitfulness and the chances of developing Pavlovs, Lorentzes and other pre-Bolshevik scientists approved by the pundits of dialectical materialism, Soviet scientists should be permitted to become *unconscious* of dialectical materialistic philosophy, instead of having it driven into them by implicit threats of the use of sanctions against them.

II

The really baffling thing about dialectical materialism of the Soviet variety is not its validity, for to the extent that it can be intelligibly stated, it consists either of a series of commonplaces, completely irrelevant to the work of science, or of downright falsities and absurdities. It is obvious that a doctrine which holds that all things are dialectically interrelated cannot be a logical guide to any scientific inquiry or experiment which holds that *some* things are irrelevant to any particular phenomena we are exploring. The scientist can only establish connections and interrelations between *specific* states of affairs and must in practice deny that everything is relevant to everything else. That he must search for some connections follows from his desire to find explanation; he therefore doesn't need a philosophy to enjoin him, in misleading language, to search for such connections when he is already embarked on a quest for understanding.

We have already seen that as a philosophy, dialectical materialism cannot justify itself as a fruitful, heuristic method of scientific discovery. Nobody knows the causes of scientific discovery, and it is conceivable that just as some literary men find tobacco or alcohol an aid in their creative labors (or imagine they do), so scientists might get on the track of new knowledge in virtue of their commitment to some private over-beliefs, like Fechner's belief in a world soul or Kepler's view that angels helped move the planets. In the absence of any evidence of statistical correlation between metaphysical belief and scientific discovery, any report by an individual scientist that such a belief played a fruitful role in his thinking would have to be considered as an interesting item in his autobiography, like J. B. S. Haldane's claim many years ago that a reading of Lenin's *Imperialism* cured him of stomach ulcers which, even if true, would hardly warrant its acceptance as a valid technique of medical therapy. Nothing in these remarks should be construed as a denial of the possibility that the private conceits of any scientist might be helpful to him in his work or that he should be discouraged from holding them. But to convert such private conceits into public law or articles of mandatory belief is a good definition of cultural barbarism.

Why, then, should the rulers of the Soviet Union set such store on the acceptance of dialectical materialism by Soviet scientists? I should like to suggest that the most decisive reason is their mistaken belief that the political strategy and social system of Communism depends upon the establishment of certain propositions about nature presumably derived by the laws of dialectic. And further, that this mistaken belief functions in such a way as to give them the illusory assurance that the cosmic process itself, as well as history, is on their side and guarantees the inevitability of Communist victory. In this sense dialectical materialism is an *Ersatz* religion.

(*1*) That the corollaries drawn from the laws of dialectic are political and social is most clearly seen in Stalin's writings. "If the passing of slow quantitative changes into rapid and abrupt qualitative changes is a law of development, then it is clear that revolutions made by oppressed classes are a quite natural and inevitable phenomenon."[7] Similarly, if development takes place through the mechanisms of objective contradiction, this is presumably the basis of the belief that class struggle and revolutionary dictatorship are "natural and inevitable phenomena."

We have already seen that *formally* this relation is a logical non-sequitur, and that the laws may be false and the specific phenomena may be true (although in *fact* the latter are false, too). Concretely, however, there is evidence that revolutions took place long before "the law of the transformation of quantity into quality" was ever formulated just as it was known that parturition takes place suddenly after nine months of gradual development. The alleged law adds not a particle of information to our knowledge about any subject matter. Indeed, the very meaning of the expression "sudden transformation of slow quantitative changes into rapid qualitative ones" alters as we go from field to field, and no generalizations about the critical points of the changes can be even remotely helpful in practice. Irritation bursts into anger, a volcano into eruption, an altercation into a brawl, a solid into gas or liquid, a retreat into a rout, and discontent into revolution. At this level of crude analogy and vague, inexact statement only the poet is licensed to instruct or entertain us by his references to them. And even he knows

---

[7] Stalin, *op. cit.*, chap. 4, sec. 2.

that not all irritations burst into anger, not all solids into gases or liquids, etc. Just as soon as we wish scientifically to understand anything about any of these specific phenomena, we court confusion unless we can dissociate ourselves from the cluster of connotations and fancies which adhere to the original analogies of our experience.

Note that the laws of dialectic are supposed to make these social phenomena "natural" as if the fact that they happened was by itself not sufficient to give them a natural status. But since the absence of these phenomena (say, revolutions) is also natural, the so-called law is irrelevant. Actually, "natural" in physics and "natural" in society do not have the same meanings. Anything which happens in physics is "natural," according to the dialectical materialists, but not everything which happens in society and history is "natural," since measures are recommended on the ground that to carry them out would be "natural," while *not* to carry them out would be "unnatural." Laws of nature cannot be violated, but presumably laws of history and social revolution can. This confusion between physics and ethics is not restricted to dialectical materialism; it goes back in Western thought at least to the Stoics and ultimately to the Platonic "form of the good." But dialectical materialism is one of the most conspicuous and persistent illustrations of this confusion since the rise of modern science. Nor are dialectical materialists unique in seeking to use applications of alleged ontological or metaphysical principles in the field of nature as a support of their social views. Some Western philosophers have argued that the sudden leap of an electron from one orbit to another is evidence for freedom of the human will. Dialectical materialists indignantly and properly deny this; they then go on to argue as if it constituted evidence for the naturalness and inevitability of the Communist revolution.

The attempt to derive social laws from physical laws is legitimate even if the history of the effort until now has been a history of failure. The validity of a social law, however, can be established independently of the validity of any more general physical law from which it is presumably to be derived, just as the laws of genetics can be established as valid independently of the success or failure of the effort to show that they are derivable from physico-chemical laws. At the very most all one can say today is that no set of social arrangements is possible which violate any valid scientific or biological generalization. But even if this be granted, *it does not follow that men will not try to achieve such a social system.* We may predict that a social ideal based upon the postulate of the indefinite fertility of the soil, or on universal, absolute chastity, or any other aim incompatible with tested scientific knowledge, will be unrealizable. But human beings may attempt the impossible, even though it may lead to rack and ruin. Now if an indefinite variety of social systems is compatible with basic physical laws, how much greater variation is allowed by dialectical or ontological laws which, granted for a moment their cognitive import, either have a wider generality than any physical laws, if metaphysics has a specific subject matter, or are as tautologous as the laws of logic, if metaphysics has no specific subject matter.

The valid arguments for democracy, capitalism, Socialism, Fascism and Communism do not rest on any metaphysics, ontology, or dialectical laws. This is true even for the ethical components and imperatives of social systems, since no ethical statement is derivable from philosophical premises unless a value term or attitude is implicit in such premises or in the situation which we accept as a point of departure. Nor, as we have seen, can social systems be derived from physical generalizations and certainly not the attempts of men to achieve such systems. It is a canonic proposition of dialectical materialism, however, that the struggle for Communism and its universal triumph are equally inevitable.

(2) Since scientific statements are corrigible, and since all predictive statements are conditional, no scientific judgment can guarantee the future. That is why the dialectical method is employed to win a kind of "truth" which is either outside the scope of science or incompatible with its very method. The more narrowly empirical Marxist-Leninist *political* strategy is, the more opportunistic its tactics, the more resolutely does it affirm that "sooner or later" the Communist goal will be achieved. One of the psychological consequences of this belief is an indifference to alternative means and methods of social change, a denial that such means and methods determine the actual ends reached in history, rather than conversely. Another is a callous disregard of the human costs of social action, since moral responsibility is shifted from human beings to the historical process working itself out with the alleged automatism of natural law. No matter what man's limitations are, no matter what his ignorance or cowardice, no matter how sustained his defeats, they cannot hold up the dialectical march of the productive forces to a Communist society. But the dialectic in history needs to be supplemented by a *Natur-dialektik,* for the history of man is also a part of the history of the cosmos. Tidal waves, earthquakes, extremes of weather have their historical effects, too, and the historical process alone cannot guarantee that a cosmic event—an accident from the standpoint of human history—may not put an end to man's career on earth. Natural development, despite all setbacks and catastrophes is, in Stalin's language, from "the lower to the higher," and the dialectical laws of development, universal and inevitable, give the emotional assurance, which history alone cannot give, that the ideal of Communism

will not be defeated. Dialectical materialists believe that if human life is destroyed on this earth, then somewhere else life will develop and resume its advance to the predestined goal.

One may regard it as a politicalized version of early nineteenth-century *Naturphilosophie* with the dialectical process cast in the role of an instrument of Hegel's *List der Vernunft*. It is not accidental, to borrow a favorite expression of this school of thought, that an English Communist, Professor H. Levy, speaks soberly of "fascism in nature" when discussing mechanics.[8] That dialectics gives guarantees is often *explicitly* claimed by dialectical materialists. Thus, one Soviet philosopher, subsequently sent to Hungary on the heels of the Red Army, writes:

> Dialectics not only points out to the proletariat its historical task, but it gives the proletariat the certainty of victory, it is to a certain extent the *guarantee of this victory*.[9]

Whoever understands the universe properly then, i.e., from the standpoint of dialectical materialism, will see (*a*) that the world of nature and society could not have been different from what it is and the victory of communism still be possible, and (*b*) that the structure of the universe is such that victory is logically already involved in the relationships discovered by dialectics. This is the promise of creation. The stars in their courses proclaim it; the ocean floor supports it; and man in his brief career realizes it. Even if life on this planet were destroyed, this philosophy offers the assurance that it would arise somewhere else and begin its pilgrimage to that one far-off event—or succession of events—towards which the cosmos is striving. Communism, it is sometimes admitted, will disappear but the same natural processes which insure its disappearance *necessitate* its coming.

> *But what passes away at one point of the universe, develops anew at another.* One solar system passes away, new ones develop. Life passes away from the earth, it arises elsewhere anew. *In this sense,* dialectical materialism asserts an eternal development; what exists evolves. It evolves because the dialectical self-movement of every thing which exists is a driving force towards development. *Decay holds in general for special cases; the endlessness of development holds only for the infinite universe sub specie eternitatis.*[10]

---

[8] *A Philosophy for Modern Man* (London, 1938), p. 125.

[9] L. Rudas, "Dialectical Materialism and Communism," *Labour Monthly* (Sept. and Oct., 1933) (italics in original).

[10] Rudas, *ibid.*, Sept., 1933.

This not only suggests the familiar consolations of religion; it is an outright expression of the theology of absolute idealism with all its attendant logical difficulties. What an ironic illustration of the alleged dialectic law of the transformation of a thesis into its opposite! Dialectical materialism, which is presumably militant atheism, is here presented as a kind of sentimental theology! The indignant repudiation of this charge by Rudas and other orthodox dialectical materialists is only a measure of their inconsistency and of their failure to grasp the essence of the religious attitude. Because they eschew the use of the word *God* or *Absolute Spirit* and insist that there is no external source of movement, but that every movement is self-movement, they feel that they have escaped religion when all they have done is to replace a transcendental theology by an immanent one. For what is essential to religion is not the use of the term "God" but the belief that the universe is somehow friendly to man and human purpose, that natural processes are such that they must realize the highest human ideals (e.g., Communism, if one believes in it), that these processes cannot be adequately understood without such reference, and that despite momentary defeats and setbacks the victory of the highest human ideals (i.e., the classless society) is guaranteed by the mechanisms of nature and society. To inspire this belief in the minds and hearts of its adherents is the precise function of the theology of orthodox dialectical materialism.

Whether dialectical materialism is an expression of the secular hunger for metaphysics or religion, it is undoubtedly a quest for certainty, a quest for what William James called "a sumptuosity of security" which no scientific philosophy can give. The animus against all deviant philosophical ideas, against technical scientific doctrines like the theory of resonance in chemistry which have not the slightest political implications, can be explained only as a fear that in some way the revolutionary faith that both inspires and consoles is being undermined if philosophy and science are given autonomy to develop as philosophers and scientists in the uncoerced quest for truth see fit to develop them.

What is new about the philosophy of dialectical materialism is not its doctrine of two truths, the ordinary scientific truth, sometimes called metaphysical, and the higher dialectical truth. It is the extent and intensity of political control of the arts and sciences to which this quest for security has gone. It is as if despairing of a rational defence of their political program with its needless sacrifice of untold millions for a problematic future which does not promise to be much better than the past and in many ways threatens to be far worse, the rulers of the Soviet Union must fall back on the authority of a mystical doctrine to whose keys they alone possess the key. "Plechanov and even Bukharin," wrote a party philosopher before the Moscow Trials, "were not in a position to give an unexceptionable exposition of dialectical materialism in the last resort also because they did not have an unexceptionable line in politics."[11] And who has an unexceptionable line in politics? Obviously whoever commands the state security troops.

No matter what else they differ about, the vocation of all scientists in the free world *as scientists* is threatened by the extension of Soviet power and its stock of ideological straitjackets. No matter what school of philosophy to which they belong, all philosophers will be compelled to bow to political decrees in epistemology, logic and methodology. The administration of philosophy will become one of the duties of the police. This is no Orwellian fantasy of the future. For it is a recapitulation of the fate of philosophy in the Soviet Union.

---

[11] L. Rudas, *The* (American) *Communist* (1935), p. 348.

13 The Literature of Political Disillusionment

IN ONE OF HIS *Dialogues in Limbo,* which in profundity and suggestiveness has been compared to the dialogues of Plato, George Santayana pictures madness as a belief in the imaginary and as a desire for the impossible. Such madness he calls normal and natural. He contrasts it with the madness which, although natural, is abnormal, subject to the chastisements of Dike, the goddess of justice. Santayana's language is peculiar, flavored as it is by a sophisticated enthusiasm for the archaic metaphysics of Democritean materialism. But what he is saying is that normal illusion or madness "comes of being alive," and that to be alive is to believe in the imaginary, to cherish and pursue ideals. For a human being to be without ideals is to be inert, dead even if unburied.

Even in the eyes of the most sober of psychologists human life is a form of goal-seeking behavior. It differs from other kinds of living behavior directed to ends, in that its consciousness and knowledge of what it strives toward, however these be analyzed, make a perceptible difference to oneself and others. Ideals are as natural to man as their absence is to other animals.

All human beings begin their career by accepting the ideals of others, first by habit and then by faith. For that is what it means to live in a community. Growth and maturity consist not in abandoning ideals but in understanding them, supplementing them, and sometimes substituting other ideals for them, more securely anchored in the flux of change.

It is in terms of its dominant ideals that the basic beliefs of any society can be defined. What is called the crisis of *our* age, whatever else it is, is a crisis of belief—not a crisis of religious belief in the conven-

169

tional sense—but a crisis of political belief in religious form. If we define religion not in terms of dogma but in terms of objects of ultimate concern, then it is indisputable that our great public religions today are political. They determine more articles of faith and belief, more objects of allegiance and devotion, than any of the traditional propositions of theology. You can infer far fewer things about a man's commitments in the way of action or belief from, e.g., his acceptance of divine existence and human immortality than you can from his acceptance of the principles of communism or fascism or, depending upon its adjective, democracy.

It is natural that the present intense struggle of political ideals should have caught up, in different ways, the artists and poets and novelists of our time as well as the philosophers. It is natural because of the pervasiveness of the political interest in modern culture, an interest which emerges from, and in turn modifies, the entire stream of human experience whose patterns and eddies and cross currents are the subject matter of art and reflection.

The contemporary struggle of political ideals has a long history. But it became focal and dramatic with the Russian Revolution of October, 1917, and the formation of the Soviet state. W. H. Auden, the English poet, in comparing the times of Wordsworth with our own, writes:

> *Like his, our lives have been coeval*
> *With a political upheaval,*
> *Like him, we had the luck to see*
> *A rare discontinuity*
> *Old Russia suddenly mutate*
> *Into a proletarian state.*

There are tremendous differences, of course, between the French and Russian Revolutions and their respective developments; and Auden would no longer refer to Russia as a proletarian state. It is undeniable, however, that the Russian Revolution has been the only historical event that has inspired in so many different fields, from philosophy to poetry, reactions of comparable magnitude to those which followed the Fall of the Bastille.

One important difference, relevant to our analysis, in the cultural responses to the French and Russian Revolutions, is the extent to which they took on a *narrow* political character. The responses that greeted the French Revolution were episodic, spontaneous, in varying degrees sympathetically *critical,* and above all *autonomous* in their subsequent development. But those evoked by the October Revolution, after the first few years, were organized, and then in divers ways moulded until their expression took the form of total acceptance.

Neither the French Assembly nor the Convention nor the Directorate nor even the Empire, which some historians view as consolidating the gains of the French Revolution, had an international organization which established political parties in other countries and channeled sympathetic cultural movements along definite lines. The Soviet regime, however, through the Communist International, organized and controlled political parties whose following provided, so to speak, the acoustic medium in which intellectuals influenced by the October Revolution could hear over and over again the echo of their own sentiments. The existence of this audience and special public was put to good use by the agencies established to effect cultural liaison between sympathetic intellectuals and the political movements inspired by the Soviet regime. Leagues of writers, associations of artists, councils of scientists, proliferated in every large country of the world. The upshot was a mobilization and concentration of intellectual talent on behalf of a political ideal unequaled in the annals of any period.

The enthusiasm generated by the October Revolution was not synthetic even though it was exploited politically to the utmost. In many cases it had the sincerity of a religious conversion. It encountered opposition, sometimes strong opposition. But it throve on it. It produced an impressive body of literature in affirmation of the philosophy, program, and practices of the Soviet regime. This literature of affirmation was in no way unique except in volume, for the American and French Revolutions, as well as the national upheavals in Italy and Germany during the 19th century, had also given rise to libraries of passionate and interpretive sympathetic studies. What seems to me to be historically distinctive about the cultural and literary phenomena associated with the Russian Revolution is the literature of disillusionment with which the spiritual Odyssey of so many converts to the Bolshevik faith has terminated, and who now recognize with Auden:

> *O Freedom still is far from home*
> *For Moscow is as far as Rome*
> *Or Paris.*

Indeed, most of them would say that Moscow is farther.

I

This literature of disillusion constitutes a distinct genre of writing in contemporary letters if only because of its international character and the common pattern of rediscovery and rededication to certain values of the Western tradition that had not been so much denied as ignored. Russell, Auden, Spender, and Orwell in England; André Gide, Souvarine and Serge in France and Belgium; Ignazio Silone in Italy; Panait

Istrati in Greece; Arthur Koestler in Central Europe; Anton Ciliga in the Balkans; Eastman, Dos Passos, Wilson, Hicks, Farrell in the United States are among the more noteworthy figures who have contributed to this literature.

As literature it must be sharply distinguished from the revelations of former members of the Communist Party who were revolted, or felt themselves threatened, by the pattern of conspiracy, espionage, and subversive infiltration which constitute an important aspect of Communist Party activity. They constitute a special group which I shall discuss later. I am not discussing the "professional revolutionists," but intellectuals who are concerned more with ideology than organization, and who in some ways are more influential than exclusively political personalities.

The evolution of attitudes in most of these men differs from the apostacies of Wordsworth and Dostoevsky, whose early revolutionary enthusiasm and doctrines became transformed into their polar opposites. We do not find in their works sentiments comparable to those expressed in Wordsworth's *Ecclesiastical Sketches* or *Devotional Incitements;* and if their writings do not reach the great artistic heights of Dostoevsky's bitter legend of the Grand Inquisitor, neither do they celebrate the central role which Dostoevsky assigned to miracle, mystery, and authority in human life.

If we ask what led so many sensitive and generous spirits to ardent and sometimes sacrificial support of Soviet communism, we find a mixture of motives inexplicable in terms of the hedonistic determinism of Bentham or the economic determinism of Marxian orthodoxy. Neither self-interest nor fear nor vanity moved them to break with the conventional pieties and allegiances of the world in which they had been nurtured. In almost equal measure, they were impelled by a revulsion against the dismal spectacle of the postwar West which tottered without faith and with little hope from one crisis to another, and by an enthusiasm for the ideals of equality and human liberation broadcast in the official decrees and laws of the early Soviet regime. Both the revulsion and enthusiasm were rooted in a moral sensibility whose fibers had been fed from sources deeply imbedded in the traditions of the West. Not one of the neophytes to the Communist faith was conscious of accepting an alien creed no matter how foreign the idiom in which it was clothed. The words in which one English convert to the Soviet idea describes her road to the Kremlin holds true with minor variations for the entire band of fellow-pilgrims:

I came to communism via Greek history, the French revolutionary literature I had read in childhood, and the English 19th century poets of freedom. . . . In my mind Pericles' funeral oration, Shelley's and Swinburne's poems, Marx's and Lenin's writings, were all part and parcel of the same striving for the emancipation of mankind from oppression.[1]

Stephen Spender, another English poet, in an effort to show that there is a continuity between the liberal idealists and philosophical radicals of the past century, on the one hand, and the Communists of the present century, on the other, between Blake, Godwin, and J. S. Mill and Lenin, Trotsky, and Stalin, wrote:

> I am a communist because I am a liberal. Liberalism seems to me to be the creed of those who, as far as it is possible in human affairs, are disinterested, if by disinterestedness one understands not mere passivity but a regard for objective truth, an active will towards political justice. During an era of peace and progress, the liberal spirit is identical not only with political discussion, but also with scientific inquiry, speculative thought and the disinterested creation of works of art.[2]

What Spender is saying is that he became a communist because he believed in disinterestedness, objective truth and justice, free political discussion and inquiry, and creative integrity—a cluster of values every one of which, oddly enough, had been vehemently denounced as bourgeois prejudices by the pundits of dialectical materialism ever since the early days of the Soviet regime. Spender has long since repudiated communism without foreswearing his liberalism.

Compare these strains of rationalism and humanism with the *motifs* in the apologies of those adherents to German National Socialism like Rauschning, Strasser, and Thyssen, who renounced the Nazi regime. What elements in the Nazi practice and doctrine magnetized *their* minds, emotions, and will? "A national awakening," "a surface discipline and order," "a vast display of energy and achievement" whose new tempos and accelerated rhythms lift men out of "the humdrum of daily life"—these are some of the things of which they speak. No ideals continuous with the heritage of either secular or Christian humanism moved these men and their fellows but only the pull of the dynamism of power. Here was no attempt to achieve either a revolution from within or a transformation of basic institutions, but in Rauschning's phrase "a revolution of nihilism." Not principle—not even mis-

---

[1] Freda Utley, *Lost Illusion* (Philadelphia, Fireside Press, rev. ed., 1948), pp. 2, 43.

[2] *Forward from Liberalism* (London, Victor Gollancz, 1937), p. 202.

taken principle—drew them on, but a frenetic national enthusiasm, and a mysticism centered on the person of Hitler. "I looked into his eyes and he into mine; and at that I had only one desire, to be at home and alone with that great, overwhelming experience." This extravagant outburst, Rauschning tells us, came not from an hysterical woman "but from a judge in a high position, talking to his colleagues."

A candid appraisal of the literature of Nazi disillusion shows that it is qualitatively of an entirely different order from that of the erst-while partisans of the Soviet idea. Those who broke with Hitler did so because their stomachs were not strong enough to assimilate, as a constant diet, the atrocities to which they had originally resigned themselves as incidental and temporary—like Rauschning; or because their private interests were jeopardized by someone who they expected would be their creature because he had been bought—like Thyssen; or because their personal ambitions were frustrated—like Strasser.

I have contrasted these two types of literature of disillusion to under-score how misleading is the simple equation often drawn between Bolshevism and Nazism. In respect to their repudiation of many features of the democratic process they are, of course, identical, but in respect to the power of the Soviet and Nazi myths to attract the liberal spirits of the West they are vastly different. One need not agree with Toynbee that Russian Bolshevism is a species of Christian heresy to recognize the seductive effect of its use of categories drawn from the Western culture it would destroy. Just as the early Christians used the temples of pagan worship to make the new religion more palatable to peoples whose rulers had been converted, so the ideology of Bolshevism parades with a vocabulary of freedoms and rights freighted with connotations precious to all genuine humanists. That is why it is a more formidable opponent of free cultures than movements openly dedicated to their destruction. It is especially formidable in drawing to itself politically innocent men and women of good will and strong emotions whose minds are unfortified with relevant information, and who have not yet learned that only an intelligence hardened by skepticism is a safeguard against the credulities born of hope.

It is worthy of note that most of those who succumbed to the Soviet myth were devoid of political experience. They were led to their first political affair by emotional compulsion rather than by sober computation of the consequences of adopting a given proposal and its alternatives, which constitutes the everyday life of rational politics. Just as the necessity for loving creates its own object, so the necessity for believing selects the myth that appears best fitted to one's need and hopes. And, given the cultural climate—the naiveté, the vague longing for "higher things," and the vast ignorance of political fact—what seemed more congenial than the Soviet idea, the apparent offspring of moral idealism and scientific law? It not only held out guarantees of fulfillment of their highest hopes but provided a metaphysics to give them cosmic support.

All the great myths of history, from Augustine's *City of God* to Sorel's *General Strike,* have been able to sustain themselves because nowhere could they be exemplified, lived with, tested in terms of their fruits in experience. The Soviet myth of a humane, rationally ordered, classless, democratic society, however, was glorified not as an other-worldly ideal but as an historical fact with a definite locus in space and time. In staking out a claim in history, it subjected not only its power but its intent to the logic of events. We have no way of knowing the actual extent to which these who are native to the Soviet Union believe in the Soviet myth, carefully inculcated as it is in every text-book from the kindergarten to the university and reinforced by an omnipresent secret police whose forced labor camps girdle the country. But we do know, judging by the literature under review, that the first doubts in the minds of the pilgrims from other countries arose when they actually lived in the land of their dreams or pondered on the critical reports of those who had.

Some day a psychologist or poet will do justice to the drama of doubt in the mind of these political believers. Few individuals ever surrend-ered their belief in God with more agony, soul-searching, and inner resistance than these latter-day apostles of revolutionary brotherhood surrendered their belief in the monolithic validity of the monolithic Soviet state system.

II

It is an elementary truth of the psychology of perception that what a man sees depends often upon his beliefs and expectations. The stronger the beliefs the more they function like *a priori* notions whose validity is beyond the tests of experience. Hopes can be so all-consuming that they affect even the range and quality of feeling. The consequence is that the shocks of reality, in terms of which the natural pragmatism of the human mind experiences actuality, lose their educational office. To say that a man is seized and transformed by an abstraction is a metaphor but it expresses the empirical fact that an idea-system, instead of functioning as a guide to conduct, can operate in such a way as to transform habits, feelings, and perceptions of the individual to a point where marked changes of personality are noticeable.

It was to be expected that the Western intellectuals who saw the Soviet Union firsthand would screen their impressions through the closely knit frame of doctrinal abstractions. It took some time before the cumulative shock of events tore a hole in this frame through which the facts of experience could pour. Only then did the agony of self-doubt begin. With varying details each one tells the same story. Once the evils of the system were recognized as evils, it was hoped they would disappear in time. When they grew worse with time, they were justified as necessary elements of the future good. When this necessity was challenged, the mind dwelt upon worse evils that could be found in other countries. But this provoked two gnawing questions. Were the evils in other countries really worse? And in any case, in the countries they came from, evils could be publicly criticized: why not here?

The process of disenchantment was all the harder because in the course of their original conversion so much tortured dialectic had been expended in defense of what now seemed to be indefensible. As a rule it requires more intellectual courage to renounce an illusion than to espouse one. For others are usually involved in such renunciations. These men and women felt a moral responsibility for those, and to those, who had been influenced by their enthusiasms. They knew that they would be showered with abuse, defamed as turncoats, that their former friends would construe the avowal of any doubt as evidence of personal fear or self-seeking despite the overwhelming evidence that neither popular favor nor material goods ranked high in their scale of values. They knew they faced loneliness and isolation. Bertrand Russell, the first of this group, and, as one would expect, the quickest to see through the myth, once confessed that he lost more friends by his criticism of Soviet terror than by his absolute pacifism during a war in which his country was locked in a battle for life and death with Germany.

Much graver considerations kept their lips sealed. They shrank in dismay at the prospect that reactionaries would seize upon their criticisms for their own purposes. More important still, a practical substitute faith to which they could wholeheartedly dedicate themselves was not available to them. They had lost their belief but not their hunger for belief. The man who cries, "Lord, I believe; help thou my *unbelief*," is usually on the way to a belief in which he may find peace, but he into whose soul the more radical acids of *disbelief* have entered can never again recapture the serenity of the original belief. He has lost his innocence, and in the end, can only be useful as a party functionary.

But as excess followed excess in a bloody succession, as intolerance and internal coercion increased in direct proportion to the strength and stability of the Soviet State, they felt compelled to make public their disavowal of their former allegiance. In every case it is clear that the ultimate grounds for their disavowal were the very same moral sentiments which had originally led them to the Kremlin. It was not the state, they discovered, which had withered away but every vestige of political freedom, and with it all the brave ideals of the heroic period of the October Revolution.

None of the writers of this school could honestly be called sentimental dreamers or Utopians. Most of them considered themselves Marxists of a sort. They had been trained to take a long view toward the stern necessities of history. Without swallowing Hegel they agreed with him that what appears evil is often the negative dialectical moment in a cycle of progress, or what Toynbee today calls the ever-renewed challenge, necessary for a creative response on a higher level at a later time. They therefore allowed many times over for the blunders and crudities and rough edges of a new social justice.

It is one thing, however, to explain a phenomenon historically; it is another thing to justify it. Where explanation and justification are confused, then whatever is, is right. But if whatever is, is right, condemnation of capitalism and Fascism, too, becomes meaningless wherever *they* exist, and the nerve of moral indignation, which led to belief in communism in the first place, becomes paralyzed. If history not only raises moral problems but settles them, then Gletkin's train of thought as he argues with Rubashev in Koestler's *Darkness at Noon* becomes inescapable. A mistake is a crime; successful might is always right; the weak are *ipso facto* wrong; every lost cause is a bad cause. Such a philosophy may be professed in words, but in experience no sensitive human being can consistently act on it. That is why, for all their historical naturalism and scientific determinism, these enthusiasts were compelled to recognize that *not* everything they saw was historically necessary, and that some things could have been *different*.

III

What, then, were the specific experiences which led to disenchantment with the Soviet myth? And at the outset it must be declared that it was *not* the discovery of the miserable living conditions of the Russian masses. Although they had been sadly unprepared for what they found by the extravagant claims made by Soviet partisans abroad, they found reassurance in the promises af future five-year plans. What struck them most forcibly was the *cruelty*, the unnecessary cruelty, which pervaded almost every aspect of Soviet administrative practice.

This cruelty was not sadistic or demonic as in some Fascist countries; it was systematic, a matter of state policy, carried out to teach object lessons to those who could not possibly profit by it because they were destroyed in the process. The use of bread as a political weapon was not unknown in the past, but its calculated withdrawal for purposes of insuring absolute conformity was something new. The same was true for the use of correctional labor camps for political prisoners. Ciliga, Serge, and others bitterly contrast the conditions in which political prisoners, including Lenin and his lieutenants, lived under the Czar with the conditions under which those charged with political offenses lived under Stalin. And in a nationalized economy under dictatorial controls almost any offense can be regarded as political. Even theft of a handful of grain from a collective farm, moving from one town to another, not to speak of crossing a border without proper papers, are crimes against the state and punishable as such.

This cruelty was manifest not only in bureaucratic indifference but by official reminders that mercy, charity, or pity were evidence of bourgeois decadence. According to our informants, there was a total absence of concern for the individual person, an attitude in high official quarters and low, which regarded the lives of human beings as if they were so much raw material like iron, coal, and scrap to be consumed in the fires of production in order to swell the figures of output.

Of course, bureaucratic indifference to the individual case, to personal need and suffering is not a Soviet phenomenon. In some degree it is found everywhere, as these men well knew. And cruelty, where state interests appear to be genuinely threatened, could be extenuated as necessary, even if harshly and mistakenly conceived. But when it was coupled with wholesale injustice, it became unendurable to those nurtured in Western traditions. Two examples of this injustice, judging by the literature, were found especially outrageous. The first was the charge of "ideological complicity" directed against anyone whose views were similar to an individual believed guilty of any offense against the regime. Thousands were in consequence punished, sometimes by liquidation, for "ideological complicity" in the alleged act of someone they never knew or heard of. The second example which particularly exercised Koestler was the practice of holding entire families hostage for the exemplary behavior of its members. One decree provided that in the case of an individual's flight from the Soviet Union even those members of his family who had no knowledge of his act were to be "deported for five years to the remote regions of Siberia." Such sentences are served in penal work camps and are renewable by administrative decision.

As if to put a doctrinal seal upon these moral outrages and answer the unuttered protests on the lips of sympathizers, the People's Commissar for Justice proclaimed in the official organ of the Soviet regime: "In the opinion of liberals and opportunists of all kinds—the stronger a country is, the more lenient it can be to its opponents. . . . No, and again no! The stronger the country is, the mightier it is . . . the more justified are we in taking stern measures against those who disturb our socialist construction" (*Izvestia,* No. 37, Dec. 2, 1936). Not long after, the man who wrote these words was liquidated for not being stern enough. If this was socialist humanism, those who in the name of humanism had fought against such practices in countries under the heel of Fascism could not swallow it.

Most of the excesses against which the disillusioned intellectuals of the West protested did not at first concern their own professional fields. They protested as *human beings* against the degradation imposed on other human beings; or as *socialists* against mounting inequalities of power and position which, in fact, produced new class distinctions; or as *Marxists* against the wilful disregard of objective historical conditions, and the blindness to the limits of endurance of human flesh. To all such protests came the reply, "reasons of state." Those who received this reply confess that although they could not *see* these "reasons of state," they were puzzled and confused by the retort. After all, there are so many variables in history, the future is so indeterminate, who knows with certainty what is necessary for what?

But there was one kind of persecution for which the excuse "reasons of state" could not be offered with the slightest plausibility. This was the cultural terror which raged in every field of the arts and sciences. All of these Western intellectuals lived in countries in which the slightest attempt to suppress a book or painting or a piece of music was sure to meet with fierce public opposition even when the censorship was tangential. And at the worst, restrictions affected sales, not one's freedom and not one's life. To undergo the exierence of a *total* censorship and control shocked and stunned them. For it was a control not only over what was written but also over what was painted and sung, not only over political thought but over thought in philosophy and science, not only over *what* was created but also over *how* it was created—the style and manner as well as theme and content. Nothing like it has ever existed in the modern world. In making art and philosophy a matter for the police, it violated the sense of dignity and authenticity among these writers and artists and thinkers of the West. It also affronted their sense of integrity as craftsmen.

It had been hard enough for them to accept Stalin's description of the intellectual as "an engineer of the human soul." When the engineer was required, however, to build not only to another's specifications but according to technical rules and laws laid down by those who had never undergone the discipline and training of the craftsman, they felt that some kind of atavistic cultural barbarism was being forced upon them. When, on top of this, the penalties and sanctions for refusing to knuckle under entailed, because of the state monopoly of all means of publication and communication, the withdrawal of the means of life for the independent thinker and writer and his family, and in stubborn cases deportation and death, mystification gave way to passionate revulsion.

They were mystified because of the demonstrable uselessness of these cultural purges to the declared objectives of the Soviet regime. What bearings, for example, on any declared social policy were involved in the purge of Soviet physicists and astronomers for expressing disbelief in absolute space and time, a corollary of the theory of relativity? Or the condemnation of abstraction in modern art, romanticism in the novel, formalism in poetry, and atonality in music? The decrees laid down with the awful authority of the Central Committee of the Communist Party and specifying the correct line in these fields must be read in order to realize how minutely this control extended to the very details of the arts and sciences. Or one could cite the dogmas of "Soviet biology"—a phrase reminiscent of the late unlamented "Nazi biology" —which renders taboo the Mendelian-Morgan theory of gene transmission in favor of Engels' Lamarckian notion, already disproved in his day, concerning the inheritance of acquired characters.

Not even this theory has any logical consequences of a political nature. Professor H. J. Muller, the famous American geneticist and Nobel Prize winner, who witnessed at firsthand the tragic purge of Russian biologists, has observed that one can just as well argue from the theory of inherited acquired characters that the children of the ruling classes, because of the advantages of their environment, become superior types of human beings in comparison with the children of the masses, as that any human being can be transformed by environmental changes into a genius. Needless to say both inferences are false. In insisting that the truth of a scientific theory had to be judged by its alleged social or political consequences, the Soviet regime, to the amazement of the Western intellectuals, was challenging what had become axiomatic since the time of Galileo.

There was another horrible consequence of the operation of the party line in cultural matters reported by those who observed it. Inasmuch as the line was a function of changing domestic and international conditions, it took sharp turns and shifts. Those who administered the party decrees often became the victims of subsequent decrees. Since there was a normal risk in any utterance, a greater risk in silence, and even a risk in ferreting out deviations, there resulted a frenzied effort to purchase immunity by professions of orthodoxy, displays of ferocity towards scapegoats, and glorifications of Stalin in language as extravagant as anything that can be found in the sacred literature of Byzantium. Everyone was caught up in an ever-expanding spiral of adulation and fear. It was this which moved André Gide, who had braved contumely in denouncing European colonial practices, to write after he returned from the Soviet Union: "I doubt whether in any country of the world, even Hitler's Germany, is thought less free, more bowed down, more terrorized, more vassalized."

There were other elements in the common saga of disenchantment which received varying emphasis in the accounts written by those who had awakened from their dream. Edmund Wilson felt that the apotheosis of Stalin had reached a point that the Russian people could react to him only neurotically both on a conscious and on an unconscious level.

One of the initial impulses which led these Western intellectuals to accept Communism was a strong feeling of internationalism. They thought of themselves as citizens of the world dedicated to an ideal of a universal parliament of free peoples. They looked to the Soviet Union as a fortress of a world movement to achieve this ideal. But when they saw that the road to power in Russia was imposed as a pattern for every other country they were disturbed. When they realized that socialist movements elsewhere were regarded as expendable border guards of the Soviet Union, active doubt set in. When, finally, cultural signs multiplied on all sides of aggressive Russian nationalism and pan-Slavism, when even Ivan the Terrible, and Peter the Great, were venerated as precursors of national Bolshevism, they felt themselves once more spiritual aliens. And with this, they experienced a new resurgence of kinship with the West and their own countries which until now they had seen only through a thick ideological fog.

The decay of faith led rapidly to other discoveries. One was that the rough economic equality which both Marx and Lenin assumed as a principle of socialist distribution was as far distant in the Soviet Union—in some respects even farther away—as in the countries of the middle-way. The other was a nausea, more acute for being so long delayed, at the falsity of Soviet propaganda, its employment of semantic corruption as a weapon, illustrated, e.g., in the use of the term *democracy* for a system in which expression of dissent was a grave penal offense.

I V

It would be inappropriate to conclude this survey of political disillusionment without some evaluation of the weaknesses in the outlook of these Western intellectuals which contributed to their tragic self-deception. Even granting the partial truth of their plea that it was not so much *they* who changed as the Soviet system, it still remains undeniable that they were at fault in not conceiving the possibilities of change. But much more than this can be said in criticism. Even when all allowances are made for human fallibility their responsibility for their own illusions remains heavy.

First, they looked to politics for something politics alone can never bring to the life of men—that absolute certainty, that emotional "sumptuosity of security," to use James' phrase, which if attainable at all, can be most easily reached through a revealed religion they had already, and properly, rejected. In identifying themselves with those in the seats of power, they abdicated their true functions as intellectuals —to be the critical conscience of the smug and contented; and to fulfill their mission as the creatively possessed, the eternal questers after truth under all conditions. There is no loyalty to any community or state or party or church which absolves the individual from loyalty to himself. Whatever good the "saving remnant" can bring to the world, it must at least save the purity of the enkindling flame which by accident of natural grace burns within them.

Secondly, in their zeal for salvation by total political faith, they forgot that politics is always made by men, and that no doctrine or institution is a safeguard against its own abuses. They were doomed to be disillusioned because they forgot that no social change can make gods or even angels out of men, that to be human is to be tempted, and that no one can be forever tempted without erring either out of weakness or ignorance. This is another way of saying that they were naive and immature about human psychology.

Third, they made the mistake of all the typically *religieux* of forgetting that in the affairs of *this* world, at least, faith can never be a substitute for intelligence. The transformation of the economic order is not a single problem that can be settled by fiat, poetic or philosophical. It is a series of problems, all very difficult, requiring prolonged study, in the absence of which a talent with paint or words or tones is not a sufficient qualification. They were immature in imagining that the field of economic behavior, from which as a youth the great physicist, Planck, had withdrawn because of its difficulty, could be stormed with the weapons of moral indignation.

Fourth, they had abandoned too soon their own heritage of political democracy. They grossly underestimated the power of the self-corrective procedures of democracy to remedy, and in time to abolish, the major economic disabilities and injustices of our age. Intent upon viewing everything *else* in historical perspective, they refused to take an historical perspective to Western democracy, and to observe the substantial progress that had been made since the time Marx described the pitiful conditions of the English proletariat in *Capital*, a book so sacred to most of them that they never read it. They failed to see that, so long as the processes of political democracy remained intact, it was possible to carry the moral imperatives of the democratic way of life just as far as our courage, effort and powers of persuasion reached.

Fifth, they did not understand the genuine sense in which the social problem is a moral problem, i.e., that no social institution or system is an end in itself but a means for realizing the primary values of security, freedom, justice, knowledge, and kindness. Since the world is just as much a consequence of the means we use as of the end we profess, the end that actually comes to be depends upon the moral qualities of the means used. They had often heard that the end justifies the means but they never stopped to examine the evidence in order to see whether the means used were actually bringing the end-in-view closer or pushing it farther away. Even if they had, it is doubtful whether they would have recognized negative evidence. For the strange fact is that despite their assurance of the scientific character of their convictions, none of them could indicate, even theoretically, what possible evidence would lead them to abandon or modify their political beliefs. Everything that happened counted as positive evidence. Until their basic attitude changed, experience could never refute what they held to be empirical truths.

Whatever the responsibility of these writers for their own illusions, the record of their disillusionment is a record of growing intellectual and emotional maturity. No one has a right to be censorious of them, and least of all those who complacently accept all social changes, whose emotions of sympathy for their fellowman are never engaged, and who leave all the risks of thought and action to others. What was possible to believe in 1919 or 1929 was no longer possible in 1939 except to the morally obtuse or corrupt. The very existence of this literature is a challenge to subsequent generations of writers who feel called to enlist themselves as foot-soldiers in a political crusade. We should be grateful to them for providing texts not only in the costs of human folly but in the grandeur of human faith and humility.

As long as there are human beings there will always be ideals and illusions. They cannot be foresworn. But perhaps the greatest lesson to which this literature points is that good sense in the quest for the good life in the good society depends not so much on *what* ideals are held as on *how* they are held; not so much on the nature of our beliefs as on the methods by which they are reached.

Underlying all other differences among human beings is the difference between the absolutist and the experimental temper of mind. The first converts its unreflective prejudices into first principles, and its shifting certitudes into a fanaticism of virtue which closes the gates of mercy against all who disagree. The second, although resolute in action, knows that finality of judgment is not possible to men, and is therefore prepared to review the evidence on which it stakes its ultimate commitments. It is this willingness to reconsider first principles in the light of relevant evidence and other alternatives which is the sign of both the liberal and the mature mind.

14 The Psychology of the "Fellow-Traveler"

ONE OF THE unique cultural phenomena of our time is the existence of Communist "fellow-travelers." Their numbers and influence wax and wane with the political climate and tend to be inversely proportionate to the temperature of the cold war. In some way their activities constitute a more serious threat to democratic life than those of Communist party members. By applying one standard of judgment to the Soviet Union and an entirely different one to every other nation, including their own, they revive and strengthen suspicion against all dissenters. Their disingenuousness calls into question the good faith of the honest critics whom they deceive.

This is the gravest evil for which the Communist fellow-travelers can be held responsible— that of giving all dissent an appearance of treason. Thus they make difficult the work of public criticism which genuine liberals must always direct against the errors and shortcomings in their own country's policies, domestic and international. Where for any reason this criticism is suspended, a free culture falls.

The term "fellow-traveler" is derived from the Russian word *poputchiki* meaning "travelers on the same road." It became current in the Soviet Union after the Bolshevik Revolution when the Communists placed a few non-party sympathizers in posts of prestige, without power, to give the impression of popular support. Within a few years the term became an epithet of abuse in the Soviet Union. To be merely a "fellow-traveler" meant to be lacking in complete loyalty to the Soviet and party regime, and therefore to be suspect. The end of the road for all fellow-travelers who did not join the Communist party was exile to a forced labor camp or physical liquidation. At present there are no "fellow-travelers" in the Soviet Union.

In countries outside the Soviet Union, however, and especially in the democracies, they are encouraged and used. Fellow-travelers are an important part of the Communist system of transmission belts by which attitudes favorable to the Soviet Union are carried to all layers of the population. They are absolutely essential for the strategy of infiltration into the commanding places, such as advisory and policy-making posts of professional organizations, trade-unions, organs of public opinion, and—when possible—governmental services. Still more important, they are the organizers and most active supporters of a far-flung network of national and local committees, leagues, councils and conferences which mobilize sentiment in behalf of the Communist line at the moment.

At the moment fellow-travelers in the United States are relatively few and quiescent. Korea and the Hungarian repressions were turning points for many. But as memories fade and new ideological offensives are launched by the Kremlin, it is safe to predict that the will to believe and the will to illusion will reassert themselves among those whose idealism is unfortified by knowledge and whose fanaticism in *the* end dries up the springs of compassion. Our discussion therefore is no mere historical excursion. It has its prophylactic uses in addition to the intrinsic interest of its theme.

Precisely how strong was the influence of the "fellow-travelers" on American thinking? This is hard to estimate, but the Communist Party itself credited them with three great propaganda successes: mobilization of public opinion for a second front when Stalin was clamoring for it; reversal of American attitude toward Mikhailovitch when the Kremlin was grooming Tito; and the transformation of Chiang-kai-Shek from a war hero battling the Japanese to the last ditch into a corrupt war lord betraying the Chinese masses. Dr. Norbert Muhlen, a profound student of the subject, on the basis of a close study of public opinion polls during 1946 concluded: "While fewer than one out of 100 Americans considered themselves Communists, at least seven out of 100 thought approximately as the Communists wanted them to think on topical issues." The magnitude of this performance can best be appreciated when we reflect on the difficult line of ideological goods the Kremlin manufactures for sale abroad. Several highly placed Soviet citizens who defected to the United States after the last war bitterly complained that Stalin had succeeded in implanting the myths about "a free and happy" Soviet Union into more American than Russian minds. But this opinion confused war-time enthusiasm for a valiant ally among naive Americans who did not distinguish between the Russian people and their dictatorial rulers and the beliefs circulated by fellow-travelers that the Soviet Union was a new form of democracy.

There is a much more disturbing indication of the power of the fellow-traveler in organizing public opinion. In 1939 a manifesto circulated by a Communist front organization denouncing Nazi suppression of science and proclaiming that "science is wholly independent of national boundaries and races and creeds and can flourish only where there is peace and intellectual freedom" was signed by 1,284 eminent American scientists. Another manifesto, distributed by the same front organization in the same year, criticizing only Fascist dictatorship, was signed by 2,169 eminent American educators and publicists. In 1949, despite a greater purge of art and science in the U.S.S.R. than any Germany witnessed, barely a handful of scientists and educators spoke out. Some of the leading spirits who had organized the demonstration against Fascist cultural excesses when confronted with the evidence of Soviet cultural terror passed some words of criticism but immediately coupled them with criticism of the United States because of the existence of silly and unenforced laws against the teaching of evolution in three Southern states. Thus Dr. Harlow Shapley, Chairman of the Scientific and Cultural Conference for World Peace, held at the Waldorf-Astoria in 1949, under the auspices of the National Council of the Arts, Sciences and Professions, denounced by Harold Ickes as a Communist Party front, declared: "Science has to be free—in our Southern states as well as in Russia." (*The New York Times,* March 20, 1949.) It is significant and characteristic that in his earlier criticism of Nazi scientific repression he did *not* couple it with criticism of the United States because of the existence of Southern racialism or the presence of these silly laws on the statute books of three states. Previously Dr. Shapley had referred to the purge of Vavilov, eminent Soviet geneticist who died in a concentration camp, and other Soviet biologists, as "demotions."

Who are the fellow-travelers? Here distinctions are essential. Every time a genuine democrat or liberal is called a fellow-traveler; every time a piece of progressive social legislation is denounced as "communistic" there is great rejoicing in Communist quarters. Here as elsewhere one kind of reaction plays into the hands of the other. Public characterization of anyone as a fellow-traveler should not be lightly made.

To identify the fellow-travelers, a study was made by the writer in conjunction with his activities as an officer of the American Committee for Cultural Freedom (an organization opposed to all varieties of totalitarianism) of members of organizations that are clearly Communist fronts, many of them actually labeled subversive by the Department of Justice. The directive for the organization of "fronts" had originally been given by Kuusinen, Secretary of the Communist International. Without concealment he wrote in *The* (American) *Communist* (May, 1931): "We must create a whole solar system of organizations and smaller committees around the Communist party, so to speak, smaller organizations working actually under the influence of our party." There were similar and more recent declarations by Foster and others. Certain well-known criteria for identifying such organizations are used: content analysis of their literature; office personnel; attitude of the party press toward them; and so forth.

For purposes of identification anyone who was a member of at least *twenty* such fronts was considered a fellow-traveler. It was discovered that of the leading hundred fellow-travelers twenty-four were college professors, twenty-one writers and editors, nine actors and producers, eight clergymen, eight lawyers. Six were millionaires.

It is instructive to compare Communist fellow-travelers with their Nazi counterparts, whose existence in their own and other countries should not be overlooked. They came from the best circles. For example, two Nobel Prize winners in physics, Lenard and Stark, were among the hundreds of distinguished German figures who supported the Nazi movement and at one time or another endorsed the policies of the Third Reich. Lenard developed the theory of "German physics," and Stark, his disciple, proclaimed, "Jewish formalism in natural science is to be rejected by all means." Other professors attacked formalism in art. All totalitarian governments tend to be allergic to formalism because it seems to transcend national and class boundaries.

The Nazi fellow-travelers, at home or abroad, were hard men, nationalistic in outlook, and illiberal in social affairs. The Communist fellow-traveler, on the other hand, at the beginning of his career is moved by generous impulses and sympathy for the oppressed. But by virtue of his beliefs he is led step by step to condone outrages which he denounced when committed by the Nazis.

The real fellow-travelers fall into two classes. The first consists of convinced Communists who have not the courage to join the party. Although extremely useful to the Communist party because of their sense of guilt, they are disliked by the rank-and-file members, who cannot live in the same style, and who, whatever else may be said of them, run great risks with little to sustain them except vicarious identification with the "laws of historical necessity" as interpreted by the Kremlin.

This first class of fellow-travelers usually function as executive secretaries of party front organizations, are assigned the most disagreeable chores, and forced into a position of insincerity and duplicity far worse than that incidental to normal concealment of membership. For while acting as a tool of the Communist party, they must go through the motions of speaking independently for the front organization, most of whose members are usually not Communists. In time they become so compromised by their actions that their usefulness to the party is limited. They must then either join up and openly do party work or they are replaced by new figures not so well known.

But by far the greater number of fellow-travelers fall into the second class. They are sincere men and women, and in their own specialized field possess intelligence, not infrequently of a higher order. They hold the following beliefs with varying degrees of intensity:

(*1*) That the Soviet Union is a progressive social order, whose imperfections are relatively minor and transitory.

(*2*) That the United States is a greater threat to world peace than the Soviet Union, which has no interest in fomenting revolution elsewhere but only in cultivating its own resources.

(*3*) That the Communist party is a legitimate part of the great movement of liberal reform, seeking by somewhat different means to achieve ends that are common to all "forward looking" people. The enemy is never on "the left" but always on "the right"—where "left" and "right" are defined not by specific actions and programs but ultimate ideals.

(*4*) That it is desirable to work together with Communists in any good cause or organization, no matter by whom controlled, and that those who are critical of such collaboration are wicked or foolish "red-baiters." (In the vocabulary of the fellow-traveler there is no term like "Fascist-baiter." The term "Fascist" is used synonymously with "reactionary" and sometimes with "conservative.")

Let us consider these beliefs in order. In this day and age to believe that the Soviet Union is a progressive society moving on a course initiated by the French Enlightenment and the American Revolution seems to display a faith invincible to any evidence. The practices of the Soviet regime are eloquent enough. All political freedoms of criticism are absent, strikes are forbidden, disparities in income and living conditions are enormous, the country is honeycombed with forced labor camps with unknown numbers of inmates, science and art are under police control. Soviet citizens until recently were not even free to choose their own wives and husbands if the latter were foreigners.

The fellow-traveler explains this away by pointing to the professed ideals in Communist propaganda. He would scoff at anyone who described conditions in Spain or our Southern states by reference to their Constitutions. But he takes the Soviet Constitution as a kind of Baedeker of Soviet reality.

In this connection a certain technique should be mentioned whose use is quite typical of fellow-travelers. In criticizing any other foreign nation, the fellow-traveler always avoids mentioning our own evils. As soon as the Soviet Union is criticized by others, he promptly brings them up. When urged to protest against evils in both countries, his invariable reply is that we must primarily deal with problems on our own door-step. But just as soon as a Communist protest movement is launched against measures taken by the English, French, Argentine, or Israeli government, the fellow-traveler will maintain that the cause of humanity or of freedom is at stake and that this cause transcends national boundaries. It is only when the outrage against humanity or freedom occurs in Communist countries that we are admonished to mind our own business and clean up our own mess. At the time of the Reichstag Fire Trials, Communist fellow-travelers roused the conscience of their American fellow-citizens. At the time of the Moscow Trials, which were more transparent frame-ups, they denounced the effort to secure a fair trial for the defendants or to discover the truth about the charges. Our task, they proclaimed, is to prevent legal injustices in the United States. Between the two wars, fellow-travelers protested discrimination against students of dissident political faiths in countries of Central Europe. When Czech students were shot down protesting peacefully against the Communist coup in 1948, they were eloquently silent. When the question was raised, they asserted that the academic freedom of American students was their first concern.

How far the human mind can go with this pattern of double-entry moral bookkeeping is evidenced by the outcry of a French Communist brutally and unjustly tortured by French paratroopers in Algeria who at the same time steadfastly defends similar and even worse tortures of innocent men and women at the hands of his Communist comrades in the Soviet Union and other Iron Curtain countries. The fellow-traveler *sometimes* goes as far as this when he condones events such as the Moscow Trials and blood purges. He *always* refuses to condemn them.

A few influential fellow-travelers gradually evolve from the mood of idealism to what they like to call "hard-boiled realism." They will acknowledge the facts of Soviet life but extenuate them as the necessary costs of progress. No price in other people's sufferings seems too high to pay.

It is indisputable that the Soviet regime has some great accomplishments to its credit, but the fellow-traveler never considers whether the tragic costs of some of these successes were really necessary, whether alternative methods, more humane and intelligent, would not have achieved the same result.

How do fellow-travelers come to believe the second proposition which asserts that their own Government is a greater threat to world peace than the Soviet regime? The answer, I believe, is that the fellow-traveling neophyte in politics is completely unaware of the existence of a vast Communist party literature, containing the blueprints of world revolution. In it is the guiding theory, the line of strategy for different situations, and the insurrectionary tactics to be followed by Communists in their bid for power.

I know of no better cure for fellow-travelers, especially if they have a feeling for style—and are not too far gone in their commitment, than a study of these documents. How necessary this education is may be inferred from the insistence of one fellow-traveler, after he had been reluctantly convinced that there was such a thing as the Communist International, that it had no relation whatsoever to the Soviet Government, on the ground that the Soviet Constitution made no reference to it.

There are many legitimate grounds for criticism of United States foreign policy. What initially arouses the fellow-traveler is some ill-advised action against which any patriotic citizen has a right to protest. This is cleverly exploited by his party mentors so that he ends up unqualifiedly endorsing the entire foreign policy line of the Soviet Union.

The most fateful of all the fellow-traveler's beliefs are the third and fourth propositions, according to which the Communist party is a legitimate part of the liberal and labor movement, and therefore acceptable as a loyal co-worker in a common cause. It is by virtue of these notions that fellow-travelers end with compromising, splitting or betraying every liberal organization in which they are found.

Party instructions are explicit on how to ensnare the fellow-traveler. "In a given community," *The Daily Worker* advises (July 16, 1944), "the Communist Club may discuss the problem of child nurseries. . . . Instead of proceeding to initiate such a movement in its own name, it will first contact community leaders of existing organizations and together with them work out a program of action." On a national level, where we find the important fronts, the concern will be with peace or civil rights or aid to anti-Fascist refugees.

The next step is to find some "big name" who half-promises one of the party's cultural liaison men to support the movement for, say, peace. Key figures in various professions are then telephoned and asked whether they wish to join Mr. Big in issuing a common statement. One name calls to another. In a few days the organization is formed, judiciously planted with stalwarts. If Mr. Big is still doubtful, the names of all the others who have been garnered by the use of his name become a powerful inducement to him to make his half-commitment definite. Sometimes Mr. Big is the captive of a fellow-traveling private secretary or of his children.

Once his name is listed, an individual has a vested interest in keeping it listed. There are almost always a few names of individuals whose company he likes to keep. He resists evidence that he has been taken in. No one likes to admit he is naive or has been a fool. To withdraw seems cowardly, as those who solicited his name originally are quick to point out. There is also the hateful publicity attached to resignation. There is no time for active work in the organization and a reluctance to get embroiled in factional controversies. Inactivity seems the best course. Those who seek to enlighten him more often earn his irritation than his gratitude. There is a profound psychology in the directive of the Organization Handbook of the League Against War and Fascism, one of the most successful party fronts: "Inactive individuals whose names command respect in the community may be put on the Provisional Committee if they are willing to lend their names for this purpose." Most front organizations are made up of inactive individuals. But by the time an individual is a member of *twenty* such fronts, he is a willing accomplice. He cannot plead ignorance of his organizational commitments because genuine liberals in an effort to dissociate themselves from the Communist effort to blur the lines of separation have probably informed him of the facts.

Active fellow-travelers are carefully watched by the office secretary and stalwarts. If they go along, involving themselves deeper and deeper in the turns and twists of the party line on peace or war, well and good. If, however, they suddenly rub their eyes, discover that the organization is being run by a tight little party caucus and protest, they are denounced as "trouble-makers," "insincere liberals," and, in stubborn cases, "Trotskyites," or "disguised Fascists," or anything else that raises the dust.

Many fellow-travelers are puzzled and have qualms when the presence and directing control of those under party orders cannot be denied. They say, and often sincerely, "After all, we are using the Communists as much as they are using us, and the cause of peace or free milk for poor children is being furthered." If this were true, a case could be made out for liberals working with Communists, Fascists or any group which at a given moment professes support of a worthy cause. But it is not true.

Here is what happens to a front organization devoted to raising funds for so innocent a cause as "free milk for poor children." First, if milk is distributed at all, it is accompanied by political propaganda. Second, children of anti-Communist parents, particularly if the milk is distributed abroad, don't get it. Third, some night when the meeting is sparsely attended the secretary introduces a resolution condemning American policy in Greece or China or Chile. If one asks what that has to do with free milk for babies, he will be discredited as a reactionary. Fourth, monies raised by the organization will be siphoned off by clever accounting methods to other party fronts and Communist political purposes.

In the end, when the facts come to light, the entire cause of free milk for poor children is compromised. Sometimes, as was the case with the Anti-Nazi Boycott League, the party line changes overnight, and the organization is spiked. Or as was the case with the American League for Peace and Democracy (originally the League Against War and Fascism) in the interest of Soviet foreign policy it is laid to rest. This happened after the Stalin-Hitler Pact.

The most dramatic and conclusive evidence that those who think they can use the Communists are themselves used, that anyone who works *with* the Communists works *for* them, and that the good cause in behalf of which the common front is established is compromised, is provided by Henry Wallace's experience as a candidate of the Progressive party of 1948. This is poignantly revealed in a letter Mr. Wallace permitted to be made public in *The New York Herald-Tribune* of February 14, 1952, to Mr. Herbert A. Philbrick after the latter's revelations about the role of the Communists in the Progressive party. What Mr. Wallace does not say is that he had waved aside both information that the Communist party had taken over the strategic organizational controls of the Progressive party and the prediction that accepting the support of the Communists would hurt his cause.

Dear Mr. Philbrick:

When I wrote you yesterday in care of McGraw-Hill I had had opportunity to read only page 245 of your book entitled "I Led Three Lives." Since then I have read the other references to me as they are indicated in your index and I must say that in the main they seem to me to be both factual and fair. Undoubtedly the Communists had no use whatever for my faith in God and in "Progressive Capitalism." You are correct, it seems to me, in saying that the Communists used their influence against me in the Progressive party. At Center Sandwich, N. H., in the fall of 1948 I recognized the damage which the Communists were doing the Progressive party when I said, "If the Communists would only run a ticket of their own, the Progressive party would gain 3,000,000 votes." Your analysis of the relationship of the Communists to the Progressive party seems to me in retrospect to be essentially correct. They did make a shambles out of a party which could have served a very useful function. They also broke the hearts of liberal, well meaning people who desperately wanted peace but who hated the force, deceit and intrigue for which Communism stands.

Mrs. Wallace and I watched you on television last night and were impressed with your evident sincerity and desire to give the facts in so far as you may have them.

Sincerely yours,
H. A. WALLACE.

South Salem, N. Y., Feb. 9, 1952.

There is no easy way of bringing the honest and sincere fellow-travelers back to the community of American cultural life in which they can play a healthy, critical role as independent minds. They should not be hounded or martyrized but educated. Not only fellow-travelers but all Americans need an education which should make clear that communism is not a progressive but a reactionary movement; and that the alternative to one reactionary movement is not another but a courageous American liberalism.

The fellow-traveler thinks he has an open mind. We must, however, bring home to him the distinction between an open mind and an empty mind. Anyone, and not only the fellow-traveler, who approaches politics without a sense of history, who does not, for example, remember Hitler's cry against encirclement as he prepared to expand, has an empty mind, not an open one. Such people are betrayed by an unscientific, narrow empiricism. Taking one incident after another, now here, now there, they do not observe the *pattern* of aggression as it is built up over the years. Expert as he is in his own field, cautious in drawing conclusions, able and willing to suspend judgment, as soon as the fellow-traveler turns to politics these excellent qualities are not brought into play. Veblen had a name for this failure to transfer training from one field to another. He called it "trained incapacity"—but it does not explain why the transference of training should be so conspicuously absent from politics.

Perhaps a more plausible explanation may be found in a remarkable passage from Lord Bryce's *American Commonwealth:*

The apparent paradox that where the humbler classes have differed in opinion from the higher, they have often been proved by the event to have been right and their so-called betters wrong, may perhaps be explained by considering that the historical and scientific data on which the solution of a difficult political problem depends are really just as little known to the wealthy as to the poor. Ordinary education, even the sort of education which is represented by a university degree, does not fit a man to handle these questions, and it sometimes fills him with a vain conceit of his own competence which closes his mind to argument and to the accumulating evidence of facts. . . . In the less educated man a certain simplicity and openness of mind go some way to compensate for the lack of knowledge. . . . At least in England and America, he is generally shrewd enough to discern between a great man and a demagogue.

This is compatible with the results of the *Fortune* poll at the close of World War II which showed that labor predicted Soviet political post-war behavior far more accurately than the college trained. But it does not explain the popular support, even though transient, for Coughlin, Huey Long, and McCarthy. Labor was more experienced with the ways of Communists.

American liberals should not be frightened off from active support of worthy causes merely because Communists and fellow-travelers profess to advocate them, too. Liberals should work harder than Communists in behalf of all humanitarian goals from free public nurseries to a durable peace with freedom. But they must work independently, cooperating only with groups which have not checked their minds and consciences with the Foreign Office of other countries.

There is plenty for liberals to do in preserving and extending the democratic way of life in the United States, whose existence is ultimately the best argument for freedom throughout the world. The implementing of the Report of the President's Committee on Civil Rights, desegregation in education, housing, transportation and other public facilities, an appropriate curb on filibustering activities which undermine majority rule, an adequate housing program, a program to insure full employment, Federal support of our public educational system where local resources are unavailable—these are some of the items that have high priority on the liberal's agenda of action.

Nor should the American liberal forget that there are other forms of authoritarianism in the world besides Soviet communism, even though the latter is the greatest present threat to free institutions. When he protests the judicial lynching of Cardinal Mindszenty in Hungary he should bear in mind the persecution of Protestant ministers in Bulgaria, Italy and Argentina, the excesses against Zionists in Rumania, and the horrible case of the Asturian miners in Franco's Spain who were hurled alive into a well and then dynamited.

There are some things in the spiritual bequest of Jefferson to American liberals that time and a machine economy have rendered anachronistic. But when Jefferson proclaimed his "eternal hostility to all forms of tyranny" he spoke for all American liberals, past and present.

APPENDICES

The following two letters illumine some aspects of the phenomenon of American Communist "fellow-traveling."

The first (A) is a letter to Thomas Mann who acted as a sponsor for the Cultural and Scientific Conference for World Peace at the Waldorf-Astoria, New York City, March 25 and 26, 1949. This Conference was a follow-up of the World Congress of Intellectuals for Peace at Breslau, Poland, from August 25 to 28, 1948, and was preparatory to the World Peace Congress, organized by the Communist movement, in Paris on April 20 to 23, 1949.

The second (B) is a letter to the Chairman of the Cultural and Scientific Conference for World Peace by another sponsor, the well-known University of Chicago physiologist, Professor Anton J. Carlson.

A. Letter to Thomas Mann

March 14, 1949

Mr. Thomas Mann
Palisades, California

Dear Mr. Mann:

I am writing to you once more about the Cultural and Scientific Conference for World Peace which is meeting at the Waldorf Astoria, New York City, March 25th and 26th. I have been refused permission to present a paper by the controlling group of the Conference. In this paper I wished to defend three theses which seemed to me of the greatest importance to-day.

1. There are no "national truths" in science, and that it is only by its deficiencies that a science can ever become the science of one nation or another.

2. There are no "class truths" or "party truths" in science. The belief that there is confuses the objective evidence for a theory which, if warranted, is universally valid with the *uses*, good, bad or indifferent, that are made of it.

3. The cause of international scientific cooperation and peace has been very seriously undermined by the influence of doctrines which uphold the notion that there are "national" or "class" or "party" truths in science.

Not only have I been refused permission to present a paper at any of the sessions, but I have also been refused permission to lead the discussion at the plenary session. I requested at least fifteen minutes. And this despite the fact that some members of the Program Committee, including Drs. Herbert Davis and Guy Emory Shipler, requested Professor Shapley that I be given an opportunity to be heard.

Since your name is listed as a sponsor of this Congress, I am appealing to you to support my request that I be permitted to read a paper at the plenary session. No arrangements have been made, apparently, by the Program Committee to have the point of view which I represent presented to the Congress. Further, no person who has in recent years ever spoken a critical word against all varieties of totalitarianism, including Stalin's, has been invited to participate in the actual program of the Congress. Neither John Dewey nor Ernest Nagel nor Horace Kallen nor James T. Farrell nor Dos Passos nor Edmund Wilson nor Meyer Schapiro nor scores of others have been invited to this Congress for World Peace.

Professor H. Muller, American geneticist and Nobel Prize Winner, has *not* been invited but A. Oparin, Acting Secretary of the Biological Section of the Soviet Academy of Science who moved to expel Prof. Muller from the Soviet Academy of Science because of his criticisms of Lysenko *has* been invited.

The *New York Times* of March 4th reports the resignation of Professor Irwin Edman of Columbia University from the sponsoring committee of the Congress on grounds that it is designed to promote "the Communist point of view or one closely approximating to it." I sincerely hope that this is not true. But the way this Congress has been organized and my experience with it suggests that it is on the order of Wroclaw-Breslau.

Sincerely yours,

SIDNEY HOOK

P.S.   Since writing the above I have discovered that the Americans who were appointed to the Continuations Committee of the Wroclaw-Breslau Communist peace conference last summer were Dr. Harlow Shapley, Howard Fast, Joe Davidson, and Albert E. Kahn, a notorious card-holding Communist and member of the Executive Committee of the New York State Communist Party. All except Dr. Shapley accepted; all including Dr. Shapley are organizers and sponsors of the Cultural and Scientific Conference for World Peace. Further, I have identified by actual count more than ninety well known fellow-travelers of the Communist Party line in the list of sponsors as published on the official stationery of the Conference.

I am confident that although you are listed as a sponsor of the Conference, your name was procured under false pretenses. At any rate, it seems to me highly desirable for the sake of your own good name to insist that the point of view I have expressed in my paper be presented at the Conference and that a place be made for me on the program. I shall appreciate it if you will send me a copy of your communication to Dr. Shapley. I am asking you to send me a copy of any telegrams or letters you address to the Conference because Professor Edman's letter of resignation was suppressed by the Organizing Committee and he was compelled to make it public himself.

It seems to me that the cause of peace would be better served if independent persons like yourself make the sharpest dissociation from any individuals or groups whose main interest is in furthering the interests of Soviet foreign policy.

B. Letter from A. J. Carlson

March 9, 1949

Dr. Harlow Shapley
Harvard Observatory
Harvard University
Cambridge, Mass.

Dear Dr. Shapley:

I agreed to sponsor the "Cultural and Scientific Conference on World Peace" on your request and on the assumption that it would be honestly scientific, that is, *all cards would be on the table, face up.*

I am greatly disturbed by the report that our outstanding colleague, Dr. Sidney Hook of New York University, has been refused a place on the conference program. The three items (see inclosure) which Dr. Hook offers to discuss at the conference are, of course, fundamental science, if I have any understanding of science. I hope that you see eye to eye with me on this issue, and that you will take steps to put this conference *on the square.* We, men of science, cannot afford to do less.

Sincerely yours,

A. J. CARLSON

AJC/mj
cc: Dr. Sidney Hook
    Mr. Thomas Mann

15 Ideological Espionage

THE CASE OF Klaus Fuchs, the Soviet atomic spy, the arrest and conviction of a half dozen of his American confederates, and the flight of others, made a profound impression at the time on American public opinion. As the fascinating stories of Fuchs and Harry Gold were unfolded, they interested not only psychologists and social scientists but everyone concerned with the preservation of freedom. They led President Truman to send a special message to Congress requesting tighter espionage laws. They also revealed a facet of the Communist movement which those who had judged it only by its ideas had until then largely ignored. Confronted by this peculiar mixture of idealism and treason many were and still are confused.

Some leading American and English statesmen schooled in the traditions of conventional diplomacy, with its stock cloak-and-dagger characters, were at the outset frankly incredulous about the extent and significance of Communist espionage. Officials in Canada scoffed when evidence was brought to them and almost refused to receive it. None of the important leads to what was going on were uncovered by government agencies. It was revealed by defectors from the Communist espionage apparatus at great danger to their very life. If skepticism was so rampant among public officials and political figures, its presence is not to be wondered at among those less active in public life. To this day some American liberals, despite two trials, a mass of documentary evidence, and affirmation of the conviction by the highest courts of the land, cannot bring themselves to believe that "a man like Hiss" could be guilty of betraying state secrets to his country's enemies. Like most decent people, they have assumed that apparent nobility of motive and an impeccable personal life are incompatible with infamous public action. This is a natural sentiment. Nor is it restricted to America. "No man," said the Romans, "suddenly becomes base."

Nothing is so disconcerting as to find one's star boarder or an ideal colleague suddenly charged with a heinous offense that seems utterly out of keeping with his personality. The reaction of Klaus Fuchs' landlady and scientific co-workers to the news of his arrest on charges of acting as a Soviet spy was characteristic. They said it was "an unutterably unbelievable surprise." The landlady described him as "a quiet man and a complete gentleman." Those who worked with Fuchs echoed her sentiments. He was "gentlemanly, inoffensive and a typical scholar." The observations of the intimates of Gold, Coplan, Slack, and others, when the news broke of their arrest, read like an absolute plagiarism of the remarks of Fuchs' landlady.

How explain this disparity between the character of the human beings involved and the character of their work?

The mere fact of espionage, of course, is not new. It is as old as organized human conflict, and there are Biblical references to it. Because of its nature, its history cannot be fully told even when the details are known which, obviously, is rarely the case. Until the twentieth century, however, espionage activities were comparatively unimportant, especially in times of peace. Espionage agents were usually creatures without honor who could be bribed by money, corrupted by women, won over by threats of exposure or promises of protection. The agent himself was always in bad odor—not only with the side he spied on but with the side he worked for. His moral status was worse than that of an "informer," for informers were often ruled by personal motives of hatred and pique, whereas the espionage agent of the past usually could be bought by the highest bidder. He knew what he was doing. It is unlikely that he had a good opinion of himself because of the nature of the things he had to do.

Espionage in recent times has been marked by two predominant features. First, the difference between military and non-military espionage, never clear-cut, has all but disappeared. Industrial and scientific data, as well as information about morale and sympathies of special groups, have potentially great value in a period of total war. Secondly, and this characterizes primarily the nature of Soviet espionage, it has now become largely ideological in the sense that political faith is the animating force of the espionage agent and not considerations of a material kind.

The far-reaching significance of this type of ideological espionage, and the tremendous advantage it gives the Soviet Union, cannot be overestimated. For it operates along different lines from the conventional kinds of espionage the Soviet Union also relies on. Like all countries, it still employs the professional spy and adventurer. But unlike all countries, it fits them, as subordinate links, into an inclusive pattern of politically motivated espionage whose existence and effectiveness is greater than anything previously known.

Chief among the many advantages it gives the Soviet Union is that it has at its disposal an enormous pool of nationals from other countries from which it can recruit agents. Hitler had to rely mainly upon non-assimilated German elements who were already suspect because of their foreign ways. Stalin could call upon indigenous elements who are as much a part of the traditional life of the country in which the espionage is being conducted as any other cross-section group.

Ideologically motivated espionage agents cost much less than others. But of far greater importance is the fact that they are more reliable and more willing to undertake greater risks. Tasks that are too hazardous for the professional spy are eagerly assumed by the political spy. Once indoctrinated with the Communist faith, there is a total dedication of purpose, sometimes to the point of martyrdom, if necessary, in carrying out assigned tasks.

Without discounting the seriousness of the offense in the least, it is none the less important to recognize that ideological espionage originates from a mixture of misguided idealism and Messianic zeal. The individual agent is seldom economically underprivileged to any noticeable degree. But he is usually carried away, at the outset of his career, by an abstract passion for social justice none the less intense for being vague and diffuse. He combines a limitless credulity in the slogans of the Soviet Union with a critical impatience for the slow processes of democracy despite their solid achievements. Or he may take, on their face value, Soviet propagandistic campaigns for "peace" and delude himself into believing that by weakening the potential military power of the Western democracies to defend themselves he is bringing closer the day of universal peace.

During the war these motives were reinforced by the easy rationalization that in revealing secret information to the Soviet Union there was no real violation of national security because the Soviet Union was our ally. By the same logic the revelation of Soviet secret data to its Western allies would have been justified, but the suggestion is repudiated with indignation by the ideological spy. This kind of "cooperation" was strictly a one-way street.

The tendency to set one's self up as a privileged judge of what is required by the national security of one's own country was very marked in the confessions that came out of the Canadian espionage cases and in some of our own. It is not merely a convenient plea employed in hopes of mitigating the severity of the sentence. It revealed the defense mechanisms of individuals reluctant to face up to the necessities of dirty work in behalf of what they felt was a higher cause.

No human being, irrespective of the original high-mindedness of his intentions, can fail to be affected in some way by the means he uses to achieve his goals. When the pattern of duplicity, lying and betrayal becomes habitual, moral sensibilities are gradually blunted and character itself becomes transformed. Not infrequently the idealist becomes a brutal cynic to whom the early ideological rationalizations are ritualistic chatter. After years of activity, these personality changes are observable in all cadres of the Communist party but, judging by recent evidence, the transition from a "gentle idealist" to a man without mercy or compunction is most rapid among those in the espionage underground.

This explanation of motivation is incomplete because it does not distinguish between those members of the Communist party who are engaged in espionage and those who perform more normal political functions. Just as not all Communist espionage agents are technically members of the Communist party, so obviously not all members of the party are qualified to serve as agents. They may, however, occasionally be called upon to perform services necessary for bringing off an assignment without always knowing how they are being used. In a sense this only reflects a shifting division of labor, but there seems also to be present a difference in personality types. Some of those recruited for espionage take up their work eagerly under the mistaken belief that it will bring them closer to the sources of power. Others are satisfied with the buoyant feeling that they are the "elect" or "chosen." But most of the agents are excessively naive persons who at the beginning are not aware of what they are involving themselves in and then find out too late. Or they are strongly romantic and imagine that the life of an espionage agent is a colorful and even a poetic career, a fantasy so far from the actual truth that it is difficult to understand how a reasonably intelligent person could believe it.

Experiences over the years have led the directors of Soviet espionage to insist that those who work for them accept some payment—even a token payment—for their services. Such payment makes it more difficult psychologically for the agent to break with the apparatus later on. At the same time, it often prevents him from passing moral judgment as a pure and disinterested idealist on directives received from the Center. Resignation from the service is not permitted to those who become full-time agents, a realization that often comes belatedly to the recruit who has taken the irrevocable first step.

Another advantage of using ideological espionage agents is their distribution and their availability at strategic points. The distribution is at least as broad as the membership of the Communist party. An engineer in a precision instrument factory, a longshoreman, a clerk in the Justice Department, a wife of a Government official, a research assistant in a physics laboratory—all of them may be strategically important in getting valuable information.

All members of the Communist party are carefully classified in terms of their vocational activity and social connections, and their records transmitted to Moscow. Before any are subsequently recruited for purposes of espionage, these records are closely scrutinized. How systematically this is done is revealed in the documents Ivan Gouzenko took with him when he left the Soviet Embassy in Ottawa, Canada. The report of the Royal Commission published the photostatic copy of the Soviet Embassy dossier on Sam Carr for 1945. After giving his pseudonym "Frank," it adds, "Detailed material on his biography is available in the Center in the Comintern."

One of the great paradoxes of Soviet ideological espionage is its impressive achievements despite the obvious crudities in its organization and its violation of simple rules of security. The best informed opinion seems to be that those who control the espionage Center in the Soviet Union are extremely inefficient as well as indifferent to the fate of those who work for them. Its phenomenal successes are a consequence of the devotion and idealism of its agents abroad. Alexander Foote, a former member of the English Communist party, who was one of the most trusted and valuable of Soviet operatives abroad before he broke, spent two years at the Center in Moscow. In his remarkable *Handbook for Spies,* he writes that the fact that Soviet intelligence continues to function is due "far more to the efficiency of its agents and organizers in the field and the facilities organized by the local Communist parties than to the driving and organizing power of the Center."

Why do ideological agents break? Almost always because of political differences. That is one reason for the absolute taboo against any political activity once the agent is enrolled. There is no conflict of loyalties in terms of national allegiance or patriotism. The real moral struggle, when it occurs, arises only when the agent has begun to doubt the wisdom of Soviet policy. Sometimes this doubt flows from second thoughts about the nature of communism; sometimes from dissatisfaction with the fidelity of the Stalinist line to Communist theory. The very idealism which leads to self-immolating support of communism not infrequently results in disillusionment with the practices of the Soviet police state. This, far more than fear or self-seeking, is the dominant motive of those agents who break publicly.

The actual organization of the espionage apparatus and the techniques of acquiring and transmitting information are closely guarded secrets. They vary with time and are subject to modification in times of war or crisis. But the general features are now clear enough.

There are three separate "firms" engaged in systematic and continuous espionage for the Soviet Union outside its borders—the foreign intelligence of the Red Army, the foreign intelligence of the Red Fleet, and the dreaded M.V.D. (formerly N.K.V.D., G.P.U., Cheka). Of these, the second is the least important, and the third the most authoritative where lines of espionage cross. A resident director heads up the espionage apparatus in each country. Sometimes he is a member of the M.V.D. but more often of the foreign intelligence of the Red Army, since most espionage activity is directed to getting information that bears upon the possibility of successfully waging war against the West. The M.V.D. usually supervises those cases which require counter-intelligence and disciplinary intervention, such as liquidation, kidnapping, and the highly developed art of making murder appear an accident or an act of suicide.

The resident director, through an intermediary or "cut-out," is in touch with the most trusted member of the Political Committee of the local Communist party. The function of this official is to screen, subject to further check, all members of the Communist party, and to send to the Center all information about likely membership prospects or strategically situated sympathizers. When an individual member or sympathizer is selected as a potentially good agent, he is approached through another intermediary who sounds him out on his willingness to perform an important service to the party or to the Soviet Union, "the fatherland of the oppressed."

When he is finally recruited after a series of tests and investigations, the agent in the field has contact with only one intermediary who in turn reports to another who is in direct liaison with the resident director. In a particular country there may be anywhere from two to a dozen rings working independently of each other connected only on the top. They are under orders never to stop working until the resident director is picked up, which has never happened anywhere. Elaborate provisions are made for re-establishing broken contacts in the event that the resident director must flee the country, which has occurred several times. The key figures in re-establishing broken connections are the military attachés of the Soviet Union or its satellite powers.

The life of an espionage agent is difficult. After the adventure and initial enthusiasm have worn off, there is little to compensate him except a lonely sense of self-sacrifice to a mission which has no end until the entire world is Sovietized, and probably not even then. Every agent is told that he holds the rank of officer either in the Soviet Red Army or the M.V.D. This is done not to bring home to him the fact that he is engaged in treasonable activity, for in his eyes it is not treason, but to give him a feeling of vicarious identification with Soviet fortunes and a fear of desertion and its well-understood penalties if he is tempted to "go private."

But these titles in fact mean very little. They are not public. They do not carry with them any material perquisites. Payment is strictly functional—in proportion to the needs of the job or the role the agent must play to get the information wanted.

If the agent is more than an occasional contact man, or if, as an occasional contact man, he has accepted money or gifts, he has no more freedom than the Center is willing to allow him—short of the risks of desertion. He cannot move or change his job without permission. He cannot take a vacation except when convenient to the apparatus. There have been occasions when agents have been forbidden to marry, or when married to raise a family.

The amazing thing is the extent to which instructions from the Center are carried out. Recalcitrance to orders is almost always interpreted as ideological disaffection—although a certain amount of leeway is allowed when women are involved. All agents who have broken are unanimous about the fact that the Center is chary of praise or reward. But there never seems to be a lack of agents.

Where there is reason to believe that an agent has become unreliable or has "gone private" knowing too much, great ingenuity is used by the Center to lure him to the Soviet Union or to a neighboring country where disappearances are easy. Krivitsky, who for some years was in charge of European intelligence for the Red Army, maintained that the readiness with which an agent heeded a call to report personally to the Center was used as an infallible sign of his reliability.

No former agent is safe who reveals what he knows, but he increases his chances of safety by telling everything about his past activities as soon as possible. The M.V.D. will go to great lengths to stop the mouth of an agent who has not yet spoken; but it is loath to risk its liquidation squads merely for personal revenge.

The odd thing is that most agents who have broken do not learn this lesson. They almost always hesitate to tell their whole story: often out of ideological compunction. For not all former agents who hate the Kremlin feel friendly to the West. There is considerable evidence that former agents who have been slain, like Reiss and others, had not told everything they knew, and the Center was aware of it.

How best to meet the dangers of ideological espionage is a difficult problem. It is obvious that there is no need for the amateur sleuth and dilettante conspiracy hunter in matters of such complexity. The greater the spy fever in any community the easier it is for the really dangerous espionage agent to escape detection. Special departments of the Government are probably well aware of the situation, although it is quite clear that no one can cope with it who has not had a thorough political training of an unusual kind. In the long run, however, the most effective way of meeting the threat of ideological espionage is to dry up its sources by public education on the nature of the Communist party. The ill-advised McCarran-Kilgore Internal Security Act is no more appropriate for this purpose than is a pitchfork for ladling water. In fact it is worse than useless because under its provisions we cannot even offer a haven of safety to former Communists whose information about our enemy's designs may be of incalculable value to us.

All educational agencies must stress the truth that no matter what the Communist movement may have once been in ideal and intention, every Communist party today is a passive instrument of one of the worst systems of despotism and terror in human history. Little can be done with those who are now in the Communist movement and who constitute its hardened core. But a great deal can be done to prevent its growth among the young and untried who are its saddest victims.

It is absurd to believe that practical idealism must be wedded to a fanatical obsession with remote goals which require the betrayal of the ordinary decencies of human life. A faith must be judged by what it does to its own adherents as well as by what it does to others. There is implicit in the American ideal of "equal opportunity for all" a revolutionary dynamic sufficient to meet and overcome every domestic challenge to our own ideals. Properly taught, which means critically taught, the democratic faith can win the rational assent and loyalty of every generation of youth before its generous impulses dry up for want of adequate expression. Communism, as we know it today, cannot thrive where a passion for freedom burns in the hearts of men.

No democracy can survive that tolerates conspiracy and espionage in a world that contains powerful nations intent upon its destruction. After Hitler once came to power all the social reforms in the world in other countries would not have prevented him from launching his campaign of world conquest. Obviously, if we stop short only with programs of social reform, it is unlikely that they will have any effect upon the Kremlin's crusade against the West. Yet it remains true that every effort made to improve the quality of our own culture, to give every group a stake, and a fair stake, in increased production and distribution of goods and services and opporunities of welfare, enhances the prospects of democratic survival. Here, as elsewhere, continuous education and continuing social reform, if not the only, are, in the long view, our most formidable defense.

APPENDIX

Statement of Harry Gold

In regard to Soviet techniques for influencing sincere people, I note only my direct experience. It is proposed to—

(*A*) First, detail certain incidents which occurred during my personal association with Soviet agents and in the course of carrying out espionage for the Russians.

(*B*) Then, to show how these incidents fit into an overall pattern. Actually, this chronological sequence was also the manner in which my own awareness came into being, i. e., first the discrete, apparently unrelated, and (on the surface) not too significant events; then the much delayed understanding of their true import.

To begin:

1. Included in the first information on chemical processes which I obtained for the Soviet Union back in 1934–35 were methods for the manufacture of various "industrial solvents"; these chemicals are used in the formulation of a whole host of lacquers, varnishes, and synthetic finishes. I was told, "our people [the Russians] eat off rough, bare boards. You can help them to live a little better, a little more as humans should, by getting us this material." And along with that idea went something else: To get this data I had to steal it from my employer, Dr. Gustav T. Reich, the research director of the Pennsylvania Sugar Co. Dr. Reich was really more than an employer, he was always a kindly mentor, and a friend, to a boy just making a stumbling start in chemistry. So this added up to violating a trust—plus theft. (But none of that meant anything, it is all for a good end. The Pennsylvania Sugar Co. is not being hurt. No one is really hurt, only good is being accomplished.)

2. In February–March of 1937 a violent strike took place at the Pennsylvania Sugar Co. Some 600 men and women stayed in the plant under a state of actual siege for about 5 weeks; at least an equal number were outside. It was worth one's life to try to cross the picket lines; food was brought in by way of the Delaware River using motor launches (the plant is right on the waterfront).

At this time there were some 30 people working in the laboratories, and though we chemists and engineers were not directly involved, it was known from the beginning that we would be used to help operate the refinery, only one of Dr. Reich's staff refused to work—Harry Gold. Now, let it not be supposed that my motives were all pure. On the afternoon that the strike broke in its full fury, I wouldn't remain because I had a "hot date" that very evening; which prospect I was much loath to forego and then I was considerably confused and upset by the circumstance that Dr. Reich, when I made it plain (after some initial wiggling and weaseling) that I would not stay in the refinery, grew terribly angry (he actually banged a water glass so hard on top of the cooler that it cracked in his hand) and said, "You're through! Get out! But you'll never work as a chemist again—I'll see to that."

I got (and ironically enough, as I was crossing the railroad yard in front of the plant, was narrowly missed by a brick hurled by a striker.) Now I was torn two ways: as one who had been reared to believe that being a "scab" in a strike was abhorrent, I was on the other hand faced with being denied further employment in the chemical field—where the Soviet Union wanted information. It was done, all right, but had I chosen the correct course? However, when I told my Soviet boss, a giant of a man known to me only as "Steve," what had occurred, he did not chide me at all. My Russian superior said he appreciated the turmoil through which I had just passed, yet I had to retain my self-respect—which would be forfeit if I worked during the strike. Steve reassuringly said that he doubted Dr. Reich's ability to carry out the blackballing threat and estimated that the research director was not vindictive, just angry. Steve added that even were the worse to come to pass and I could no longer work in the chemical industry, my efforts would still be utilized (in some unnamed fashion). (Here the Soviet Union was being forgiving and understanding, bearing up nobly under a loss—though actually Pennsylvania Sugar had been pretty well looted by this time. If all this sounds fantastically foolish and naive, all I can say is it was another day and age and I am relating it just as the event happened.)

As a matter of record, the union won the strike and one of the provisions of the settlement was that no one be fired for having stayed out; this included the laboratory, even though we never became union members. In fact, Dr. Reich treated me most agreeably when I returned and I rose fairly rapidly in the research setup.

3. In March–April of 1942 I was due to be drafted into the Army. I told my Russian mentor ("Sam," since identified as Semen Markovich Semonov) about this so we could make arrangements for my successor. Frankly, I had expected a "chewing-out," or a plea to use any means to stay out of the service and avoid disrupting our efforts at obtaining technical information. Instead I received a "Go, and God bless you" type of sendoff. The gist of Semonov's remarks was that the Soviet Union (not he, mind you but the Soviet Union) understood my desire to fight fascism (to me fascism was directly equal to anti-Semitism) as a frontline soldier and it was well realized that were I to avoid such duty, I could never again regard myself as an entire man. I ate it up.

Well, when I was rejected because of hypertension (April 20 (?), 1942) I rushed in to the commanding officer (Major Keough?) at the Lancaster Avenue Armory and pleaded to be taken into the Army. He said I was wasting his time. I made two subsequent efforts, first the Navy and then the Marines, but neither would look at a 4–F.

And I was welcomed back by Semenov—a Harry Gold all the more anxious to aid the Soviet Union in its struggle with the Nazis. I was ready to do any bidding, to obey any command.

4. This is a bit difficult to place in time. It did occur somewhere about 1943, but it also took place on many other occasions, both before and after this date; and in more or less the same form. I'm sure this technique was used beginning with my very first contact with a Soviet agent in 1935 (I

started industrial spying for the Soviet Union back in 1934, but did not actually meet a Soviet agent till well over a year later.) Thus, in 1943 I was experiencing difficulty in getting information from Abe Brothman, an American chemical engineer. It was not that Brothman was unwilling to furnish data, but that he insisted on giving what we didn't want (i.e., his own work) and would not supply what we wanted (that is, chemical processes in successful operation in the United States—"successful operation" was defined as "making money" and that, curiously enough, was the Russian criterion: if a plant operated at a profit in the United States, then the exact process used was what the Soviets desired—they refused to hear about any theoretically better, but as yet untried method).

* * * I had made some 3 or 4 trips in 1 week between Philadelphia and New York (after working a full day at the Pennsylvania Sugar Co.) and, on the last of these journeys, I was horribly tired again: Abe had nothing for me. A little later in the evening I met Semenov to report another failure and on this occasion he too appeared weary. We spoke of the inherent troubles in attempting to get individuals to supply technical information and of the many disappointments; of the necessary cajoling and flattering; of the importuning and of the deceit; of the promises never meant to be kept; of the outright threats—when required; of the dreary, but apprehensive, waiting on street corners for appointments never kept; of the whole discouraging business. It was deadeningly—dull, dirty, sullying work Semenov said, and here we were, I a chemist, happiest when working in a laboratory, and he a mathematician and a mechanical engineer, both pursuing a shabby course we only despised, both longing just to be allowed to do the work we liked and for which we were trained. A dismal job, this espionage, but a vital job, one which had to be done, and by implication we were to be commended for sticking with it. Then, one glorious day in the future, Hitler would be destroyed, there would be peace on earth, and no such depressing endeavor would be required. Neat.

5. About this same time, 1943–44, and carrying through to 1945, Semenov and his successor "John" (since identified as Anatoli Antonovich Yakovlev) occasionally would introduce another theme. This related to Semenov leaving America to return to the Soviet Union. But it was not "Goodbye," I was told. Surely, when it was all over, this dreadful war, that is, all nations would be friends again and people could travel freely; then I could openly go to the Soviet Union and in Moscow (yes, this city was special) would renew acquaintance with all my old Soviet "friends" (by which was meant the men who had directed my espionage activities). Oh, we would have a fine old reunion.

And I remember Yakovlev's enthusiasm—early in the spring of 1945— over the impending organization of the United Nations in San Francisco. Actually, the subject came up before I was due to meet Klaus Fuchs in Santa Fe in June of that same spring and Yakovlev was reminding me of the need for early travel reservations what with all the people heading for the west coast about that very time. Please I am not faulting the U. N. here. It is the only hope for world peace. All I wish to point out is the attempt to foist upon me the idea of: "We're all going to be friends forever right soon now. So what's it matter if meanwhile I engaged in a little illegal activity. Just a dab of espionage, huh?" * * *

6. There were a great many other manifestations of the Russian devices for influencing me, some in constant use during the 11 active years of my spying, from 1935 to 1946. I mention just:

(a) If the Nazis triumph, the Jews are done. Extermination. The Soviet Union is the one unyielding opponent of Hitler's fascism. Therefore, anything that strengthens the Soviet Union helps save the Jews. . . . This was in reality the big drive that kept me so resolutely working in espionage. Yes, I'm fully aware of the loopholes in such a stand and I was conscious even then of the illegality of many of my actions, but I continued to put all doubts aside 'til 1946 (when for about 3 years the contract with me was abandoned and I saw no Russians).

(b) Contempt for paid agents: at times I acted as paymaster and I was constantly reminded that, while people who gave information for money were to be valued, Harry Gold, motivated solely by idealism, was a much more laudatory character (and the idea here was not to save a few dollars).

(c) Contempt for the Communist Party of the United States: I was told, "Hah! you call this a revolutionary party? These fools! What do they think they accomplish by standing on street corners and selling the Daily Worker?" (This was a really slick shot, one with plenty of reverse English on it—you see, I was never a Communist Party member, in fact, I always felt a revulsion at the thought of joining it.) The one quote given here, as I recall it, dates from late 1942, when we were having more vexation with Abe Brothman and he kept talking of wanting to give up espionage and go back to the Communist Party.

(d) Open and direct flattery:

Incident 1. Three people are involved. About December 1942 or January 1943, a meeting between Abe Brothman, Semenov, and myself was arranged. It took place in a suite of rooms at the Hotel Lincoln in New York City (45th Street and 8th Avenue?). I introduced Abe to "George" (Semenov) and the latter, as an "important visiting Soviet official," praised Abe's most recent technical data as being equivalent to a "full brigade of men" (or was it "several brigades"? my memory is dimming, and a side note on the care used, viz, the alias "Sam" with me, and "George" with Abe). The real purpose of this rendezvous was to get Abe to abandon his own firm (the recently formed Chemurgy Design Corp., in which he was a partner with two other men, Henry Golwynne and Artie Weber) and renew working for any large American chemical process company, preferably a petroleum refinery—so the Soviets would have the latest American techniques again fed to them (as they had when Abe was employed by the Hendrick Co.). What an awesome respect they had for the technical ability of the United States, and how the Russians worshiped largeness in United States corporations.

Incident 2. This has been given much publicity. It was the award to me of the "order of the Red Star" in about October–November of 1943. Just one point here. In December of that same year I was asked ("asked," mind you) would I accept the most important assignment any agent had ever had, one where I would have to think 3 or 4 times before I uttered any word or made any move, and in January of 1944 I met Klaus Fuchs.

(*e*) The human touch: In the middle of 1942 I was trying desperately to get Abe to assemble some badly wanted information on the design of chemical process mixing equipment. After several fruitless trips to New York on successive days, I met Semenov and told him, "Saturday is it. Abe promised faithfully."

"The hell with him," Semenov stormed. "He [Abe] won't have it ready this Saturday or the next one or for months to come." (An accurate estimate. The material was finally sent to the Soviet Union in November 1942.) Semenov continued, "Look at you! You not only look like a ghost, you are one. What must your mother think? Come." And we went to a quiet restaurant where I had a sandwich and a couple of drinks; then Semenov put me in a cab, took me to Penn Station, and insisted that I buy a parlor-car ticket to Philadelphia, and left me with firm instructions to stay home over the weekend. Nothing really. Just a decent concern (it seemed), and it worked so beautifully with me.

Also, on my part, I was enjoined to be certain that, when I visited any of my sources of information, to regularly bring along a small gift. I was told to give much thought to this matter and to make each gift (be it book, wallet, flowers, candy) reflect a genuine liking and not appear just a routine courtesy gesture.

(*f*) In the very beginning, on the occasion of my first meeting with a Russian contact (about October 1935), this man, "Paul," wanted a "history" of me and my family: all I knew, from my earliest recollections—and going back before my birth to the origins of my father and mother (and their beliefs). Then later, I in turn submitted careful "personality evaluations" on each of my primary (American) sources of espionage data, . . . and I always was given to understand that no decision was made by my immediate superior above (except for the most humdrum items). There was ever the reply, "I'll talk it over with our people." Yes, there must have been a committee.

This ends phase 1 of this writeup, the detailing of certain incidents. There is more that could be related, but to get to, as Somerset Maugham has put it, "The summing up":

The overall pattern is the deceptively simple one of, "Tell 'em what they want to hear"—but because of its obviousness, it disarms and thereby becomes tremendously effective. The simplest and most used idea is to espouse an incontrovertibly decent cause, one really of solid worth and undeniably correct. In my case, the ready-made one of anti-Semitism. Did I have a horror of anti-Semitism? So did the Soviet Union—actively so (as far as the face was presented to me). And, as with a symphony, there are minor themes, all building up to the crescendo of the coda. Such are:

(*1*) Let's start them [the gulls] in a small way, any way at all, but let's start. Have them get the habit of working for the Soviet Union.

(2) Bolster up the [phantom] of the courageous individual who dares disagree, the man of true moral fiber * * * and from there one can easily go on to a lack of respect for the properly established procedures and authority * * * and then, inevitably, to take matters into one's own hands.

(3) Feeding the individual's self-esteem: This appears so plainly a sucker play, that it doesn't ever seem likely to succeed. But see how nicely it was accomplished. Me and my lofty idealism and let's not forget the neat back-spin on the item of contempt for the Communist Party of the United States.

(4) Reaction to kindness: This doesn't have to be anything big or of great moment and, preferably, little, if any, monetary value should be involved. We humans seem to most appreciate the small, considerate, selfless gestures and such an event binds one even closer to the donor.

(5) Where the Russians positively wanted to make certain, they just crashed ahead with blunt, out-and-out flattery. This works too, because a person won't believe that anyone would try such a brash approach. It's as if a man's closest friend were to say (for no apparent reason), "I'm going to kill you," and forthwith does so—the victim would probably laugh and turn his back at just the moment before the tragic event.

The last element in the Soviet structure requires a place by itself, right along with the overall pattern given earlier (it's too important, especially right now, to be relegated to a minor theme status). I refer to the Russians dwelling on the prospect that all nations would live in peace. It's sort of, "Look, Mom, no brass knuckles," gambit. Plus, "See, I smile and make jokes—Ergo, I'm no monster; I'm human." This is the deadliest of all.

But, remember: "Tell 'em what they want to hear."

With this goes also the decision that I was always to regard myself as an American citizen, working under cover for the Soviet Union solely because of the obstructive tactics of industrialists and politicians. Even that much-belabored trip to Moscow carried with it the explicit understanding that I was to return to the United States. The Russians nurtured this idea most carefully: Harry Gold—loyal American. To me the true horror underneath "buying" the Soviet way of life resides in the inevitable, completely inexorable demand for a payment—but the currency in use is the human soul and there is the awful corollary, the fact that a man becomes willing, even eager, to do any bidding, no matter how loathsome.

I am aware that the portrait given here of my reactions to the Soviets' maneuvering of my personality is delineated in harsh strokes. Looking back, as I said before, it does seem as if it were another day, another age, almost another world. Yet I know what occurred and what I did.

HARRY GOLD, *No. 19312.*

Lewisburg, Pa., July 27, 1957.
Entered into the record of the Hearings Before the Senate Internal Security Subcommittee, August 15, 1957.

16 The Problem of the Ex-Communist

ACCORDING TO reliable estimates, approximately three quarters of a million Americans have at one time or another been members of the Communist Party. This is about ten times as many as have ever been members at any one time, and a much larger number than have ever voted for open Communist candidates. For different reasons these ex-Communists are a source of profound concern both to Communists and non-Communists. To the Communists here and abroad they are objects of fear, rage, and contempt. To the non-Communists, they are a puzzling phenomenon, provocative of mixed reactions which are likely to be strong, emotional, and undiscriminating.

The reaction of Communists to ex-Communists is not hard to understand. Except for those who dropped out of the Party merely because of excessive demands made on their time and energy, no other group is so immunized against the virus of Communist conspiracy. No other group knows so much about it. No other group has done it so much harm. They are the first to be destroyed wherever the Communists come to power.

Normally the enemies of our enemies are welcomed as our allies. But not in this case. Although ex-Communists as a rule serve as black snakes in relation to the Communist rattler, the non-Communists are far from friendly to them. This is sometimes a tepid understatement: there have been many occasions in which non-Communists have refused to make any distinctions at all between them and have damned ex-Communists as a species of Communists.

There is a wry truth in an apocryphal anecdote of a meeting at which General Clay, recently returned from Berlin, was scheduled as chief speaker, and which was invaded by Communists. They had come early, filled the front rows, and tried to break up the meeting. A large group of democratic workers, mobilized from the New York garment center, rushed to the hall only to find the entrance blocked off by the police. "Officer," pleaded one of the original organizers of the meeting, "let us in. We are the anti-Communists."

"I don't care what kind of Communists you are," came the reply. "Communists can't go in!"

The ex-Communist is a phenomenon that has always attracted more attention in the United States than in Europe, where his existence is taken for granted and he is judged by present performance rather than by past allegiance. Malraux in France, Silone in Italy, Spender in England, Plivier in Germany, are among the better-known figures who, having broken with the Communist movement, have taken their place among the defenders of the open society without offering humble apologies for their former lives or expecting acclaim as prodigal sons. And on the whole they have been treated neither as heroes nor villains but as individuals.

The most gallant figure in the West-European struggle for freedom in recent years was Ernst Reuter, mayor of Berlin. He was once a Communist but no German McCarthy ever threw that up to him, even though on occasions Reuter would say it was not so much he who had changed as the Communists. On the other hand there have been Communists like Jacques Doriot who on breaking became collaborators of the Nazis.

Ideologies have always been treated more seriously in Europe than on this side of the Atlantic. Nonetheless there is a certain refreshing, common-sensical attitude taken by Europeans toward former Communists. It is based on an appraisal of their dignity as human beings, on whether they talk sense or nonsense, whether they are driven by desire for revenge or gain, whether they permit themselves to be used as tools in the hands of a politician's drive for power, and whether their testimony of disillusion has the ring of authenticity.

Unfortunately the same cannot be said of the attitude toward ex-Communists in the United States. And this despite the fact that one of our most vital democratic traditions is to judge a person not by his origins or past beliefs but by his achievements and the present direction of his thought. In the supercharged atmosphere of the cold war, the problem of the ex-Communist like the problem of the Communist has become a political football. Different political camps seem to have posted signs reading *Wanted: Ex-Communists Only if Useful*—useful either to prove that the New Deal was a willing host to Communist conspirators and subversives, or to prove that the Communist Party was only a harmless social club whose ideas accidentally paralleled those of the Kremlin.

The result has been that such elementary and necessary distinctions have been ignored as the distinction between members of the Communist Party and functionaries; between casual fellow-travelers, who were never members and who long since have turned away in disgust from the Communist associations to which their generous-hearted impulses once led them, and hardened collaborators who suddenly proclaim themselves ex-Communists when the glaring light of exposure focuses on them and who revert to customary ways when the light shifts. An ex-Communist who speaks the truth is invariably denounced as an "informer" by those who find these truths unpalatable or embarrassing to them. On the other hand, let him regale a Congressional Committee with unsubstantiated fantasies and he becomes an infallible "authority" in the eyes of those who wish to make political smear-capital out of it.

Just as in ages gone by professional anti-Semites would have their favorite Jew, so today different groups of anti-Communists have their favorite ex-Communists. One group's "high authority" is the other group's "base informer." Even among ex-Communists there are feuds and recriminations depending on the vintage year of their break with the Communist movement. Usually the earlier the year the greater the degree of self-righteousness, but not always. Not so long ago a leading collaborator on a top level with the Communist-organized League of American Writers, who had remained mute even after the Hitler-Stalin Pact of 1939, sought to pillory as a Communist fellow-traveler the poet, Max Eastman, because of the latter's associations, long since renounced, in the early twenties.

The upshot of all this has been a growth of hostility on the part of the American public to all ex-Communists irrespective of their present character, credibility, and allegiance. As one former Communist, a novelist who had been a professor, put it recently: "I was less condemned for being a Communist than I am now for being an ex-Communist."

This explains why, although approximately three quarters of a million Americans have at one time or another been members of the Communist Party, comparatively few ex-Communists have identified themselves in the public eye. The social penalties for disclosure about past membership are heavy, and many avenues of employment are barred to them irrespective of the period, grounds and circumstances of their break with the Communist Party. An ex-Communist has almost as difficult a time getting a government job as a Communist, even if because of his experience he is in a much better position to combat Communism.

When we discuss the question of ex-Communists, there flashes before our mind a limelighted figure testifying in Court or before a Congressional Committee. But these are rare and special cases. They do not represent the actual situation or history of the overwhelming majority of ex-Communists who, although they would once have been willing, never enjoyed positions of leadership or played seemingly romantic but actually grim roles in the underground.

What should our attitude be toward former members of the Communist Party as distinct from those who are alleged to have been only former "fellow-travelers"? What role should ex-Communists have, if any, in the public life of a democracy? Shall we treat them as prodigal sons whose testimony can be used to glorify the democratic institutions which made it possible for them to survive and learn the error both of their faith and works? Or shall we spurn them as traitors *manqué,* as tamed fanatics, cowards who lacked the guts to persist in an infamy so black that no river of confession can wash them clean? Or shall we ignore completely their political past, pretend it never existed, give them access to jobs of confidence or trust on the same terms as their less erring fellow-citizens? Or shall we suffer their presence, as one ex-Communist, Mr. Deutscher, suggests, on the sole condition they keep their mouths shut on matters political? Or is there a more discriminating and intelligent way of handling the issues? These questions cannot be answered unless we keep certain facts clearly in mind.

Once individuals join the Communist Party, they are subject to a careful winnowing and disciplining process so that in time, if they remain in the party, their modes of thought and feeling, and especially their behavioral responses, become very similar. Although individual differences never disappear, it is possible to predict with considerable accuracy the behavior of present and active members of the Communist Party at any definite moment in a given situation. That is why it is a reasonable and completely justified policy to exclude them from certain posts, in and out of government, even though there is no mathematical certainty that all members of the Communist Party will carry out their instructions.

Once individuals leave the Communist Party, however, they revert to a pattern of behavior almost as individualized as other members of the community. The differences that set them off from others are the result of the traumatic shock of cutting themselves loose, or being expelled from, an institution around which they had organized their entire lives, and served with a fervor and dedication more complete than that with which most individuals serve their church. One cannot make reliable predictions about how they will behave, except that at the beginning they tend to run both from themselves and from others. They either cultivate a purposeful forgetting and blot out the memories of their own naiveté and credulity, or recast the past so as to appear to themselves as victims or heroes of history. Oddly enough, judging by the record of individual cases, it is psychologically much easier to join the Communist Party than to break with it on any grounds whatsoever. The break seems always to be a time of anguish and of deep soul searching. Some individuals carry the stigmata of the experience for years. Threatened by the social ostracism of the non-Communist world if he publicizes his break and thus reveals his past membership, and hounded often by agencies of the Communist Party which secretly denounce him to his employers as still a Communist, the ex-Party member is often overwhelmed by a feeling of being lost, of spiritual loneliness. If he is not too well known, he seeks to ease his mind and conscience in an underground of anonymity until he comes to terms with himself.

More important than the psychology of the ex-Communist is his political thinking after he recovers from the shock of his political rebirth. The evidence shows that there is no such thing as *the* politics of the ex-Communist, for ex-Communists are divided among all the colors of the non-Communist spectrum. Some are liberals, some democratic Socialists, some are Democrats, some Republicans. Some eschew politics but rarely for long. Some of the most ardent supporters of Senator McCarthy were ex-Communists, but so were some of his earliest and bitterest critics. Those who overlook the extreme variations in the thinking of ex-Communists tend to generalize from a few conspicuous illustrations. The Communist generalization that most former Communists embrace the fanaticism of some other totalitarian creed or party is false. Most of them return to an earlier form of liberalism.

The most fundamental division among ex-Communists today, regardless of their political labels, is between those who still believe that the ideals of social justice, progress, freedom, and scientific intelligence, which led them mistakenly to embrace the Communist Party, are still valid; and those who believe that the historical degeneration of the Communist Party and the emergence of the Soviet Union as the completest and most tyrannical despotism in history establish the bankruptcy of the liberal philosophy, the alleged parent of the ideology of communism. Both groups face difficulties. The first cannot give a plausible account of their egregious error without convicting themselves of serious political incompetence. Genuine liberals should have anticipated the kind of crop which would develop from the seeds planted by Lenin and Stalin. The second group cannot explain why the liberal philosophy did not lead to dire totalitarian consequences in any country except where Communists or Fascists, who were emphatically not liberals, seized power and destroyed democratic institutions.

It should now be clear, assuming no question arises about the sincerity of ex-Communists, why a uniform policy towards them is unwise even if it were feasible. The ex-Communist is as he believes and does. No obstacle should be placed in the way of his returning to the free community. But his experience does not automatically qualify him as an expert on the best way to save democracy. It goes without saying that he is a better citizen as an ex-Communist than he was as a Communist, but it is sometimes overlooked that the best citizens have been neither Communists nor ex-Communists. It would be inhuman, not to say undemocratic, to shut the gates of compassion and understanding in the face of someone who has made the awful discovery that the "workers' democracy" of Communism is in reality the equality of forced labor. Nonetheless we must guard ourselves against sentimentality and insist that a decent period of reflection and re-evaluation follow the burial of dangerous illusions. Overnight repentances are shallow and not always lasting. The fact remains that the ex-Communist, whether out of defect of heart or intelligence or both, was once an enemy of the democratic society which nurtured him. This is especially relevant if he was a leader or official and cannot plead naiveté. He bet on his hunches against our liberties and lost. He may find consolation in the ironical truth that only in the open society he sought to destroy can he quit the Communist Party without being liquidated. He is in luck that his cause did not triumph. Even the unrepentant Earl Browder must bless his stars that he is an American. How much more so the repentant Communist. Had he been a citizen of the new Soviet "democracies," he would now be a corpse.

If no permanent bars should be erected against the ex-Communist, not even temporary ones should fence out the former fellow-traveler from the democratic community or even from branches of the government for which his training qualifies him. A fellow-traveler is someone who on occasions either agreed with the Communists or participated in their front organizations. Their number is legion. Leaving aside the fact that the Communists sometimes supported good causes, for their own nefarious political purposes to be sure, the right to be wrong, to make honest mistakes, especially when the mistakes are acknowledged, is part of the birthright of every American citizen. It is easy to have twenty-twenty hindsight. More significant than the errors of the former fellow-traveler are his courage and willingness to acknowledge that he has made them. For the latter are a sign of political growth and maturing and make future lapses less probable. To penalize the former fellow-traveler precisely when he knows better and is on guard against further snares is a gratuitous folly, much worse than the wholesale condemnation of the ex-Communist Party member with whom we are here mainly concerned.

The English are a traditional people; but they never let a man's political past stand in the way of his political service in the present if his gifts fit him for urgent work at hand. John Strachey was once a follower of Oswald Mosely, the British Fascist, and subsequently an even closer fellow-traveler of the English Communist Party. Nonetheless, when he clearly broke with both he ended up as Secretary of War in the Labour government.

To the community the chief value of the ex-Communist is the knowledge he has of the myriad ways in which the Communist Party functions in its never ceasing activities to undermine society. He can supply information, sometimes very valuable, on the points of successful infiltration. The more discreetly and quietly it is given, the more likely is it to be helpful. Pressure put on him by some government officials and Congressmen to make public recantation and public identification of his erstwhile fellow-members is unwise. At best it is an unedifying spectacle, and, if repeated to a point where the ex-Communist becomes a professional witness, tends to discredit him even if his testimony is accurate. If an ex-Communist has useful information, it should be possible to get it without glorifying him or holding him up to obloquy. Those who would refuse to listen to him and reject information that may help us in our war for survival, or who say, "If there is anything worse than a Communist, it is an ex-Communist"—which they never said of Fascists—are either Communist sympathizers or simply lack mother-wit.

The former Communist knows, as no other can, that the Communist Party means business, deadly business, especially when it puts on a smiling visage for innocents and dupes. His most frustrating experience is to encounter incredulity, and sometimes abuse, when he warns the intended victims or tools of Communist intrigue that they are being used for purposes which in the end will encompass their destruction. He sometimes exaggerates and grows frantic somewhat in the way a lineman might when he sees someone reaching for a live wire at a distance just beyond the range of his voice.

Few ex-Communists talk, and as a rule only when their refusal to talk threatens to be more prejudicial to their future than their willingness to do so. It is a little unreasonable to expect, as some ritualistic liberals do, former Communists to permit themselves to be jailed on grounds of contempt of Court or Congress for refusing to answer questions about the Communist Party in whose eyes they are fit only for liquidation. It is a very eloquent commentary on ritualistic liberalism that it is much more hostile to former Communists than to those who remain faithful to their dogma and party.

But when they do talk are ex-Communists reliable? How can we control the truth of what they say? How can we discount, or safeguard against, personal vindictiveness? How do we even know that they are not really plants or secret agents of the Communist Party seeking to demoralize us? Senator Fulbright once wondered whether men like Chambers and Budenz were still not secret Communists.

To take the last question first. No secret agent would publicly denounce the rulers of the Kremlin, not only because this violates the Communist "holy of holies," but also because the Party could never be sure that its agent didn't really mean it. The agent himself would be mad to provide the verbal evidence for his subsequent purge as a double-agent. This may be hard to believe for those who have not closely studied the documents of the Communist movement, but members have been dropped from the Communist Party who to all intents and purposes were sincerely criticizing Trotsky, Norman Thomas, or the enemy of the moment, on the ground that they were quoting too extensively from the writings of the devil and in this way secretly propagandizing for him. The Communist Party and its masters in the Kremlin do have their secret agents, but their task is always of such a nature that it requires them to lie low. They do not have to make exaggerated and irresponsible charges about the extent of Communist penetration into government services because this demoralizing work is done for them as a free gift by some political demagogues, of whom McCarthy was only one, and some mindless anti-Communists.

The more difficult questions are raised, not by the fanciful hypothesis of the double agent, but by the degree of credence we should extend to the genuine ex-Communist. Common sense should tell us that no one is infallible, that memories vary in their retentiveness, that a perfectly coherent story may be false, and a slightly inconsistent one substantially true, that in the end we must size up a witness somewhat in the way jurors do. But common sense must be fortified by knowledge of how the Communist Party is organized, how it functions, what it instructs its members to do. For much of this knowledge we are not dependent exclusively on the ex-Communist. It is available in the official literature. But the ex-Communist can offer to supply crucial details.

The first thing to remember is that it is the Communist Party member who is under official instructions to commit perjury when it is in the Party's interest, and not the ex-Communist. Many Communists have been convicted of perjury, and were it not for the protection given them by the Fifth Amendment, undoubtedly many more would be convicted.

It was fear of prosecution for perjury if they lie and contempt if they remain silent which led so many Communists to invoke the Fifth, although the converse is not necessarily true. So far there is only one case in which an indictment of perjury was brought in against an ex-Communist who identified a man who was at most only a fellow-traveler as an actual member of the Communist Party. His subsequent history suggests that he was a psychotic. Other charges of perjury have been made against ex-Communists, but so far they have not been substantiated. There probably are cases of genuine confusion of identity, or of identifications made on the basis of insufficient evidence, in which although not guilty of perjury an ex-Communist may be mistaken. Members of the Communist Party have a penchant for exaggerating their successes in reporting to each other and to their Party superiors. An individual will be told by a fellow-member that "X," active in some Party front organization, is "one of us." When the individual who has received this information leaves the Party, he will be sincerely convinced that "X" is actually a member of the Communist Party, although his only evidence, aside from his Communist front activities, is an identification by another Communist. On the other hand, when testimony is not of this hearsay character but based on personal knowledge it may prove extremely valuable.

That an ex-Communist says something, doesn't therefore make it so; neither does it make it *not* so; nor is it suspect merely because he says it. The whole context must be considered, particularly the number of times past identifications have been confirmed or not confirmed by supplementary testimony and documentary evidence. Patient investigation buttressed by knowledge of what is relevant will usually confirm or deny any man's story. Neither patriotic fervor nor the hand-wringing of hysteria-mongers who deny that some things could be true because if they were, "it would be awful!" help the process of inquiry.

Why do not even more members of the Communist Party break away as its ties to the Kremlin become exposed, and why do not more of those who break away reveal what they know? The testimony is almost unanimous on the part of ex-Communists that the Communist Party seeks to punish those who wish to escape from it. Since large sections of the community do not distinguish between the Communist and the ex-Communist—"once a Communist, always a Communist" runs one foolish slogan—anonymous denunciation of former members of the Communist Party is a potent instrument of intimidation.

When ex-Communists speak soberly and responsibly, democratic society can learn a great deal from them, both positively and negatively, about the psychology of conversion, the attraction of the Communist myth, the techniques of political infiltration, and the most effective educational remedies to apply. One of the best methods of keeping down membership in the Communist Party without any police measures whatsoever is to keep open the avenues of employment for those who have been members of the Communist Party, once it is clear that their desertion is not a matter of personal convenience to ride out a storm but is genuine and principled. In addition to some influential trade unions who set the lead in this respect, some churches have accepted the ex-Communist as a human being on the same terms as others. But having fled from what they regard, rightly or wrongly, as a political church, most ex-Communists are not likely to embrace another church, or to accept any source of spiritual authority except their new and hard-won faith in free intelligence and autonomous morality.

The world has certainly changed a great deal since the time when some of these ex-Communists, impatient to abolish the social evils around them, and left defenseless and ignorant by an education which gave them no insight into the still greater evils of Communist practice, thought that joining the Communist Party was testimony of their seriousness about helping their fellow-men. Frustrated idealists, some have become egocentric and politically indifferent cynics. But a whole library of literature seems to suggest that most of them, like people who have been disappointed in love but still have a deep capacity for loving, long to serve in the struggle for freedom, and all the more resolutely because of their tragic and mistaken choices in the past. Their early idealism is now more reflective. It is purged of its Machiavellianism and the impulse to improve other human beings against their will, and tempered by the knowledge that a Utopia laid up in a Platonic heaven may be a better guide to progress on earth than one believed to be just around the historical corner. To bar them from employment, not to avail oneself of their talents and experience, seems absurd on every count.

Learning about the past from ex-Communists and listening to their suggestions about the present is one thing. Leaning upon them as guides to the future is quite another. It certainly does not follow that a democratic society must necessarily look to ex-Communists for *leadership* in the political struggle against Communism, and in devising the positive programs required to meet the threat of the Soviet challenge. For as we have seen, the ex-Communists politically by no means agree among themselves. Rarely, as in the case of Ernst Reuter, have they the stature and moral authority to inspire wide confidence.

In their interesting book on the ex-Communists and Communism, Ernst and Loth quote a former Communist as saying that "Ex-Communists and those fellow-travellers who studied Marxism-Leninism-Stalinism are best equipped to combat Communism." This is especially true on the operational and organizational level for the same reason that an ex-poacher makes a good game warden. On the political and theoretical level, however, it is possible for those who are not, and who have never been, Communists to study and master the ideology of the enemy. Intelligent ex-Communists may make intelligent advisers, but their advice must always be weighed in the light of a positive social and political faith which has sources other than a disillusioned Marxist-Leninist and the negations of sectarian ideology.

PART THREE . . . Problems

of

Security

and

Freedom

17 The Fall of the Town of Usher:

A Political Fantasy

THE HISTORY of the Town of Usher was hard to reconstruct from its ruins. Only when some manuscript scrolls, dug up from the silt that covered an old well, had been deciphered, was it possible to get a coherent account of the last years of the town, whose very existence had been previously unsuspected. The Chronicler was obviously a participant in the events. Although there was no way to check up on his bias, the fact that he seems to have been on the inside of things, that he is temperate in his judgments of those with whom he disagreed, that he makes no claim to omniscience but actually seems puzzled by what overtook his beloved town, and finally that he has a sense of humor, lends a certain credibility to his story. This credibility is enhanced by what has been observed in other cases in recent history.

The Town of Usher, situated on a plateau on the highest ridge of rolling country, was impregnable to any kind of frontal attack. That is why it had survived the periodic waves of invasion in which the barbarian hordes from the South, led by able and crafty commanders, laid waste the countryside, killing the men and enslaving the women and children. At the time the narrative begins, a new Southern chieftain had come to power who relied more upon ruse and stratagem than violence to gain his ends. He sent emissaries to the Town of Usher offering an alliance on the sole condition that his own troops be permitted to man the strategic places so that the town could be more effectively defended against a still bigger tyrant who, the Southern Chieftain warned, was on his way with almost irresistible forces from the North. Until that time, no one had heard of this bigger tyrant. Most of the countries to the North were inhabited by uncouth tribes whose rude chieftains perpetually squabbled with each other.

Opinion in the town was overwhelmingly opposed to such an alliance or to any of its conditions. Particularly so, since memories were still alive of the duplicity of earlier invaders, which had resulted in the destruction of neighboring towns. Nonetheless, there were some trusting souls who believed in the existence of the new tyrant in the North and who proposed to capitulate in the hope that the Southern Chieftain would live up to his promises. The latter, however, did not attempt to force the issue. Over a period of years, he invited several disgruntled members of the town to his camp, banqueted them, plied them with gifts, extended even a conjugal hospitality to them—strange but not unpleasant to those accustomed to the strict monogamy of Usher culture—and offered to deputize them as trusted lieutenants. His most persuasive argument was that, in accepting this role, they would be serving not only themselves or him but also the ultimate welfare of their kin, their friends and the good townsfolk of Usher. Those who accepted were sworn to utter secrecy, given the names of their fellow-townsmen who had also accepted, and trained in the use of certain codes and techniques of operation for different types of situations that might arise. Those who refused this role were told by the Chieftain, with an air of admiring wonder, that he had been unable to induce anyone in the Town of Usher to act as his deputy. Never, he said, had he met such incorruptible patriots.

Meanwhile, in the town itself, because of the increasing rigors of life which the burden of preparation and defense entailed, a number of well-meaning and perfectly loyal citizens began to urge that official negotiations with the Southern Chieftain be undertaken. They called themselves the Party of Good Will. They argued that there might conceivably be a still greater tyrant in the North, that nothing that the Southern Chieftain could do would be worse than what would befall the town if this tyrant triumphed, and that the lessons of history, although instructive, were not decisive. They asserted that it was not necessary to yield to all the demands of the Southern Chieftain, that reasonable people could always find a compromise. They also pointed out that if all the time, energy and resources which were being invested in the frenzied search for new weapons and methods of defense were devoted to civilian pursuits, not only would the Town of Usher prosper but the Southern peoples, too. When this happened, they predicted that there would be no need of soldiers, of catapults, battering rams and all the paraphernalia of war. A new era would dawn. Needless to say, the deputies of the Southern Chieftain joined this group in a body and told everyone that what it was saying was true, only more so.

Now things began to happen which, according to the Chronicler, were new in the history of the Town of Usher. Those who were deputies of the Southern Chieftain seized every opportunity to advance themselves to key roles in the governing and defense agencies of the town. As soon as they came across plans, they would copy them and send them to the Southern Chieftain through most ingenious methods. Ropes were cut, wells polluted, food stores spoiled, certain houses fired. No one was ever apprehended committing those acts and an influential school of thought proclaimed that these were a series of unusual, but not unnatural, coincidences. But as the continued communications from the Southern Chieftain began to show a striking familiarity with what was going on in the town, the disposition of its forces, the details of its administrative measures, the people became apprehensive. It was soon said that the Southern Chieftain was the best informed man on what was going on in Usher.

From time to time, one of the members of what we today would call the Southern Chieftain's fifth column, frightened by what he observed on visits to the Southern encampment, broke away and revealed what he knew. But corroborative testimony was difficult to obtain. Since such individuals were self-confessed traitors, little credence was placed in what they said and they usually came to a bad end. They died by accidents that looked to some like murder, to others like suicide. Whenever these revelations were made, someone whom the Southern Chieftain had vainly tempted to become his deputy was almost always sure to come forward and recall that the Southern Chieftain himself had bemoaned the incorruptibility of the citizens of Usher. Those who believed this testimony and who also believed that the Southern Chieftain was telling the truth—he had a genial manner and warm eyes and smile—were naturally inclined to believe that the allegedly repentant fifth columnists were making their story up out of whole cloth, and that they were either, again to use current terms, psychotics or exhibitionists. Some townspeople who had been recruited by the fifth columnists never had seen the Southern Chieftain or visited his headquarters. They joined the Party of Good Will as part of a fraction controlled by the leaders in touch with the Southern Chieftain, but they sincerely regarded themselves, even when ready to engage in subversive actions, as loyal members of the Party of Good Will, only more advanced. They called their fraction the Caucus of the Better Will.

A reaction soon manifested itself, particularly when an emissary from the Southern Chieftain was found with detailed written instructions to do all sorts of mischief—instructions which he tried desperately to destroy at the cost of his life. The Southern Chieftain denounced these instructions as obvious forgeries of the Tyrant from the North, and called attention to his own official messages to the townspeople of Usher, which uniformly breathed friendliness and good will to all of them except their misguided leaders. But the circumstantial evidence was too damning and the Town Council, dominated by a middle-of-the-road group which had always been a little distrustful of the naive idealism of the leaders of the Party of Good Will, undertook to strengthen the town of Usher by cleansing its government and defense services of the members of the Caucus of the Better Will. Since no one in such positions would confess to membership in this Caucus, the Council sent out its own agents to join the Caucus and to discover who was who. It also secretly dispatched some individuals to contact the Southern Chieftain and to pretend to join him. None of these were ever heard of again, so it was presumed that the wily Chieftain had a trusted agent in the highest councils of the town.

As the evidences of danger began to multiply, a large and noisy group began to protest what they called the coddling policy of the Council of Usher. The Chronicler's sense of humor is apparent in the peculiar names—obviously nicknames—he gives the leaders of this group: McRuth, McRath, and McPurge. They denounced all members of the Caucus of the Better Will as traitors; all members of the Party of Good Will as potential traitors; and the ruling middle-of-the-road party as "muddle-roaders," which is the nearest equivalent to the archaic pun the Chronicler uses. (The expression he uses is literally translated as "muddle heads buried in muddled roads.")

Even before this outburst, the Party of Good Will had called a protest meeting against the policy of the town government in ordering the dismissal of members of the Caucus of the Better Will from strategic services. The Chronicler dubs the leaders of the Party of Good Will—again with a play on words—McMushy, McWordy and McSappy. They argued that the real cause of the difficulty with the Southern Chieftain was the hysteria in the Town of Usher. They asserted that the cause of the hysteria was the alleged revelations of his intentions by those who allegedly had been members of the Caucus of the Better Will. They did not deny that what was said about the Southern Chieftain *might* be true. But there were some things that were worse than the role of the Southern Chieftain—for example, the rule of the Tyrant of the North. Bad as the Southern Chieftain might be, the Town of Usher should not imitate him.

At this point, they become most eloquent. To dismiss members of the Caucus of the Better Will from positions of defense and strategic Government services *before* they had committed acts of treason was morally just as bad as behaving in the way the Southern Chieftain allegedly behaved toward those who, for any reason at all, incurred his displeasure.

He threw them and all members of their family to specially trained wild beasts, which tore them to pieces. This treatment was just as bad as the dismissals in Usher, because in both cases the families had to suffer hardships for the problematic guilt of individual members. In the Town of Usher, families suffered from the loss of the employment of a member who—traitor or not—might be their only breadwinner; in the domain of the Southern Chieftain, families lost their lives. Superficial people who thought the differences more significant than the similarities ignored the fact that life was impossible without bread, and therefore breadwinners.

McMushy, McWordy and McSappy protested that they were just as much opposed to treason and conspiracy as McRuth, McRath and McPurge. They argued that members of the Caucus of the Better Will should be dismissed from Government service only *after* they had committed acts of treason. They were even willing to increase the severity of such laws if only they were applied *after* such acts were committed. To the argument made by the "Muddled Roaders" that this was locking the stable after the horse was stolen, that the function of the measures taken by the Council was to prevent disloyalty and not to punish it, and that it was more humane to punish a declared conspirator by depriving him of the opportunity to betray the city than to punish him by taking his life after he succeeded—to all this the leaders of the Party of Good Will replied with scorn and rhetorical vigor.

First—they ticked the points off on their fingers—they were not convinced that each and every member of the Caucus of the Better Will (for whom, understand, they held no brief) was a conspirator. It was a fact that the Caucus officially denied the charge as a malicious libel circulated by McRuth, McRath and McPurge for their own ulterior purposes. Second, without assessing the rights and wrongs of these charges and counter charges, the fact that a man declared his intent to commit treason did not mean he would necessarily commit it any more than a man who comes all prepared to cheat at a gambling game necessarily cheats. Intent is by no means an index to action, they declared. How often did even the worthy members of the Council, when chasing their children for some mischievous prank, threaten to break their legs when they caught them? But how many ever did? Therefore, what guarantee was there that a member of the Caucus in possession of secret information would live up to his pledge to transmit it to the Southern Chieftain? Finally, it was logically possible that someone who was not a member of the Caucus of the Better Will should be a traitor. After all, conspiracy and treason were as old as man himself. They concluded with the observation that the town was in the grip of hysteria, and warned that, unless the measures taken by the Council were repealed, the town would be delivered over to chaos and pandemonium. Portents of doom already abounded on all sides. McMushy wept; McWordy ranted; McSappy swooned.

McRuth, McRath and McPurge were not long in drawing their conclusions. Not for a moment could they imagine that anyone would be so stupid as to sincerely believe all this. They reasoned—loud-mouthed but modest men, adds the Chronicler in a sardonic aside—that, since no one could be more stupid than they themselves were, and since *they* realized the utter absurdity of these arguments—and they were absurd, comments the Chronicler—that therefore the whole campaign by McMushy, McWordy and McSappy was an elaborate pretense to disguise the latter's deliberate complicity in the conspiracy against the Town of Usher—in which inference, according to the Chronicler, they were profoundly mistaken. Nonetheless, they now demanded that the proscription from Government service be extended to the Party of Good Will, and denounced its leaders and members for double-dyed villainy even more vehemently than they did members of the Caucus. This convinced the leaders of the Party of Good Will, who were aware of their own rectitude but not of the limitations of their intelligence, all the more of the justice of their position. They rushed precipitately to the defense of every one of their members, even those who belonged to the Caucus. When a member of the Party who had once opposed the Caucus was dropped from the Town Council Privy Guard because he was confused with his identical twin or who actually was a member of the Caucus, many members of the Party of Good Will began to wear mourning. When asked by their fellow-townsmen what they were mourning for, they dolefully replied: "We mourn for our liberties. We mourn for the Usher that used to be." Some of them said that, in the unlikely event that the Southern Chieftain attacked the town, they would not bear arms in its defense, for life in Usher was now no different from life under the Southern Chieftain. He, at least, was no hypocrite. It was commonly observed that the members of the Caucus were most vociferous in lamenting their lost freedoms. They no longer criticized McMushy, McWordy and McSappy, but rose in a body when they appeared at meetings, and forced all other members of the Party to rise. "We still have our differences," they declared, "but we honor them for their courage. They are truly men of good will who some day will become men of better will."

The Muddled Roaders were angry with both of the contending factions. They were angry with McRuth, McRath and McPurge because of their unbridled attack on the Party of Good Will, whose support the Muddled Roaders sometimes enjoyed in the Council. They were angry with McMushy, McWordy and McSappy for interposing themselves between the Town Council and the deputies of the Southern Chieftain, and thus frustrating the elementary measures of security the Council adopted. But they refused to yield to the demands of the intransigent critics to summarily dismiss all members of the Party of Good Will. Whereupon McRuth, McRath and McPurge turned on the Muddled Roaders and charged them with coddling traitors, with not knowing their own minds, and with sacrificing the Town of Usher for the support they expected to get from the Party of Good Will. This so infuriated the Muddled Roaders that their leaders joined McMushy, McWordy and McSappy in a common meeting in defense of the freedoms of Usher, a meeting in which, to speak truthfully, says the Chronicler, the exaggerated slogans of the Party of Good Will were most in evidence. Emboldened by this apparent solidarity, members of the Caucus became more brazen in their acts of subversion. Unfortunately for them, one of their most daring men was caught *in redhanded delicti* and, at the same time, a leader of the Caucus suffered a change of heart and named his confederates, some of whom were highly placed in the Town's defense setup. This conjunction of events caused a popular clamor which led the Muddled Roaders to tighten their controls. But this infuriated the leaders of the Party of Good Will, who now turned against the Muddled Roaders and accused them of spineless capitulation to their arch-enemies. Things came to such a pass, writes the Chronicler, that no group could agree with another about anything. There was one exception: The group headed by McRuth, McRath and McPurge, and the group headed by McMushy, McWordy and Mc-Sappy, both agreed that the Muddled Roaders were unfit to rule.

The Muddled Roaders were sorely distressed. The situation was unprecedented. Only the wise and informed men of all parties, says the Chronicler, could have solved the problem, if it were soluble, and he seems to leave that question unanswered. But these wise and informed men were not consulted by the McMuddled Headed. (The Chronicler seems impatient with them, judging by this new appellation he bestows upon them.) Instead, the time-honored method was adopted of combining all positions at once. On Monday, Wednesday and Friday, the Muddled Roaders would proclaim that McRuth, McRath and McPurge were character assassins, alarmists, men made out of the same cloth as the Southern Chieftain; on Tuesday, Thursday and Saturday, the Muddled Roaders would declare the need for stricter and stricter controls, not merely against those who were members of the Caucus or of the Party of Good Will, but against anyone who for any reason at all might prove untrustworthy. The Muddled Roaders in charge of the Government services became more suspicious and more adept at uncovering the deputies of the Southern Chieftain. But they refused to admit that they had once been remiss, or to acknowledge what they were doing at present. They asserted they were carrying on as usual, with the result that no one knew what they were really doing. And they ended up not knowing themselves.

The town remained in a state of turmoil and went from alarm to alarm. The animosity among the three main groups exceeded their fear of the Southern Chieftain.

The manuscript scroll at this point comes to an end and the next numbered scroll, if it was written, has not come to light. There is no record of subsequent developments. We know the town was destroyed, but not the proximate causes of its destruction. But at the bottom of the last section of the existing scroll, the Chronicler reports briefly an ironical comment of one of the few independent members of the Council:

> Our only chance of survival is to send an emissary to the Southern Chieftain and give him an account of our domestic debates and the full text of the speeches of the leaders. He is sure to die laughing. Although such a death will be an undeserved piece of grace for a savage butcher of the innocent, it is a small price to pay for the salvation of the Town of Usher.

18 Security and Freedom

THE QUEST for security in human life, like the quest for certainty in human knowledge, has many sources. All are rooted in man's finitude in a complex world of danger and mystery. Of the varied methods man has pursued to reduce the dangers and cope with the mysteries, the way of piecemeal knowledge and continuous experiment has been most fruitful. For it is in the fields in which human knowledge has foresworn the quest for absolute certainty, as in the scientific disciplines, that it has proved both reliable and capable of winning universal agreement. On the other hand, in the fields in which the strongest claims to certainty have been made—politics and philosophy—there is the least agreement.

Because absolute certainty in human affairs is impossible, absolute security is impossible. Unless we are aware of this, the price we pay for straining to achieve an impossible ideal may result in netting us less security than would otherwise be attainable. This is not an unusual phenomenon: it is observable in large things and small. The man who strives for absolute health may end up a valetudinarian. The man who won't venture on the highways until they are accident-proof may as well not own an automobile; and if he crawls along playing it supersafe, traffic-enforcement authorities tell us he adds to the dangers of the road.

The real problem, then, is not one of absolute security, or security in general. It is always one of achieving more and better security in meeting specific hazards in a particular area of risk and uncertainty—and meeting them in such a way that we do not lose more by the methods we use than by the disasters we would prevent.

As a rule we feel more insecure in our personal relations than we really are. About public affairs, on the other hand, when times are normal, we are apt to feel less insecure, because less interested, than we have reason to be. But we are living in times which are not normal. It is in such times that the expert and the insider, the savior and demagogue, command an audience merely by assuming a posture of authority.

Most political commentators and analysts sustain their reputation, and continue in their vocations only because their audiences have neither memory nor a sense of history. Everyone can and does make errors. One can be wrong and yet, because of the evidence at hand, have a right to be wrong. The man who takes a long chance and wins is lucky, not intelligent. It is because of the grounds on which judgments are made in the light of knowledge of the past and present that we appraise their validity. Subsequent experience tests the reliability of these grounds.

The McCarthy episode in American history was a test of political judgment and political morality. Those who dismissed him as an unimportant phenomenon or extenuated his methods in the light of his goals failed the tests of both judgment and morality. So did those who exaggerated his power, who proclaimed that he had transformed America into a police state, and who fought McCarthy with the weapons of McCarthy instead of the weapons of truth. Even at the height of McCarthy's power a more rational view was not impossible.

One of the questions most frequently asked me during an extended trip abroad in 1953 was: "Why is there so much ado about the problem of Communist infiltration in the United States?" My interlocutors usually added, "After all, look at Austria which in part is actually occupied by Soviet Russia; look at France and Italy in which huge mass Communist parties exist. No one in these countries seems disturbed about Communist penetration or regards it as a serious menace." The question is a legitimate one, but before attempting an answer, I wish to discuss some preliminary topical as well as theoretical questions.

Let us examine the phenomenon of Senator McCarthy. Partly because of the findings of the Senate Investigating Committee on the McCarthy-Stevens imbroglio, McCarthy's influence, even his news value, radically declined from that time on. His previous influence in the United States had been pernicious, although few Europeans realized in what fields it had a major impact. The chief victims of his undiscriminating investigations were government employees. I am not referring here to members of the Communist party or to those who have invoked the Fifth Amendment on the ground that their truthful testimony would tend to incriminate them and whose actual loyalty is in doubt. I am referring to the immeasurably greater number of government officials, genuinely liberal, enlightened and knowledgeable, who have been intimidated into playing it safe by the threat of a public inquisitorial investigation. Even a loyal and efficient bureaucracy does not court criticism. Because he wielded the power of investigation which in turn commanded all the nation's resources of publicity, Senator McCarthy could make life grim for public servants who disagreed with him not about Communism but about the best methods of combating it.

That grave injustices were done to some individuals who distinguished themselves by their intelligent opposition to Communism abroad (Kaghan) and at home (Wechsler) is undeniable. These injustices have been mitigated to some extent by the ultimate public vindication accorded to innocent victims of Senator McCarthy's attacks. But there has been little mitigation of the far greater evil of lack of critical independence, initiative and originality in government service as a direct consequence of Senator McCarthy's invasion of the Executive domain. No absolute taboo, of course, can be placed upon the constitutional power of the Congress to investigate scandals in any department of the government, and in the past some investigations have been necessary. But to embark on an unlimited inquiry into all executive agencies of government is to generate a climate not merely of conformism—since conformism even to an administrative policy disapproved of by Senator McCarthy was risky—but of neutrality, protective coloration and unconscious accommodation to McCarthy's own prejudices and aggressive ignorance about the most effective way to combat Communism.

If McCarthy's influence in the United States has been pernicious, his effect abroad has been disastrous. He grieved genuine friends of American democracy and was a positive godsend to the much more numerous and articulate Europeans who are looking for pretexts to rationalize their neutralism or their hostility to the United States. With explicit reference to McCarthy, some European commentators suggested that the United States in 1953 stood where Germany stood in 1932 when Hitler waited in the wings to be called on stage by General von Hindenberg. "It is useless to pretend that the United States does not now face a rather similar danger," Mr. Vernon Bartlett sadly warned his British readers in *The Listener*. That such fantasies could grow in the heads of not unfriendly critics is a measure of the damage McCarthy did.[1]

On the other hand, many Europeans are under the impression that

---

[1] This ignorance about the United States seems to be supplemented by ignorance about the U.S.S.R. The same commentator feels that the Soviet-controlled, one-party elections are a dull and undemocratic way of filling a parliament. He then adds—"but I do not criticize the Russians for choosing (*sic!*) it." It is a pity he did not indicate when the Russians *chose* the system under which they are ruled.

American intellectuals, as a group, were affected by McCarthy in the same way as government officials, and that the whole of American cultural life breathed in the shadow of fear. The nightmarish picture often painted in the European press of McCarthy stalking up and down the country intimidating writers, educators, newspapermen, and other professional groups suggests the vision of delirium rather than the results of sober reporting. It is eloquent evidence that the United States is still an unknown country abroad. All the great organs of American public opinion with the exception of one midwestern newspaper were hostile to McCarthy; all the Luce magazines with their fabulous circulation damned him for his demagogy; almost all church bodies denounced his methods; most radio and television commentators were caustic or savagely critical.

At the time I visited the campuses of more than thirty colleges. Far from discovering that McCarthy had unleashed a reign of cultural terror, I found fewer professors than could be counted on the fingers of one hand who had anything to say in his behalf. And their voices were drowned in a thunder of denunciation which poured in on him from all sides. McCarthy and his friends were aware of the extremely vocal and almost total opposition to him on the part of American intellectuals. They attributed to intellectuals the turn in the tide of public opinion against him. Government agencies remained somewhat cautious, if not demoralized, and undoubtedly McCarthy had considerable grass roots support. All this is deplorable enough. But to exaggerate his influence, to speak of a reign of terror, or a climate of fear, is to do the sort of thing which has come to be associated with McCarthy's name.

The American public was not altogether unaware of the effects of McCarthy at home and abroad. Why, then, did it countenance his antics for so long and to the extent it did? What was the source of McCarthy's popular support? The obvious answer is that public concern about the apparent indifference to national security on the part of previous administrations had reached a point where the demagogic methods of McCarthy were waved aside as unessential or dismissed as a small price to pay for a security long delayed. Those who spoke in this fashion, and at one time they were many, were profoundly in error. The methods by which a democracy defends itself are never unessential, and the price of McCarthy's methods, it is now apparent, is much too high to compensate for the dubious securities they have won. It is not necessary to deny that McCarthy uncovered a few Communists in government service and called attention to some administrative bungling. All this was far outweighed by the harm he did in dividing the country more than Henry Wallace ever succeeded in doing, undermining American prestige abroad, and intimidating American officialdom.

Nonetheless, this does not answer the basic question. Why should the public, especially a public liberal enough to have followed Roosevelt and Truman, have been so much concerned with security? For without this concern McCarthy would never have captured his audience.

I

"Security is like liberty," writes Mr. Justice Jackson in one of his dissenting opinions, "in that many are the crimes that have been committed in its name." Yet he would be the first to admit that this is no more warrant for abandoning the quest for reasonable rules of security than for relinquishing the struggle for a more humane conception of liberty.

Nonetheless, in the past, problems of security were never considered seriously by lovers of freedom except in the guise of *social* securities. In pre-totalitarian days many did not care if these social securities were achieved by undermining to some extent the *political* securities with which special privilege was hedged. After all, "law and order" was the traditional slogan of social reaction; and the social gospel, whether secular or religious, considered itself above the call of patriotism.

Not until a democratic law and a democratic order were firmly established, and not until they were threatened by Fascist and Communist movements, operating in some countries as Fifth Columns of powers bent on world domination, did it dawn on liberal thinkers that without political security the very social securities, so painfully built, might be lost. They had long since understood that the abstractions of *economic* liberalism under modern historical conditions were semantic fetishes. That the same might be true of some of the slogans of *political* liberalism, when used for purposes of conspiratorial evasion by one's own nationals in the service of a foreign power posing as a universal church, was a disturbing thought. The actual facts were not so much a challenge to the principles of political liberalism as to the intelligence of the liberals to apply their principles to the relatively new problems created by conspirators masquerading as heretics.

With some notable exceptions, American liberals were particularly insensitive to the problems of ideologically motivated subversion of democratic institutions and processes. This was in part due to the fact that until the Roosevelt era twentieth-century American liberalism was in the main an opposition movement sympathetic to any group opposed to entrenched political power without paying too much attention to the grounds of its opposition. It was in part due to the absence of a politically mature conservatism which could recognize the abysses that separated the opponents of the status quo from each other. Herbert Hoover characterized socialism as "the weak sister of Bolshevism" at the very time when the socialist movement was more hostile to the Kremlin than the business community. Until surprised by events, the conservatives were no more aware of the problems of ideologically motivated subversion than the liberals. By indiscriminately tagging progressive ideas and the New Deal as "communistic," they had blinded themselves to the genuine article.

After the Seventh Congress of the Communist International, the Communists kidnaped the vocabulary of American liberalism. This "corruption of the word," as I called it then, made it easier for some sentimental liberals to interpret sharp criticisms of Communism as oblique attacks on liberalism, if not a first step towards Fascism. In liberal circles to be an anti-Fascist was always honorable. But to be anti-Communist, especially during the war years, invited distrust. That liberals had a stake in the survival of the democratic system whose defects they could freely criticize under the ground rules of the Bill of Rights was granted, of course. That they therefore also had a stake in preventing the ground rules from being abused, that they had a responsibility to think about the problem, was resolutely ignored. This was something for the state to worry about. To this day most liberals tend to dismiss questions of political security as subjects only police minds are fit to consider. On the Continent even a theoretical discussion of the *principles* of political security is regarded with suspicion as a kind of collaboration with the police. In view of the actual situation in some European countries, this makes as much sense as saying that the discussion of theories of capital punishment is a kind of collaboration with the executioner. There is a certain logic in the refusal to think about problems of political security if one regards the state as nothing but the executive committee of the ruling class. But this dogma of vulgar Marxism is certainly unacceptable to any genuine liberal. It is rejected even by intelligent Marxists.

The preeminent intellectual concern among liberals in the United States was with the question of civil rights which, however justifiable, led to a paradoxical situation: since it went hand in hand with an intellectual taboo against a consideration of the question of political security, the defense against ideologically motivated infiltration, espionage and sabotage came to be entrusted to the police mind. But the police mind is helpless in dealing with it. For the problem is not one primarily of detection and punishment, but of prevention and avoidance. Unless this is understood, nothing is understood about the unprecedented type of ideological espionage organized by the Kremlin, whose operatives are totally dedicated, and because of a large reservoir of replacements, totally expendable. Yet precisely because the professional police mind centers on detection and punishment, it is unable to cope with the complex problems created when Machiavellianism is harnessed to fanaticism. The police mind seems constitutionally incapable of distinguishing between heretics, whose criticism is essential to the health of a democratic community, and conspirators playing outside the rules of the game, sometimes with deadly effect. In this respect, the military mind is hardly different from the police mind. Both can recognize and judge actions which formally violate rules and regulations. Neither is in a position to assess qualifications for employment, especially for employment in which political motivation and political beliefs have a bearing upon security.

The results have been what any politically sophisticated person could have expected. On the one hand, inefficiency in preventing widespread espionage and subversion; and on the other, frenzied efforts either to conceal the situation for narrow political purposes or to retrieve the situation by hasty executive decree. And as usual when confusion rules, individual hardships and injustices result.

This was not helped by ritualistic liberals whose protests against genuine abuses in security programs were coupled with an almost willful ignorance of the facts that make such programs an unpleasant necessity in times of emergency. Instead of offering a viable alternative to eliminate or reduce these injustices, they wrote as if the only problem was to develop more efficient methods of detecting acts of espionage *after* they had been committed. They thereby revealed the extent of their misunderstanding. Not the acts prevented but those which are discovered create public disquietude, because they give the impression that many more remain undiscovered and beyond the reach of prosecution in virtue of the statute of limitations.

The liberal mind has recently been criticized as inherently unable to grasp the facts of political evil, especially the ancient wisdom that the corruption of the best may give us the worst. This type of mind is reflected in Lord Jowitt's book on the Hiss case which argues in effect that because it is incredible that a man like Hiss would pick his neighbor's pocket, it is therefore absurd to believe that he would commit dishonorable acts in the service of a foreign cause. This is no ground, however, to identify liberalism with gullibility or with invincible belief in the natural goodness of man. On the contrary, the liberal mind can bring to this problem a specialized knowledge and a certain attitude. The liberal of all people should have an understanding of "the ideological man" afire with zeal to destroy and reform, since he is destined to be among the first victims of ideological fanaticism. Recent experience, or a study of recent history, should make it possible for the liberal to acquire a reliable knowledge of the whole costumer's shop of organizational masks cleverly designed by Communist technicians to take in the unwary until the time comes for the sacrificial slaughter. If he believes that there is a foreign threat to the survival of the liberal community, he cannot withold assent from the dictum of Roger Baldwin, former head of the American Civil Liberties Union, that "a superior loyalty to a foreign government disqualifies a citizen from service to our own." It does not disqualify the citizen from protection of the Bill of Rights, but the right to government service is not an integral part of the Bill of Rights.

It is the liberal *attitude,* however, which is most crucial in the reasonable administration of a security program. Just as only those who love children can be trusted to discipline them without doing psychological harm, so only those who love freedom can be trusted to devise appropriate safeguards without throttling intellectual independence or smothering all but the mediocre in blankets of regulations. No safeguards are appropriate or even efficient which impose conformity of belief or inhibit intellectual spontaneity. The fresh and unfamiliar solution to difficulties depends on a certain imaginative daring and a receptivity to such solutions by those in a position of authority. A liberal with a sense of history is aware of the possibility that in a specific situation there may be a sharp conflict between the legitimate demands of national security and the freedom of the individual. But on balance, and in perspective, he is convinced that the two are not in opposition. In the very interest of a freely expressed dissent, some security measures are required to protect the institutional processes which, however imperfectly, reflect a freely given consent. At the same time, the faith and practices of freedom, indeed, an almost religious veneration for the *élan* of the free spirit, may generate a sense of security even in the shadows of war.

II

It may seem odd to have to justify the necessity of a security program at the present juncture of world affairs. My experiences, however, in England and western Europe have convinced me that in the eyes of a great many people in those countries it certainly needed justification. Parents who would not entrust the care of their children to anyone without the most painstaking investigation of character references, businessmen most meticulous about whom they would employ even in minor posts of trust, professional men who set absurdly high qualifications for their assistants, scoffed at "all this fuss" about security in positions assuredly more important to their community than that of nursemaid or cashier or dental aid. Repeatedly I was told when discussion arose about the Burgess and McLean case or Pontecorvo or French Communist scientists in official posts, "England (or France) is not America!" I do not think my experience was unrepresentative. Not only did my friends shrug off the question of security in their own countries, they regarded concern about security in the United States as nothing but downright hysteria. But why, I asked, were Americans "hysterical" about Communists and not Nazis? Why did no hysteria develop in the United States toward the Japanese after Pearl Harbor or toward the Germans during World War II? Indeed, I found it possible to present the argument and evidence for the necessity of a security program only in the puzzled silences with which those questions were met.

The argument and evidence can be put briefly. The one unshakeable dogma in the Bolshevik faith is that the Soviet Union is not safe from attack so long as the "capitalistic democracies" of the West—and not only the United States but also countries like Great Britain and France —exist. Let not those who in the past assured us that Hitler's racial myth and ideology of world conquest were "just words" tell us again that ideologies do not count in politics and history. If anything, the Kremlin has gone further than Hitler because it has publicly proclaimed that "encirclement" is a *political,* not a geographical, concept. The Communist parties of the West, affiliated with the Cominform, have as their *first* function the defense of the Soviet Union. Instructions are explicit to all of them to organize secretly (as well as publicly) even in "the freest" and "most democratic" countries and to infiltrate into strategic centers. This type of activity has been extensively carried on for years especially during the days of the popular front struggle against the Nazis. Even during the war which Hitler forced on the Soviets, the Kremlin engaged in the most comprehensive types of espionage against its Allies as part of the underlying struggle which, according to their fanatical conviction, must end either with the victory of the West or the Soviet power.

Because it can count on the devotion *à outrance* of Communist nationals of other countries, many of them highly trained, intelligent and inspired by a misguided idealism which does not see under the flowers of official rhetoric the chains of Soviet control on its own people, the Kremlin possesses an incomparable advantage over the West. For one thing, it is the best informed regime in the world. It knew the date of Pearl Harbor but did not notify the United States government from whom it was receiving generous aid at the time. It was even informed by its agents about the scheduled German invasion of Russia though it gave the reports no credence. It knew that General Clay's proposal to arm military trains and fight his way through to feed Western Berlin in the event of a Soviet blockade had been vetoed by the State

Department, so that the blockade could be clamped on the city with absolutely no risk. If the Soviet government did not know that the United States would propose to the United Nations to fight in the event that South Korea were invaded, it was only because the United States government didn't know it either. It is amusing to note Truman's confession of astonishment at Stalin's impassivity when he was informed at Potsdam that the United States had manufactured an atomic bomb. For we know today that at the time Stalin was being kept at least as well informed about some of the details of the progress of American research on atomic weapons as Truman. Although one would hardly suspect it from present attitudes to security in many circles in those countries, it is from Canadian and British sources that we have the most incontrovertible, if not the weightiest evidence, of how Communist Parties are involved in the espionage nets the Soviet Union has spun around the free world.[2]

Since the Kremlin combines this belief in the inevitability of war with a dialectical conception according to which a sudden attack or offense, as in Korea, is the best method of defense and because of the centralized organization of western industrial life, the location of America's undispersed plants, and the evolution of thermonuclear weapons, an attempt at a sudden knockout blow cannot be ruled out as a possibility. Since Bolshevik morality is confessedly subordinate to what will further the victory of the "proletarian dictatorship"—indeed, this is *the whole* of their morality—the possession of information about strategic weakness on the part of the West, or the hope that a sudden blow may prevent instant retaliatory action, may make a decisive difference to the Kremlin in resolving to launch the Blitzkrieg which will end "the final struggle." It does not require many persons to betray the key secrets of the radar defense of a nation.

The consequences of less extreme suppositions may be equally disastrous. The free world cannot deploy its defense forces everywhere. Its decisions where to stand, where to fight, once known to the Kremlin, give the latter a flexibility that it can exploit most skillfully to draw the world bit by bit into its orbit. On the other hand, there is no possibility for the free world to build up a counterweight within the Soviet sphere to redress the balance. No democratic Jeffersonian or Millsian International exists with affiliated parties in the Soviet world.

Does it follow that *every* member of the Communist party is an

---

[2] Cf. *The Report of the Royal Commission to Investigate the Facts Relating to and Circumstances Surrounding the Communication by Public Officials and Other Persons in Positions of Trust of Secret and Confidential Information to Agents of a Foreign Power* (Ottawa, 1946); also Alexander Foote's *Handbook for Spies* (London, 1949).

espionage agent ready to do the bidding of his superiors and betray his country? Is it not possible that some members of the Communist party may be loyal to their own government rather than to the Soviet Union? The best answer to these questions was made by Mr. Clement Attlee, Prime Minister at the time when Pontecorvo, scientifically a much more gifted man than Fuchs, fled from England. "There is no way," said Mr. Attlee who never chased a witch in his life, "of distinguishing such people [hypothetically loyal Communists] from those who, if opportunity offered, would be prepared to endanger the security of the state in the interests of another power. The Government has, therefore, reached the conclusion that the only prudent course to adopt is to ensure that no one who is known to be a member of the Communist party, *or to be associated with it in such a way as to raise legitimate doubts about his or her reliability* (my italics) is employed in connection with work, the nature of which is vital to the security of the State." It is well to remember that a clerk in a code office or even those who empty trash baskets may have access to material bearing on national security. Mr. Attlee apparently believes that if we distinguish between legal guilt and *moral* or professional guilt or unfitness, and between association by happenstance and association by cooperation, then there certainly can be and is "guilt by association."

III

We now return to the question from which we started: why was the United States, in contradistinction to other countries, so alarmed about Communist infiltration? The question has two facets: one concerns the reasons for the state of American public opinion; the other, the reasons for the relative unconcern of other nations.

It is the gravest error to imagine that anyone in America, even Senator McCarthy who helped the Communist cause throughout the world, believed for a moment that the Communists constituted a domestic danger. But American public opinion was aroused by a series of incidents over a span of three years which seemed to show that in the international field the position of the American government was being weakened by Soviet agents.

The first was the Hiss case and the revelation that several interlocking rings of Communist conspirators had been active in high places for years. It remains mystifying that many of these individuals continued working in strategic places, one even at the Aberdeen Weapons Proving Grounds, many years after the chief operatives had been identified by former members of the Communist party. The worst of these revelations came after Mr. Truman had dismissed the Hiss case as a "red herring." Following Hiss's conviction, Wadleigh's confession, and a long line of refusals to answer questions about espionage on the ground that a truthful answer would tend to be self-incriminating, the implication was natural, and in part justified, that the government had been lax or indifferent in taking intelligent safeguards. As the Dexter White case shows, the Truman administration feared that its opponents would make political capital out of the presence of Communist espionage agents in the government and tried to hush up matters. This narrow political partisanship by no means warranted the charge of "treason" or of coddling treason hurled by some Republicans against the Democrats. There is no reason to believe that had the former been in power, they would have acted more wisely. But the country never really recovered from the shock of learning that publicly sworn testimony, some of it legally substantiated where the charges were contested, showed that persons holding the following positions were members of the secret Communist underground apparatus:

> an Executive Assistant to the President of the United States
> an Assistant Secretary of the Treasury
> the Director of the Office of Special Political Affairs for the State Department
> the Secretary of the International Monetary Fund
> the Head of the Latin-American Division of the Office of Strategic Services
> a member of the National Labor Relations Board
> Secretary of the National Labor Relations Board
> Chief Counsel, Senate Subcommittee on Civil Liberties
> Chief, Statistical Analysis Branch, War Production Board
> Treasury Department Representative and Adviser in Financial Control Division of the North African Board of UNRRA, and at the meeting of the Council of Foreign Ministers in Moscow
> Director, National Research Project of the Works Progress Administration

These were not the only, but only the most conspicuous, positions Communists filled. The *actual* amount of damage done, however, is difficult to assess and probably will never be known. But no reasonable person can doubt the existence of a planned pattern of infiltration whose significance can be better gauged by the European reader if he draws up a comparable list of posts in his own government and fills them, in his mind's eye, with Communist espionage agents.

The second series of incidents began with the Fuchs case which broke after several outstanding scientists had dismissed the idea that atomic espionage was possible. "There are no secrets" declared the very scientists who in 1939 and 1940 had imposed upon themselves a voluntary secrecy in publications to prevent Hitler from developing nuclear power. Subsequent trials in the United States of the Communist spies associated with Fuchs produced evidence that there were others deep underground.

All this was still very much in the public mind when Truman announced that the Soviet Union had exploded its first atomic bomb, thus eliminating the monopoly of atomic power which, according to Churchill and other Europeans, had prevented the Red Army from marching west after American and British demobilization. The head of the United States Atomic Energy Commission observed that Soviet espionage had made it possible for the Soviet Union to save years of costly experiment (an observation officially repeated by President Eisenhower on October 8, 1953, after the U.S.S.R. had exploded a thermonuclear bomb).[3]

Finally came the loss of China and the charge that some of the advisors and consultants to the State Department on Far Eastern affairs not only had long records of Communist association but had followed the twists and turns of the Party line. Some like L. Rossinger who fell back on the Fifth Amendment were identified as members of the Communist party. Although there was no legal proof of the identification by Budenz of Lattimore as a top Soviet agent, there could be no reasonable doubt that he was a fellow-traveler whose justification of the Moscow frame-up trials was very brazen. Whatever the degree of their Communism, it seemed indisputable that a group in the State Department had been urging the abandonment of all support to Chiang Kai-shek despite the absence of any alternative to Communist triumph. The defeat of Chiang may have been unavoidable, but the evidence that American Communists and their sympathizers had actively worked for his downfall by attempting to influence official channels was unmistakable.

These events, together with other trials involving Communist espionage and perjury, and the multiplication of cases of refusal to answer questions on the ground that a truthful answer would tend to be self-

---

[3] As early as 1950 some scientists holding high official positions had charged that the Soviet Union had acquired through espionage the "know-how" to make hydrogen bombs. *The New York Times* of July 20, 1950, quoted Francois Perrin, Joint Commissioner for Atomic Energy in France, as saying that Russia, through its espionage network, had certainly obtained the know-how to make the hydrogen bomb. The same report appeared in *The San Francisco Chronicle* of July 23, 1950. At the time Professor Perrin's co-commissioner was Irene Joliot-Curie, wife of Frederic Joliot-Curie, later dismissed from the post as High Commissioner for Atomic Energy because of his pro-Soviet activities. Frederic Joliot-Curie subsequently charged that the U.S. was waging bacterial germ warfare in Korea and spurned the proposal of a Committee of Nobel Prize Winners to conduct an objective international inquiry into the truth of his charges.

incriminatory, contributed to the prevalent feeling that the United States was being weakened in the cold war on whose outcome so many things, both domestic and international, depend. The Korean war exacerbated the mood. Had these events, especially the pattern of their succession, occurred in other countries, it is not likely that they would have been met with complacency.

The concern of the American people with the question of Communist penetration, in the light of the evidence, was legitimate enough. Questionable only was the character of the reaction to it on the part of the government. Buffeted by cultural vigilantes on the one side and ritualistic liberals on the other, it swung from one position to another, pleasing no one with its eclecticism. Almost all of the excesses of loyalty and security programs are attributable to the incredible political ignorance and naiveté of the personnel of the Review Boards. It was not the procedures themselves which were at fault, because oddly enough American procedures in crucial respects are fairer than the English. For example, in hearings before English boards, civil servants under investigation are rarely, if ever, told of the evidence against them. They are also denied rights of legal counsel, and even of representation.[4] Nonetheless, American procedures worked hardship and injustices because instead of being administered by knowledgeable men and women with a little common sense who had some political experience, they were entrusted to investment bankers, corporation lawyers, army and navy officers, small town officials, or Republican or Democratic party regulars to whom Communist language was gobbledegook, Communist ideas suspiciously like the ideas of socialists, dogooders and even New Dealers, and Communist organizations with the distinctions between member, sympathizer, front, dupe, innocent, and honest mistaken liberal, as mysterious as the order of beings in the science of angelology.

In the light of the above, the answer to our final question regarding the relative unconcern of other nations to the problem of Communist penetration is not hard to give. The greatest Soviet effort was directed against the United States as the Kremlin's chief and strongest enemy. Since 1939 the United States has been the center of atomic weapons research and development. Its policies are more fateful for the U.S.S.R. than those of any other single nation. To make these policies miscarry, to delay, distort and abort government directives pays rich political dividends. The Kremlin is quite aware of the fact that a defeat or paralysis of the United States would mean the end of the independence of Austria, France and Italy. Further, the Communist movement in the United States is not a mass party and, in all likelihood, will never become one.

---

4 See Appendix to this chapter.

But it has a solid core of some thousands of hardened "professional revolutionists." From the Soviet viewpoint they are expendable. What is more natural, therefore, than to employ them for all sorts of conspiratorial purposes from direct espionage to the capture of small but key unions, to the seeding of government services with "sleepers"? A few thousand totally dedicated persons, working underground with the help of a sympathetic periphery of several times that size, can cause a great many headaches. Countries like Austria need not worry about the problem, one is tempted to observe, because it wouldn't make a difference if they did. There isn't much the Kremlin can learn from them and an attempt at a Communist putsch on Czechoslovakian lines, so long as the United States is still strong, risks a war for which at the moment the U.S.S.R. is unready. Countries like France and Italy, on the other hand, which have mass Communist parties and where infiltration and underground organization are not inconsiderable can hardly solve the problem without facing crippling strikes and extensive public disorders. Too weak to act they sometimes pretend that there is no need for action. *They can live with the Communist menace only because the United States is free of it and only so long as the United States is strong enough to restrain the Soviet Union from overrunning the free world.*

Only those who are ignorant of the stupendous extent of Soviet infiltration and espionage over the years, the complexity of its patterns and its potential for harm, can sneer at the problems of security in the free world. It is not enough to shout slogans—whether of security or freedom. What is required is creative intelligence to devise just and effective procedures which will protect the free cultures of the world from their hidden enemies without making less free those who are not its hidden enemies. These procedures must be flexible. They cannot be formalized into a code without inviting abuses. They must be devised and administered by civil libertarians who are familiar with Communist theory and who have studied Communist conspiratorial practice. They must be applied discreetly, without fanfare, without developing a climate of public concern. And their primary function must be effective prevention rather than exemplary punishment.

APPENDIX

Security Measures for Civil Servants in England

Since security measures for civil servants in England have often and unfavorably been compared with measures adopted in this country, I present the situation as it exists there today described by Douglas Houghton, M.P., in *The Listener* of February 7, 1957:

The security measures in the Civil Service are by no means entirely new. A complete ban was put on the employment of members of the Communist Party on secret work nearly ten years ago. This also covered those associated with the Communist Party in such a way as to raise reasonable doubts about their reliability. At the same time, a tribunal of three advisers was set up to hear appeals. Rules were made about suspensions from duty, transfers to other work, and dismissals where unavoidable.

All that we have had for nearly ten years. Then came the shock of Burgess and McLean, the two Foreign Office men who left their posts, crossed over to France, and disappeared. In November, 1955, the Government set up a committee composed wholly of Privy Councillors to examine the security arrangements and consider whether any further precautions were called for. The substance of their report and recommendations were published in a White Paper in March, 1956. This was debated in the House of Commons shortly afterwards. The Government accepted the recommendations of the Privy Councillors, and these have been given effect in the new security arrangements announced.

So much for the background. Now for what the Privy Councillors said should be done, and has now been done. First, they accepted the basic principle of the earlier security measures, which is the belief that "the Communist faith overrides a man's normal loyalties to his country." What the Privy Councillors added to this was their view that the risk from communists is not confined to party members, either above or underground, or their associates, but extends to sympathisers with communism. So now the ban covers one who has sympathy with communism, or association with communists or sympathisers with communism, or is a likely subject of communist pressure in such a way as to raise reasonable doubts about his reliability. That obviously opens up a wider field of investigation and a good deal more room for matters of opinion and judgement of reliability.

Second, on the recommendation of the Privy Councillors, security measures have been taken into the wider field of defects of character and conduct. Their view was that today it is of great importance to pay attention to character defects as factors tending to make a man unreliable or expose him to blackmail or influence by foreign agents. They said it was the duty of departments to inform themselves of serious failings of character or behaviour, such as drunkenness and drug-taking, or of any loose living that might seriously affect a man's reliability.

They also said—and this is very important—that in deciding these difficult and often borderline cases "it is right to continue the practice of tilting the balance in favour of offering greater protection to the security of the state rather than in the direction of safeguarding the rights of the individual." In their opinion an individual who is living with a wife or husband who is a communist, or a communist sympathiser, may for that reason alone have to be moved from secret work.

The Civil Service does not question the responsibility of Government and Parliament in these matters. Nevertheless, the Civil Service is properly concerned with the way this far-reaching oversight over their political activities and private lives is to be exercised. Individual liberty is at stake as well as security, and a sensible balance must be kept between the two.

The Privy Councillors themselves acknowledge that some of the measures which the state is driven to take to protect its security are in some respects alien to our traditional practices. "Nothing could be worse," they said, "than to encourage tale-bearing or malicious gossip." That is one point of uneasiness in the Civil Service now. There are two more: one is the vagueness of some of the charges which can be made against a man (what, for example, is a communist "sympathiser"; or an "associate"?) These are questions left to the tribunal of three advisers to decide in the light of the particular facts. The other is the absence in the new arrangements, as in the old, of any provision for an appellant to the three advisers to take a friend or staff association representative with him. Mainly on that account perhaps, the three advisers are now to be required to report fully to the Minister if they are in doubt whether the charges are substantiated or not: and Ministers have accepted full personal responsibility for coming to a final decision.

These new security measures extend and tighten up the old ones, but they are no witch-hunt. Fortunately they are of practical concern to few people, because the overwhelming majority of Civil Servants are decent, loyal, and hardworking folk. They are very jealous of the good name and integrity of the public service.

19 Liberalism and the Law

THERE IS A ROOT ambiguity in the word "liberal." It is reflected in the fact that its opposite is in some contexts "illiberal," which no one will own up to being, and in other contexts "conservative," to which, if it is kept in lower case, everyone in some respect can make a claim. A resort to history is not likely to be decisive in establishing the proper usage of "liberal," primarily because in the past the term was preempted by particular social and political programs. To this day in Europe the predominant connotation of "liberal" is of laissez-faire economy, free trade, and opposition to government measures of welfare. And in the United States there are those who, like the adherents of the Liberty League in the 30's and the followers of Von Mises and Hayek today, regard freedom from government intervention as the key to all freedom.

Nonetheless there are two historical figures of the American past who in doctrine and temperament stand for what is commonly meant by liberalism: Jefferson and Lincoln. Jefferson is forever associated with the Declaration of Independence; Lincoln asserted that he had never had "a feeling, politically, that did not spring from the sentiments embodied in the Declaration of Independence." The Declaration was not only a pronouncement in favor of freedom but of equality. The notion that there is a necessary conflict between freedom and equality, current in their day as in ours, was dismissed by both Jefferson and Lincoln, perhaps too simply, as a prejudice of those who believed that nature itself was organized along aristocratic lines. There were certain *historical* reasons, however, that led many to fear that political equality could be achieved only at the cost of individual freedom. At any rate, no scheme of political equality is conceivable or practicable without some form of majority rule. That is why, among other reasons, both Jefferson and Lincoln were passionately devoted to the principle of majority rule. Lincoln, especially, recognized what some of the sophisticated critics of the principle, who feared the tyranny of the majority, have failed to see: that the only alternative to majority rule is either despotism or anarchy, the tyranny of the individual (or cabinet, mistress, junta, council, or court) or the tyranny of the mob.

At the same time neither Jefferson nor Lincoln believed that the majority was necessarily right or wise. Nor did they embrace Rousseauistic nonsense about the general will. For both of them a democracy which was not enlightened could not long remain free. It is this recognition of the importance of creative intelligence in the functioning and defense of a free society, and in the liberation of human personality, which constitutes the link between John Dewey and Thomas Jefferson.

American liberalism owes to Jefferson its acceptance of the principle of majority rule, its trust and faith in the free play of intelligence as the means by which not merely programs of political action emerge, but, beyond that, institutions fostering enduring sentiments of freedom. As Justice Frankfurter puts it: "This was the essence of Jefferson's social philosophy and the devotion of his life. It is the permanence of his meaning—to establish sentiments of freedom as the enduring habits of a people." These sentiments were not to be exercised vicariously or held in trust for the people by their betters.

From this principle Jefferson derived his well-known opposition to the doctrine of judicial supremacy. This opposition he bequeathed to contemporary liberalism; its most distinguished legal representative in our time, and possibly all time, was Justice Holmes. Although differing in their economic views, Holmes, Brandeis, Cardozo, and Frankfurter have been the great Jeffersonians on our bench. All of them recognize the necessity of a supreme *court* as well as a supreme *law*—else forty-nine different state legislatures and court systems would generate conflict and chaos. But at the same time they recognize that the supreme *law* in a democracy must express the legislative will of the nation as a whole and not merely the judicial will. The Constitution provides the guide lines to Congress, but cannot be made a fetish without violating the American spirit of government. Holmes recognizes the differences in the functions of the Court when he observes: "I do not think that the United States would come to an end if we lost our power to declare an act of Congress void. I do think the Union would be imperiled if we could not make that declaration as to the laws of the several states."

What embarrasses the Jeffersonians on the bench, however, is that the Supreme Court, which is not responsible to the electorate, has the power, won for it by John Marshall, to nullify the acts of a Congress which is responsible to the electorate. No honest mind can contest Justice Frankfurter's reminder that "judicial review is a deliberate check upon democracy through an organ of government not subject to popular control." But the contention that such a check is necessary to prevent the tyranny of the majority, and that without such a check the civil liberties of minorities would necessarily be destroyed, is sheer rationalization: it was property, not freedom, that the Supreme Court safeguarded throughout most of its history. Nor has that history been distinguished by the valiant defense of civil rights.

In England, where a proposal to give the courts the power to pass on the constitutionality of an Act of Parliament would be regarded as comparable to restoring the doctrine of the divine right of kings, civil liberties and minority rights flourish more luxuriantly than elsewhere. To be sure, majorities in a democracy may be foolish and tyrannical. But so may minorities if they have power. And the Supreme Court is the smallest of all minorities. If judges are to be our rulers, Morris R. Cohen used to say, they should be elected.

The Supreme Court has, of course, sometimes spoken out very effectively in behalf of civil rights, most notably in *Brown v. Board of Education,* which outlawed segregation in the nation's public schools. But let us not forget that in doing so it reversed the deplorable decision of *Plessy v. Ferguson* upholding "equal" and "separate" facilities, a decision that for fifty-eight years gave legal sanctification to a pattern which the more recent decision cannot easily modify. If the reasoning of the Court in 1954 had been followed in 1896, by this time we would be much closer to rectifying the social and civil injustices from which our Negro fellow citizens suffer—and not only in the South. And if history is relevant, there are few if any Supreme Court decisions on civil rights whose beneficial effects begin to compare in importance with the grievous consequences of the Supreme Court's decision in the Dred Scott case, which some historians regard as one of the causes of the Civil War. Only historical myopia can see in the Supreme Court a consistent defender of civil liberties.

Justice Holmes and his Jeffersonian colleagues have met the embarrassment in which their power to nullify acts of Congress has placed them by a severe self-restraint. They have resolutely refused to impose their own conception of social and economic policy on the country in the guise of interpreting the wisdom of Constitutional fathers who never even conceived of the character of contemporary problems and issues. What Justice Frankfurter says of Holmes is only in slightly lesser measure true of himself. "Probably no man who ever sat on the court was by temperament and discipline freer from emotional commitments compelling him to translate his own economic or social views into Constitutional commands." That is why he frequently speaks of the need for humility and detachment lest "limitations in personal experience are transmuted into limitations of the Constitution."

This has led to considerable criticism of Justice Frankfurter by a highly articulate group of liberals whose attitude toward the Supreme Court is frankly opportunistic—critical when they disagree with the Justices, as in the 30's, and approving when they agree, as in the present. Some of the unjust aspersions upon Justice Frankfurter's liberalism reflect the extent to which principles that should guide democratic *process* are conceived of merely as useful instruments toward specific *programs*. One reviewer, not the worst, of Justice Frankfurter's recent collection of miscellaneous papers and addresses[1] (from which I have already quoted) interprets his emphasis upon the need for "dominating humility" in judges as signifying that the judge "must not follow his own conviction but must derive his judgment as a spokesman, vicar, or proxy of some authoritative outside voice" (*New York Times Book Review*).

Nothing could be further removed from Justice Frankfurter's meaning. A judge who does not follow his own conviction is unworthy of his post, but his conviction must not be arbitrary or molded only by what he is famliar with in his personal experience. He must have a sense of the limits of his knowledge and of his power. He may, for example, be convinced that the free enterprise system is more efficient than any form of planned economy, and that all the freedoms of the Bill of Rights ultimately rest upon it, but he has no business reading that conviction into the Constitution by exegetical exercises on systematically ambiguous expressions like "due process." A judge without convictions should step down from the bench. But the conviction that he is not there to legislate; that the spirit of the democratic process gives this power to Congress; that on specific matters of policy he is not likely to be less foolish or more informed than most legislators; that although interpreting law is to some extent inescapably making law, there is a difference between adjudication and outright legislation—this according to Justice Frankfurter should be a judge's overriding conviction, and the source of his humility.

Justice Frankfurter pleads guilty to the charge of entertaining an "old-fashioned liberal's view of government and law." It is the liberalism with which we all grew up—even those who opposed it. If there has been any change, it has not been in Justice Frankfurter but in those sophisticated neo-Machiavellians who believe, despite the historical evidence, that in the long run courts are better guardians of the liberties

---

[1] Felix Frankfurter, *Of Law and Men* (New York, 1957).

and welfare of the people than a democratic legislature. They could well chew on his words: "If judges want to be preachers, they should dedicate themselves to the pulpit; if judges want to be primary shapers of policy, the legislature is their place." To make one's philosophy of judicial review dependent upon the composition of the Court at any definite time is cynical. Worse than cynical, it is foolish, for death and the pendulum of history are sure to place on the bench not merely conservatives but illiberals.

Justice Frankfurter, like Holmes, recognizes the difference between what I have elsewhere called "the strategic freedoms," those upon which the functioning of the free market in ideas depends, like freedom of speech, press, and assembly, and those freedoms which are required, say, for the functioning of the free market in commodities. But since the strategic freedoms are themselves not absolute and on occasion conflict, it is sometimes necessary to abridge a particular freedom in order to safeguard the entire complex of freedoms on which the democratic way of life rests. Here is the really troublesome area in which the justification for judicial review of Congressional legislation seems most plausible. Where Congress clearly acts in haste or panic, or in anticipation of having the Supreme Court save it from its own folly while it reaps electoral dividends, the Justices of the Court can exercise with an easy conscience the power John Marshall won for them. Justice Frankfurter, as I read him, would no more hesitate than Justice Holmes, under the *existing powers* of the Court, to put a brake upon Congressional action, to nullify legislation that clearly violated the strategic freedoms, even though he believes that the best appeal from majority rule, drunk and unenlightened, is to majority rule, sober and enlightened.

Such cases, however, are extremely rare. The more usual cases are those involving, as does the Smith Act, conflict between legitimate concern for the security of our system of freedom and legitimate fear that one or another strategic freedom has been too tightly circumscribed. Here, according to Justice Frankfurter, the issue is not whether the legislation is wise or justified, or whether the individual Justice agrees or disagrees with the way Congress has resolved the conflict of rights and interests, but whether the legislation was sufficiently reasonable in the light of the evidence and the spirit of deliberation. If the Smith Act is unwise, amend or repeal it, but do not invalidate it on the ground that you as an individual Justice personally do not appraise the Kremlin and its fifth column as a serious threat, or that if you had been a Congressman you would have voted against it. It is even conceivable that a Senator Douglas may understand the nature of the Communist threat better than a Justice Douglas. There are obvious difficulties in interpreting the rule of "reasonableness," but they are less formidable than those involved in any alternative rule.

It betokens no lack of deference for the Supreme Court to recognize that Justices are capable of talking and writing nonsense like lesser mortals, including Congressmen; that the appearance of a Justice Holmes is the result of a mutation, not the operation of a rule; that many judges in the lower courts, such as Justice Learned Hand (whose opinion upholding the constitutionality of the Smith Act was much more profound than Justice Vinson's), know more law than do most Supreme Court Justices; and that the opinions of the Supreme Court are not unaffected by the winds of doctrine that blow in the market place. Every system of law needs a Supreme Court: but a truly democratic community does not need a Supreme Court as an arbiter of its destinies.

Despite his detractors, Justice Frankfurter's stature will grow with time and with the increasing political maturity of the American people. Though he, too, is capable of lapsing into absurdities—as in his recurring references to nature as democratic—he manages to keep them out of his judicial opinions. And although he admires Harold J. Laski, that smart silly man who never understood the United States (despite many visits, he described it as if it were still in the 1890's) and who divined in Stalin's Russia the future of civilization, his admiration is not for Laski's unoriginal ideas but for the good show Laski put on, tall stories and all.

I I

In turning to Professor Zechariah Chafee's collection of speeches and articles we encounter a different kind of liberal spirit.[2] For many years a distinguished colleague of Justice Frankfurter's at the Harvard Law School, learned in the history of the Bill of Rights, free from that judicial gravity which inhibits quick and spontaneous judgments on men and events, Mr. Chafee radiates a breezy confidence that he incarnates the liberal tradition and that those who differ with him about problems, especially security problems, are suspect in their devotion to freedom.

When Mr. Chafee defends free speech as a general principle he is magnificent, especially in his rhetoric. But we are living in an age one of whose paradoxical features is that in the abstract everyone is in favor of free speech, just as everyone is in favor of democracy. No longer is there honest opposition to free speech as a principle, or to democracy as a form of government. In the case of totalitarians like Communists and fascists, this defense of free speech, or claim to be democratic on occasion, is largely dishonest, and consciously so. But genuine differ-

---

[2] Zechariah Chafee, *The Blessings of Liberty* (Philadelphia, 1956).

ences among most Americans today arise not over the justification of free speech but over its *problems:* where free speech can be limited and when, and above all what *constitutes* a problem of free speech or a violation of free speech. And here the issue around which almost all contemporary controversy revolves is whether the problem of security is one involving free speech. Does barring a man from a government job because he belongs to a subversive organization *ipso facto* constitute a violation of free speech? Does barring a man from a position because he expressed opinions which bear relevantly upon the job he is expected to do—though he is left free to shout these opinions from a housetop—constitute a violation of free speech? Does the occasional stupidity and injustice of the security system mean that we do not need one or that we must think up a better one?

It is a pity that in his sense of exaltation as a champion of freedom, Mr. Chafee tends to regard almost the entire problem of national security as a simple one of freedom of speech. It would follow from some of the positions he takes that any intelligent and effective security system is incompatible with the Bill of Rights. In consequence, he is often careless in his writing, defective in his logic, and emotional about problems that invite stubborn and prolonged thought. When he does reach sound conclusions it is sometimes in the fashion of someone who concludes that since the Mississippi rises in the French Pyrenees, and since France is a country in North America, therefore the Mississippi is a river in North America.

Ironically enough, the valid criticism which Mr. Chafee makes of the deplorable excesses committed in the quest for security do not require the rhetoric and debating devices he employs. For example, discussing the ill-considered McCarran Act of 1950, and approving the sound objections contained in Truman's veto message, Mr. Chafee concludes with the pious observation: "We must choose between freedom and fear—we cannot have both. If we persist in being afraid, the real rulers of this country will be fanatics. . . ."

Now this is sloppy thinking. No one chooses to be afraid; if we *persist* in being afraid—that is the surest sign that we are not afraid. There is a sense in which we can choose to be free but there is no proper sense in which we can *choose* to fear. Further, freedom and fear are perfectly compatible, just as are wisdom and fear. If we did not fear tyranny, we would not safeguard our free institutions. Mr. Chafee's own language indicates this. If he did not fear the rule of fanatics, he would not write his indignant essays. Not fear but unintelligent fear is the enemy. It is just as bad as unintelligent complacency.

This is a minor point but there are so many of them that they indicate a consistent style of thought. Another example illustrates this from a different angle. Mr. Chafee is discussing the unimportance of the Communist party. And, of course, considered independently of the Soviet Union, as Mr. Chafee considers it, the party is hardly more than a nuisance. But the absurdity is to consider it independently of the strength of the Soviet Union. To establish the insignificance of the Communist party, Mr. Chafee compares the number of members of the Communist party in the United States with that of the rest of the population. Historians, aware of Spartacus and Cromwell and Lenin, would scoff at this way of estimating the power of a revolutionary movement. Indeed, some of the fanatics whom Mr. Chafee fears argue that since the Bolsheviks were only a few thousand strong in February 1917 and were able to lay a mighty empire of tens of millions by the heels, they are a comparable menace everywhere. This is the counter-absurdity to Mr. Chafee's own procedure.

But it is the specific argument that Mr. Chafee offers in defense of his position which is instructive here. Writing in 1949, he compares the 70,000 members of the Communist party to the 150 million Americans and turns to his readers with the triumphant observation that the odds are almost 2,000 to 1 in favor of free institutions. Now, whatever the strength of his point, it would not be affected if the odds were 1,000 to 1 or even 100 to 1. But so indifferent is Mr. Chafee to the amenities of valid argument that he commits the statistical outrage of comparing 70,000 adult, dedicated, hardened, professional revolutionists, resting on a periphery of perhaps ten times that number, with a population which includes babes in arms, little children, the aged, infirm, sick, and confined. The same statistical method would confirm the claim of the old enlistment poster that it was safer to be a sailor on board Uncle Sam's battleships in the Spanish-American War than a civilian in the streets of New York.

I come now to matters that are more serious. The excesses of the security program with which Mr. Chafee, like all American liberals, is legitimately concerned may partly be attributed to angry reactions to the absence of an effective security program in the palmy days when Hiss was a red herring. So long as there is no intelligent security program, excesses and injustices will be plentiful. The best remedy for the latter is thoughtful consideration of the former. In places Mr. Chafee tends to dismiss the question of security as if it were simply a game of cops and robbers: wait until the criminal act is performed and then leave it to the FBI to catch the offenders. But certain actions connected with Communist infiltration, although highly undesirable, technically may not be criminal; and the function of a security program against espionage and sabotage is to *prevent* these activities from taking place, not to punish those guilty *after* they have taken place. Not only has Mr.

Chafee nothing to say on this question: his point of view is such that it would actually prevent any security program from operating.

This comes about as follows. Mr. Chafee "detests" Communists. But even more than Communists he detests spies and government agents. Most of all, he detests renegade Communists. "The worst spy of all is the renegade. He has already double-crossed the community by engaging in wrongdoing and then double-crossed his associates by deserting them and helping to punish them." You cannot be sure that spies tell the truth—and certainly not that renegades will! Therefore he would not use them or place any trust in their testimony. How, then, would Mr. Chafee keep members of the Communist party—70,000 strong or even much less—out of sensitive agencies like the many connected with the State Department, the military departments, the Atomic Energy Commission, or prevent them from having access to the secrets of our radar defense? (I assume that he would regard it as a legitimate measure of security, and not an expression of McCarthyism, to bar members of the Communist party from sensitive posts.) He rightly scorns hearsay evidence and dismisses membership in "alleged" Communist front organizations as worthless. How, then, tell whether X is a member of the Communist party? Presumably, the only method which meets with Mr. Chafee's approval is to ask him!

Mr. Chafee's emotionalism is apparent at every point in the discussion except the first. He detests Communists. "I have confronted a good many of them in the United Nations at Lake Success and Geneva. Some of them are menaces, a good many others are nuisances. They are opposed to every ideal of freedom which I hold dear. . . ." But the problem of security is not fundamentally one of Soviet diplomats at Lake Success or Geneva. It is one of fellow citizens under known instructions to infiltrate into strategic and sensitive posts in government and society in behalf of a foreign government which is the spearhead of an international movement to destroy the society Mr. Chafee holds dear. Mr. Chafee seems unaware of these instructions. For all his knowledge of the propaganda of Communism, he is apparently unfamilar with its organizational literature including specific injunctions to members to commit perjury when necessary in the party cause.

Mr. Chafee declares he wants "to prevent Communists from taking over our government and our lives and destroying our freedoms"—he has forgotten that he has told us there is no danger of this—but the actual problem is much more modest. For there is no danger, nor was there ever the remotest one, of Communists taking over the American government. The problem is much more modest. It is merely to keep them out of places where they can do harm, where as agents of a foreign power—and all members of the Communist party are potentially such

—they can weaken the free world in its struggle with the Communist world. But how can Mr. Chafee keep Communists out of positions of trust if he is more distrustful of ex-Communists than of Communists, and rejects with burning scorn the testimony of FBI agents like Philbrick, and others who were never Communists, not because their testimony has been shown false but because of the nature of their roles?

Mr. Chafee leaves no doubt that he puts far less trust in the Communist who recants than in the Communist who does not, because the first, as we have seen from the quotation above, is twice damned. Mr. Chafee makes so much of the fact that many well-meaning individuals got involved with Communist party organizations because of idealistic leanings that it is surprising to read his denunciation of them as "having double-crossed the community by engaging in wrongdoing." Very well. Let us accept Mr. Chafee's recognition of the fact that all Communists have double-crossed the community and engaged in wrongdoing. What, now, shall our attitude be toward them when, having realized what they were doing, and seeking to make amends to prevent further wrongdoing, they turn, not without risk, on their former fellow conspirators? It is precisely when they do this that they incur Mr. Chafee's intensest displeasure. One act doesn't cancel the other in his eyes: it only aggravates it.

This is not a normal moral reaction. A sincerely repentant criminal who reveals and forestalls, at great risk to himself, further crimes by his associates is, morally, surely not worse than the unrepentant criminal. Those followers of Hitler who finally saw where he was leading Germany, broke with him, and tried to kill him were surely not worse than the unreconstructed Nazis who fought for Hitler to the last.

With such ideas about Communists, government agents, and ex-Communists, no security program is possible. If Mr. Chafee had the courage of his passionate resentments, he would, like Alan Barth (or, as he interprets Mr. Barth), make no bones about scrapping the whole program. This would rekindle the fires of McCarthyism.

How deep Mr. Chafee's emotionalism goes is evidenced by the positions it leads him to take on two legal matters—one involving the question of Congressional investigations, and the other his interpretation of the privilege against self-incrimination in the Fifth Amendment.

On the first question, again it is not Mr. Chafee's conclusion which is at fault. The activity of some Congressional committees, aside from possible criticism of them on grounds of their constitutionality, warrants strong rebuke. The recent harassment of Mr. Cogley and Mr. Javits typifies what is most objectionable in the procedure of these committees. It is, however, the reasoning which attends Mr. Chafee's conclusion that is puzzling. It is not enough for him to point out that a Congressional committee is not a law enforcement agency. Nor is he satisfied with distinguishing, as some committee chairmen from Dies to Walter unfortunately have not, between inquiry into matters relevant to legislation and inquiry into personal opinion. He attacks Congressional committees for asking questions which result in the crimes of perjury and contempt, "crimes which would never have been committed at all except for the investigations." He charges that "the committees did not unearth the offenses, they created them." It is not the actions of the witnesses which are responsible for their plight—their words in the case of perjury, their refusal to speak in the case of contempt—but the actions of Congress which have "turned scores of previously law-abiding citizens into criminals."

To realize what egregious legal nonsense an illustrious professor of law can sometimes talk, we must recall that questions about membership in the Communist party, the source of its funds and related affairs, are perfectly relevant to the kind of information Congress should have in order intelligently to legislate—or not to legislate—about a variety of matters connected with Communism. A witness who fears that he may be prosecuted under the Smith Act or who fears that his answer would tend to incriminate him, whether in fact it does or not, whether he is a Communist or not, may invoke the Fifth Amendment with complete legal impunity. No Congressional committee has ever denied a witness that privilege except when he himself has waived it. If anything, these committees seem to be too eager to increase the number of those who invoke it.

We must remember that the witness found guilty of committing perjury or contempt must first be tried. The courts may not recognize the relevance of the questions to the scope of authorized Congressional inquiry. They may throw out the charge. The jury may refuse to convict. Mr. Chafee is talking about witnesses who have been legally convicted after a fair trial on the basis of their lying words, or for defiance of a properly constituted legislative body. The committees, whatever one thinks of them, did not compel the witnesses to lie, or to withhold testimony. No system of law or government can permit the witness to be the final authority on what evidence is relevant or admissible.

To be sure, if no questions were asked, no perjury or contempt would be committed by refusal to answer. Should we therefore blame the questioners for these crimes? As well say that law is the cause of crime, marriage of divorce, property of theft; for if the first did not exist, neither would the second. The Congressional committees do not *make* the laws which govern perjury and contempt. And not *they,* but the courts, find witnesses guilty of breaking them. To lay the responsibility for the voluntary actions of the offenders at the door of the committees is comparable to holding the tariff laws responsible for the crime of smuggling. Since under the same laws, some smuggle and some do not, the laws cannot be the cause, or the most decisive part of the cause, of the crime of smuggling. Since only a handful of witnesses before Congressional committees commit perjury or contempt when questioned, the questions cannot be the cause, or the most decisive part of the cause, of these crimes.

Space does not permit a detailed analysis of Mr. Chafee's discussion of the privilege against self-incrimination and of the inferences which may legitimately be drawn from its invocation. His treatment is shot through with errors—some of logic, some of psychology, and most of common sense. It will be sufficient for our purposes here to focus discussion on an issue which divides Mr. Chafee from the position taken by Harvard University toward a professor who invokes the Fifth Amendment in answer to a question which bears on the fulfillment of his professional trust.

Harvard University has had a magnificent record in defense of academic freedom. On May 20, 1953, it declared:

> We think membership in the Communist Party by a Faculty member today, with its usual concomitant of secret domination by the Party, goes beyond the realm of his political beliefs and associations. It cuts to the core of his ability to perform his duties with independence of thought and judgment. By the same token it is beyond the scope of academic freedom. In the absence of extraordinary circumstances, we would regard present membership in the Communist Party by a member of our Faculty as grave misconduct, justifying removal.

> We deplore the use of the Fifth Amendment by a member of our Faculty. . . . *Furthermore, since we are not conducting a criminal trial, we will not shut our eyes to the inference of guilt, which the use of the Fifth Amendment creates as a matter of common sense. Hence, the use of the Fifth Amendment by a member of our teaching staff within the critical field of his possible domination by the Communist Party makes it necessary in our judgment for us to inquire into the full facts.* We regard it as misconduct, though not necessarily grave misconduct [my italics].

Mr. Chafee takes issue with the reasoning of the Harvard Corporation. He denies that the claim of the privilege is misconduct. "As one who has sworn allegiance to the Constitution, I think this is a very inappropriate phrase to apply to the use of a right given by the Constitution."

What Mr. Chafee is saying is that the exercise of a Constitutional right can never be an instance of ethical or professional misconduct; that because one is privileged to exercise a legal right it can never be morally wrong to exercise it. Mr. Chafee is demonstrably mistaken. What is legally permitted may be morally inadmissible. Depending upon the circumstances under which a legal right is exercised, the activity it involves might be the object of severe and justifiable moral censure.

Suppose a professor publishes something written by someone else, which is now in the public domain, under his own name. He is exercising his Constitutional right to freedom of the press. Plagiarism is not a crime. Yet although he is legally not liable, professionally and morally he is guilty of misconduct. Suppose a scientist cooks his experiment for pay. There is nothing illegal about his action. He has a Constitutional right to do business this way. But he is guilty of the grossest professional and moral misconduct. Suppose a teacher abuses his students and colleagues with the vilest epithets, but stays just within the libel laws. He is exercising his Constitutional right to free speech, but professionally and morally this is conduct unbecoming a teacher. Like many others, Mr. Chafee hasn't the faintest notion that the objection to Communist party teachers does not lie in their "heterodox opinions" but in their *violations of professional ethics*.

The declaration of the Harvard Corporation goes to the heart of the matter in its assertion that sheer common sense indicates that invocation of the Fifth Amendment creates an inference, or presumption, of guilt. This presumption, of course, is not a conclusive one. But *unless resolved* in a hearing, which should be granted to all who invoke the privilege, it is normally sufficiently strong to justify the refusal of employment to someone in a position of trust who invokes the privilege against self-incrimination when asked questions bearing on the performance of his duties—a cashier, a nurse, a policeman, a guide, or even a newspaper man. Mr. Chafee's discussion of "the right not to speak" indicates that he flatly refuses to acknowledge that there is any legitimate inference of guilt, as a matter of common sense, whenever the privilege is invoked. Here he is in good company. The *obiter dicta* of several Justices of the Supreme Court show that they, too, have failed to see that because there is no *conclusive* presumption of guilt when the Fifth Amendment is invoked, it does not follow that it is illegitimate to infer a *presumption* of guilt.

There are three alternatives here to choose among, not two: no inference of guilt whatsoever, according to Mr. Chafee; a *conclusive* presumption of guilt, according to McCarthy; a presumption of guilt warranting further inquiry, according to common sense—and I say common sense because everybody makes this presumption in ordinary life when he is not trying to prove a legal point.

It is in connection with his discussion of the Fifth Amendment that Mr. Chafee makes one of the most horrendous statements ever leveled against the system of American justice and the character of the American government. In explaining the position of a witness embarrassed by a question, he points out that if he answers falsely he may be convicted of perjury. Mr. Chafee then adds: *"And a perjury conviction may follow even if he answers truthfully; the witness may expect, with good reason, that the jury will disbelieve the truth, being persuaded by government witnesses who hate him and are themselves perjurors"* (my emphasis).

Mr. Chafee obviously believes that this is no mere possibility but occurs sufficiently often to represent a danger to innocent and truthful witnesses in American courts. I doubt whether the author grasps the clear import of the charge he is making not only against the courts but against his government. Not only does he fail to substantiate it as something which frequently occurs, he does not cite a single case (and as horrible as it would be, a single case would not prove the charge) in which an innocent man truthfully denying Communist connections was convicted of perjury. That he could bring himself to make such a charge impugning in this wholesale way the American system of justice, with all its imperfections, is a measure of his emotionalism. It blinds him to obvious facts such as that instructions to commit perjury are issued by the Communist party to its members, not by the government to its witnesses.

It remains to explain how a scholar of such learning, and one so passionately devoted to the traditions of freedom, should be so profoundly in error about the nature of the Communist problem in the world today. The explanation, I believe, is provided by Mr. Chafee himself when he writes: "It is now more than thirty-five years since my work as a student of freedom of speech led me to pay considerable attention to the activities of Communists in this country. My considered opinion is that they are far less dangerous today [1949] than they were in 1919–1920, soon after the Russian Revolution."

Few opinions ever had less foundation in fact. The American Communist movement in 1919–20 was mainly a group of national sections which had split away from the Socialist party. They were completely isolated from American life, and most of their members could hardly speak English. With no mass organizations and without even the tiniest foothold in a trade union, they spent their time debating the merits of "mass action" over "action of the masses." For all their flaming manifestoes, it was *opéra bouffe*. They were torn apart by sectarian factionalism which did not end until 1929 when, under Browder, the original instructions of the Comintern began to be implemented, and infiltration on a large scale was undertaken, front organizations developed, and dual trade unionism finally abolished.

Most important of all, Mr. Chafee does not understand that, from the beginning down to the present, the threat of Communism to the United States was never endemic. Only as the foreign arm of the Soviet Union could the Communist party threaten American security. But in 1919–1920 the Soviet Union hung by a thread. There is no evidence that so much as a single cell was organized by the Communist party in any government service in 1919 and 1920. The Communist party became strong in this country only as the Soviet Union did. Mr. Chafee has obviously not studied the structure of Communist organization and the multiple threads which bind it to the greatest aggregation of power on earth. He would do well to read some of the literature published by the Congressional committees at which he scoffs. He would understand that in 1919–1920 it would have been far more accurate to regard the Communists as thoughtless heretics made feverish by their own rhetorical extravagances than as dangerous conspirators. They were more appropriately objects of satire and laughter than of Palmer's lawless and inhuman raids.

The paradox is that at a time (1949) when the Communist party was a powerful Fifth Column, not only organized underground but entrenched in large unions, able to launch a Progressive party that could snare more than a million votes, Mr. Chafee writes of Communists as if they were still primarily heretics rather than conspirators. He compares those who invoke the Fifth Amendment today when asked about their participation in Communist activities with honest and independent spirits like Thoreau and Garrison. But the words: "I am in earnest —I will not equivocate—I will not excuse—I will not retreat a single inch and I will be heard," sound worlds apart from "I refuse to answer on the ground that a truthful reply would tend to incriminate me."

For all his reading of Communist literature, Mr. Chafee understands the nature of the Communist movement no more in the small than in the large. He cites the Joint Anti-Fascist Refugee Committee as an organization dedicated solely to helping the widows and orphans of Spain, a victim, alas! of Congressional persecution. He seems unfamiliar with the evidence that not only was it a notorious Communist front but that a considerable portion of the money it raised "for widows and children" was actually diverted to Communist party purposes. Photostatic copies of the committee checks paid to Gerhard Eisler, under the alias of Eiseman, representative of the Comintern in the U.S. and the Kremlin's link with the American underground, were published in the newspapers. They seem to have escaped Mr. Chafee's notice. It would have been more appropriate for an intelligent liberal to denounce this fraud on the American public than the Congressional investigation into what was transparently a part of the American Communist movement.

Despite the mountains of evidence about the character of the Communist movement, Mr. Chafee basically sees Communists in the same light as he saw Soviet diplomats at the United Nations: as mostly "nuisances." No one can question his liberalism. But liberalism is sentimentality unless its sentiment for freedom is nurtured by reason. It is not enough, as Mr. Chafee does, to praise reason. Better than praising reason is using it.

No one can put down Mr. Chafee's book without the feeling that, according to him, the greatest overt threat to American institutions comes not from the Stalins and the Khrushchevs, not from the Hisses, Fields, and the Dexter Whites, not from the Fuchses, Golds, and Rosenbergs, not from the Browders and Fosters and Dennises, but from the Chamberses and Philbricks, from the Brownells and Hoovers, from the House Committee on un-American Activities and the Senate Judiciary Sub-Committee on Subversive Activities. One can be a severe critic of the views and activities of all the latter without countenancing the absurdity of regarding episodic folly and stupidity as more reprehensible than systematic subversion of free institutions. Happily McCarthyism is dead —killed not by such criticisms as these of Mr. Chafee, on which it throve, but by its own excesses. It is time to inter with it ritualistic liberalism which cannot distinguish between heresy and conspiracy.

20   The Fallacies of Ritualistic Liberalism

RITUALISTIC LIBERALISM is the reliance upon rhetoric rather than logic, slogans rather than analysis of problems in defense of freedom. It does not rethink situations afresh but makes a ritual of phrases, principles, and solutions which have come down from the past as if they were sufficient guides to complex and novel issues. No issue is completely novel, and the complex is sometimes an organization of simples viewed in a fresh way. That is why the past is relevant. But there may be a profound difference between what is relevant and what is reliable.

The reactionary social thinker is a stand-patter who uses the past as a model for excellence. The ritualistic liberal is a stand-patter who when he invokes the past draws different lessons from it. That the past can be invoked as an authority for conflicting positions indicates that in the end the use we make of the past, actual or imagined, is determined by what we regard as desirable in the present.

The genuine liberal who faces problems as they arise, instructed by experience but without recipes, is a lone thinker usually uncomfortable even in an organization of liberals. For as necessary as they are, organizations tend to make fetishes of their programs, to stop thinking in the interests of action, and therefore sometimes to act unwisely or hastily.

The intelligent defense of freedom during the last decade in the United States has been hampered by two movements, which I have called cultural vigilantism and ritualistic liberalism, which in their failure to make proper intellectual distinctions have more in common with each other than they are aware. Cultural vigilantism, since the eclipse of Senator McCarthy, is on the decline. Today ritualistic liberalism is growing in strength. This makes all the more relevant the following study of the ideas of one who may rightfully be regarded as among its chief spokesmen—Robert Maynard Hutchins.

Florence Nightingale's great reforms in the care of the sick are said to have begun with the resolution that hospitals should not be breeders of disease. According to Robert M. Hutchins, the aim of the Fund for the Republic, of which, for a number of years, he has been President and chief spokesman, is to shed light on the Bill of Rights. Surely it is not unreasonable to expect that whatever else Hutchins does, as the chief spokesman of the Fund he should not generate confusion about the Bill of Rights. But this is precisely what he has succeeded in doing. And he began even before he was selected to replace Clifford Case as President of the Fund.

Robert Hutchins has been a positive boon to groups and individuals not overly solicitous about civil liberties ranging from Communists and their sympathizers to Senator McCarthy, his friends and allies. Just before he became President of the Fund, the Communist-dominated Teachers Union of New York (expelled from both the AFL and the CIO) offered him its annual award, which he first accepted and then declined under pressure from officials of the Ford Foundation, with which he was then associated. On the other side, right-wing extremists have seized upon certain fundamental confusions in his thinking and flaunted them as typical of liberalism generally. The most notable of his confusions is his apparently incorrigible belief that efforts to bar members of the Communist conspiracy from positions of trust in Government and society must necessarily lead to the abandonment of the Bill of Rights.

In addition, Hutchins has unweariedly asserted for years that civil liberties have been eclipsed in the United States, that our schools and colleges, our leading universities and newspapers have capitulated to the witch-hunters. In a speech before the American Jewish Congress, he assured the guests that it was a dangerous thing not only to speak up for the Bill of Rights but to put in an appearance at the banquet in his honor.

We are accustomed to the unedifying spectacle of the professional patrioteer who, whenever he is attacked, wraps himself in the flag and denounces his critics for being un-American. It is no more edifying to watch Hutchins, under fire for foolish and extreme statements, wrap himself in the Bill of Rights and, instead of replying to responsible criticism, imply that all his critics are enemies of freedom. The truth is that the existence of a Communist conspiratorial movement exploiting the institutions of freedom in order to destroy the defenses of freedom, in coordination with the most powerful state in Europe and Asia, poses extremely difficult problems. They cannot be met with the empty rhetoric of denunciation whether it comes from cultural vigilantes or ritualistic liberals. One expects from Hutchins more intellection, more illuminating analysis, just a little more wisdom about how to reconcile conflicting freedoms than from his noisy and ignorant detractors of the Right. He has preached so much about education of the intellect that it is not unfair to expect him to exercise it on the problems of how to survive and remain free. Instead, we witness almost a complete failure to recognize that we have any problems except those created by too much concern with Communism, and dogmatic pronouncements about the meaning of the Constitution and the Bill of Rights which would make incredible the growth and defense of the Union, the great court decisions on civil rights, and much of our common law.

The patrioteer who hides behind the flag can enjoy the illusion of covering himself because the flag is all of a piece. But one who wraps himself in the Bill of Rights covers himself in one place only to expose himself in others. For the Constitution and Bill of Rights defend an entire complex of freedoms. Intelligent political life in a democracy consists in resolving conflicts of freedoms in such a way as to strengthen the security of the entire structure of our freedoms. This means that when right clashes with right, one or the other right must be given priority depending upon historical circumstances and a vague but meaningful concept of the public welfare and common good. It is absurd to speak as if any particular right is absolute or unlimited or can be exercised independently of its effects on social welfare and the whole complex of freedoms. For example, the Bill of Rights guarantees to the individual a right to a fair trial. It also guarantees free speech and press. What shall we do if the exercise of the right to free speech and press prejudices a man's right to a fair trial? Which yields to which under what conditions, and in the light of what guiding considerations? Our laws seek to protect individuals against slander and libel, incitement to violence, treason and foreign conquest, which may entail some limitation on freedom of speech. The problem is where, when and how. Even "the free exercise" of one's religion must sometimes be balanced in relation to other moral goods and values, as voodoo worshipers and pious believers in plural marriages know.

In a discussion of civil liberties, it is not unreasonable to expect of the responsible head of a foundation devoted to understanding them some fruitful analysis. But to Hutchins all this is an unnecessary and sophistic complication. Rights are absolute, inalienable and sacrosanct, and that's an end on't. In a recent speech, he caustically criticized someone's statement that individual rights "do not supersede the right of the [democratic] state to protect itself against subversion, sabotage or treason." Hutchins objected to this on the grounds that "the rights of the individual remain perpetually sacrosanct. They may not be subverted under any circumstances, least of all in the name of safeguarding the Republic. The preservation of these rights is the purpose of the state."

One is left aghast at the extremism and irresponsible judgment which denies that the Bill of Rights is not a protection for subversion. This plays right into the hands of those who would limit our freedom even when it is not necessary to protect the complex of our other freedoms. Does not Hutchins know that the Constitution itself provides for the suspension of the writ of habeas corpus in order to safeguard the Republic? Is he trying to tell us that Abraham Lincoln is a precursor of Senator McCarthy? Is he implying that Justice Holmes in elaborating the "clear and present danger" doctrine was betraying democracy because he indicated the conditions under which freedom of speech could and should be abridged? But that doctrine was enunciated in the course of a most eloquent defense of free speech! As well say that the existence of traffic rules is illegitimate because it restricts absolute freedom of movement, despite the fact that such rules enable us to get where we want to go faster, more safely and therefore more freely.

Who makes more sense, Hutchins with his claim that the right of the individual to free speech is "perpetually sacrosanct," or Justice Holmes in his observation: "The most stringent protection of free speech would not protect a man in falsely shouting fire in a theater"? And shouldn't we add that the most stringent protection of the Bill of Rights would not protect a man in engaging in subversion, sabotage or treason—or inciting a mob to lynch Negroes? Or have we failed in extending the rights of due legal process to those charged with subversion and treason—to the Rosenbergs, Gold or Coplon?

Why should Hutchins even give the appearance of contesting this? Whatever the reason, McCarthy and his friends had in him a perfect foil for their campaigns against liberalism. If Hutchins did not exist, they would have had to invent him.

In what follows, I propose to discuss a number of confusions which mark Hutchins's thinking about Communism, civil liberties, and the nature of freedom. I will show why all liberals, together with Hutchins, must disagree both with McCarthy and with the Communists. I shall also try to show why liberals who are informed and intelligent about the nature of Communism must also disagree with Hutchins.

Before doing so, I wish to state as clearly as I can that although the problems of domestic Communism cannot be separated from world Communism—we are dealing with one movement—these domestic problems have been blown up into dimensions out of all proportion to their true significance. The problem of Communist penetration into positions of trust is difficult but *minor*. It can be compared to having cinders in the eye. If one keeps on rubbing the eye instead of removing the cinders by expert and delicate treatment, the eye swells and becomes inflamed to a point where we can no longer see the big things on the horizon. This is the McCarthy treatment. The Hutchins treatment is to deny that there are any cinders in the eye and to attack any attempt at their discreet elimination as a violation of our natural right to see. But a minor infection incorrectly treated may cause a major infection.

The failure to handle problems of security adequately, ranging from original laxity to overcompensating stringency and stupidity, has resulted in scores of cases of injustice to individual non-Communists and sometimes even anti-Commuists who have lost their careers because of innocent involvements with others. Nonetheless, the way to avoid injustice in treating security cases is not to deny that there is any problem of security. Hutchins calls for "righteous indignation" with administrative abuses of security rules, as in the cases of Chasanow, Radulovitch and Ladejinsky. Excellent! We need more righteous indignation. But one will look in vain for a flash of righteous indignation on Hutchins's part against Communist abuses of trust and the conditions which made them possible in the Hiss case, the Rosenberg case, the Marzani case, the Coplon case, the White case—to mention only a few—whose cumulative impact panicked Democrats and Republicans equally into transforming an alleged "red herring" into an entire school of flying whales.

Fallacy Number One

Suppose the President of the American Jewish Congress, an organization devoted to combating anti-Semitism, were to declare publicly: "I certainly am prepared to hire an anti-Semite or a member of an anti-Semitic organization to work for the Congress provided he is competent and I can supervise his work." We can well imagine the outcry which would arise from the Jewish community, whose memory of its six million co-religionists massacred by anti-Semites is still vivid. Or suppose the Executive Secretary of the NAACP, an organization devoted to the defense of the human and civil rights of Negroes, were to declare that he was prepared to hire a member of the Ku Klux Klan, provided, of course, that the Klansman was efficient in his task and could be watched. Even if there weren't a Till case to exacerbate its feelings, the Negro community would be justifiably indignant and resentful.

But no one should be judged without a hearing. And we can well imagine the mythical President of the American Jewish Congress making the following defense:

"Not so fast. We believe in civil rights not only for Jews but for non-

Jews and even for those who are anti-Jewish. After all, our very existence is proof that we are opposed to judging people by labels. Haven't we ourselves suffered from labeling? The term 'Jewish' is a label which bigots affix to an entire group of people and then proceed to judge members of the group irrespective of their individual differences—forgetting that there are all kinds of Jews. Well, if there are all kinds of Jews, there are all kinds of anti-Semites, too, and merely because a man is a member of an anti-Semitic organization pledged to liquidate Jews is no reason why we should assume that he is automatically unfit to work for an organization devoted to defending the civil rights of Jews. To make such an assumption is to believe in guilt by association. It really is a form of blacklisting. For us to say 'anti-Semites not wanted' is like others saying 'Jews not wanted.' We must judge each individual case strictly on its own merits and not by an organizational label. For all we know to the contrary, the individual in question may be a 'bad' anti-Semite; perhaps he doesn't agree with Hitler even if he has heard of him. There are various degrees of membership in anti-Semitic organizations and varying intensities of belief. He may not believe in gas chambers to solve the Jewish problem but exclusively in legal process and education to exclude them. Guilt is personal or it is non-existent. If an anti-Semite is more competent for a job in our organization than any other candidate and if we can supervise his work, morally we cannot discriminate against him. And any Jew who disagrees with this position is as much opposed to civil liberties as the anti-Semites! He is a kind of anti-Semite himself."

It would not be long before the fallacies in this kind of argument were laid bare. Let us list some of them:

(*a*) First, the denial of a job to an anti-Semite in an organization devoted to fighting anti-Semitism is not a denial of his civil rights. The right to a *specific* job is not part of the Bill of Rights but depends on the fulfilment of certain qualifications—in this case, the acceptance of the ends of the organization. If the candidate professes to accept the ends of the organization—defense of Jewish rights—what is he doing in an organization whose program is liquidation of Jewish rights and of Jews altogether?

(*b*) Labeling Jews (or Negroes) and judging their *beliefs* and *character* in virtue of their *being* Jews (or Negroes) is intellectually and morally vicious. People are *born* Jews or Negroes. They *acquire* their specific beliefs. But individuals are not born members of anti-Semitic organizations. They acquire membership by a *voluntary* and personal *action* for which they are morally responsible. It is not blacklisting a person when justifiable moral grounds exist for excluding him. His voluntary and personal act of membership constitutes such a ground.

(c) What does it mean to say that a man is a "bad" anti-Semite? It can only mean that he has repudiated the principles and program of anti-Semitism. If he did, he would not be likely to remain in an anti-Semitic organization or be tolerated in one.

By this time, the reader must be wondering about the pertinence of all this to Robert Hutchins and his views about Communists and civil liberties. Surely I am not suggesting that the simplistic thinking of our hypothetical President of the American Jewish Congress in any way represents Hutchins's ideas on the subject. Unfortunately, if Hutchins's public declarations and writings are an indication of his thinking, I am not only suggesting that he is guilty of these egregious fallacies but I propose to demonstrate it. Substitute the term "Communist" for "anti-Semite," and the Fund for the Republic for the American Jewish Congress, and the foregoing sounds like a complete plagiarism on the hiring of Communists by the Fund.

I present this criticism in the stubborn hope that Hutchins—if I may take him here to stand not only for himself but for all ritualistic liberals —will come to see that his position is really a disservice to the cause of civil liberties, that it makes the defense of our democratic institutions from conspiratorial infiltration more difficult and permits cultural vigilantes, who are opposed to Communists and civil libertarians alike, to exploit his confusions for their own purposes.

My criticism of Hutchins's notions is not to be construed as a criticism of the Fund for the Republic, which has a great opportunity to serve the cause of civil liberties and of understanding civil liberties. Nor, on the other hand, is this an endorsement of all its activities. But that is a story for another day. . . .

In a well-publicized interview with the press, followed by a coast-to-coast telecast on November 20, 1955, Hutchins declared that he would be willing to hire a present member of the Communist party to work for the Fund for the Republic, provided the individual in question was qualified and could be supervised. To appreciate the significance of this declaration, we must remember, first, that the Communist party is a conspiratorial organization one of whose purposes is the establishment of a Communist dictatorship which would destroy the civil liberties of all but those who agree with the dictatorship. That is to say, the victory of Communism would have the same effect on the preservation of our liberties as the victory of anti-Semitism would have on the rights of Jews. Second, membership in the Communist party is voluntary. Third, the check upon membership by the various control committees of the Communist party is severe and periodic, and among the grounds for expulsion are not only disagreement with the party line but inactivity.

Now why should any reasonable person declare that as head of an organization devoted to civil liberties he would hire a Communist party member to work for it? Several reasons suggest themselves. One may believe that members of the Communist party are like members of other political parties and therefore that it is an invidious distinction to discriminate between them and the members of these other parties. Or perhaps it might be imagined that the nature of the work to be done is such that membership in the Communist party is some qualification for that work or at least not patently a disqualification.

Is it possible that Hutchins still seriously believes that the Communist party is like other political parties? Why, then, has he himself carefully qualified his statement of willingness to employ members of the Communist party by asserting that, in addition to being competent, they must be carefully supervised or watched? This would indicate that he does not regard them as trustworthy. He obviously is not prepared to repose the same confidence in them as in non-Communists. Why, then, should he proclaim that he would be prepared to hire Communists, meaning present members of the Communist party, to work for the Fund for the Republic?

This brings us to the underlying reason which explains Hutchins's position not only with respect to employing Communists in an anti-Communist organization but with respect to employing them in other capacities in which their doctrines and organizational directives instruct them to abuse their professional trust. Hutchins maintains that, after all, it is not inconceivable or impossible that a member of the Communist party may actually not believe in Communism. He may be a "bad" Communist. And even if a party member is a "good" Communist and believes in the Communist program, it is possible that he will never attempt to indoctrinate for it or carry out its instructions.

Speaking specifically of teachers, he wrote a few years ago: "A man who is a bad member of the Communist party may conceivably [*sic*] be qualified to be a professor because he has retained his independence; and a good member of the party may be qualified to be a professor if he retains his independence in the field in which he teaches and conducts his research." (*Ethics,* 1951, reprinted in *Bulletin of the AAUP,* Vol. 37, pp. 244–45.)

What Hutchins believes true for teaching he applies to Government service generally; and what he believes true for Government service he believes true—as his telecast showed—even for posts in an organization pledged to defend freedom. In his telecast of last November 20, he said in answer to a question as to whether he would hire members of the Communist party for an organization which is fighting Communism:

"What this question amounts to is this: Is it conceivable that you could possibly think that in any capacity at any time an individual who belonged to the Communist party could possibly be associated with any enterprise with which you're connected? I don't see how you can say such a conclusion is absolutely inconceivable any more than you could say that a thousand-to-one shot is absolutely inconceivable."

Now it is certainly true that it is conceivable for a member of the Communist party to disbelieve in Communism in the sense that it is not logically contradictory or logically impossible to be a member of the Communist party and opposed to Communism. It is also logically conceivable that a man may be a member of Murder, Inc. and fervently opposed to murder. It is logically conceivable that a bottle labeled "poison" may be mislabeled and actually be a nourishing substance. It is possible that pigs may fly in the sense that it is not "absolutely inconceivable."

However, we are dealing with situations in which we must use that degree of probability which in our judgment is appropriate to the particular subject-matter. And when we lay down a *policy,* our formulation must center not on abstract logical possibilities, not even on remote probabilities, but on the weight of evidence as it has been historically established. Where men are concerned, it must agree with the knowledge we have of human beings and their motives. Certainly it is conceivable that a member of Murder, Inc. may never commit a crime or be tempted to commit one, but no reasonable person would rely on it or hire him for a bodyguard. Of course, a bottle labeled "poison" *may* contain a nourishing substance, but what person in his right mind would base a policy on that recondite possibility? Pigs might conceivably fly, but who would therefore take off from the Empire State Building mounted on a porcine charger? Abstract possibilities, when applied to concrete, historical, especially political situations, represent fantasies. *That means the abandonment of evidence when confronted by the problem of formulating a reasonable policy.*

To talk about what is logically conceivable—about examples which Hutchins himself admits have never "occurred in my experience or are likely to occur"—is to talk about what is irrelevant as a guide to action. Anything not self-contradictory is logically conceivable, but wisdom consists in recognizing which alternative among all logically conceivable ones is the most likely to be true. To be sure, all generalizations of fact may be disproved by an exception and there is no logical guarantee that an exception will not crop up. But a policy cannot be based on the abstract possibility of an exception.

The error which is at the basis of Hutchins's thinking was exposed long ago by Aristotle, who observed in the *Nicomachean Ethics*—one of the "hundred great books"—that "it is the mark of an educated man to look for precision in each class of things just as far as the nature of the subject admits: It is evidently equally foolish to accept probable reasoning from a mathematician and to demand from a rhetorician scientific proofs."

In human affairs, we cannot reasonably require certainty, and in a political context we must be satisfied with much less than certainty.

To charge Hutchins with sympathy for Communism or Communists because of his misplaced sense of methodological nicety is absurd. All it indicates is a lack of common sense. But it is lack of common sense whose consequences are prejudicial first of all to the individuals engaged by the Fund for the Republic on research projects.

After Hutchins's broadcast in which he indicated he was prepared to hire members of the Communist party who were qualified for the post, some of my neighbors who heard it asked me how many Communists I thought were working for the Fund. I replied, "None." "Why, then," they rejoined, "did Hutchins go to such trouble to make the point about their employability?" The effect of Hutchins's foolish remark was to raise a doubt in the mind of a number of people about the *bona fides* of the Fund's investigators. In time, these doubts may grow. An honest research worker for the Fund, discovering that here and there Communist influence has been exaggerated or that Communists have been unjustly treated, will feel some reluctance to broadcast his conclusions. He may fear that his results will be interpreted in such a way as to raise a question, planted by Hutchins's injudicious observation, as to whether or not he falls into the category of a "qualified Communist," and whether, in reply to another suggested doubt, he has been properly watched.

What Hutchins should have said to defend the reputation for professional integrity of the men working on the Fund for the Republic projects was something quite different. He *should* have said:

"The public can be quite confident that our investigators who are conducting research to establish the objective truth about the state of civil liberty in this country and/or the degree of Communist influence in this or that cultural field will be qualified and free of any pro-Communist bias." If Hutchins had then been asked whether membership in the Communist party would be considered *prima facie* evidence of pro-Communist bias, his answer should have been: "Yes—and although it is not logically impossible for a member of the Communist party to be free of pro-Communist bias, this is such a remote possibility that we cannot take it seriously even aside from whether it would be worth taking a risk on him. After all, we don't take a thousand-to-one shot even in a horse race! And we are not running a horse race but fighting for freedom."

It will be remembered Hutchins said that not only must a Communist be qualified to work on a project but his work must be of such a nature as permits of supervision. Here again, Hutchins's proposal makes no organizational sense. Consider a member of the Communist party hired to investigate the degree and modes of penetration of Communists into a particular field. Since he cannot be trusted, he must be watched or supervised constantly. In effect, Hutchins is saying that for every qualified Communist who is hired a non-Communist must be hired (or assigned from those already hired) to watch him. To what purpose? Why not hire (or assign) the qualified non-Communist in the first place? Subsequently, Hutchins pretended in a newspaper interview that what he really meant was that he would employ members of the Communist party for non-ideological work like that of window-cleaner or messenger boy. This is a disingenuous evasion. In that case, why make such a point about watching them?

Fallacy Number Two

Members of the Communist party are members of a conspiracy one of whose goals is the destruction of all civil liberties. This should bar them from employment in any organization devoted to the preservation of civil liberties. But the difference between a democracy and a totalitarian Communist dictatorship is that in the first even Communists (and fascists) are recognized as human beings, whereas in totalitarian countries democrats are destroyed like vermin. And not only democrats. Khrushchev recently referred to the unhappy executors of his agricultural policy as "human filth." They had failed in achieving the norms.

On the other hand, in a democracy even Communists have certain legal and human rights, among the latter being the right to some kind of employment. In a democracy, not *all* kinds of employment can or should be denied them. Nonetheless, this does not give them a right to a *specific* job.

Hutchins's second material fallacy is to confuse the *ethical* demand a person may make on society for opportunity of employment with a right to a specific kind of employment. This is the source of his failure to realize that membership in the Communist party normally constitutes a bar to posts in the government which the Communist party has sworn to overthrow. This does not mean that a security check should be made of all who fill Government posts—a needless, cumbersome and inefficient procedure which is the current practice. It does mean that where membership in the Communist party is established, or where an individual refuses to answer questions concerning such membership on the ground that a truthful answer would tend to incriminate him, he should be barred from Government positions. No one has an ethical right to be on the payroll of the government he has sworn to destroy. Or, as Roger Baldwin once put it: "A superior loyalty to a foreign government disqualifies a citizen from service to our own."

This is the present practice, and Hutchins minces no words in criticizing it. "Why," he asks, "should the Government demand that a man convict himself out of his own mouth instead of requiring the prosecution to make the effort to establish the charges it has brought against him?" He then goes on to add that "Injury is added to insult if there is no pretense that the questions asked must be relevant or proper." And, as an illustration of the kind of questions or considerations which would be irrelevant to the duties of Government employment, Hutchins writes: "If the President were to refuse to employ bald-headed men in the Federal establishment, the Supreme Court would find, I believe, that the bald had been deprived of their Constitutional rights." (*Annals of the American Academy of Political and Social Science,* 1955.)

The significance of these observations can be assessed only if we recall that they are made in the context of discussion of whether membership in the Communist party should bar a person from working for the Government or holding a teaching post in the public schools. That as late as April 2, 1955, Hutchins should believe that membership in the Communist party is as relevant to the performance of one's duties as a Government employe or teacher as is baldness is astonishing. It can be explained not in terms of Hutchins's total political depravity but only of his total political innocence. For it is unreasonable to assume that anyone familiar with the nature of the Communist party, with the established fact that it owes its primary allegiance to a foreign government, and with its specific instructions to its teacher-members, could believe that membership in such an organization is irrelevant to serving in a governmental and/or teaching post. It is unreasonable to assume that any informed person could believe that a question from a legally authorized source, designed to elicit an answer about membership in such a group, is improper. The real question is: How could Hutchins have escaped learning about Communism all these years?

It is not surprising that when Hutchins discusses the question of whether members of the Communist party should be permitted to teach, he should dismiss the question of their "political affiliations" as irrelevant. What is surprising is that his views on this subject are today more extreme than ever before. He criticizes Harvard University, despite its liberal stand, for abandoning the *one* test, for failing to ask "the right question" about a teacher, *viz.,* "whether he is competent." He protests the dismissal of members of the Communist party in Philadelphia and elsewhere on the ground that their actual incompetence has not been established.

Fallacy Number Three

Now where positions of trust are involved, there are *two* questions which are normally asked, not one. The first is: Is the candidate competent? The second is: Is the candidate honest and will he abide by the ethics of his calling? A competent bookkeeper is not necessarily an honest one. If he is not honest, his competence makes him even more unsuitable. A man may be a competent soldier, but what if he is disloyal? Fuchs and Pontecorvo were competent physicists. A competent physician or a competent lawyer may be guilty of a breach of professional ethics. And a competent teacher may be guilty of a breach of trust. He may be under instructions to violate the ethics of teaching. In arguing as if the violation of professional trust is incompatible with the achievement of professional competence and as if disbarment for such violation of trust is tantamount to dismissal for holding unorthodox opinions, Hutchins is guilty of a double confusion—between competence and trustworthiness on the one hand, and between untrustworthiness and ideological non-conformity on the other. The objection to Communist party teachers is not on the technical ground of their competence or incompetence in the *skills* of teaching a specific subject matter, but on grounds of their moral and professional integrity in accepting instructions to use their skills to indoctrinate and recruit.

We have previously seen that Hutchins himself was aware of the distinction between competence and trustworthiness. In stating his willingness to hire for the Fund for the Republic a member of the Communist party who was qualified, he added that he would do so only if he could watch him. But in discussing the case of Communist party teachers Hutchins disregards the distinction, and says: "The standard of competence would have protected us against teachers following a party line or conducting propaganda." This is false not only because the standard of competence has failed to prevent Communist party teachers from following the party line or conducting propaganda (see for evidence my *Heresy, Yes—Conspiracy, No*), but because it is apparent that the more skilful a teacher is, the more effectively he can indoctrinate, the more he is able "without exposing himself to inject Marxism-Leninism into every class." (The last phrase is from official Communist instructions.)

I have discussed this question often and at length. I content myself here only with pointing out that, in every other common-sense situation, we would say that membership in an organization which gives specific instructions to its members to violate their trust—a trust which is relevant to the performance of their duties—would be considered *prima facie* evidence of unfitness to occupy that position of trust. Only where

Communists are concerned do some ritualistic liberals fail to draw the same inferences which guide them in other instances of the same class.

Sometimes it is said that the following two propositions are logically equivalent to each other:

(*1*) Membership in the Communist party in and of itself is not a sufficient ground for dismissal.

(*2*) Membership in the Communist party is *prima facie* evidence of unfitness to hold a teaching post.

If these propositions are logically equivalent, why should anyone object to the second formulation? My objection to the first formulation is that it is misleading since it is also true to say that membership in the Democratic or Republican or Socialist party is not in and of itself a sufficient ground for dismissal and thus it overlooks the distinctive conspiratorial and educationally unethical character of the Communist party. On the other hand, the second formulation is at present true of only one political party—the Communist party—and the statement would be false if other political parties were substituted for it.

The difference between these two propositions is operational. In neither case would dismissal be automatic. But the second formulation would require the member of the Communist party to refute the *presumption* of unfitness, *i.e.,* to convince an elected academic committee of his peers that, despite his voluntary membership in an organization which gave him instructions to act dishonorably, he was worthy of being retained as a teacher. If anyone at this point retorts: "A man must be considered innocent until he is proven guilty," the answer is twofold. First, this is not a court, and outside a court, say in a game of cards, a man detected with an ace up his sleeve cannot ask *us* to prove that he intended to use it—*he* must prove that he didn't intend to use it. Second, a man who is proved to be a member of a group which gives him dishonorable instructions is *ipso facto* under a cloud. That fact itself constitutes weighty if not decisive evidence of guilt. He must then prove to our satisfaction that he doesn't intend to carry out the instructions.

Fallacy Number Four

Another typical fallacy which runs through Hutchins's writings is the belief that, if common-sense defensive action is taken against infiltration by members of the Communist party, in the end everyone's liberties will be destroyed. In connection with Pastor Niemöller, he writes:

"When the Nazis attacked the Communists, he [Niemöller] was a little uneasy, but he was not a Communist and he did nothing. When they attacked the Socialists, he was uneasy, but he was not a Socialist and he did nothing. They went after the schools, the press and the

Jews, but he was not directly affected and he did nothing. Then they attacked the Church. Pastor Niemöller was a churchman. He tried to do something, but it was too late." (*Annals of the American Academy of Political and Social Science,* 1955, p. 75.)

Before analyzing this, two peripheral remarks must be made. First, Niemöller was an anti-Semite who was never interested in freedom until the Nazis backed pagan religion. Even then, he offered to fight for Hitler against the West. He is now a neutralist and apologist for the East German regime who is as little interested in freedom as he was during the Weimar regime. Second, the Nazis and their precursors like the *Schwarze Reichswehr* and *Fememörder* did *not* begin by attacking only the Communists. They began by assassinating Rathenau, attacking Jews and Socialists, and before they took power often collaborated with the Communists.

But now let us look at the passage and its implications. It begs the question in two ways. First, it draws an equation between the *legitimate* efforts of democrats to prevent conspirators from destroying freedom and the criminal outrages of the Nazis against all their opponents. Second, it assumes that what begins in a justified effort to save democracy from fascism and Communism *must* end in one or the other. (Take a drug on the best medical advice in an emergency and you *must* end up a raving dope fiend or worse!) Both assumptions are clearly false!

It is positively monstrous for Hutchins to imply that the few measures adopted by the United States against the Communist conspirators are comparable in any significant way with the measures adopted by the Nazi hangmen against their opponents or those employed by the Communists, before the Nazis and after the Nazis, against the innocent and helpless victims of their terror. Due judicial process has been denied to no Communist in the United States. Judith Coplon is at liberty despite the court's judgment that "her guilt is plain." Whatever the wisdom of the Smith Act, Communists are not treated as if they were outside the law. American Communists actually enjoy more freedom in the United States than they would in the U.S.S.R.

There is always a danger, to be sure, that any act of a punitive nature, even if justified on the highest moral grounds, *may* coarsen our sensibilities so that we impose more restraints when fewer will do. The desire for retribution *may* become a cloak for cruelty as well as an expression of our sense of justice. That is why we must not approach the problem in blind anger against Communists or smug, self-righteous scorn of anti-Communists, but responsibly, seeking primarily to *prevent* infiltration, espionage and treason rather than merely to *punish* after the acts have been committed. Nothing can help us here but hard thinking about safeguards that will not inhibit fresh creative ideas and even dissent on the part of public servants. But Hutchins is no help at all. In one mood, he says we should do nothing lest we become like our enemies. In another mood, he advises us to wait until the worst happens and the infiltrator strikes. His speeches are full of slogans, with not a single idea which points to a creative solution of any serious problem.

Characteristic, too, of the quoted passage from Hutchins is his failure to realize that one of the causes of Nazi triumph was the degree and extent of secret Nazi infiltration into the strategic places of the Weimar Republic's political and social life. If the appropriate measures had been taken to cope with the Nazi conspirators against the democratic Weimar regime, the latter's chances of survival would have been immensely strengthened. And when I say "appropriate" measures, I do *not* mean that they should have been treated the way the Nazis treated their opponents. I mean that the same measures should have been adopted to curb their infiltration into Government and other sensitive agencies—including schools, where the Nazis were very powerfully entrenched—as intelligent liberals advocate against Communist conspirators sworn to abuse their trust.

Those who think like Hutchins would undoubtedly have cried out in the Weimar days: "If you begin with excluding Nazis from Government posts, you will end with beheading Jews and liberals." Some legal cretins in Germany actually took this view and argued that, since Hitler had declared that he stood on the basis of legality, his underground army, his governmental fifth column—the classic use of their operation was subsequently to appear in Austria—were no concern of the democratic government until they actually took up weapons for direct assault. The same cretinistic attitude which believes this to be a profound expression of liberalism instead of a declaration of intellectual and spiritual bankruptcy was manifested in Czechoslovakia, where the Communist action committees were tolerated until it was too late.

In all this I do not mean to suggest for a moment that freedom and democracy can be destroyed *only* by conspiratorial means, or that the danger of Communist infiltration in the United States, past or present, was anything remotely approaching the danger of Nazi infiltration in Czechoslovakia. All I am saying is that when a fifth column, no matter how small, works in conjunction with the most powerful aggregation of military force on earth, fanatically intent upon the destruction of the chief bulwark of the democratic world, devotion to freedom requires a certain prudential vision and elementary wisdom apparent to all who are not blinded by Hutchins's fallacies.

Further, I am prepared to grant that, although the Communist movement is a conspiracy, it does not therefore follow that every man jack in it is a hardened conspirator prepared to do anything. But since one cannot tell *in advance* who will or will not obey his party instructions, and since members are selected and purged in terms of their willingness and past performance in obeying instructions, it is elementary common sense not to employ them in positions where they can violate their trust. A pinch of common sense in preventing such violations is worth more than a ton of indictments and prosecutions afterward to punish violators.

Fallacy Number Five

Why is it that Hutchins appears unable to see all this? I believe there is a fifth material fallacy which prevents him from thinking clearly on these matters—his continued reiteration of the ambiguous phrase "guilt by association." This rhetorical bromide or slogan has been analyzed again and again by Professor Arthur Lovejoy, myself, and others, apparently without effect on Hutchins's use of it. The terms "guilt" and "association" are ambiguous. There is "legal" guilt and "moral" guilt. There is association merely by "happenstance" or irrelevant juxtaposition, and association by "cooperation." Refinements aside, we do not recognize "legal" guilt by association. We do, and properly, recognize "moral" guilt by association where the association is a form of voluntary cooperation. According to Hutchins, any inference based on a man's membership in the Communist party is an illustration of invoking guilt by association. This would make sense *only* if the association were accidental or irrelevant, but certainly not if it were the continued voluntary kind of cooperation with the purposes and activities of the Communist party which defines its membership.

Even outside of a political context, moral guilt by intimate voluntary association in behalf of common goals may be legitimately inferred where there is no evidence of dissociation. To take an extreme case: If one were to write an introduction to a book by a Nazi apologist who criticized American treatment of Negroes and remained silent about Nazi treatment of the Jews and the author's record in condoning it, one could legitimately be charged with the moral guilt of political collaboration with an enemy of freedom. This is not, of course, anything for the law to concern itself with. But if such a person were then to be considered for the post of president of an organization devoted to defending freedom against the Nazis, would it be persecution, thought control, or a lapse into "guilt by association" to regard this as relevant evidence of professional unsuitability for this particular post?

To drive this point home, I shall take an actual illustration. In 1950, Jerome Davis published a book entitled *Character Assassination*. Davis is a man who has been an out-and-out apologist of the Soviet terror regime, as witness his unqualified endorsement of the Moscow Trials, not only before the Dewey Commission of Inquiry brought in its verdict but even after, at which time, together with other well-known sympathizers with the Soviet cause, he threw mud at those liberals who opposed all varieties of totalitarianism. In his book, Davis singles out for criticism only those who justly or unjustly have attacked individuals for being Communists. Why this should be considered "character assassination" in Davis's eyes, in view of his views about Communist Russia and his intimate collaboration with Communists in the Teachers Union, is a little obscure. In the book, he also defends Harry Dexter White ("one of the most patriotic men of our generation"), as well as Silvermaster, Perlo, and Ullman, against "the notorious spy, Elizabeth Bentley." The character of the book may be gauged by the following passage from a review in *The Saturday Review* by Roger Baldwin, who certainly cannot be described as a "Red-baiter":

"Since I go along in general with most of his condemnations of these measures, it is disheartening to find them compromised by partisan special pleading. Whatever value they might have *is destroyed by total omission of any reference to character assassination by the masters of the art, the Communists*. Nor is there reference to assassination of character of conservatives or reactionaries; they are evidently fair game in a continuous open season. Thus, Professor Davis's declaration of his faith in freedom becomes a partisan expression of the case for 'our side' . . . it is evident that he accepts Russia and Communism as progressive forces. His is the dilemma familiar among the captive Wallaceites, posing as the progressives they think they are *and acting like the party-line apologists others think they are*" (my italics).

Lest this appear as an aberration of one particular liberal, here is another comment on Jerome Davis's book by a reviewer in the *New Republic*:

"Just as minority groups tend at times to adopt and practice the stereotyped prejudices of the majority, thereby furthering the evils they profess to oppose, *so Jerome Davis appears to have mastered and now to advance the vile art of hysteria. If we are to judge by this book, Davis is the John T. Flynn of the Left*" (my italics).

This book appeared with an introduction by Robert Maynard Hutchins, identified as Chancellor of the University of Chicago. Not by so much as a single word does Hutchins dissociate himself from Davis. The weight of his name and his post is used to reinforce Davis's partyline apologetics in the reader's mind. It is certainly safe to say that Hutchins would never dream of writing an introduction to a book by John T. Flynn against Communism. It is also safe to say that he would judge harshly any individual who did so and did not at the same time dissociate himself from Flynn's views. And yet Flynn's views, as mistaken as they may be, do not begin to approximate in baseness Davis's defense of the Moscow Trials.

There is no room here to analyze the content of the introduction, which makes some valid points in addition to exemplifying some of the fallacies discussed above. Hutchins quite rightly protests against "labeling something or some man Communist because Communists happen to favor it or agree with him." Unfortunately, he does not protest against the practice of labeling liberals "fascists" for criticizing the Communist conspiracy.

The point here is that in writing the introduction Hutchins voluntarily chose to associate himself with Davis by giving him and his book a virtual endorsement. How would Hutchins himself judge others who wrote introductions to the works of those whom *he* regards as enemies of freedom? Why shouldn't Hutchins himself be judged in the same way —not, of course, as a Communist or a sympathizer, but, charitably, as a foolish man, scornful of all criticism, whose arrogance has prevented him from learning the elementary facts of political life? If this is moral guilt by association, it is conspicuously deserved. Despite the critical reception Jerome Davis's book received from liberals, Hutchins never withdrew or qualified his introduction to it.

Fallacy Number Six

The final illustration of Hutchins's fallacies may be considered as a variation of the fallacy of *accent*. The ordinary fallacy of accent consists in emphasizing or italicizing a word in such a way as to give a completely misleading and sometimes blatantly false impression of the meaning of a sentence. DeMorgan pointed out that even Holy Scripture is not safe from this type of fallacy. For example, in the commandment "Thou shalt not covet thy neighbor's wife," emphasis on any one of the words "thou," "covet," "thy," "neighbor" and "wife" produces interesting variations, all false to the intent of the sentence.

This fallacy of accent is found in connected discourse, where it consists in giving such a disproportionate emphasis to some details rather than others that, despite the fact that none of the details is strictly false, the picture as a whole is violently distorted. From this point of view, almost every theme which Hutchins treats illustrates the fallacy of accent, whether he is discussing the state of American education or the state of American civil liberties. This is an extremism of statement which reflects not merely temperamental bias or the legitimate exercise of what Auden calls the esthetics of controversy, but an intellectual impatience or violence in imposing a position that cannot be sustained by judicious inquiry. The result is that the truth is often a casualty of rhetorical cavalry charges. Furthermore, Hutchins's laudable objective, the defense of freedom, is itself thereby weakened. For if everything stinks to high heaven, why insist on fresh eggs for breakfast? If our present practices, as Hutchins puts it, are "hardly better than the purges and pogroms" of Nazi Germany and Communist Russia, why bother defending merely the reputation or job of someone who, although falsely accused, can find employment elsewhere? The strategy of over-statement and misstatement makes it more difficult to win the battles for freedom.

Let me give one illustration of Hutchins's method. A few years ago, Hutchins wrote: "Everywhere [*sic!*] in the United States, university professors are silenced by the general atmosphere of oppression which prevails." This was no casual judgment, since he has repeated it in one form or another again and again. In 1954, he insisted that "professors everywhere [*sic!*] will hesitate before they express opinions contrary to those of Senator McCarthy, or before they will say anything that can be twisted—somehow, sometime, by someone—into an unpopular statement."

When other individuals, right-wing extremists, have charged, on the basis of the fact that some professors have been members of the Com-munist party, that our universities are hotbeds of Communism, they have been regarded as creatures of the intellectual underworld. Even a few hundred teachers—the maximum estimate ever made—is a very small percentage of the total. But what shall we say of the statement that *all* professors have been intimidated by McCarthy into silence at a time when any honest observer on the campuses of America could testify to the loud, continuous and unrestrained criticism of McCarthy voiced by students and teachers alike? Actually, it is the lone and rare supporter of McCarthy who has been the genuine non-conformist in academia. Dean Griswold, Mrs. Eleanor Stevenson, President Cole, President Shuster—all educators and all directors of the Fund for the Republic—know that at Harvard, Oberlin, Amherst, Hunter and else-where professors have *not* been silenced. I am not suggesting that they silence Hutchins. I am suggesting that they hold him to the minimum standards of intellectual responsibility that they expect of their other colleagues.

Criticism of Hutchins is made awkward by the fact that it may be construed by those of bad faith as support for right-wing criticism of the Fund for the Republic. This criticism is often unjust and un-founded, but if Hutchins had deliberately set out to provoke it he could not have succeeded better. The trouble is that Hutchins is weakening the position and prestige of the Fund. Since it is rumored that the Fund is to be investigated by the House Committee on Un-American Ac-tivities, I wish to avoid associating myself with those who, like the

Reece Committee, have charged foundations with support of subversive ideas. Hutchins has been guilty of nothing except the promulgation of foolish ideas. A foolish idea, like a foolish general, can cost us the battle. But the antidote for a foolish idea is not investigation but a better and wiser idea. I believe Hutchins can learn. If he can't, surely the directors of the Fund for the Republic can. If they can't, the whole cause of American freedom may suffer in the barrage of undiscriminating criticism which will be launched against their organization.

21 The Ethics of Employment

Is THE RIGHT to a job a part of the Bill of Rights? Obviously not, otherwise we could call on the state to enforce it. The right to a job, as distinct, say, from the right to speech and the right to worship according to one's conscience, depends upon certain merits or qualifications. Freedom of speech does not depend upon the possession of merit or truth or even the will to speak the truth. The right to a job depends not only upon merit or qualification but sometimes, perhaps always, upon certain standards of ethical behavior. It is not enough to be an expert salesman; one must be an honest salesman. Expertness and honesty are two independent variables, not only in salesmanship but in most pursuits. Sometimes the requisite standards of conduct to qualify for a particular post may be, not minimal, but very high, especially when individuals are serving in a confidential capacity.

Granted that an individual has both the technical and moral qualifications for a job, does this give him a right to one? Obviously not, if there are no jobs or if there are jobs and some law or trade-union provision (concerning veterans or seniority) prescribes an additional qualification. It is apparent that the term "right" when we speak of the right to a job does not mean the same thing as it does when we refer to the right to freedom of assembly or publication.

Nonetheless, when all qualifications are met by an applicant and there are jobs, denying him employment would universally be regarded as an injustice. The only exceptions possible are to be found in the field of personal service, which are privileged because of the inescapability of subjective criteria of selection. We would regard denial of access to a job as unjust if the ground given were failure to meet qualifications which are arbitrary and discriminatory.

289

This becomes even more evident when we make a distinction between those who are only applying for jobs and those who already have them. If an individual is deprived of his job on an arbitrary, irrational, or discriminatory ground such an action would be clearly unjust. Even if technically we may not be able to say that his civil right has been violated, in the same sense as if he were denied the right to speak, we may legitimately speak of a violation of his human right. And this for two reasons. First, because the right to live carries with it, or should, the right to the means to live, and the means to live for most human beings are acquired through some possibility for employment. Second, to be deprived of one's job because of the arbitrary action of another, a job for which one may have prepared oneself for many years and in which one's personality finds expression, is to be treated like a thing, without human dignity. The first does not give a right to a specific job: the second does. The law may not recognize this because it lags behind our sense of what is morally just or appropriate. The difficulties of legislation of fair employment practices and costs of enforcement must be taken into account, but some states have already moved in this direction.

Recognition of the distinction between private employment and public employment does not invalidate the judgment that dismissal, or even refusal of employment on arbitrary or discriminatory grounds is morally unjustified. Legally, there is nothing to prevent an individual from organizing a typing agency and adding in addition to his specifications for eligibility: "Only Blondes Need Apply." In government or civil service this would be ruled out as a violation of the rights of brunette citizens. Morally the situation is the same. Property is power and the administration of private property should no more lead to the arbitrary use of power over other human beings than the administration of government property. The argument assumes there is no correlation between expertness in typing and being blonde. If there were, the additional qualification would not be arbitrary.

These general considerations do not take us very far, because most of the problems concerning the ethics of employment bear upon the question of what constitutes a legitimate qualification. Sometimes the rule, "No Women Need Apply," or "No Unmarried Women Need Apply," is justified by the nature of the work; at other times it is a form of discrimination. If the Democratic Party Election Committee is setting up headquarters and hiring organizers, no one can reasonably object if it chooses only Democrats and rejects highly persuasive talkers about whose politics it is uncertain. But whatever the law may be, the rule "Democrats only" in private employment would be as unjust as in public employment. The same is true for any other legitimate political organization. (By this time it should not be necessary to prove that the Communist Party is not a legitimate political organization.)

In this chapter I wish to consider the ethics of employment in one branch of the private sector, in the entertainment industry, partly because of the many controversies associated with it, and partly to illustrate how the nature of the industry affects the warranted judgment of what is ethically justified and unjustified in the way of employment practices. The specific conclusions cannot be automatically applied to other employment fields, but the general considerations have implications wider than the entertainment industry.

I shall take as my point of departure a discussion of a two-volume work, *Report on Blacklisting,* sponsored by the Fund for the Republic and directed by John Cogley, former executive editor of *Commonweal.* The one indisputable merit of this study is that it served to focus attention upon a whole cluster of problems bearing on the ethics of employment in the entertainment industry. This industry, to understate the case, is much more sensitive to public opinion than most other industries. What is true, therefore, for democratic culture as a whole is pre-eminently true for it. Ultimately we must look to the education of public opinion to give effect to enlightened policies on employment as well as civil liberties.

Unfortunately, this report is more likely to generate fruitless controversy than to contribute to public enlightenment. And for a very simple reason. Although it professes to offer only a *factual* study, it does much more. Despite the claim of Paul Hoffman, chairman of the Fund, in the preface, that the report supplies only data for consideration, it contains a stinging indictment, much of it deserved, of current employment practices, and an implicit defense of a thesis or point of view. It is a pity that Mr. Cogley, who was given complete discretion and takes sole responsibility for these volumes, did not choose to discuss frankly and boldly the principles involved in the inquiry instead of organizing the facts in such a way as to make them argue for his own position—a position not so much explicitly stated as assumed. The consequent impression is one of needless disingenuousness and manipulation aggravated by the fact that so many incidents are anonymously reported, permitting no objective check. We need the facts, but to be significant they must be relevant to ideas. Some pages might better have appeared in a book called *Black Channels* since they are every whit as questionable as Mr. Cogley alleges are some pages of *Red Channels,* a compilation of the Communist involvements of screen, stage, and video personalities.

It was hardly necessary to undertake a survey to confirm the fact that some individuals had been unjustly denied employment because their names had appeared on a list of real or alleged Communist membership or affiliation. (Some notorious instances of injustice in the past motivated the inquiry.)

Nor is it important whether the practice of barring such individuals is technically a "blacklist." An injustice is an injustice under any name. Nonetheless, even discounting for inaccuracies and exaggerations, and they are many, Mr. Cogley shows that the practice is widespread, that movie studios and radio and television networks have often abdicated their responsibility to outside groups in making decisions about employability, that screening in the past has gone to absurd lengths, and that although the situation is improving, there is neither clarity nor consistency in policy.

What Mr. Cogley does not explicitly discuss is the nature and ground of the injustice. Is it the *false* accusation of communist affiliation which makes the denial of employment unjust or would it be unjust even if the accusations were *true?* Mr. Cogley obviously believes that, true or false, all such accusations are irrelevant and that any policy which bars Communists as such from employment in entertainment industries is unjust if not a violation of their civil liberties. Instead of explicitly stating and defending this position, Mr. Cogley concentrates on cases of false or doubtful accusations which have led to denials of work that no one would or should defend in order to achieve by emotional transference, rather than straightforward argument, sympathy for his general position. This compels him to marshal his facts in such a manner as to lump Communists and anti-Communists together as equally undemocratic in intent, and to make the latter in effect the real villains whereas the former appear as innocent victims. These absurdities were not necessary to Mr. Cogley's valid indictment of current employment practices. Nor does one need to agree with columnist George Sokolsky and others on general questions to recognize, without sneers or smears, their role of good Samaritans in aiding some who were innocently victimized.

Now it is perfectly possible for someone who is vehemently opposed to communism, as is Mr. Cogley, to argue that members of the Communist party should be permitted to work in the entertainment industry. Even though wherever they come to power, Communists deprive democrats of the right to eat, we must treat them by *our* moral standards not by theirs. If they have a right to eat, they have a right to work. But have they a right to work in any special industry and in all positions within that industry?

The chief difficulty in holding the view that members of the Communist party should be permitted to work everywhere in the entertainment industry on the same terms as others is the evidence presented by Mr. Cogley himself. Believing that the popular arts are important instruments in the class war and the struggle between the Soviet Union and the democratic world, Communists infiltrate into positions of influence, favor party-liners and, wherever possible, carry out a blacklist of anti-Communists which does not hurt its victims any the less for being sporadic and unorganized. Communists cannot control the content of films and network programs even when they try but they can easily prevent, by devious means, themes and books of which they disapprove from being used.

It is surprising to learn from Mr. Cogley how powerful an influence they exerted in Hollywood—happily no longer. Membership in one of their most important front organizations, over which they had iron-clad control, reached 4,000, which testifies not to the number of Communists, of course, but to their influence. The pitch of their fanaticism may be inferred from the fact that: "In Hollywood, philosopher John Dewey's investigation of the Moscow trials was publicly denounced in newspapers and by party members and sympathizers."

How can unethical professional practices by members of the Communist party or those under their discipline be prevented? It is difficult to draw the line with respect to where they can be tolerated and where not. But in the very interest of professional integrity, it must be drawn somewhere: roughly between posts in which they have authority and can hurt others, make decisions, etc., and performance roles. That some line must be drawn is suggested in the independent study of Professor Marie Jahoda of New York University, printed as an appendix. It is not clear that Mr. Cogley believes a line should be drawn anywhere. If it is drawn, it should be drawn openly, not secretly, in terms of a code of professional behavior administered by representatives of the producers and artists, whose associations must be prepared to defend their decisions against hostile pressure groups.

To draw the line anywhere against Communists will appear outrageously unjust to those who regard them merely as another political group like Democrats or Republicans and not as conspirators. But to regard membership in Communist organizations as merely an expression of political difference one must be outrageously uninformed. If some screening is necessary, the program and activities of the Communists are chiefly responsible for it.

A very difficult problem, not squarely faced by Mr. Cogley, is the extent to which a sponsor, concerned mainly in the sale of his product, is under obligation to accept a performer who antagonizes his potential buying public. It is a knotty problem to which there are no easy answers or analogies. One expects a restaurateur to serve his Negro patrons even if he loses the custom of prejudiced people because the civil rights of our fellow-citizens should take primacy over any economic interest. But if, say, in a highly competitive market an automobile manufacturer sponsors a show whose talented performer has endorsed the Protocols of Zion or some congruent libel against Roman Catholics or Protestants which may result in a boycott of his cars, would he be guilty of unfair practice in insisting on another performer? Mr. Cogley might have benefited from consultation with Mr. Hoffman on this point. Suppose, now, the performer in question had endorsed the Communist libel about American germ warfare and Americans felt outraged as patriots and not as members of a particular church—would refusal of sponsors to use or agencies to employ be a morally illegitimate blacklist? There are some who would justify refusal to employ in the first case but not in the second, and vice versa, but it is hard to see any justification for making the distinction.

So long as the radio and television industries operate under commercial sponsorship, it is both unrealistic and unfair to compel sponsors whose income position is being undermined by a popular boycott of Communist or Fascist performers on their programs to continue their sponsorship, or to drop the show and thus harm other performers. Paradoxically, only a publicly owned radio or television system, as in Great Britain, could withstand a popular boycott of entertainers who had outraged the conscience of the country. The Minister in charge, however, would have to answer for it in Parliament.

Under existing conditions of sponsorship no general theoretical solution is possible. It may be that with time and increasing sophistication, no matter what the politics of an entertainer, the audience will react to his talent and not to his prejudices. After all we laugh with Chaplin despite his politics, enjoy Picasso even though he is committed to communism, and listen with pleasure to Wagner without being upset by his virulent anti-Semitism. There is a kind of *Narrenfreiheit* customarily extended to artists which does not license them to violate the moral decencies but which makes for greater charity in judgment on the part of audiences. This in no way jeopardizes our right to criticize artists and our right not to listen. Where no position of executive trust is involved, it would be wiser as well as more generous, especially since no question of national security enters, to leave all careers open to talents subject to the criticism of audience response. In the entertainment industry no one can survive the audience's refusal to listen. Only the great are likely to escape the consequences of violations of basic community values. And when they do, we should forgive them their bizarre morals and politics, within the law, because of the joy they give us in enriching the human legacy.

At the moment the popular arts suffer more from low standards of taste and achievement than from threat of communist penetration. Problems flowing from the latter can best be solved by working out a code of ethical procedures *within* and for the industry. They are not a legitimate concern of any Congressional committee unless it can be shown that a definite issue of national security is involved. If it is true, as it once was true, that a large portion of the financial backing for the Communist Party comes from its Hollywood contingent and sympathizers, this is certainly a relevant question for investigation. But this could be more effectively accomplished not by an investigation of the entertainment industry but by an investigation of the financial resources of the Communist Party.

22 Academic Freedom and Academic Integrity

JUST AS almost everyone, including totalitarians, professes belief in "democracy," so in the field of education there is an almost unanimous expression of belief in "academic freedom." That differences of a strong and stubborn kind exist among the defenders of academic freedom suggests that the phrase is interpreted in widely different ways. By "academic freedom" I understand "the freedom of professionally qualified persons to inquire, discover, publish, and teach the truth as they see it in the field of their competence, without any control or authority except the control or authority of the rational methods by which truth is established."[1] This differentiates it sharply from the position of those who believe that this freedom should be subject to ecclesiastical or public or private control and restraint no matter what the level or kind of instruction.

By and large, the academic community of this country, including administrators as well as teachers, accepts this broad and, to some conservatives, too liberal conception of academic freedom. Nonetheless the arguments for it seem to me overwhelming in their validity.

All the more surprising therefore it is to find that in the academic community itself, as well as in the liberal political community which supports this conception, there are sharp differences of opinion. These arise not merely from disagreements about specific applications of the principles of academic freedom and which are traceable to different assessments of fact. They center on the very meaning and implication of the principles themselves. And they derive from conflicting views as to whether freedom to teach is primarily a political question to be

[1] Cf. my *Heresy, Yes—Conspiracy, No* (New York, 1953), pp. 154 ff. and *passim*.

296

considered in the same way one would consider the freedoms of the Bill of Rights or whether freedom to teach is a special kind of freedom, earned by qualification, and forfeited by violation of professional and ethical standards of conduct determined, as in the case of physicians and lawyers, by their peers. It was widely hoped that a Special Committee of the American Association of University Professors, the largest organization of college teachers in the country, would offer a definitive analysis of the whole complex of problems.

The Committee released its report on "academic freedom and national security" and it was accepted by the Council of the AAUP and adopted at an annual meeting. (Whether it represents the point of view of the membership is another question.) It is the first report that has been made on the subject of Communist party teachers in colleges and universities since the issue was raised several years ago at the University of Washington. Cases had been piling up with no action taken by the AAUP. Not even investigations were launched. Finally, a Special Committee was appointed to bring in a comprehensive report on all the cases to date in which the issue of Communism was directly or indirectly involved and to formulate general principles to guide action with respect to them.

Of the eighteen institutions reported on, only two were visited by a committee. This would normally be extraordinary, because hitherto in the investigation of run-of-the-mill academic freedom cases the reports of the investigating committee of the AAUP have been exemplary in every respect. They commanded great moral authority, and university administrations were very sensitive to their findings. The report of the Special Committee, on the other hand, has been severely criticized because the Committee did not visit all the institutions it censured, conducted itself like a kangaroo court, and based its findings on "facts of public knowledge" even though these admittedly did not represent all the facts.

However, there are two reasons why these criticisms are not very significant. First, the principles enunciated by the Special Committee made visits or detailed investigations in most cases unnecessary. Secondly, the censures were based primarily on the failure of administrations to follow certain *procedural* principles. Even if different and more sensible principles had been expressed in the report, it is clear that some of the censured institutions deserved condemnation for violating canons of proper procedure.

My concern in this chapter is with the principles of the report, the grounds given for the AAUP's attitude toward employment of Communist party teachers, the knowledgeability of the Committee, and the pertinence and validity of its observations and recommendations on the issue before it. I approached this report with no hostility and, indeed, with some sympathetic interest. Dr. Ralph F. Fuchs, AAUP General Secretary at the time, had written me a few days before the report was printed: "Although the Committee's approach probably differs from yours in some respects, I believe its conclusions do not differ substantially in practical effect from yours regarding the matters covered."

It may well be that the recommendations in particular cases may not be very different from what my own would have been, but the principles enunciated will inevitably be interpreted as a guide to future cases and as a short compendium of the ethics of the profession.

The basic weakness—it would not be too strong to say the basic evasion—of the report is apparent in its very title: "Academic Freedom and Tenure in the Quest for National Security." The problem of Communism and Communist teachers in colleges and universities has little or nothing to do with national security. It has everything to do with the question of professional ethics and professional integrity. At no time was the number of Communists in colleges sufficiently high to warrant the slightest concern that they would undermine our national security. Today, there are no or hardly any Communist party teachers active on American campuses. In none of the cases considered by the Special Committee were individuals charged with weakening or even working against the security of the country. On the contrary, they were usually charged with lack of professional integrity, with undermining not our national security but the principles of academic freedom.

These charges, first formulated at the University of Washington, set the pattern elsewhere. They were the charges which the Special Committee should have considered. After all, John Dewey, first President of the AAUP, and Arthur Lovejoy, its first Secretary, made it very clear that the group was founded not merely to defend the narrow professional interests of college teachers, important as they were, but to develop and uphold the highest standards of academic integrity. And it was fundamentally on this ground that both of them were opposed to tenure for members of the Communist party or any other group organized under similar disciplines for unprofessional purposes.

It was the business of the Special Committee to assess these charges against members of the Communist party thoroughly and honestly in the light of the ideals of professional ethics which the AAUP always stressed. They did nothing of the sort. They made no study of Communist party activities in the colleges. They made no study of Communist party directives to its members to abuse their professional trust. They cited no literature on the question. They met none of the arguments showing why supervision and observation of the behavior of Communist party teachers in the classroom was morally undesirable and pedagogically impractical. They contented themselves with the pious statement that the academic community has a duty "to defend itself from subversion of the educational process." But they did not even ask whether, as a first commonsensical measure of defense, those who were under explicit instructions to subvert the educational process should not be regarded as *prima facie* (not automatically) unfit for their posts. After all, academic freedom and common sense are not irreconcilable. When physicians, lawyers or any other professional group set up standards to defend the integrity of their profession against those who would undermine it, membership in any organization which gives instructions to proceed dishonorably or to subvert standards of decent practice is of immediate concern to the character committee or committee on professional ethics. Are teachers to be less concerned with the honor and integrity of their profession? Why, then, the "red herring" about national security?

Even as concerns national security, the Special Committee evinces an extraordinary naiveté which reflects its ignorance of the Communist party and its ways. It has one paragraph on "Military Security" which starts bravely with the admission that the Committee accepts "unhesitatingly" the application of safeguards, where secret research is going on, against misuse of classified information important for military security. It makes the reasonable request that these safeguards should extend only to individuals who have access to such information. It then adds: "In no degree do they [the safeguards] justify the proscription of individuals because of their beliefs and associations, unless these persons were knowingly participants in criminal acts or conspiracies, in either the past or present." If this means what it implies—the report is not a model of clarity or precision—then members of the Communist party *as such* cannot be proscribed or barred even from work on restricted projects no matter how important to the security of the nation. They must first be caught acting as good Communists do in such situations! No one who has the slightest acquaintance with the enormous documentary evidence of the role of Communist parties as fifth columnists and agents of Soviet subversion could hold such an absurd position.

This is not the first time that a committee of the AAUP has betrayed either ignorance of, or indifference to, the nature of Communism and the Communist party. As late as 1948, the Committee on Academic Freedom reported that "the evidence that the Communist party in the United States is subservient to the dictates of international Communism, which means the Communist Party of the Soviet Union, is not conclusive (*Bulletin,* Spring 1948, p. 123). One wonders what in the light of the record available at the time, this Committee would regard as conclusive.

Ignorance about Communism, however, is not the decisive feature of the report, but rather a disregard of the standards of professional integrity. So that there may be no doubt that the instructions given to Communist party teachers do violate the rudiments of professional ethics, I cite several lines from the official instructions:

"Party and YCL [Young Communist League] fractions set up within classes and departments must supplement and combat by means of discussions, brochures, etc. bourgeois omissions and distortions in the regular curriculum. . . . *Marxist-Leninist analysis must be injected into every class.*

"*Communist teachers must take advantage of their positions, without exposing themselves,* to give their students to the best of their ability working-class [i.e., Communist] education. . . .

"Only when teachers have really mastered Marxism-Leninism will they be able skilfully to inject it into their teaching *at the least risk of exposure* and at the same time conduct struggles around the school in a truly Bolshevik manner." (*The Communist,* May, 1937; my italics.)

Although often criticized for giving these instructions to its teachers, to this day the Communist party has not withdrawn them or qualified them in any way.

The retort usually made—that accepting these instructions is one thing, while carrying them out is another—is quite specious. One might as well say that a boxer who has indicated his willingness to throw his fight, or a basketball player who has promised not to score, is not morally culpable until it can be established that he has actually carried out his instructions. The rules governing examination procedures in most colleges indicate clearly that evidence of *intent* to commit dishonest acts is a ground for disciplinary action. Membership in the Communist party, which issues specific instructions to act dishonestly, is certainly *prima facie* evidence of intent warranting at the very least close inquiry and professional indictment. But not according to the AAUP. The very principles of ethics which teachers expect their students to follow, they cast aside in assaying the professional misconduct of their colleagues.

The notion that members of the Communist party can be detected by their classroom practices is mistaken, and I have detailed the reasons at length elsewhere. Some professors say that, if members of the Communist party carry out their instructions, they are thereby establishing their incompetence and can be dismissed on grounds of incompetence rather than betrayal of professional trust. But has anyone ever heard of a professor losing his job on grounds of incompetence? Harold Taylor, President of Sarah Lawrence, who believes that members of the Communist party have a right to teach on the same terms as any other teachers, has frankly admitted that "once a man has received tenure, the tenure rules and the academic policies of the university community are usually strong enough to sustain him in his post indefinitely, *no matter what level of achievement he may subsequently reach as a teacher or thinker.*" (*Annals of the American Academy of Political and Social Science,* July, 1955, p. 79; my italics.)

The non-professional reader may be startled by this, since it seems to put the college teacher in a highly privileged position. Nonetheless, there are good and sufficient professional reasons for this state of affairs, the chief of which is the difficulty of formulating objective criteria of performance. Academic freedom would be imperiled were teachers to be dismissed on vague grounds of incompetence. This further reinforces the conclusion that the nub of the whole matter is one of professional honor and integrity. Once a teacher has won his spurs, neither supervision nor snooping can detect whether or not, if he is a member of the Communist party, he is carrying out its instructions. His primary offense lies in his voluntary act of membership in an organization which gives him such instructions, and, although this should not be an automatic ground for dismissal, it should constitute a presumption of unfitness. *Mutatis mutandis,* the same principle should be applied to members of any group bound by a similar discipline and under similar instructions.

As if the failure of the AAUP Special Committee to come to grips with the basic issues were not bad enough, it goes on to advocate a policy which seemingly suggests that a college is actually failing in its educational duty unless members of the Communist party are teaching on the campus:

"To maintain a healthy state of thought and opinion in this country, it is desirable for adherents of Communism, like those of other forms of revolutionary thought, to present their views, especially in colleges and universities, so that they may be checked by open discussion. How else are Americans to know the nature of the ideological currents in their world? If representatives of Communism from abroad were to be employed under an exchange program in American institutions of higher learning, as has been proposed, the unwisdom of the present academic policy would quickly become evident." (*Bulletin of the AAUP,* Spring 1956, p. 199.)

Now the above reference to "the unwisdom of the present academic policy," in the light of the context, can only be to the policy of barring Communist teachers. The Committee cannot mean that there is a policy of barring people who hold Communist views from speaking on the campus, for there is no such policy. Dr. Herbert Phillips, dismissed from the University of Washington as a member of the Communist party, presented his case on almost every major campus of the country and admitted that he could not accept all the invitations he received. Not only are Communists permitted to speak before student groups on campuses; they are often invited to speak before classes as *open* representatives of their views. Although some adverse publicity sometimes results, this does not occur much more often today than in the years before "the quest for national security" began. The Special Committee is certainly aware of all this—or should be. (Objections are usually raised to *convicted* Communists appearing as speakers, but that is another question.)

What shall we say, then, of the implied proposal of the Special Committee? Simply this: The notion that, in order to learn objectively about Communism, it is necessary to hire members of the Communist party to teach it is just as absurd as the notion that, to give an objective report about Communist activities in the press, it is necessary to hire members of the Communist party as reporters. If we do not need to employ racists in order to study objectively the claims of racism, fascists to study fascism, or bankrupts to study the laws of bankruptcy, then surely it is not necessary to employ Communists to study the doctrines and conspiratorial practices of Communism.

The odd thing about the position of the AAUP on this question is that it has never permitted its membership to discuss the issue fairly in the pages of its *Bulletin* or to hear it debated by competent representatives of both sides before a national meeting. It has loaded the pages of the *Bulletin* with only one position. It has refused point-blank to invite any speaker known to differ with the official position. It is not too late to conduct a fair debate around the question of professional responsibility and ethics. Is there any reason why the American Association of University Professors should not adopt as its own the statement of the New School for Social Research:

"The New School knows that no man can teach well, nor should he be permitted to teach at all, unless he is prepared 'to follow the truth of scholarship wherever it may lead.' No inquiry is ever made as to whether a lecturer's private views are conservative, liberal or radical; orthodox or agnostic; views of the aristocrat or commoner. Jealously safeguarding this precious principle, the New School stoutly affirms that a member of any political party or group which asserts the right to dictate in matters of science or scientific opinion is not free to teach the truth and thereby is disqualified as a teacher."

APPENDICES

A. A Letter from Dr. Ralph Fuchs, Former Secretary of the American Association of University Professors

Professor Sidney Hook's discriminating appraisal of the report of the Special Committee of the American Association of University Professors on "Academic Freedom and Tenure in the Quest for National Security" deserves thoughtful consideration. I continue to believe that Professor Hook's viewpoint and the Committee's differ only slightly; and the difference between his stand and the position taken by the Association's Annual Meeting (which formally approved only one section of the report) is even less.

I am sure that all members of the AAUP would agree, as do I, with Professor Hook that professional ethics and integrity are a primary concern of the academic profession. But it seems evident, too, that the search for national security has generated problems which are important in relation to academic freedom and tenure and cannot be left out of account. The Special Committee's report, although it focuses upon these problems, asserts the duty of the academic community to defend society and itself from subversion of the educational process by Communist tactics, and the duty of faculty members to disclose the truth concerning possible Communist affiliations to their institutions when questions are raised. Such a report cannot be said to disregard professional ethics and integrity.

On another point, there is a genuine difference between Professor Hook's views and the position stated by the Committee, but not between his views and those formally approved by the Annual Meeting. Professor Hook takes issue with the statement in the Committee's report that it is desirable for adherents of Communism, like those of other forms of revolutionary thought, to present their views, especially in colleges and universities, so that they may be checked by open discussion. "How else," the Committee asks, "are Americans to know the nature of the ideological currents in their world?" The portion of the report which takes this position was not presented to the Annual Meeting for adoption and so remains simply an expression by the Committee. The policy expressed in the report would have the merit of stripping the mystery from student awareness of Communism and substituting honest, open study for the present hush-hush approach. It does not mean, of course, that members of the Communist party who engage in illegal or unprofessional conduct should be employed as teachers; for the report is clear in saying that they should be dismissed.

On the question of the significance of membership of teachers in the Communist party, there is conflict within Professor Hook's article between a passage from a statement of the New School for Social Research, which he quotes with approval, and his own statement. The former asserts that "a member of any political party or group which asserts the right to dictate in matters of science or scientific opinion is not free to teach the truth and thereby is disqualified as a teacher." Professor Hook himself says that membership in such an organization "should not be an automatic ground for dismissal," but "should constitute a presumption of unfitness." I fail to see wherein this position of Professor Hook's differs from the position taken by the Special Committee of the AAUP and by the Annual Meeting.

The report of the Special Committee does not use the word "presumption," but it says that "indications of past or present Communist associations or activities" by a teacher create "a possibility of his involvement in activities subversive of education itself, or otherwise indicative, to an important degree, of his unfitness to teach." This possibility, according to the report, calls for an inquiry by the employing institution into the teacher's fitness. The Annual Meeting adopted this position. The Committee also refers with approbation to the position taken in these matters by the Corporation of Harvard University, including the stand that "in the absence of extraordinary circumstances, we would regard present membership in the Communist party by a member of our faculty as grave misconduct, justifying removal." The Committee notes that recognition of the possibility of special circumstances which might render the removal of a member of the Communist party inadvisable "implies the right to a full hearing"; and the maintenance of this right in each case where party membership is involved, as well as generally, is the Committee's principal concern. Professor Hook's "presumption" similarly preserves the right to a hearing as to the individual's fitness.

Whether "presumption" is a good word to use in this connection presents an additional question. In law, the word is one of many meanings. It may mean that the person against whom a presumption operates can avoid an adverse decision only if he comes forward with opposing evidence, but that, if he does so, the effect of the presumption is eliminated and the decision is then based on the evidence, without further reference to the presumption. The word "presumption" may mean, on the other hand, that the person against whom the presumption operates must also counteract it in the mind of the deciding authority by the superior weight of the evidence he adduces. If the word is to be used, it must be defined; but very possibly its use should be avoided, so as to leave the decision in each case simply a professional one on the merits as they appear. The Association and its Committee clearly mean, in any event, that the teacher who is shown to be a member of the Communist party, or who has given indications that he may be, can properly be required to come forward with an explanation.

An additional point should be made clear. The AAUP has never maintained, and its Committee does not now assert, that a commitment by a faculty member to use deception or concealment, whether the commitment is made through acceptance of organizational policies or otherwise, must be followed by actual misbehavior before his dismissal can be justified. Such a commitment is clearly inconsistent with professional objectivity and integrity, upon which the Committee specifically insists. Therefore, Professor Hook's analogy between boxers or basketball players who have undertaken to throw the contests in which they engage, and the teachers whose party membership the Committee does not regard as in itself a disqualification, is inapplicable.

The question is: How shall the commitment to dishonesty be shown? The answer should be: By evidence that it was consciously made, including evidence that it was acted upon and evidence that a denial of it is not made in good faith. The Association subscribes to Professor Hook's view that "membership in the Communist party, which issues specific instructions to act dishonestly, is certainly *prima facie* evidence of intent warranting at the very least close inquiry," if not to his view that a "professional indictment" should necessarily follow. If, in the trial upon such an indictment, organizational membership is not made in itself conclusive evidence of professional malfeasance, there is no quarrel between us.

Washington, D.C.

RALPH F. FUCHS
General Secretary, AAUP
(*Reprinted from* The New Leader, *June 25, 1956*)

B. A Reply to Professor Fuchs

I wish to express my deep appreciation for the courtesy and sympathetic understanding of Professor Fuchs's response to my criticism of the report of the Special Committee of the AAUP. Its tone and substance are a refreshing contrast to the strictures against my views by certain ritualistic liberals who believe that heartily reiterated slogans are a substitute for knowledge and thought about the subject.

I want to say at once that if Professor Fuchs's interpretation both of the AAUP's position and of the report of the Special Committee is correct on the key matters of (1) *prima facie* ineligibility of Communist party members, and (2) the absence of *necessity* in establishing actual misbehavior in addition to establishing commitment to deception or concealment, then there is little difference between us. However, I would be less than candid if I failed to point out that most interpretations of the AAUP's position and of the meaning of the Special Report are greatly at variance with Professor Fuchs's reading. I am referring now not to blatantly dishonest distortions of the report such as are featured in the official Communist organ, *Political Affairs* (May, 1956), or in the organs of the Trotskyite sects, but to versions appearing in reputable intellectual and cultural circles and, indeed, in colleges and universities generally.

Although aware myself that as a purely logical exercise the formulations of the AAUP and its committees could be construed as expressing the same policy I have been defending, until now I have seen not the slightest evidence that this is the actual policy of the AAUP. On the other hand, unless one has read my books and articles on the subject with a positive will to misunderstand, the main propositions of my position are clear enough.

In order to obviate misunderstanding in the future, it is imperative, if Professor Fuchs's interpretation is the canonic one, for the AAUP to adopt some statement equivalent in meaning to the position taken by Harvard University. This is all the more desirable since, according to Professor Fuchs, Harvard's position is approved by the Special Committee, to wit, ". . . in the absence of extraordinary circumstances, we would regard present membership in the Communist party by a member of our faculty as grave misconduct justifying removal." The trustees of the New School have applied the provision I quoted in a similar fashion. The intent is unmistakably clear.

I am still bewildered by the contention of the Special Committee, re-affirmed by Professor Fuchs, that in order for "Americans to know the nature of the ideological conflicts in their world," it is *necessary* to have adherents of Communism teach in our colleges. I presume he does not mean members of the Communist party, or else the endorsement of Harvard's position would make no sense. Even so, I do not see the *necessity* of a teacher believing in Communism in order to study it objectively any more than the *necessity* of a teacher believing in fascism or anti-Semitism in order objectively to study anti-Semitism or fascism. Why is Communism in a different class from everything else? If a teacher honestly reaches the conclusion that the Communist or fascist position on any subject is valid, that is one thing. He should be staunchly defended in his right to present his view, among other views, in an acceptable pedagogical manner no matter how mistaken we believe his view to be. But if the teacher is pledged in advance to indoctrinate, as members of Communist and fascist parties are, that is something quite different.

In conclusion, I am happy to point out a basic agreement between Professor Fuchs and myself which I regard as more significant than any of our differences past or present. This is that the faculties of all institutions of higher learning, or their representative committees, should be the guardians and the sole judges of the professional integrity of their members. For obvious reasons, this procedural principle is more basic than differences on the specific question of infiltration by Communist party teachers, especially since the question no longer has any *actualité*. It has seemed to me that in the past a fundamental ambiguity, if not confusion, on the part of the AAUP about the significance of Communist party instructions to its members to violate their professional trust—*viz.,* the failure to treat forth-rightly the issue of professional *ethics*—has obscured the wisdom of its stand on the procedural issue and slowed its acceptance.

Higher education in the United States owes Professor Fuchs a debt of gratitude for making a major step toward the clarification—to some it will appear a rectification—of the position of the AAUP.

(Reprinted from The New Leader, *June 25, 1956)*

C. A Dissent by Arthur O. Lovejoy, Founding Secretary of the American Association of University Professors, Emeritus Professor of Philosophy, Johns Hopkins University

In the discussion between Professor Sidney Hook and Dr. Ralph Fuchs, General Secretary of the American Association of University Professors, about that organization's policy on the eligibility of Communist party members for membership in university faculties, two distinct questions are involved. One has to do with principle—what *should be* the position of the Association on this issue? The other concerns fact—what *is* that position, as formulated in the report of the Association's Committee on Academic Freedom in the Quest for National Security?

Dr. Hook's real answer to the first question is obviously stated in the concluding sentence of his May 21 article, "The AAUP and Academic Integrity" (quoted by him from the declaration of the New School for Social Research): "A member of any political party or group which asserts the right to dictate in matters of science or scientific opinion is not free to teach the truth and is thereby disqualified as a teacher." For the acceptance—or reaffirmation—of this principle by the Association he presents, in my opinion, entirely sound and adequate reasons. On the second question, Dr. Hook charges that the Special Committee's report not only fails to reaffirm that principle unequivocally, but even asserts what seems to him its opposite: that nothing can "justify the proscription of individuals, unless these persons were knowingly participants in criminal acts or conspiracies, in either the past or the present."

Dr. Fuchs, in a conciliatory spirit, seeks to show that the position on the question of principle expressed in the Special Committee's report is really the same as Dr. Hook's. To this end, he quotes Dr. Hook's admission that "membership in an organization" such as the Communist party "should not be an automatic ground for dismissal," but should only "constitute a presumption of unfitness." Dr. Fuchs clearly scores a point here, for this admission is undeniably inconsistent with Dr. Hook's concluding sentence, quoted above, which plainly calls for "automatic" dismissal of CP members. But the point is a trivial one: It amounts merely to a dubious argument *ad hominem,* to show that Dr. Hook apparently expresses two incompatible views on the main issue. It does not even show which of these views he actually holds (he certainly does not hold both), and it does nothing to rebut his strictures on the Special Committee report.

What *is* significant about Dr. Fuchs's argument is what it tells us indirectly about the AAUP's position as understood by its General Secretary, *viz.,* that admitted or proved present membership in, or support of, a political party or group which asserts the right to dictate what its members may teach or write should *not* be considered *ipso facto* ("automatically") a disqualification for membership in a university faculty. On *this* question of fact about the present position of the Association, Dr. Hook and Dr.

Fuchs appear to be in complete agreement. That it *is* a fact I, like Dr. Hook, consider deplorable. That Dr. Hook's view (which is also mine) on the question of principle is identical with the Committee's is not a fact, as should be patent to every reader of his article as a whole.

I do not, however, attribute to the distinguished drafters of the report such dubious, not to say sinister, intentions as he appears to ascribe to them. I do not believe that they really *want* to facilitate the admission of active CP members to the teaching staffs of their own or other universities. The occasion for this report was the current tendency among hysterical persons and reactionary politicians to represent all academic teachers whose political affiliations have even the slightest tinge of "liberalism" as "Communist sympathizers"—and thereby to frighten them into silence. The report, I think it fair to assume, was designed as an exposure of and protest against this tendency.

But in their defense of the professional freedom and civil liberties of non-Communist teachers, the drafters, in some passages, have seemed willing also to permit the infiltration of the worst and most insidious conspirators against both academic freedom and civil liberties. But I assume that these unfortunate passages in the report are due to simple, though surprising, ignorance of the actual policy and methods of the Communist party—as Dr. Hook himself suggests.

It is, finally, important to note that, in one respect, Dr. Hook's information about the present policy of the AAUP is not up-to-date. He writes: "It has never permitted its members to discuss the issue fairly in the pages of its *Bulletin*, or to hear it debated by competent representatives of both sides before its annual meeting." That was, apparently, once true under a previous administration; but I am assured by Dr. Fuchs that it is not true at present. "The pages of the *Bulletin*," he writes me, "are not closed to a point of view different from the Association's," and "I contemplate the possibility of an article or articles expressing both [Professor Hook's] point of view and that which the Annual Meeting has adopted on the basis of the Special Committee's report."

I hope, therefore, that, after such discussion, some member will move the reconsideration and amendment of that report and the adoption of a declaration on this issue equivalent in substance to that of the New School for Social Research. I should perhaps explain that I cannot myself make such a motion because *emeriti* are (wisely, perhaps) excluded from the privileges of active membership.

ARTHUR O. LOVEJOY
Baltimore, Md.
(*Reprinted from* The New Leader, *July 2, 1956*)

Comment by Sidney Hook.   Both Professors Fuchs and Lovejoy regard as inconsistent my acceptance of the New School principle and my conviction that membership in any organization which instructs its members to violate their professional trust is *prima facie*, but not necessarily conclusive, evidence of unfitness. The latter has been my position from the outset of the discussion. Like the Trustees of the New School I have always interpreted the first principle in the light of the second. If the first principle is read and accepted literally, then I abide only by the second because I cannot accept the principle of automatic dismissal. This makes all the more important my view that the burden of proof must rest upon the individual who has accepted instructions to violate his trust, to show cause why he should not be declared unfit. Subsequent statements and actions by the AAUP, after Professor Fuchs resigned his Secretaryship, have in effect repudiated his agreement with my general position and confirmed my criticisms of its confused stand and its grave disregard of the basic principles of professional ethics.

23 Academic Freedom in the United States:

Two Views

A FEW SHORT years ago there appeared within a few weeks of each other two studies of academic freedom in the United States written from antipodal points of view. Although the educational landscape since then—and, indeed, at the very times they appeared (late in 1955)—revealed them to be grandiose works of imagination rather than sober accounts of fact, the pictures they drew of the state of American education are still carried around in the heads of different groups of American citizens. As most American scholars who have traveled abroad will testify, one of these pictures is the standard conception of academic freedom in American higher education which prevails in intellectual circles in Western Europe and Eastern Asia. This justifies our continuing concern with these interpretations.

I

The first is presented in a two-volume work, *The Development of Academic Freedom in the United States* by Richard Hofstadter and Walter Metzger and *Academic Freedom in Our Time* by Robert M. MacIver.[1]

The first and larger of these books, on the history of the academic freedom in the United States, is a valuable and brilliantly written study, especially Part One. It is both analytical and informative. More important, it provides the indispensable perspective from which to see the tangled complex of problems associated with the principles and practices of academic freedom. Professors Hofstadter and Metzger, both in

---

[1] New York, 1955.

the History Department at Columbia, warn against the distortions produced by treating the story of academic freedom as if it were mainly the story of academic repressions. This would be like "a history of science telling only of the encroachments of theology" or a history of the American economy merely in terms of its bankruptcies.

The authors unfold a fascinating and richly documented tale. A hundred years ago academic freedom was nonexistent in this country, despite the democratic vitality of our political institutions. The whole notion was foreign to the conception of education which then prevailed. Academic freedom was an "un-American" import from Europe, preeminently from undemocratic Imperial Germany, which took root here in the latter part of the nineteenth century. It was modified to meet the peculiar conditions created by the fact that American higher education was in the main privately endowed and governed. In its short career academic freedom underwent many vicissitudes, was almost completely eclipsed during World War I, but emerged hardened and strengthened. Since then it has developed to a point where, despite episodic tribulations and outrages, and occasional public suspicion, it enjoys more professional and administrative support than ever before.

Because it is written with perspective, balance and a sense for the nourishing forces in American life which have transformed the tender plant of academic freedom into a robust flower, the volume by Messrs. Hofstadter and Metzger, despite a weak final section, is a creditable achievement.

It is rather a bewildering experience to turn from the first volume to the second. The authors of the first volume disclaim writing "a full-throated polemic." Whether or not this is a reference to the companion volume by Prof. Robert M. MacIver on *Academic Freedom in Our Time,* it is an apt characterization of it. Although it contains some good things, large portions read like the work of an angry partisan, and in a tone incompatible with the manner of judicious inquiry one expects of so distinguished a scholar, now Professor Emeritus of Political Philosophy and Sociology at Columbia. In addition, it manifests a selective bias in the material examined, more appropriate to a partisan attempt to prove a predetermined thesis than to an objective survey. This will puzzle some admirers, among whom this writer is one, of the author's other works.

The upshot of Mr. MacIver's study is that, except in a few islands, academic freedom in the United States has virtually been destroyed. Speaking of the relationship between faculties and governing bodies, he writes: "In what other country, outside the dictatorships, would the members of college faculties be regarded, and treated (*sic!*) as hired men whose job it is to teach whatever and howsoever they are bidden to teach by their comparatively uneducated employers?" And elsewhere, in referring to the transgressions of authority against the limits which safeguard academic freedom, he writes: "In fact, it is hardly an exaggeration to say that the weight of authority in the United States is now adverse to the principle of intellectual freedom." We are not told when it was ever favorable.

As a description of the actual state of academic freedom in American colleges and universities today, "it is hardly an exaggeration to say" that Mr. MacIver's words are a gratuitous libel on the overwhelming majority of self-respecting teachers, administrators and trustees in American institutions of higher learning. With the exception of some minor provisions of state laws governing public colleges, *what* is taught and *how,* are determined by the faculties themselves without dictation by anyone. Save for denominational colleges, what President William Rainey Harper once said of the University of Chicago is the general rule for the vast majority of institutions. "It is a firmly established policy of the trustees that the responsibility for the settlement of educational questions rests with the faculty." Mr. MacIver furnishes no evidence that this policy is not generally observed.

Most violations of academic freedom have arisen from unwarranted interference with extracurricular utterances, activities and associations of teachers, not from the attempt of trustees to usurp the educational prerogatives of the faculty or to lay down a line on what to teach or how in the classroom. After all, the Association of American Colleges and the Association of American Universities are in substantial agreement with the American Association of University Professors on principles of tenure and academic freedom. And although in the past business groups have sinned grievously against academic freedom elementary fairness requires us to recognize that the extensive and much-needed financial aid now offered by such groups to private colleges is completely unrestricted. Sad to relate, faculties in state-subsidized institutions have suffered more from incursions on their educational autonomy than those in private institutions.

In the very interest of the defense of academic freedom we must distinguish between current violations of its principles, and the rejection of the principles themselves. Mr. MacIver confuses the two and goes to great lengths in an effort to establish the existence of a concerted attack on the validity of the very principles of academic freedom from the point of view of opposing *doctrines*. But no informed educator with a sense of humor will take seriously the contention that Allen Zoll and Merwin Hart are important influences on the academic community. And although the author makes great play about a school of thought which refers to "the superstitions of academic freedom," the only individual who can be cited is a recent Yale alumnus, William F. Buckley Jr., whose brilliantly wrong-headed book, *God and Man at Yale,* has been laughed out of court at Yale and ignored elsewhere. The mass support that Mr. Buckley has won for his views seems to consist, according to Mr. MacIver, of Max Eastman. One is reluctant to cavil, but alas! this turns out to be a calamitous lapse in Mr. MacIver's research scholarship. For Mr. Eastman, although praising the nonconformist and challenging character of Mr. Buckley's ideas about academic freedom, severely castigates them as both mistaken and dangerous.

The extreme right-wing "pseudo-educational" associations mentioned by Mr. MacIver are small, have interlocking directorates, and are so fanatical in their pronouncements as to be self-defeating. In any event, no evidence is adduced that they carry any weight in American higher education. When Mr. MacIver states that "these are the forces that in our time most seriously threaten not only academic freedom but the whole broad freedom of thought," the unhysterical reader cannot help reflecting that if this is so, the future of academic freedom is safe, indeed. The conclusions remain the same even if we add to these "pseudo-educational" associations, special interest organizations and militantly patriotic groups. And although some congressional and legislative committees have caused uneasiness by unbridled exaggeration concerning Communist party infiltration in the colleges, which was never a major problem, it is foolish and unscholarly to react by unbridled exaggeration of the effects of Congressional investigations on academic freedom.

Mr. MacIver is on much stronger and perfectly justified ground in his criticism of the absurdities of the intellectual underworld. He also deserves commendation for his vigorous reprimand of those few members of the academy who have permitted their names to be exploited by right-wing groups which do not believe in academic freedom. "When members of distinguished universities have allowed their names to appear, say, as consultants, on the staff of * * * or as members of the Advisory Committee of * * *, we submit they are dishonoring their calling and betraying the faith reposed in them."

An excellent sentiment! One is therefore all the more taken aback to find that Mr. MacIver has not a word of criticism of the much more numerous and much more eminent members of distinguished universities who have lent their names and prestige to all sorts of Communist party causes and Communist party front groups, ranging from the defense of the Moscow trials to the latest partisan Communist "peace" movement. After all, such groups are opposed not only to academic freedom but to every other variety of political and cultural freedom. But I very much fear that Mr. MacIver would dismiss such criticism as a charge of "guilt by association" despite the fact that his own strictures prove there is such a thing as *moral* guilt by association—especially when association takes the form of cooperation.

Mr. MacIver has a powerful and acute vision in one eye which looks through the microscope that magnifies by a hundred diameters the antics of peripheral, extremist right-wing groups. He seems totally blind in the eye which should have observed the professional derelictions of Communist fellow travelers. Objective research requires in this field normal vision in both eyes neither one of which is color blind.

The author himself indicates that a false conception of the amount of intolerance in the United States has been promulgated, and cautions against it. But with respect to the state of academic freedom today, his entire book sins against his own warning and the methodological insights of his younger colleagues. There is nothing in it which indicates that although the number of criticisms against colleges and universities from outside their walls has increased, never in the history of American education have teachers cared more for academic freedom, never have they been so resolute and embattled and, despite some defeats, so successful in its defense.

It is true that conditions are still far from ideal, even though they are better than they used to be. It is also true that conditions vary regionally with the South still lagging behind. But by and large Mr. MacIver would have gone far less astray had he taken the history of academic freedom at Columbia University as a paradigm of the *tendency* in the situation of the country as a whole. For despite the fact that members of the Communist party or of any other group, who are under instructions to betray their professional trust, are quite properly regarded as unfit to teach, the faculty of Columbia University enjoys greater academic freedom than it ever did in the past, even in periods less stormy and hazardous to democratic survival than our own.

II

The second interpretation of academic freedom is contained in *Collectivism on the Campus, A Battle for the Mind in American Colleges* by E. Merrill Root.[2]

The great English philosopher F. H. Bradley once remarked that the opposite of an absurdity can be every whit as absurd. *Collectivism on the Campus* points up the maxim. For some time now we have been regaled with blood-chilling horror stories of reactionary witch hunts that have everywhere reduced American college teachers to a cowering and fearful silence. Merrill Root, an English professor at Earlham College

---

[2] New York, 1955.

in Richmond, Indiana, argues that the precise opposite is true. It is the "collectivist Left," he says, that has terrorized and intimidated conservatives and noncollectivist professors, set the goals and pace of instructors and indoctrinated an entire generation.

The charge is leveled even against trustees. Afraid of being labeled "illiberal" and "reactionary," they lean over backward in suffering collectivist intellectual monopoly. The conservative student, it is alleged, encounters sneers when he attempts to break out of his isolation—or incurs penalties at the hands of the vehement minority who dominate the American campus.

Mr. Root is an earnest man of undoubted sincerity who has read widely, if not discriminatingly, but whose very zeal defeats whatever is laudable in his purpose. His use of the catch-all term "collectivism" to cover Communists, fellow-travelers and those he calls "state liberals" (some of the "state liberals" are resolute critics of the Communists) is an invitation to confusion.

Parts of the book are not without merit, particularly where Mr. Root treats of the antics of the comparative handful of Communist party teachers. He is justly caustic of those who professed to have joined the Communist party mainly out of opposition to Hitler and fascism but who remained stanchly loyal after the Nazi-Soviet pact. He also establishes clearly that Communist party teachers are not intellectually free —a fact still not understood by those who argue that because an individual is "free" to leave an organization he is therefore "intellectually free" while he remains in it. This confuses two senses of the word "free" —free as "voluntary" and free as "honest quest for truth."

A person is free to accept instructions, join or not to join a group that pledges him to indoctrination for a predetermined party line. But when he joins he is not intellectually free. Indeed, it is precisely because the Communist party teacher freely (i.e., voluntarily) accepts membership in a party that presumes to dictate in matters of science and scientific opinion that he is culpable of betrayal of professional trust.

Granting all this, Mr. Root exaggerates both the number and influence of the Communist party teachers. More important, he does not seem to recognize that today the group has practically disappeared from the campus.

Of the second group, "the fellow-travelers" (who still exist), Mr. Root also has some true things to say. Some of the quotations from their writings make hair-raising reading. Here, too, he does not distinguish clearly enough between those who are sympathetic with the aims of the Communist movement and help Communist activities and those who do the work of the Communists unwittingly and drop their association when they see how their names, positions and academic prestige are being organizationally exploited. And he overlooks the elementary fact that it is possible to disagree with wise and informed critics of Communism, and sometimes even to agree with some proposal supported for their own purpose by the Communists, without incurring the deserved stigma of moral guilt by association.

The obsessive character of Mr. Root's book is clearly apparent in his denunciation of "liberals," a category that includes all except fervent believers in a completely free economy as "collectivists," too. This would make most Democrats and Republicans "collectivists." The oddest thing in all this is Mr. Root's assertion that the key heresy of liberalism is belief that economics determines everything in social and political experience. For he, himself, by making everything turn upon free enterprise or collectivism (which includes the New Deal) falls victim to this very same belief. As economic systems, either or both can be politically democratic or nondemocratic. In terms of Mr. Root's personal philosophy one would have expected him to recognize that the basic issue of our time is not capitalism or socialism—for this is everywhere a matter of more or less—but whether our culture, our minds and our basic choices are to be free. In other words the primary issue is moral and political.

Those to whom Mr. Root looks for salvation, the advocates of a completely free economy, share the key proposition of orthodox Marxism, according to which the economic system uniquely determines a culture. Without denying the enormous influence of economics, it is especially clear in our own century that political ideas and ideals are often more decisive and therefore of greater concern. The author overlooks the fact that the Declaration of Independence and the Constitution do not prescribe our mode of economic production but only our mode of political decision.

Mr. Root is convinced he believes in academic freedom and asserts he has no objection to "collectivist" teaching. All he wants, he tells us, is a fair deal, a hearing for other kinds of teaching. But he presents no persuasive evidence that any professionally qualified teacher who believes in free enterprise is therefore prevented from teaching or that students are not permitted to learn about the theory and practice of free enterprise.

When Mr. Root goes on to assert that parents, alumni and educators should demand that "50 per cent of the faculty passionately and articulately uphold free enterprise" before a college can be given a clean bill of health, he reveals a most lamentable misconception of the meaning of academic freedom. It is not the business of a faculty passionately and articulately to uphold any doctrines whether collectivist or free enterprise. Their business is free inquiry, the enterprise of the free mind, to teach without prior commitment and extraneous control whatever conclusions appear valid in the light of the available evidence and argument. And despite hysteria-mongers from both extremes, that is what most teachers are doing day by day, oblivious to the noise and din waged over them by excited partisans within and without academic walls.

The pity of it is that, for all his sincerity and belief in freedom, Mr. Root has not sufficient faith in the processes of intelligence. And, supreme irony, by coupling Communists with their liberal critics Mr. Root is unwittingly aiding the work of the Communists who at present are exploiting the spirit of Geneva for another campaign of infiltration.

The useful information the book contains is overshadowed by its exaggerations and misleading insinuations. It should be required reading only for those who maintain that academic freedom is well on its way to being destroyed by the sinister forces of reaction. They will find in it a precise mirror image of their own thinking.

PART FOUR . . . Socialism,

Freedom

and

Survival

24 The Challenge to Freedom

"FREEDOM" is a fighting word. But like all fundamental terms it is ambiguous in use and application. When human beings stake their lives in defense of freedom, few can state what they precisely mean and still fewer will ever agree on what that meaning is. In this respect, "freedom" is no different from such words as "justice" or "security" or "love." From this, together with the historical evidence which indicates that different groups are often in conflict with each other under the same slogans, I conclude that concern with freedom in practical life is always concern with specific freedoms in particular historical contexts.

As a rule human beings do not struggle for freedom because they subscribe to one or another ideology. They first become conscious of some need, of a hindrance or obstacle to some desired fulfillment, and then find a congenial ideology which seems to justify the fullfillment. Ideological beliefs in time may affect one's consciousness of needs, and strengthen the conviction of the desirability of gratifying them. But in the end, conflicts of ideology become irrelevant when conflicts of needs or interests disappear, or when some peaceful method of adjudicating them wins common acceptance. What unifies free societies is not a common ideology or a set of common interests but a commonly accepted *method* of legally and peacefully resolving conflicts of interests. If all the nations of the world were freely to accept a common method of settling the issues which divide them, their ideological differences, no matter how extreme, would have only a peripheral effect, if any, on the political shape of things. To use an analogy, such differences would have no more bearing on political conduct than conflicting metaphysical views about the nature of matter—whether considered as a complex of sense data, a colony of souls, or prime substance—on the problem of how to construct a seaworthy ship.

Failure to take as our point of departure the specific freedoms for which men struggle, and the methods of resolving conflicts among freedoms, usually results in immersion into an arbitrary dialectic of concepts unrelated to the world of historical experience. Sometimes this is productive of bizarre results, such as that no one is free even in the most democratic of societies or that everyone is free even in totalitarian societies.

When I speak of the "future of freedom" or "the challenge to freedom" I refer to free societies, not to the concept of freedom. Instead of formally defining what I mean by "free societies," I shall designate them. They are the societies of Western Europe and America and some other regions of the world in which institutions exist that rest directly or indirectly upon the freely given consent of the majority of the adult population. The test of whether a free society exists is the presence or absence of legally recognized instrumentalities by which changes in conformity with the wishes of the population can be carried out— wishes that are molded and expressed in the free interchange of opinion. This entails, of course, that no group enjoys a monopoly of the means of education and communication. In this sense, a free society is not necessarily a good society—a majority may be foolish or rash—but to the extent that a society is free, other things being equal, it is better than an unfree society since it is marked by less coercion.

The historical development of free societies has shown that most economic challenges, especially in the twentieth century, can be met by political action. Whatever may have been true in the past, *today it is the mode of political decision rather than the mode of economic production which is of primary significance.* This does not deny that they are interrelated at many points. But my contention is that a sober assessment of free societies will show that, despite the use of traditional slogans, issues that center around the mode of economic production, around the principles of "capitalism" or "socialism," have receded in relative importance. They are approximating the status of questions like that of free trade or protection. Many avowed socialists no longer regard it as sufficiently descriptive of their aims to say that they believe merely in collective ownership or socialization of instruments of production. In the United States even advocates of free enterprise not only accept, but agitate for, a large variety of public controls and price supports. Whenever the discussion leaves the realm of abstractions, it turns out to be not a question of *either* socialism *or* capitalism but of *more or less* social control.

Through the slow accommodation of dogma to the intractabilities of men and events, we have discovered that a whole spectrum of socially viable alternatives exist with respect to legal forms of both ownership and managerial control. Socialism and capitalism as classically defined may be mutually exclusive, but even as definitions they are not exhaustive, and as soon as any one of them has any commerce with historical reality it loses its exclusiveness and borrows principles and methods hitherto associated with the other. The principle of co-determination in Western Germany or a guaranteed annual wage in the United States is as far removed from traditional capitalism as the piece-work, speed-up, Stakhanovist wage system of the Soviet Union and its satellites is removed from the socialist society envisaged by Marx and Engels.

On the other hand, in such countries of the world as the Soviet Union, where socialization of the means of production is complete, the moral, political, and cultural ends of socialism are systematically violated. The effective control which workers exercise over their own lives, including their conditions of work, is far less in the Soviet Union than in the so-called capitalist democracies.

The development of specific freedoms in capitalist countries cannot be simply explained in terms of the development of productive forces or of the mode of production. A relatively *autonomous* psychological and moral demand played a great role. As the capitalist economy became more centralized, the political power of the workers in most countries increased instead of decreasing. Just as those who professed belief in Marx's historical materialism in Russia helped refute it by building the economic foundations of what was supposed to be the pre-condition of political activity, so in a different way those who accepted Marxist orthodoxy in the West, by helping to achieve major reforms, invalidated his catastrophic economic predictions. Whatever heuristic value the theory of historical materialism may have for historians and sociologists, the history of capitalism shows that an economy does not uniquely determine any one social or political system, that at most it limits possibilities, and that the desire for freedom to speak, to assemble, to petition, although related to the desire to buy cheap and sell dear in the market, is not derived from it nor always nurtured by it. History is replete with doctrinal ironies. Some writers who predict the direst consequences to political freedom as necessarily ensuing from a centrally planned economy seem to have accepted, despite themselves, the cardinal tenet of historical materialism and have overlooked the plurality of political and cultural systems which are compatible both with a planned and an unplanned economy.[1]

Whether one accepts or rejects historical materialism or any other of Marx's specific theories, it seems to me undeniable that the original inspiration of his thought was humanistic and libertarian. Property for him was a source of power, not so much to use as to exclude others from use. Consequently private property in the means of life carries with it power over those who must live by their use. To a large extent the source of popular support of socialism is not poverty but the feeling that one's destiny is determined by decisions over which one has no control. Marx absolved the individual capitalist from all responsibility, but the worker whose means of livelihood is affected by a decision to close down a plant because it is unprofitable, even if he is saved from extreme want by some form of insurance, projects his resentment against those whose decisions in his eyes are not socially responsible. Perhaps in any large-scale economic order the ultimate decision could not be his to make, but if he can control even indirectly those who make the decision, he does not feel completely helpless.

Another of Marx's powerful indictments against capitalism which is indicative of his humanistic concern is his charge that it alienates the worker from conditions which make labor a means of creative fulfillment. But it is an open question whether, except in the imagination of those who glorify the past, labor was ever a means of creative fulfillment save for a comparatively small group of craftsmen, artists and officials. Since the advent of the technological revolution, size of plant, degree of division of labor, possibilities of promotion and increased earnings, a voice and vote in industrial affairs have a far greater bearing on the sense of significance in one's work than the legal forms of ownership.

What Marx apparently did not appreciate is that on both counts a collectivist economy in which the mode of political decision is undemocratic is a greater threat to individual freedom and dignity than a non-collectivist economy in which there is no monopoly of political power and in which plural aggregates of power bargain and negotiate with each other over all issues in dispute including the distribution of wealth. In a totalitarian culture even if the rulers have no legal title to property they have absolute power to exclude workers, or anyone else, from their means of livelihood. The material basis for the human dignity which Marx once said, perhaps too optimistically, the worker values more than his daily bread is thus destroyed. And even though the complexities of advanced technology and mass production rather

---

[1] Cf. my discussion with Max Eastman on pp. 349–374.

than the legal forms of ownership deprive the worker of creative satisfaction, it is obvious that a system in which he is denied the right to help determine the conditions and rewards of work can only intensify his sense of alienation. The more industrialized a totalitarian economy becomes, the more difficult his plight. He becomes not merely an appendage to a machine but an appendage to a factory—a set-up which Oscar Lange, before he returned to Communist Poland, aptly characterized as "industrial feudalism."

The future of freedom in modern society everywhere depends upon the extension of the democratic process into industrial affairs even when this involves some sacrifice of efficiency. Although it has been maintained that participation in the processes of decision-making on some levels actually enhances efficiency, and some evidence exists that this is the case, it is not necessary to assume it is always true. The possibilities of abuse are always present and it is notorious that even in purely political matters democracies on occasion are less efficient than dictatorships. But it is not unreasonable to believe that where participation carries with it genuine power, and is not merely a deceptive promise accompanying propagandistic exhortations to increase production as is the case in Communist countries, the individual worker may develop something of the feeling of responsibility, pride and satisfaction which in the past were associated with individual ownership or the performance of some honored social service.

One would be tempted to regard some of the foregoing observations as an obvious commentary on the political experience of the last generation were they not implicitly denied by recent arguments according to which the issues of freedom are subordinate if not irrelevant in underdeveloped and industrially backward countries. Nations in which there is not sufficient capital accumulation cannot afford, it is said, the slow processes of democracy to reach Western standards of living. Once the forces of production have reached sufficiently high levels, the cultural and political institutions distinctive of a free society will gradually and inescapably be added to it. It is sometimes claimed that even in the Soviet Union democracy stands in the wings ready to make an entrance as soon as the country's economic progress reaches a point where emphasis can be placed upon the production of consumption goods. Freedom can wait upon the distribution of refrigerators and television sets, and it is the veriest parochialism, it is held, to expect economically underprivileged nations to adopt modes of political decision characteristic of the West.

What this overlooks is that not a single economically advanced country in the world has ever reached freedom by following this path. Free institutions have never come into existence in consequence merely of large capital accumulation and an industrialized economy. Where they are found today they are the result of long developments which accompanied the process of economic evolution, and sometimes preceded it. Whence is derived the confidence that if a totalitarian society can produce enough goods and services to rival current standards of distribution in Western countries it will therefore modify its political and cultural institutions, too, and move toward freedom? Here, too, we see operating in a crude way one of the assumptions of historical materialism. The capacity of totalitarian societies to provide a high standard of material life for the masses is yet to be demonstrated. It certainly is not inherently impossible; but if and when it succeeds in doing this, that very fact may constitute a very powerful argument to let "those who know best," those who have engineered the nation to higher levels of material prosperity, determine not only the pattern of production but the basic design for living. What we have learned of the interdependence of historical means and ends, and of the pervasive effects of monolithic cultural conditioning make it unlikely that an improvement in material standards of life, if actually attained under unfree institutions, will give rise to a strong desire for a new political order. It may give rise to a desire for more of the same.

The main point, however, is not whether better material conditions will inspire a desire for freedom among the people—signs indicate that in the Soviet Union and the satellite countries it has always been there—but whether it will inspire it among their rulers. Here hope may be legitimate but belief is the sheerest wish-thinking. No ruling group voluntarily surrenders its power is a Marxist maxim which must be qualified wherever democratic processes exist. But where they do not, the insight is still valid. We should know by now that it is far easier for free societies to lose their freedom by supineness and foolishness, and as in Czechoslovakia by a failure to distinguish between heresy and conspiracy, than for totalitarian societies to regain it. To ignore the fact that as totalitarian countries have become more stable they have increased the pitch of political and cultural repression is to invite a crop of illusions. Under Lenin when the Communist regime was still shaky it was possible to murmur and make political jokes. Under Stalin, when Western Europe was shaky, even the Soviet circus was purged and party-lined.

And although some degree of cultural thaw seems to be setting in today among communist countries, it has not even reached the level of restricted freedom which existed in the first decade of the Soviet Union. The current strategy of the Kremlin is no more fundamental than the turns it made when it joined the League of Nations, inaugurated the Popular Front, and initiated the Nazi-Soviet Pact. Genuine signs of freedom will appear in the Soviet Union, not when it opens its doors to tourists and tolerates differences of opinion in some non-political spheres (features also found under the regimes of Hitler and Mussolini), but when it abolishes its concentration and slave-labor camps, abolishes a one-party dictatorship, and permits open political criticism by a legally recognized political opposition.

The position I am criticizing sometimes takes a more vicious form when it is asserted that the *peoples* of economically backward or colonial countries are not prepared to accept the burdens and responsibilities of free societies, that nothing in their past has prepared them for democratic community life. One sometimes hears this view expressed not only with respect to peoples of Asia and Africa but of East European countries, some of which, before they fell to Communist aggression, enjoyed far more freedom than they possess today. It used to be said of colonial peoples that they were ill prepared for national independence and that the very concept of the Nation was a Western notion foreign to the thoughtways of the Asian or African. Today although we do not regard nationalism as an unmixed blessing, we see in it an expression of a universal and thoroughly justified desire on the part of a people to determine its own destinies in independence of foreign sovereignty no matter how benevolent. We may reasonably expect a nation to surrender some of its sovereignty to an international authority but not to the authority of a foreign nation. Even if national independence meant liberation from foreign exploitation in order to give native rulers a freer hand to exploit their own compatriots, we would extenuate it as a first step in the awakening of a people to the possibility of liberation from all economic exploitation. We have reached a point of recognizing that under their skins all literate peoples today are nationalist to some degree. Why should anyone assume that in this age of rapid communication people of economically backward countries are more indifferent to the elementary rights of a free society than they are to the right of national independence. Does the Yugoslav peasant desire to have less say in communal affairs, to speak less freely than the Indian peasant or the Italian peasant? Or does the Soviet man like administrative sentences to slave labor camps any better than the Yugoslav? Do the North-Koreans or Vietnamese or the Chinese prefer to leave control of their property and life to Communist social engineers? If they did why should apologists for Communist regimes insist that a dictatorship is necessary? If one argues from the fact that Communist dictatorships have remained in power that therefore they enjoy popular favor, every tyranny in the past could be called a forerunner of the new "Communist democracies." There is a tendency in the West to speak as if Communist rule in Asia is the natural result of a popular movement, and to read the *military* defeat of opponents of Communism as if it were in some way a political judgment as well. This seems to me to be a capitulation to the rhetorical clap-trap of the so-called "popular democracies." How does anyone know what the masses want or prefer in the absence of an honest registration of consent? Those observers who say that Communist regimes "satisfy the needs" of the masses are either guessing or have embraced the totalitarian principle that the rulers are better judges of the interests of their subjects than the subjects themselves.

Those who patronizingly declare that the people of economically backward or formerly colonial countries are not yet ripe for free institutions are substituting a new kind of imperialism for the old. The "white man's burden" or the burden of the West is now become "the burden of freedom" just as in the past it was the burden of Empire or Christianity or Trade. There is no special "gene" for freedom possessed by Americans and Europeans but lacking in other peoples. One does not have to embrace the Rousseauistic nonsense about compelling men to be free to recognize that the practices of freedom tend to be contagious. I am not speaking of primitive tribes, of course, but of peoples of ancient civilizations with written languages. Granted that free institutions do not spring full-blown into existence overnight. Neither does science nor medicine nor industry, the beginnings of which we assume can be naturalized in all countries. We are living in an age in which different historical periods are being telescoped, and free institutions may develop more rapidly in economically backward countries than was the case in countries of their origin. It may be that their parliaments or representative bodies without being rubber stamps for local despots will avoid the riotous scenes which used to mark the sessions of the Reichstag in the last years of the Weimar Republic and which erupt, it is rumored, even in the assemblies of democratic France and Italy.

We are sometimes told that the peoples of the East care more for the things of the spirit than do the materialistic civilizations of the West. At the same time we are informed that they pant for the higher material standards of life of the West, indeed to a point where they are prepared to trample upon those freedoms which represent the Western spirit at its best—its respect for the individual, the rule of law, and the democratic mode of political decision. Without denying that the life of the spirit can take many different forms I am skeptical of both reports. I cannot see that except perhaps for holy men and saints freedom of speech and freedom from want are incompatible with respect for the things of the spirit. Nor is it evident that the spiritual values of the West to the extent that they are embodied in the institutions of a free society imperil the central religious or spiritual traditions of the East.

The more industrially advanced free nations of the world must shoulder the responsibility of aiding underdeveloped countries to combat poverty, famine, and disease not only to help preserve peace but also to show that economic progress can be achieved at less human cost under free institutions than under Communist or Fascist dictatorships. I am not convinced that this requires mechanization and industrialization of all countries. If the danger of war recedes, a better international economic comity may lead to a more intelligent husbandry of resources. But where mechanization and industrialization are required we should not be unduly impressed by the charge, more fashionable in prosperous than poor countries, that these processes as such are hostile to free institutions. What is usually meant is that they affect the sense of spontaneity, undermine the joy of work, substitute large impersonal enterprises for small and intimate ones, and imposes a drab uniformity on consumers.

It is hard to establish or refute such large and vague claims but it seems to me just as plausible to argue that the *absence* of mechanization and industrialization is just as great a threat—indeed, a greater one—to the possibility of a full and abundant life as is their presence. This is particularly true for those who actually do the toil in any society. If one recalls the conditions under which, say, miners have labored from ancient times down to the last century, or the conditions under which "the man with the hoe" as distinct from the gentleman farmer has wrestled with the soil, one will be chary of such wholesale generalizations. Except where jobs have been imperiled, it is usually literary men and not those who have done the back-breaking work on roads or docks or dams who are most eloquent about the dangers of mechanization.

Many of the evils attributed to mechanization and industrialization are a consequence of urbanization and the growth of slums. But these are no longer necessarily bound up with each other. The pace of urbanization can be controlled. Rural electrification, express highways, automobile, and airplane make it possible to decentralize many industries and provide a mode of life for those who do not share Socrates' preference for the culture of cities.

There is more substance to the charge that mechanization and industrialization standardize products of use and enjoyment and make for an appalling sameness in style and form. Here, too, the indictment is largely overdrawn. In many ways machines can diversify and multiply patterns. There is far more variety in machine-made clothing today than clothes showed at a time when most people wore homespun and a few wore silk. In an age when we can construct "thinking" machines, the main reason our machines do not produce greater variety is that we do not want it.

For these and many other reasons, it seems to me to be, if not a complete mistake, a diversion from our main concern to regard mechanization and industrialization as threats to a free society or to significant experience within it. At most they are challenges to human ingenuity and creative intelligence. In principle, the issue posed by the invention of any machine is morally no different today from the one faced by primitive man when the first tool gave him the power to destroy life or conserve it. It betokens a lack of historical imagination to fail to see that by and large the impact of science and technology on culture has been humanizing. It has liberated human beings from the squalor, misery, disease, and needless cruelties under which until recently all but a comparative handful have lived. It holds out indefinite (not unlimited) possibilities of achieving more if our wisdom can keep abreast of our knowledge and power.

There is also the notion that the prospects of freedom are dimmed by the growth of social and economic equality and that the rule of democratic majorities spells in the end uniformity and conformity in the life of culture. These conclusions rest upon a faulty dialectic of concepts and a misreading of historical events. Modern totalitarian states are not exactly distinguished for the variety and vigor of their arts and sciences, and "egalitarianism" is a capital heresy under Communist regimes. "Freedom" and "equality" cannot be simply counterposed for the obvious reason that all may be equally free or equally unfree. Free institutions presuppose political equality and therefore measures designed to reduce those inequalities, particularly economic inequalities, which give groups or individuals disproportionate *political* influence, are not only legitimate but necessary. There are, of course, other powerful moral grounds for social and economic equality. When we speak of a conflict between freedom and equality analysis will show that we are confronted as a rule with a conflict of freedoms. In the resolution of these conflicts, the political freedoms—of speech and press, assembly and petition, of minorities to become majorities—are the *strategic* freedoms. I call them strategic because they not only have intrinsic worth but because they define the process by which we can discover what, in case of conflict, our preferred freedoms are, the order of their priority, how to maximize and share them, and what the ultimate limits of compromise and conciliation are.

Free societies may not be good societies and one does not have to be an extreme cultural relativist to recognize as a possibility that historical situations may exist in which democratic modes of political decision are impossible or undesirable because of their consequences.

From the point of view of any humane ethic, however, free societies in our era have proved themselves inmeasurably better than any alternatives.

Although it may sound old-fashioned in the present climate of opinion to say it, I feel that the chief threat to a free society in our time is the spirit which contributed so much to the rise and spread of Hitlerism. It is expressed in the belief that security can be won by the sacrifice of the strategic freedoms and that because Communists possess the nuclear weapons to destroy the world, the cause of freedom is less urgent. But in an unfree world only those who have resigned themselves to being slaves can feel secure. And even for them, since there is no institutional restraint on their master's will, security may prove to be an illusion. If Hitler had possessed nuclear weapons, free men would not have regarded it as an overwhelming argument for a super-Munich; and since Hitler was mad, it is much more likely that he would have used such weapons, regardless of consequences, than the coldly calculating tacticians of the Kremlin. I am *not* saying that any agreements concluded with the Kremlin necessarily represent the Munichs of our decade. I am saying that the belief that survival *at all costs* is the be-all and end-all of political wisdom does not guarantee survival, and to the extent that it does it tends to make a casualty of the free life in an open society.

25 Karl Marx in Limbo

IT WAS NOT difficult to find the shade of Karl Marx in limbo. His spectral beard was trimmed, his monocle was gone and he seemed much more benign than his pictures show him—indeed, almost grandfatherly. Flanked by Engels and Kautsky, he was arguing a technical point with Keynes, Veblen and Schumpeter. Lenin was not in the circle. Later my guide told me he was waiting with brooding impatience for Stalin, who, although due, was still missing; there were rumors that limbo would not receive him.

Marx detached himself from his fellow shades when he learned that a visitor from earth had arrived. Instead of introducing myself as an author of several studies of his thought (I had heard that biographers and critics sometimes got an unspiritual reception when they met their subjects face to face), I announced at once that I had news for him.

"News?" he said. "I hope it's agreeable for a change. For the last twenty years or so, it has been uniformly unpleasant. Almost every new arrival prominently connected with public affairs has picked an argument with me, as if I were responsible for what's happening on Earth."

"My news is more personal," I replied. "The Marx-Engels-Lenin Institute at Moscow is issuing a new corrected edition of your works at the command of the Central Executive Committee of the Russian Communist party."

"Corrected edition, indeed!" he remarked bitterly. "They have been correcting me by word and deed ever since 1917. Every last outrage they commit is laid at my door—even by people who should know better."

"Well," I pointed out. "Isn't it natural? You called yourself a Communist at one time and they call themselves Communists."

332

"That, my dear Professor," Marx interrupted, "is known as the fallacy of the undistributed middle term, according to the logic you teach, whose laws, I gather from our cosmic news ticker, the Kremlin has just rediscovered. As well say that, because both sides in the Thirty Years War called themselves Christian, they really were in agreement with each other. Soviet Communism and mine are quite different."

"In what respect?" I inquired.

Marx's retort surprised and alarmed me a little because it indicated either that his reading habits were still omnivorous or that the cosmic ticker paid attention to him. "You ought to know, since you've read the material. We called ourselves Communists in order to differentiate ourselves from sentimental socialists who had their eyes so fixed on a Utopia that they couldn't see what the necessary steps were in the process of realizing it. As you recall, when my friends and I were members of the Communist League we wrote that *'we were not among those Communists who were out to destroy liberty and who wished to turn the whole world into one huge barracks or into a gigantic warehouse. There certainly were some Communists who with easy conscience refused to countenance personal liberty.'*[1] But for me personal liberty was the very oxygen of any decent society. My criticism of capitalism was based on my desire to diffuse freedom among those who were suffering from lack of it."

"But if that's true," I objected, "why have the leaders of Communist Russia canonized you and built a cult around you? Surely, to use a favorite phrase of theirs, it is no accident that—"

"It's a long story," Marx interjected, "and there *are* accidents in history even if this isn't one. The Russians were always difficult and different. More than once I had to say *'I am no Marxist.'* Bakunin, who also once called himself a Marxist, I disowned on Earth. The Communists are people of *his* kidney, and even Bakunin rages against them up here. I don't recognize the present-day Communist brood as my legitimate offspring no matter what they call themselves."

"I've heard other fathers *say* that," I replied, "but saying it is not enough to disprove parentage. Legitimate or not, they claim to be inspired by your ideas and to have built a socialist society. You may not like *how* they got there, but they *are* there, are they not?"

"By no means," Marx replied with a vehemence that seemed to make his beard-tip glow. "A Socialist society as I always conceived it is one in which *'the free development of each is the condition of the free development of all.'* That excludes the dictatorship of a party, and especially the rule of despots. A socialist society is based on equality,

---

[1] All italicized material is quoted from the writings of Marx.

even if it cannot be absolute, and, in the beginning, on equality of wage payments for equal working time. The Communists have substituted a new and worse system of exploitation of the workers—through piece-work, speed-up devices, and differences in earned income and living conditions greater than existed in the early days of capitalism. Why, they claim to be Marxists and socialists and yet they frankly admit that labor power is still a commodity subject to the law of value. The surplus value sweated out of them goes to their masters. . . ."

Fearing that Marx was going to ride his ancient economic hobby horse, I interrupted. "Surely not all of it. Some of it goes into new plants, and they do have trade unions."

By this time Marx's whole beard was incandescent. "Trade unions!" he burst out. "Their trade unions are worse than company unions. They are auxiliaries of the secret police whose function is to intimidate the workers into producing more. I have always taught that the working class *regards its courage, self-confidence, independence and sense of personal dignity as more necessary than its daily bread.*' How is this possible under a regime of a ruthlessly censored press, regimented schools from kindergarten to universities, forced labor, juridical frame-ups, mass deportations and executions? No, the Soviet Union is not a socialist society."

"Nor is it a capitalist society," I added while he paused to draw a fresh breath, "since all the major instruments of production, distribution and exchange are collectivized. What kind of a social system is it, then? Your theory of social development seems unable to account for it."

"This is a terminological matter," Marx declared with a touch of asperity. "The main point is that Soviet society, wherever it exists, out-rages all the democratic traditions for which the socialist movement fought as well as those of the great revolutionary movements of liberation whose heirs we always considered ourselves to be."

"Very well," I said hurriedly, "I grant your social philosophy is not theirs. But there is nothing in the notion of a completely collectivized economy which insures that *your* social philosophy will prevail rather than theirs. What I am asking you to explain, however, is the origin and development of the Soviet social system on the basis of your own theory of history. Didn't you say over and over that '*no social order ever perishes before all the productive forces for which there is room in it have developed*'? There was certainly plenty of room for the development of productive forces in Russia in 1917, even more than in the United States of 1917, which was decades ahead of Russia and which has enormously increased its productive capacities since then."

"Quite right," retorted Marx with a triumphant air. "I predicted that socialism would come first to England and the United States because those countries are ripe for it. And certainly not in a backward, undeveloped, semi-barbarous country like Russia. You see how presumptuous the Communists are in calling themselves Marxists."

I wondered why he sounded so triumphant. "I see," I exclaimed, "that the Communists are not Marxists as they claim to be and that, if you came to life again in Moscow, the Grand Inquisitors of the Kremlin would probably throw you into the cellars of the Lubianka as an agent of American imperialism. But it seems even clearer to me that the Communists have refuted the central doctrine of Marxism in the name of Marxism. According to that doctrine, the mode of economic production determines political events, not conversely. But the Communists seized political power, nationalized the economy, industrialized the country, collectivized agriculture. Their culture may not be democratic, but their economy is collectivist. It is quite apparent that it was not, as you proclaimed, *'historical laws working with iron necessity toward inevitable results'* which were the driving force of events in Russia but the driving will of the Communists. Doesn't this show that men control economic forces, for good or evil, wisely or unwisely, and are not controlled by them to the extent that you taught? In other words, haven't the Communists refuted the central proposition of the theory of historical materialism?"

"Not so fast, Professor," Marx quietly replied. "If you take my words literally, you may be right. But let's look for the meaning behind the mere words. When I wrote about what was historically necessary or impossible, I assumed that there was a certain level of civilization which we could take for granted, certain basic human needs and values which would guide human action, or at least limit what human beings would do to other human beings. I was a humanist before I became a socialist, and therefore I believed it was impossible to build a socialist economy in a backward country like Russia except at a morally prohibitive cost. But if we are completely indifferent to questions of human cost and suffering, only physical and biological necessities limit our action and we are all reduced to the level of clever beasts of prey."

"Nothing can grow in a desert," he continued after a pause, "but we can make even a desert bloom like a flower garden if we are prepared to fertilize it with human corpses and water it with rivers of blood. A country which doesn't grow into socialism on the basis of an already prepared economic foundation, a tradition of skill, management, democracy and culture, will defeat the very ends in behalf of which the socialist movement came into existence."

"It is a pity," I observed, "that you didn't spend more time in elaborating on these ends. By concentrating mainly on the economic conditions of achieving them, you gave the impression that collectivism was the be-all and end-all of socialism; that, once it was achieved, all the other virtues would be added to society. The fault is not completely attributable to those of your disciples who converted a necessary condition into a sufficient one. The sentimental socialists may have ignored the means, but *you* lost sight of the ends. It seems to me that your fault is graver."

"No," said Marx, "my Hegelian teachers had convinced me that means and ends are so intertwined that they couldn't be separated. It may be I took too much for granted. But, remember, I wasn't writing textbooks or manuals or recipe books for revolutions everywhere at any time."

"Then tradition becomes an important constraining force in what men can make of man," I pointed out, "and under some conditions as decisive in influencing the direction of social change as the mode of economic production."

"I have never denied it. On the contrary. *'Men make their own history, but not just as they please. They do not choose the circumstances for themselves, but have to work on circumstances as they find them. The legacy of the dead generations weighs like a nightmare upon the brains of the living. At the very time when they seem to be creating something perfectly new, the past often creeps back.'* The Russian past could not be wiped out by any Commissar's decree; it still lives in the present. As of old, for the Russian ruler progress consists in extending the domain of their despotism. What I said at the time of the suppression of Poland by Tsarist Russia is even truer today: *'The policy of Russia is changeless. Its methods, its tactics, its maneuvers may change, but the polar star of its policy—world domination—is still a fixed star.'* "

Not wishing to discuss foreign policy in limbo, I shifted to another question.

"Well, now," I asked, "what about China. Surely here is something you didn't foresee. Do you think China can build socialism, even with the help of the Soviet Union?"

"My analysis of the Soviet Union," Marx spoke scornfully, "is even more valid for China. I predict that the attempt to introduce socialism in China will fail even more badly than it has in the Soviet Union."

"Agreed," I replied, "but what you didn't predict is that the attempt would be made! Since the consequence of the attempt, whether it fails or succeeds, is bound to give rise to momentous historical changes—indeed! it already has—something important about history is left unexplained."

"My main interest, as you should know," Marx patiently explained, "has always been in the Western world, and the truth or falsity of my theories rests primarily upon developments there. I predicted *the growth and centralization of large-scale industry, increasing mechanization, the concentration of capital and monopoly, the entanglement of all peoples in the net of the world market, and periodic crises of production.* By and large, all these things have come to pass."

"Quite true," I rejoined, "but there are a number of other things you predicted which didn't come to pass. You predicted the pauperization of the working classes, the disappearance of the middle class, the atrophy of nationalism and patriotism. Large groups of workers in Western Europe, and especially in the United States, enjoy a standard of living higher than the privileged classes of some previous societies. Nationalism is as strong as ever. The middle class has not disappeared. And the plain fact is that the workers in non-collectivist economies have incomparably more freedom, political power, and a greater share of what they produce than the workers in presumably collectivist economies."

"I cheerfully admit it," Marx smilingly responded, "but I believe I can take some credit for it since I taught the necessity of political action and called attention to the influence of factory legislation."

"But, in addition to the predicted things which didn't happen," I objected, "there are other things which happened that you did not predict —the birth of new industries, the expansion of productive forces, the rise of fascism, the emergence of the welfare state."

"I underestimated the vitality of capitalism," said Marx, "and the extent to which the democratic process could be used to strengthen social control and responsibility. But this is a matter of detail and degree. I always argued that *in countries like Great Britain, Holland and the United States the transition from capitalism to socialism could be effected peacefully.* Similarly with the development of the technological revolution. I believe I was the first to recognize the impact upon society of *'conscious technical application of science to industry and agriculture.'* "

"But you claimed that technology was always a subordinate instrument to war and industry," I protested. "Yet neither you nor anyone else guessed that some day the choices we would have to make concerning its dread uses might affect the very existence of civilization as such."

"The effects of certain discoveries," he agreed, "as well as their significance, cannot always be measured by their origins. Whatever the causes of technological change in the past, unless men today think and plan better than they have in the past, they may not even survive. Limbo will become rapidly overpopulated."

I turned to ask a last question. "Do you believe the basic issue of our time is still between capitalism and socialism?"

Marx spoke deliberately. "Capitalism and socialism as they were traditionally conceived are today irrelevant abstractions in understanding social reality. Wherever free institutions exist, they have been used to make capital more socially responsible and labor more powerful and prosperous. Aside from the defense of freedom itself, the great problems arise in the West not from a quest for new forms of property but for new modes of democratic human experience which will enrich human life and multiply the possibilities of creative fulfillment. The choice is not between *either* capitalism *or* socialism but of *more* or *less* insofar as they bear upon the possibility of maximizing in each specific situation the opportunities of freedom. Socialism must today be conceived as a principle of welfare and fraternity integral to the democratization of culture on every level—economic, educational and social. It is democracy as a way of life. It relies on creative intelligence to conceive, modify or transform any or all institutions with one goal in view: the development of a community of free persons—each one different from the other and yet enjoying or respecting one another's differences.

By this time, the space ship which was to take me back to Earth had arrived, and Marx escorted me to the ectoplasmic gangplank. I told him that it was not likely that credence would be given to my report of our conversation. His last words to me were the sentence from Dante with which he completed the preface to his chief work: *"Segui il tuo corso, e lascia dir le genti—follow your own course and let people talk."*

26 Socialism and Freedom

_____ _____

SINCE THE FIRST WORLD WAR the Socialist movement has undergone one crisis after another. With the triumph of Hitler and the consolidation of the Russian dictatorship, the succession of crises seemed to be culminating in a death rattle. Many Socialists, men of integrity and intelligence, reluctantly came to the conclusion that they had been on the wrong track. Experience and reflection reinforced their conviction that the iron heel of totalitarianism had stamped into the ground, together with millions of Socialist lives, the very ideals of Socialism as feasible options in the present era of history.

In order to safeguard the democratic ethos of Socialism, they surrendered their belief in a planned collectivist economy. Some became New Dealers, others advocates of a "mixed economy," a phrase that covers a whole spectrum of social forms; still others became defenders of the capitalist status quo.

What united these retreats from democratic Socialism was the absence of a _positive_ social philosophy that furnished a directive to long time action. Thinking went on a day-to-day basis except in relation to the beloved illusions which had borne such bitter fruit. From a justified critique of many dogmas of orthodox Marxism, some of these thinkers went on to an indictment of Marx as the father of totalitarianism, and from there to the view that Socialism as an ideal of the good society was invalid because one of its essential elements is a planned economy. Gradually they found themselves allied, at first unwittingly and then

_____

Note to the reader. Some anachronistic references appear in this essay and the subsequent exchange with Max Eastman which reflect the period in which they were written. I have let them stand in order to preserve the flavor of the discussion.

339

consciously, to conservative forces and groups whom, as Socialists in the past, they had combatted in behalf of democracy. The human being in yesterday's enemy was rediscovered—he should never have been forgotten! —and tentative hopes for a cooperative solution of our major social ills under capitalism blossomed in the most unexpected quarters.

There was no apostacy in this development. Its motivation was a passion for democracy, heightened by a sense of the dangers to which the great liberal tradition of the western world was exposed by the monstrous concentration of power in existing collectivist economies. There was no blind panic or emotional revulsion. What took place was a reexamination of first principles that seemed too weak to withstand the crushing impact of historical events. Indeed a high order of intelligence was displayed in the appraisal of the multiform ways in which a planned economy *could* be used as an engine of repression—a subject to which the mass of "totalitarian liberals" was indifferent.

Nonetheless it seems to me that the conclusions concerning a planned economy which were drawn from the ghastly experiences of Germany and Russia were not warranted, and that the case for a democratic Socialism, instructed by past errors and present dangers, is stronger than for any other alternative.

There are certain historical events and situations which make the abandonment by genuine democrats of a planned economy seem a little premature. First of all, there is the problem of postwar reconstruction in the liberated European areas. It is a commonplace that the peace of Europe depends to a large extent upon the establishment of a workable *domestic* economy. But capitalism in any of its recognizable forms has practically disappeared in most of Europe. The forms and titles of ownership are badly scrambled. Hardly anyone envisages a return to the prewar capitalist system of production, if only because of the dearth produced by the widespread destruction of productive forces. Privation and need are so acute that they will not wait until the process of capitalist accumulation has run its course. On the contrary, it is clear that some of the purely economic devices and organizational forms of the existing system in Europe can be redirected by democratic political control to get production going, and to insure a more equitable distribution. If we define property in a functional, rather than an absolutist sense, as the power to control the disposition of things and services, the role of "government" or "public" property in the organization of the resources of every European country is going to be *more,* not less. And this is a development which cannot be reasonably opposed by democrats who realize that chaos, hunger, and chronic unemployment are the seedbed of totalitarianism.

One cannot consistently (a) maintain that capitalism is a *sine qua non* of democracy, (b) entertain hopes for a democratic Europe, and (c) admit that the swan song of capitalism has already been sung.

It will be admitted by all who have studied the history of left-wing movements, particularly by those who have foresworn Socialism out of love for democracy, that the greatest threat to democratic liberties in existing democratic countries are the Communist groups and parties. Their influence is now growing by leaps and bounds. We know that they stand for the most ruthless kind of terrorism. Yet at the present time Communists are the most impassioned defenders of private enterprise, especially in the United States. In the light of their staunch defence of the rights of capital and their vicious attacks upon even traditional forms of militant labor action, the mildest Fabian appears to be a be-whiskered revolutionist. The Communists are *now* the most "conservative" social group within any coalition they may join. Tomorrow they may reverse their line again.

Let us suppose for a moment—what is not beyond the limits of historical possibility in some countries—that the Communists and their confidence men in other parties, actually come into possession of state power pledged to a defence of free enterprise. *Can there be any reasonable doubt that politically they would act in precisely the same way as if they came to power on a collectivist program?* Spain is a case in point. Their terror was directed not so much against capitalist Republicans with one foot in Franco's camp as against the revolutionary POUM and those elements among the left-wing Socialists and syndicalists who pressed for mild social and agrarian reforms. The current scene should recall, to those who have despaired of Socialism because of Hitler and the Kremlin, the truth *that political terror can be systematized under free enterprise, too.*

The great strides the Communists have been making in democratic countries of the West are possible only because influential sections of the capitalist class have *voluntarily* allied themselves with Communist-controlled organizations. From machine politicians of both parties to members of the House of Morgan, from government officials to representatives of business organizations, from trade union bureaucrats to conservative publicists, we observe an amazing number of non-Socialists willing, and sometimes, eager, to "play ball" with the Communists. And this despite the historical record of planned political terror in every country in which the Communists have shared power. Among the motley array of supporters of free enterprise, there are substantial groups which are not so much interested in democracy as in power. It is very instructive to watch how readily they are prepared to throw overboard ideological ballast to save the precious cargo of property, status, and power.

It does not require a feverish mind to imagine a situation in which a business executive irked by government restraints and an unruly labor force, comes to the conclusion that he has nothing to lose and something to gain as a "Commissar" of production. (Rickenbacker tells us that he feels perfectly at home in Russia. There are no labor troubles; the unions know their place!) It does put a strain on one's imaginative powers to see people of this character fighting for the democratic rights of the workers, or protecting democrats and Socialists against Soviet terror. They are not as dangerous as the actual fellow-travelers, who open the gates to the Stalinists, because they are not as sophisticated. But they are certainly weak reeds for democrats to lean on.

How safe, then, is democracy in any capitalist country of Western Europe which calls in Communists to stabilize its economy or restore peace and order? The newly won converts to free enterprise are not as tough-minded as they think. They are overestimating the strength of capitalist allegiance to democracy despite the history of Germany and Spain. There *are* capitalists who are genuine believers in political democracy just as there are workers who would betray it. But one cannot take this on faith. By works alone must we judge.

There is an analogue to this naiveté in the field of foreign policy. It is expressed in the belief that because the consequences of the war against Hitlerism *may* be the preservation of political democracy in western Europe and America, the decisive cause of the war was the desire to preserve or extend democracy throughout the world. From this confusion the illusion was born that the democratic statesman would remain faithful to the provisions of the Atlantic Charter (which is certainly not an ideal democratic document) in respect to countries coveted by their totalitarian ally. The utterly callous betrayal of Poland and Yugoslavia shows how futile it is to expect a consistent democratic foreign policy from non-Socialist democrats who still think in terms of balance of power. And when we observe the conservative press, which editorializes eloquently about democracy in the abstract, abet this betrayal either openly or by judicious silence, we understand that we are dealing not with a personal phenomenon but a social one.

But the above merely highlights by way of introduction some of the aspects of the current social and political scene which should give pause to those who fear Socialism as a threat to democracy.

The question, can a planned economy be democratic, is empirical. It is one that cannot be settled by definition alone, but which permits of an answer in terms of historical evidence—past and present. Too many treatises on the subject define "socialism" and "democracy" in such a way that the notion of a "democratic collectivism" becomes a contradiction in terms: or they define these terms so that they logically imply one another and rule out in advance the relevance of any historical case in which either democracy or a planned economy is not found.

The historical evidence must be specific in nature and not some vague historical generalization from which the conclusion is deduced. It is very curious to observe that despite their rejection of the dogmas of orthodox Marxism, many who assert that a planned society must historically result in totalitarianism, unconsciously reflect one of the crudest of these dogmas. Orthodox Marxism believed that the economy of a culture was the decisive, if not the sole, determining factor of its political form, so that if we know the relation of economic forces at any period we could predict that one, and only one, political form was historically possible. In respect to the past, critics of orthodox Marxism recognized this as an error, or at the very least, a misleading oversimplification. *More than one political form—obviously not all—are compatible with capitalism in many stages of its development. Yet it is ofttimes assumed that given a collectivist economy, politically only a totalitarian state is compatible with it.*

There is, to be sure, evidence of the most tragic and palpable kind that in *some* specific cases such a development *has* taken place. That is the starting point of our inquiry. But before we leap to the conclusion that these cases prove democratic Socialism to be historically impossible anywhere, we should investigate the antecedent conditions of the cases in question to see whether the totalitarian features of their culture were actually a consequence of their planned economy.

The historical evidence shows that in the countries which manifest totalitarianism in their most repugnant forms—German and Russia—a planned economy did *not* precede the death of political democracy. The Bolsheviks and the Nazis were undemocratic political groups organized to seize complete power; they *first* destroyed political democracy and then organized collectivist economies. The destruction of democracy was implicit in the totalitarian character of the parties, not in the ideal of collectivism. In the philosophy of Bolsheviks and fascists there is no value set on freedom. When a "socialist" economy is built by men who despise democracy and freedom of personality as illusory bourgeois forms, it is not surprising that their "socialism" develops along totalitarian lines. Many of the objectives of their planning, as well as many of their organizing techniques and methods of planning, can be traced to the politically undemocratic form of their governments. Can we justify an inductive inference from these cases to situations in which planning would be undertaken by democratic governments?

By itself, however, this argument is not very strong, for after all, we do not have anywhere in the world a politically democratic community which engages in social planning to a degree commensurate with totalitarian countries. But we do have an *approximation* to such a situation in the war economies of the United States and England.

The First World War was characterized by two features: the practice of business-as-usual, on the one hand, and the practice of a very unusual terror. In the present war there is hardly any business-as-usual. The government has taken over the control of the productive forces of the country to a degree not even remotely approached during the First World War. Yet despite this tremendous growth in overall and piecemeal planning, there has been far less cultural and political repression than there was in the war years of business-as-usual. To anyone who remembers the atmosphere of the First World War and its immediate aftermath, the spectacle of representatives of two Socialist parties addressing the armed forces, with radio time equal to that given the two major parties, is both astonishing and encouraging, especially since both the Socialist and the Socialist Labor Parties are anti-war.

How account for the fact that despite the existence of a war economy which has more planned control than anything that existed in the past, and which *could* have been used as a weapon of cultural totalitarianism, the watchdogs of civil and cultural freedom have had *comparatively* little to do. (See the American Civil Liberties Union Report for 1943–44.) The answer, it seems to me, must recognize *the present effects of consciousness of the past*. Past history as remembered and interpreted contributes to history as presently enacted. Our knowledge of past evils as signposts of present dangers may guide us to a safer future. The excesses of the First World War produced a widespread revulsion. Memories were still quick and sensitive when World War II broke out. There was better organization and, potentially, a greater militancy by liberal and labor groups against excesses. *The economy was not a decisive, but only a limiting condition.* It tolerated a certain range of cultural variation in relation to which human knowledge, ideals, and valor, such as they are, became selective and creative factors.

In the same way it seems to me that knowledge of how a planned economy has been used to choke off freedom in Germany and Russia (and other totalitarian countries) can become not only a motivating force, but a positive guide, in developing the democratic possibilities of planning. It teaches us not only what to avoid but in what areas we must further experiment. Here everything depends not so much on this or that specific detail—although details are important—but *on how they are planned and carried out*.

The terms "planned economy" and "property" are not free from ambiguity. Their meaning shifts with different social contexts. In the past, economic planning for a society as a whole was envisaged on the model of planning in a modern mass production factory. Every last item and effort were to be coordinated by one total plan emanating from one central office. But a planned economy need not take this form, and the reasons are obvious. The aim of a planned factory-economy in a system of free enterprise is primarily profit; everything else is incidental. The aim of the planned economy of a Socialist society is public welfare. The two chief components of public welfare are social efficiency and the strengthening of these rights of personality which are associated with the ideals of democracy. The question *how far* planning must go is yet to be decided. Even if *total* economic planning were socially more efficient than any other form, it would not necessarily follow that it would be acceptable if it seriously interfered with those rights and freedoms of the person which we wish to see preserved.

Assume we want to retain the freedom of individuals to choose occupations, for which they can qualify, to move freely around the country, and to select from among a wide *variety* of goods and services in clothes, furnishings, books, amusements, etc. In line with these preferences we could organize a system of planned economy that would be less efficient, in the sense that a part of the products of human labor would be unused and wasted. But this waste or relative insufficiency would be a small price to pay to secure these freedoms. We don't want six different milk delivery wagons servicing one block, because here the waste of energy is foolish and adds to the cost; we do want six different radio stations and newspapers competing with each other, even if it involves a considerable duplication and waste of materials. The notion that a planned society *must* inevitably be a totally planned society, down to every nook and cranny, and that therefore there can be no room for variety, seems to be an invincible belief of conservative sociologists who believe that the values of democracy are indissolubly associated with those of free enterprise. One of them has called me a "zealot" because in an essay a decade ago, I urged the possibility of encouraging "diversity, creative individuality and catholicity of tastes" in a planned society. (Kimball Young, *Sociology: A Study of Society and Culture,* pp. 949–50.)

However, it is far from having been established that a completely planned and centralized economy is in fact the most socially efficient system of production. For many commodities and services, a decentralized system of planning by regions and municipalities might be more efficient despite some overlapping and conflict. All this remains to be determined. In the nature of the case, even when a community accepts planning in principle, it cannot be carried out *en bloc,* but from sector to sector. Some sectors might even be *planfully* omitted from a planned economy and left to private ownership or individual initiative. This, if I understand it, is involved in Professor A. P. Lerner's idea of a "controlled economy." But a mixed economy of this kind, assuming it to be workable, would be a variant of democratic collectivism.

This brings us to the concept of property. Once a community undertakes a scientific organization of its productive resources to achieve public welfare under democratic political controls, "private property in instruments of production" (as distinct from private property of articles of personal use) changes its meaning. To the extent that it exists within such a framework, it does not mean what it does in a system of free enterprise. For its function and nature are different. It becomes a kind of competitive control on possible bureaucratic inefficiency in publicly owned sectors of industry. Where it is not competitive, it is prevented from exploiting its monopolistic position. It must justify its independence of the sector of public ownership by the contribution it makes to social welfare. For the first time it becomes true that ownership is held in trust, and that any profit earned is a consequence of genuine contribution to the community. In a mixed economy of this kind the role of the government as stabilizer and regulator between the various sectors of industries and the different levels of planning is just as great as in a totally planned economy.

Some of the specific provisions which, it seems to me, should be an integral part of any planned economy, if the democratic values of Socialism are to be preserved, are: a vested right in a job (or a minimum income or annual wage) which cannot be alienated once certain qualifications of skill have been met; trade unions independent of the government, to pass on these qualifications, whose primary function is not to stimulate production but insure the best working conditions and to protect their members from arbitrary administrative power; an independent judiciary to check administrative excesses both of government and trade-union officials against individuals; control (without the right of disposal) of newspaper plants, news and wire services, radio stations, by organizations like cooperatives, political parties, trade unions, scientific and cultural societies. These are "public properties" but yet not "government" property.

With this must go a realization of the central importance of a democratic philosophy of education. The educational curriculum on every level must be rethought and reorganized to develop intelligent citizens who do not merely "tolerate" cultural and individual differences within the community but who accept these differences as a basis for an enriched cooperative experience. Love of freedom is best nurtured by living *and* by learning. It cannot be easily lost where men are prepared to fight for it when it is threatened.

No specific device, or any set of them, is by itself sufficient to insure the preservation of democracy in a planned society. Those who clamor for guarantees should ask themselves what guarantees freedom in the unplanned system of free enterprise. Indeed, what guarantees that free enterprise will remain free? At best they fall back upon some degree of government intervention and control to prevent monopolistic combination from throttling, first, free economic activity, and then cultural freedom. But the hump of the totalitarian camel can just as readily follow its nose into the tent of regulated capitalism or of mixed economy as of Socialism. Both Mussolini and Hitler flourished in a capitalist milieu.

Human beings cannot live together in this world without conflicts of interests arising at some point. Planned society or not, there is not enough of everything for everybody at the same time. The heart of a social philosophy lies in its conception of the institutions and methods that can be relied upon to negotiate these conflicts. The heart of the democratic social philosophy is found in its dedication to those institutions and methods that negotiate conflicts with a minimum of coercion, overt or implicit, and a maximum of collective participation.

It is not a question of absolute equality or absolute inequality. Both are unattainable. But every social philosophy must accept either one or the other as a *regulative* ideal. Equality as a regulative ideal is necessary but not sufficient for democratic Socialism. For it may be interpreted in such a way as to make it hostile to freedom and the development of free personalities. Democratic Socialism interprets equality not as a pattern of uniform treatment in all respects—although there are good reasons for making the basic wage payments for *all* types of socially useful work identical—but as an equality of concern. In a family it is easy to see how it is possible to treat all individuals equally and yet not uniformly. A society, of course, can never be knit together by the same emotional bonds as the family. In a society the only feeling that can play an analogous role is one that develops in and through democratic traditions and practices. To find the devices and mechanisms which in one specific situation after another reconcile equality and freedom is the task of intelligence or scientific method. That is why scientific method as applied to human values may reach its greatest fruition under Socialism.

Despite the current dispraise of Marx, whose ideas and ideals are uncritically identified with those of Lenin and Stalin (and by Monsignor Sheen even with those of Hitler!), it should be clear to any careful reader of his writings that he was a fighter for freedom as well as for equality. In short, he was a democratic, not totalitarian, Socialist.

Only one piece of evidence must suffice us here. Marx assumed that the historic development of planned society would lead to the disappearance of the state or organized coercion in every form. In ultimate belief and allegiance he was one with philosophical anarchism. In this he was a mistaken Utopian. But his very mistake testifies to the genuineness of his belief which was not compromised, as in Lenin and Stalin, by the Machiavellian advocacy of a dictatorship of a minority political party. Marx was a true son of the Renaissance, the Reformation, and the French Revolution. He sought to discover the material conditions wherein the ideals of cultural, religious, and political freedom, formulated during these progressive periods in human history, could reach their greatest fulfillment. The picture of a totalitarian planned economy, with its workers enslaved to a class more ruthless than the capitalists, would have appalled him as a great betrayal of Socialism, all the more so if it were glossed over with words and phrases torn from his writings.

Historically it is true that modern democracy as a political system came into the world with capitalism. Crude economic determinists, who are happy that they are liberated from the dogmas of Marx, therefore infer that with the decline of capitalism, democracy is doomed, too. *But they overlook the pluralistic character of the historical process and the distinctive role that human knowledge or ignorance can play within that process.* The whole of human history in unplanned societies may be read in terms of the effort to preserve what is valuable to man out of the complex of unintended effects of the causal process. Sometimes the effort succeeds, sometimes it doesn't. Where it succeeds, the material conditions must be transformed to support the valuable effects, and give them a direction man can morally approve. At any rate, modern technology, some fields of science, universal literacy, the desire for a higher standard of living, are likewise children of capitalism. But who will argue that they must disappear with the disappearance of capitalism? These are in no danger of being lost but their expression in the future may lead to terrible results unless they are wisely controlled.

Democracy may be lost in a planned society. If it is, its loss will not be an economic fatality but a moral failure, a failure of man to use his intelligence to liberate the great possibilities of plenty and freedom in a planned economy.

27 Socialism and Freedom:

A Criticism of Sidney Hook

by Max Eastman

SIDNEY HOOK's defense of democratic Socialism is refreshingly good-natured. Socialists usually blackjack each other when they disagree, even about so secondary an article of faith as Marx's whiskers. And Sidney Hook can wield the blackjack, not to mention the rapier, with the best of them. Yet here, when the dispute is about Socialism itself, he enters the lists with a bow to his opponents and a tribute to their "integrity and intelligence." Speaking of us who have decided that democracy and collectivism are incompatible, he says:

"There was no apostasy in this development. Its motivation was a passion for democracy, heightened by a sense of the dangers to which the great liberal tradition of the western world was exposed by the monstrous concentration of power in existing collectivist economies. There was no blind panic or emotional revulsion. What took place was a reexamination of first principles. . . . Indeed a high order of intelligence was displayed in the appraisal of the multiform ways in which a planned economy *could* be used as an engine of repression."

Such comradely behavior is itself almost an argument for Socialism, although one that its apostles have rarely employed. It does, however, need following up either with some cogent proof that the planned economy *will not* be used as an engine of repression, or with some plan to *prevent* its being so used. Nothing of this kind emerges from Sidney Hook's discourse on "Socialism and Freedom" (Published above). It is an intriguing discourse enlivened with penetrating remarks on

349

many subjects, but I must say it has for me a lack of punch more significant—in our most brilliant debater—than anything it says. I have the impression that Sidney Hook is defending his logical right to "believe in" democratic Socialism rather than declaring his allegiance to any practical effort to produce it.

"It seems to me," he begins, "that the conclusions concerning a planned economy which were drawn from the ghastly experiences of Germany and Russia were not warranted, and that the case for a democratic Socialism, instructed by past errors and present dangers, is *stronger than for any other alternative*."

[I underline the anti-climax.]

That certainly is not the mood in which one rips up the foundations of society and sets out to build a new one. The case will have to be stronger than that!

In the next sentence, instead, it grows weaker:

"There are certain historical events and situations which make the abandonment by genuine democrats of a planned economy *seem a little premature*."

Premature from the standpoint of meticulous inference, perhaps, but from the practical standpoint recklessly belated. For their woe is not only that democratic Socialism is impossible, but that adherence to this utopian notion is diverting the energies of some of the best men of this epoch from the real fight for freedom.

Hook exemplifies this in his "introduction" where he declares that "capitalism in any of its recognizable forms has practically disappeared in most of Europe," and that privation and need are so great that there is no time for "capitalist accumulation" to "run its course." The existing "economic devices and organizational forms" must therefore be "redirected by democratic political control to get production going."

Those economic devices and organizational forms are totalitarian. They were created by a gang of Nazis and fascists to be run by a one-party police state. A gang of Communists is organized and armed to take them over and run them the same way. How is "democratic political control" going to gear in and "redirect" them? Democratic political control is an abstract idea. An abstract idea can not redirect, much less direct, anything. If Sidney Hook would say "the people" instead of "democratic political control," he would begin to sense the problem in its concrete terms. It is surely legitimate to ask a pragmatist what he is going to *do*—what are those who want the state to run the industries, but the people to run the state, going to do in the existing and imminent situation in liberated Europe? What action, unless they form a countergang to resist the Communazis, can they take?

The main thing the democratic Socialists *are* doing now is oscillating.

They are switching back and forth between the totalitarian Communists and the democrats who believe in free enterprise, turning up now in one camp, now in the other. Politically they are nobody and nothing, except on trivial issues an ignominious "balance of power." And that, it seems to me, is not accidental. It is the whole affirmative meaning of their program.

And the reason for this, to a mind trained in Marxism, ought to be obvious. The struggle in progress is economic, and their program, in its divergence from Communism, is purely political. They want democracy, but refuse to defend the economic set-up in which democracy has its roots. They want "human freedom," but refuse to fight for free buying and selling and free enterprise, which is not a little part of it, but the rock-bottom on which it rests.

I don't know where Marx's perception of the prior importance of the economic factor ever seemed more cogent than in the countries liberated from the Nazis. The whole political future of Europe, and perhaps of mankind, is contained in the question: *What are you going to do with the industries?* If you believe in free competition and the state as a regulative mechanism, then you will turn them over, to the extent compatible with regulation, to private owners. That will create many small powers over against the single power of the state—and over against the Communist Party which is boring from within, with its expertly unscrupulous technique, to control the state. But if you believe in democratic Socialism, then you have only the power of the state. You have no choice but to increase that power by taking over more and more industries. And you have no choice but to share that increased power with the Communists, for that is the meaning of democracy. If you organize to exclude the Communists, your organization is not democratic. If you admit them, they will soon be in totalitarian control.

Even where the state is still essentially political it is hard enough to hold them off, because they appeal to the immediate passions rather than the foreseeing minds of men, and they appeal to these passions with a program of affirmative action. Power for the gang is an affirmative concept, liberty for mankind is, politically, a negative one. That is the gist of our dilemma in the sphere of politics.

But if the state goes into business, there is another reason why the Communists will take control: namely, that they are organized for it. They are all ready and fixed by rigid discipline under a dictator to function as an individual. It takes an individual to run a business. And this is more true, the more complex the business is. The idea of running the whole economy of society by democratic process, or by a process that can be called "representative" and have the word mean anything, has been a fantasy all along. And with industries to run, and these implacable totalitarians right there hitching up their pants to run them, the fantasy evaporates—that is all. Sidney Hook is right when he says there is no "apostacy" involved. All that is involved is practical imagination.

If Sidney Hook will place himself in one of those European countries where a civil war arises, as in Greece, between a "capitalist" government and the armies of totalitarian Socialism, and try to find himself something significant to *do* as a democratic Socialist, he will understand what I mean. And Greece is a foretaste of what is to come. In the postwar restoration the primary struggle of all who believe in freedom, humane culture, and above all in a genuine labor movement, will be *against the Communists and their drive for the totalitarian state.*

The Communists will be strong, especially in fascist countries, because they will offer the masses a new allegiance without a change of political habits. In the struggle against them, there can be no genuine compromise, for their sole aim is total control. And some of the strongest forces on the side of freedom in that struggle—however you like it—will be found in the business class. The struggle will be primarily for a regime of free enterprise. A concern for genuine labor unions, gigantic cooperatives, social security, moderation of unemployment, etc., will be essential to this struggle. *Without them it will fail.* But it will fail also, and more rapidly, if the central issue in its economic aspect is blurred—the issue between democracy's program of free competition and the Communist program of the totalitarian state as the sole employer.

I ask Sidney Hook of what use, on this battle field, will be a pious belief in state-ownership under a different kind of state from that which has put it over once, and is under construction by a gang of fanatics to put it over again. The pious believers, it seems to me, will do one of three things. They talk themselves into thinking that the totalitarian state which actually puts the thing over *is,* or *is going to be,* democratic. That is what a lot of G. D. H. Coles, Julian Huxleys, Harold Laskis, and Max Lerners are doing about Russia, and no doubt will do when the question arises, in their own countries. They will sell out democracy for the sake of their faith in Socialism. Others will sit honestly in a corner wringing their hands, as Norman Thomas and Lillian Symes do: "Oh dear no, you've the right idea, but you're doing it the wrong way!" That will be of small help, but at least it is clear-headed.

Still others will try—and these are the Trotskyists—to take both attitudes at once. To defend the Soviet Union as a Workers State and denounce it as a Bureaucratic Usurpation in one and the same breath, is certainly the most extraordinary gymnastic ever put forth by a logical brain as a political program. But it was logic exactly that drove Trotsky into this ridiculous position. He saw that, in order to go on believing in Socialism he had to declare the Soviet experiment a success; in order to go on fighting for Socialism, he had to declare it a failure. With characteristic courage—the courage of a dedicated mind—he seized both horns of the dilemma. A free mind as bold and brilliant would have dared to see that Socialism is a failure.

The dispersion of power, the dispersion of property—defined wisely by Sidney Hook as "power to control the disposition of things and services"—is the sole practical scheme for defeating the Communists in their grab for the "economic devices and organizational forms" created by the Nazis. *We must meet them on the economic field with a real program, not in the political super-structure with an abstract notion.* The fight is for human freedom, and those are its terms. People who lack, through dying loyalties, the heart to see this, and speak it boldly, are out of the fight. They are out of the future. The future is for those who know that private enterprise is *not dead* in Europe, and that where it has been wounded by fascism, it can be revived. Between them and the totalitarian gangsters it is no-man's land. And that is where the democratic Socialists, forgetting the truths and preserving the pipe-dreams of Marxism, are pitching their camp.

I do not mean that the pre-existence of these Communist gangs ready to take over is the sole or basic reason to beware of large-scale "socialization." The end-result will be much the same, in my opinion, whether the gang comes first or the "socialization" first. I merely wish that the present picture in Europe might drive home to Sidney Hook's imagination what his mind seems loth to learn: that if many little bosses don't run independent enterprises and control our work, one big boss will run the state and control our whole lives.

Thomas Jefferson was right when he said, or implied, that a government which is to be democratic must not govern very much. Mosca was right (and Aristotle) when he said that *only where opposing social forces are in equilibrium can freedom or justice flourish.* Hayek is right when he says: "There is no other possibility than either the order governed by the impersonal discipline of the market or that directed by the will of a few individuals; and those who are out to destroy the first are wittingly or unwittingly helping to create the second."

Sidney Hook makes the point in his introduction that the "capitalists" can not be relied on to defend political freedom against a regime of terror. That is indeed true—nor the workers either. The struggle against totalitarianism is not a struggle between two classes. But he is mistaken when he says: "The newly won converts to free enterprise are . . . overestimating the strength of capitalist allegiance to democracy. . . ." It is not "capitalists" but a capitalist economy on which we base our hopes. And we are not relying on it to guarantee political freedom, either. We are asserting that *under a free economy political freedom is possible, under a state-controlled economy it is impossible.*

The social forces on which we rely to defend political freedom are diverse and not well determined: the farmers, the "conservative" trade unions, the cooperatives, the individualistic business men, that part of the intelligentsia (regrettably small in America) who have political intelligence and love honesty better than power. Scientists and artists ought to be solidly on our side, but they are, alas, in great part pushovers for political hokum. Artists are swayed more by notions than by fact; and scientists, too cruelly confined to fact in their specialties, relax the more easily into credulous dupes upon public questions. Nevertheless, it is the task of the intelligentsia primarily, the task of those with trained understanding, to save the day in this new struggle that is not of classes.

Political freedom will be defended, I believe, by a majority of those in every class who understand its peril. But if their understanding is profound, they will defend not only political but economic freedom—private property in the means of production and a genuinely competitive market—for that is so bound up with political freedom that the two will stand or fall together. That is our thesis. That is what we have learned from "the ghastly experiences of Germany and Russia."

We do not argue against public ownership of any specific enterprise. The roads, the post office, the schools, the national parks—nobody would dream of turning them over to private control. Many communities own their power-plants, street car lines, water-works and other public utilities, and run them efficiently without too much damage to democracy. But to infer from the success of these state-run undertakings *within a system* of private enterprise that the *system* can be abandoned, and the whole economy, or a major part of it, run by the state with like success, is a wild, and I now think, fatal jump. Instead of wasting our mental energy in this jump, we should expend it in a minutely specific examination of every particular proposal of "socialization," to make sure that it genuinely promotes the public interest, makes private industry function better (as in the case of the TVA), and protects it from strangulation by monopolies that are inevitable.

The rest of our "socialist" energy we would pour, I think, mainly into the movements for Consumer's Cooperatives. An overgrowth of the state is our chief peril. The older, and lesser, peril of domination by "Big Business" is held in check by the cooperatives *without recourse to the state*. That is why Socialists should channel their energy into the cooperatives—yet here too without the false inference from part to whole, without the dream of making them absorb the entire population, which would be another road to totalitarian gang-rule.

In a previous section I discussed what Sidney Hook describes as an introduction to his main argument for democratic Socialism. His main argument begins as follows:

"The question, can a planned economy be democratic, is empirical. It is one that can not be settled by definition alone, but which permits of an answer in terms of historical evidence. . . . The historical evidence shows that in the countries which manifest totalitarianism in their most repugnant forms—Germany and Russia—a planned economy did *not* precede the death of political democracy. The Bolsheviks and the Nazis . . . *first* destroyed political democracy and then organized collectivist economies."

That is true, of course, and if you wish merely to defend a faith, it is sufficient. Collectivization by a democratic state has never been tried, and its possibility has not been empirically disproven. The Golden Rule as a solution of our problems has also never been tried, and you can still "believe in it," if belief is what you want.

To a practical mind, however, anxious about the real destiny of human freedom, the behavior of men and institutions throughout this change of relations (especially in Russia where it was thorough-going) teaches a general lesson. The fact that it *was* a superclass party-state, and not the masses (to say nothing of the proletariat) which expropriated the capitalists, when at last a revolutionary situation arose, is not merely a doctrinal heresy. It is a natural phenomenon of primary importance. The fact that, after this expropriation was completed the party-state grew more, not less, dictatorial, is still more important. No natural kinship between democracy and collective enterprise was found to exist. On the contrary "complete collectivization," the old panacea program of world socialism, became the slogan of armed war waged by a state against the masses of the population. Under complete collectivization the last vestige of democracy disappeared.

To confront these facts, and others like them, by merely noting that the Bolsheviks were anti-democratic, and adding in italics the word *democratic* to the word socialism, is inadequate to wisdom. It is doing tricks with concepts where perception of facts is called for.

Sidney Hook admits that "by itself" his argument from historic sequence is "not very strong." It is not really an argument at all, but only a refutation. Even in abstract logic, the fact that the Bolsheviks killed political democracy before establishing totalitarian socialism does not add to the probability that democratic socialism would succeed. It merely removes a hindrance to the belief that it might. What Hook needs for an argument, as he himself suggests, is "a politically democratic community which engages in social planning to a degree commensurate with totalitarian countries." This, of course, he can not find, but he does think he finds "an approximation to it in the war economies of the United States and England." And the sum-total of his empirical argument is that, in these countries, while state-planning went *much further* in this war than in the last, democratic liberties were *much less* infringed on. He thinks this was due to "the present effects of consciousness of the past," or in simpler terms, that we learned a lesson from World War I. He bases his hope of socialism on the fact that such lessons can be learned.

I think it is risky to make inference about state-planning from wartime to peace. It is the diversity, perhaps, as much as the nature, of men's wills that compels the planning state to be coercive. A war tends to unite men's wills and make extreme coercion unnecessary. That union of wills was far more perfect in America in this war than in 1917–18. At that time the nation was really in a state of inner conflict—a cause of hysteria in society as well as individuals. I should say that the curtailment of constitutional rights in wartime varies roughly in inverse proportion to the solidarity of the nation at war. And I would remind Sidney Hook that for American citizens of Japanese extraction constitutional rights in this war disappeared completely—the first such event in our history.

Still I hope we learned a little from the last war. I like to think so, but I don't feel sure enough of it to gamble on the fate of civil liberties under a different administration in a third World War. Do you? Does anybody? And yet Hook rests on this frail change in public opinion the hopes of a new and revolutionary social system that is to endure through ages.

"In the same way it seems to me that knowledge of how a planned economy has been used to choke off freedom in Germany and Russia (and other totalitarian countries) can become not only a motivating force, but a positive guide, in developing the democratic possibilities of planning. It teaches us not only what to avoid but in what areas we must further experiment."

That is his empirical argument.

I wonder if Sidney Hook realizes how completely, in order to defend the abstract notion of socialism, he has abandoned the concrete dynamics of Karl Marx. Who, exactly, is this "we," to whom the experience of Germany and Russia is going to teach so much? Not Henry Wallace certainly, not Harold Laski, not H. G. Wells, not any of the big guns who are really in the saddle and riding hard for state-planning. Is it then some social class? Could it conceivably still be "the proletariat" to whom Hook looks to learn this lesson? I am pretty sure it is not.

I think the "we" involved here is the "we" of the utopian socialists. It is "reasonable and good men"—the kind of men who read *The New Leader* and perhaps the *Call* and *Common Sense*. I don't know where you can find so much as an "I" anywhere else who wants to inaugurate a socialist economy and yet *whole-heartedly rejects* the choking of freedom in Russia. In general, those eager for a planned economy are equally eager *not to learn* what to avoid, or learn anything else, from the Russian experiment. Their main intellectual occupation is kidding themselves about Russia.

I hope I will not seem to be cavilling about grammar, if I point out that when Sidney Hook abandons that bastard "we," a personal pronoun which refers to no person, he does not put a living force in its place, but an abstraction: "the planned economy."

"The aim of the planned economy of a Socialist society is public welfare. The two chief components of public welfare are social efficiency and the strengthening of those rights of personality which are associated with the ideals of democracy."

In the name of Karl Marx, I want to ask Sidney Hook how a planned economy can have an aim? Only living beings have aims. And in just what class or kind of beings does he put his trust when he says that in a "socialist" planned economy, as against those of the Russians and Germans, the aim will be "public welfare"? Is it not solely in his own intellect that this so surely happens?

I mention Karl Marx for poignancy's sake, but I might as well say Aristotle. "Everyone thinks primarily of his own, hardly at all of the common interest; and of the latter only when he himself is concerned as an individual." That was Aristotle's comment on Plato's demonstration of the *logic* of collective ownership. The point of the comment lies in the fact that individual interests differ and conflict. As a consequence of that, and over and above it, individual *opinions* conflict about what the public welfare is. As Hayek has pointed out, terms like "public welfare," "common interest," "social goal," "common good," etc., "have no sufficiently definite meaning to determine a particular course of action." They serve only to "conceal the lack of agreement about specific ends."

"The welfare of a people, like the happiness of a man, depends on a great many things that can be provided in an infinite variety of combinations. It cannot be adequately expressed as a single end, but only as a hierarchy of ends, a comprehensive scale of values in which every need of every person is given its place. To direct all our activities according to a single plan presupposes that every one of our needs is given its rank in an order of values which must be complete enough to make it possible to decide among all the different courses which the planner has to choose. It presupposes, in short, the existence of a complete ethical code in which all the different human values are allotted their due place."

How much more sagacious that sounds than Sidney Hook's recitation that "the aim of the planned economy of a socialist society is public welfare," and that "the two chief components of public welfare are social efficiency and the strengthening of those rights of personality which are associated with the ideals of democracy." If a strengthening of the rights of personality will be the aim of the planned economy when we get it, let us give thanks to God, for it is certainly not the aim of any of those now rabidly hepped up about giving it to us. How many of them, though they number millions, ever gave a thought to strengthening the rights of personality? How many times in history did that aim enter the mind of any person, or any group, wielding that power? When it comes down to facts, if "historic evidence" is worth anything, the main component of public welfare in the view of the state power will usually be military might.

I am not despairing of the rights of personality. I merely observe that, for the purposes of effective action, they must be associated, not "with the ideals of democracy," but with the realities of economics.

It is one of the queerest in many queer turns of events that I should be recalling Sidney Hook to the wisdom of Karl Marx. But he leaves me no choice. He has abandoned that mystic faith in the "historic mission" of the proletariat, which enabled Marx to read the socialist ideal as inevitable end-term into the current struggle of social forces. But therewith he seems also to have abandoned all thought of social forces. Supposedly he is answering us who assert that a totalitarian gang is the only force that can take over a national economy and run it on a plan, and that the replacement of the abstract metaphysical notion of a triumphant proletariat by this concrete actual force was, and will always be, the way in which socialism fails. But he does not answer by naming any other force. He does not go forward from Marx to a more scientific dynamics. He retreats from Marx to the abstract evangel of the utopians, resting his faith explicitly on education—on the ability of "man" to learn by experience—and by implication on man's learning to be a democratic socialist.

Let us read a little further, if only for the pleasure of converse with so civilized a mind:

"Assume we want to retain the freedom of individuals to choose occupations, for which they can qualify, to move freely around the country, and to select from among a wide variety of goods and services in clothes, furnishings, books, amusements, etc. In line with these preferences we could organize a system of planned economy that would be less efficient, in the sense that a part of the products of human labor would be unused and wasted. But this waste or relative insufficiency would be a small price to pay to secure these freedoms. We don't want six different milk delivery wagons servicing one block, because here the waste of energy is foolish and adds to the cost; we do want six different radio stations and newspapers competing with each other, even if it involves a considerable duplication and waste of materials. The notion that a planned society *must* inevitably be a totally planned society, down to every nook and cranny, and that therefore there can be no room for variety, seems to be an invincible belief of conservative sociologists, who believe that the values of democracy are indissolubly associated with those of free enterprise. . . . One of them has called me a 'zealot' because in an essay a decade ago, I urged the possibility of encouraging 'diversity, creative individuality and catholicity of taste' in a planned society.

"However, it is far from having been established that a completely planned and centralized economy is in fact the most socially efficient system of production. For many commodities and services, a decentralized system of planning by regions and municipalities might be more efficient despite some overlapping and conflict. All this remains to be determined. In the nature of the case, even when a community accepts planning in principle, it can not be carried out *en bloc,* but from sector to sector. Some sectors might even be *planfully* omitted from a planned economy and left to private ownership or individual initiative."

It is all benign and lovely, *but who is going to do it?* Who but the "zealots" are going to do it? And how are they going to do it, in a society the majority of whose members are not interested in benign and lovely programs, if they don't organize to seize the state power? And once a sufficiently compact and determined gang has seized the power, who is going to make them care about "variety," about "diversity, creative individuality and catholicity of taste"? Or to put it more mildly: What is to be done if they don't happen to care about these things?

These are the questions you have to answer if you are going *forward* from Marxian dynamics and not drawing back into the quieting dreams of the utopians. It is really out-of-date now, when civilization itself is on the defensive, to dismiss sociologists, or anybody else, as "conservative." The main job of real radicals today is to conserve the freedoms that mankind has gained. None of the old cliché methods, the stamping of opinions and tossing them into bins marked "Left—Right," "Red—White," and so on, have any meaning left.

Unluckily for Sidney Hook, he published his defense of democratic socialism just a few days before Friedrich Hayek's *The Road to Serfdom,* which brilliantly answers him, came out. That gives me an advantage in this debate which I am loath to exploit to the full. I will only say that to a mind nourished on Hayek's mature study, *both* empirical and theoretical, of the nature of the planned economy, Hook's notion that society might stop halfway in adopting this mode of life, or that anyone would be the gainer if it did, seems especially impractical. It seems a little like hoping a boa-constrictor will eat only half of your cow. The issue is between two distinct mechanisms for accomplishing one and the same task—broadly describable as adjusting production to human needs. If the impersonal mechanism of the market is employed, there must be free buying and selling, freedom of entry into all trades, free movement of prices, and no control of the quantities of goods produced. If the mechanism of the personal directing center is used—and used sufficiently to solve the problems it is invoked to solve—these conditions can obviously not be met and the market cannot function as a guide to production. As Hayek puts it: "planning and competition can be combined only by planning for competition, but not by planning against competition."[1] He also points out that the power which controls half an economy directly (as in Germany) controls it all indirectly. And he reminds us that control of an economy is control of the *means* to all ends. He explodes deftly the notion of Stuart Chase and others that, by surrendering our freedom in a sphere called "economic," we can retain it in other and "higher" spheres.

In the opinion that private enterprise and a planned economy conflict in principle, Hayek has the support of the one man in history who ever totally created a planned economy. Here is Stalin's dictum as expressed in a conversation with H. G. Wells (July 23, 1934):

"Without getting rid of the capitalists, without *abolishing the principle* of private property in the means of production, it is impossible to create a planned economy" (my italics).

Of course, this is only one essay, and Sidney Hook may have more to say. He may not have drifted as far from his Marxian "activism" as I

---

[1] Abba P. Lerner, reviewing Hayek's book in a recent *New Leader* professes to find some obscurity in Hayek's distinction between planning in the good sense, and planning in the bad. The above sentence, I think, makes it perfectly clear. These others may be added:

"Everybody desires, of course, that we should handle our common problems with foresight. But it is not in this general sense that our enthusiasts for a planned society employ the term. For their purposes it is not sufficient to design the most rational framework within which the knowledge and initiative of individuals are given the best scope, so that *they* can plan successfully. What our modern planners demand is a central direction of all economic activity. They want the resources of society 'consciously directed' to a social goal."

It is upon good planning—planning to regulate the spontaneous activities of men instead of directing those activities from a single center—Hayek's whole hope of civilized and democratic culture rests.

think. In this article, however, Marx's strong sense of the economic factors which condition (and in his metaphysical pontifications "determine") political forms, is cited only to be pushed out of the way of that faith in increased "human knowledge" upon which the utopian socialists rested their hopes.

"Historically it is true that modern democracy as a political system came into the world with capitalism. Crude economic determinists, who are happy that they are liberated from the dogmas of Marx, therefore infer that, with the decline of capitalism, democracy is doomed too. But they overlook the pluralistic character of the historic process and the distinctive role that human knowledge and ignorance play within that process."

I don't know who those "crude economic determinists" are who, though thinking themselves liberated from Marxian dogma, "infer" the future from Marx's account of the past. I was among the first, I think, to remark that Marx's understanding of the historic relation between democracy and capitalism might, if he had deigned to consider the future, have made him less reckless about abolishing capitalism. There was no economic determinism in my remark, and no "inferences" from past to future. It was on the basis of "empirical evidence" found notably in textbooks of psychology, in the communist colonies, and in the "ghastly experiences" of Russia, that I abandoned the misleading notion that Socialism could be democratic. No doubt Sidney Hook has other writers in mind, but I should like at least to demonstrate my own invulnerability to his thrust. Here is my remark in full:

"If these things [psychological findings] are true, it is no accident that Owen's community—and the others like it—throve only so long as the founder stayed on hand to boss it. It is no accident that 'complete collectivization' in Russia, instead of setting the workers and peasants free, set free the hands of a complete tyrant. It seems obvious to me now—though I have been slow, I must say, in coming to the conclusion—that the institution of private property, the dispersion of power and importance that goes with it, has been a main factor in producing that limited amount of free-and-equalness which Marx hoped to render infinite by abolishing this institution. Strangely enough, Marx himself, as an historian, was the first to see this. He is the one who informed us, looking backward, that the evolution of private capitalism with its free market had been a precondition for the evolution of all our democratic freedoms. It never occurred to him, looking forward—with Owen's dream in his eyes—that if this was so, those other freedoms *might disappear* with the abolition of the free market." (Italics inserted.)

Sidney Hook has some authority in Marx, or rather Engels, for asserting the causal, or at least accelerative, effect of knowledge on the historic process. It was, as I remember, the knowledge of Marxism to which, specifically, Engels attributed this effect. Still there could be no more complete drawing back from Marx to his predecessors than this resting of the essential argument for democratic collectivism on man's ability to learn. From Marx's first question: *Who is going to educate the educator?* to Engels' last word over his grave: *the phase of development is to be explained by the method of production, and not vice versa,* this kind of talk was ruled out. That, of course, does not make it invalid. But it makes Sidney Hook's peroration, in which he invokes the blessing of Marx on his argument for democratic socialism, a little unpersuasive.

And when, in a final paragraph, he seems to rest his hope, not only on man's ability to learn, but on his moral character, the hunch that he is only defending a sort of unreal intellectual *right to believe* becomes a conviction.

"Democracy may be lost in a planned society," he says. "If it is, its loss will not be an economic fatality but a moral failure, a failure of man to use his intelligence to liberate the great possibilities of plenty and freedom in a planned economy."

I may be overworking my intuitions, but to me this is the speech of a man who is all but ready to say that democratic socialism will fail, and will fail because it is not suitable to human nature. I do not think the adjective "moral" or its opposite can be meaningfully predicated of "man" in general, or of what "man" succeeds or fails in doing. The word derives its meaning from distinctions we make among men and their doings. Therefore, to say that if democratic socialism fails, it will be a moral failure, is tantamount to saying that it will fail for psycho-biological reasons.

I myself once expressed the opinion that socialism will fail, and has failed, because of "the size and complexity of the administrative problem" and "the basic drives or tendencies in human nature." My socialist critics dismissed me with the remark that human nature is too various to permit any inference in conflict with their views. I wonder what they will say to Hayek, who proves that socialism must fail because of the complexity of the administrative problem and *the variety* of human drives or tendencies!

(Reprinted with the permission of the author, and Editor of *The New Leader,* Jan. 27, Feb. 3 and 10, 1945. Mr. Eastman has made some slight changes in his original text.)

28 Socialism Without Utopia:

A Rejoinder to Max Eastman

WHATEVER THE MERITS of his arguments against me, Max Eastman has put all Socialists in his debt for making them face squarely the problem of sharply defining their present allegiance and beliefs. My original criticisms were not addressed primarily to him, for until recently his grounds for rejecting Socialism were mainly psychological. The impossibility of democratic Socialism was derived from alleged facts of human nature, not from the incompatibility of economic planning and political democracy. In his rejoinder to me, all the weight is now put on administrative and economic reasons for believing that "free buying and selling and free enterprise . . . is not a little part of [human freedom], but the rock-bottom on which it rests." I am happy to join issue with him and am grateful for the seriousness and courtesy with which he has conducted the discussion.

Before coming to grips with his analysis, there is one preliminary matter I must mention. Throughout his essay, Eastman supplements the many relevant things he has to say with a kind of psychoanalysis of my style. Time and again he suggests that at heart I really do not believe in the possibility of democratic Socialism, that I have shut out from my will and mind the bitter wisdom which my subconscious has distilled from experience. Lest my present remarks be similarly construed, let me state flatly that Max Eastman is overplaying his hunches and intuitions about the significance of my style. I wish I had the patience to improve it so that it would acquire the limpid flow that makes Eastman's writing so interesting even when what he says is clearly wrong. But in every case he cites, there is a much simpler explanation of my meaning than his psychoanalytic one—an explanation to be found in the literal sense of my words.

For example, at the outset of my article I wrote that "the case for democratic Socialism instructed by past errors and present dangers is stronger than for any other alternative." Eastman underscores the phrase "stronger than for any other alternative," dubs it an anti-climax, and adds: "That certainly is not the mood in which one rips up the foundations of society and sets out to build a new one."

But why? More important than any belief a man holds is the *way* he holds it. Any fool or fanatic can embrace a doctrine. Even if true, it remains a *dogma* unless it is evaluated in the light of its alternatives, and the relevant evidence for them. The whole enterprise of intelligence consists in envisaging alternatives before embarking on action. And my point was that those who, like Eastman, would narrow our choice between the chaos of *laissez faire* capitalism on the one hand and the deadly totalitarianism of Hitler or Stalin on the other, have not adequately evaluated the alternative of democratic Socialism.

Nor is it true, as Eastman implies, that action on the best alternative cannot be resolute and vigorous. Consider a military decision made after the advantages and dangers of alternative campaigns have been thoughtfully explored. Or to cite a more pacific illustration, consider a medical decision to operate on a patient as the best warranted alternative for effecting his recovery. Once the decision is made, its success depends upon our carrying it out with all our might, with all our heart, with all our soul—and still not blindly but with the eyes of the mind open *to subsequent alternatives which our own action helps to create.*

I am all the more convinced that the case for democratic Socialism, as a live option worthy of support by those who love democracy, is still stronger than for any other alternative because of the weaknesses and inconsistencies of the alternative Max Eastman presents in its stead. This I now propose to show.

In my original article I argued that those who were defending capitalism as the only safeguard of democracy against statism were overlooking at least two important things. One was the development of capitalist economy which required the state to intervene more and more actively in business, to consolidate monopolies and cartels or else to control them, in either case increasing the area of state control. The other was the fact that political terror can be systematized under free enterprise, too, and that the dominant capitalist groups, as modern history has shown, have been more interested in property, status and power than in the preservation of democracy. To rely upon them to defend democracy is even more unrealistic than to expect the democratic statesmen of the big powers to defend the democratic rights of small nations.

The first point Eastman ignores. The second he admits as "indeed true," but retorts: "It is not 'capitalists' but a capitalist economy on which we base our hopes." This is very curious. Why did a capitalist economy deny our democratic hopes in Germany, Japan and Italy? Why is the *direction* of capitalist economy in every large nation following the same general pattern? *More and more, the allocation of materials, of manpower and money, is coming under state control in order to prevent disastrous crises. These crises plow under human hopes for security and fertilize the ground for totalitarian creeds.*

But what does it mean to say that you don't base your hopes on "capitalists" but on capitalism? Were Socialists to say that they don't base their hopes of democracy on "Socialists" but on Socialism, Eastman would laugh their mysticism to scorn. His position logically is just as exposed as theirs to the charge of mysticism. Social institutions are not abstract forces independent of men. They are ultimately relations between men. As objective social relations, they condition human behavior and are themselves influenced by the human ideals and interests which arise in the course of that behavior. Whether it be capitalism or Socialism, the presence or absence of political democracy depends not only on the economy but on social and historical traditions, human intelligence and courage. The groups, other than capitalists, which Eastman enumerates as forces that can now be enlisted in the struggle for political freedom will also be found in the kind of planned society I sketched. Why should they love liberty less under a planned society than under an unplanned one?

Eastman's answer is involved in what is really the key sentence of his piece. "We are asserting that under a free economy, political freedom is possible; under a state-controlled economy it is impossible." The assertion that anything is historically impossible logically entails the proposition that its contradictory is historically inevitable. Specifically, to say that democracy under a planned society is impossible, no matter what human beings believe or do, no matter what safeguards they erect, is to assert that it is inevitable that Socialism will fail to be realized.

This *is* an ironical reversal of positions! For years Eastman has maintained that Marx taught the inevitability of Socialism, and that to believe in historical inevitabilities is to substitute metaphysical and religious faith for scientific thinking. I agreed with Eastman about the metaphysical character of belief in historical inevitability but denied that Marx actually held this view. I do not wish to stir up the embers of this argument which is only of historical interest. But to discover

Eastman suddenly accepting the metaphysical doctrine of historical inevitability in reverse, so to speak, is at first very startling. If it is mystical to say 'It is inevitable that Socialism will be realized,' is it less mystical to say 'It is inevitable that Socialism will fail to be realized'? Can it be that Eastman's lapse into metaphysics at this point indicates that he is reading not his wishes into history—only Socialists do that!—but his fears? Scientifically what difference does it make? For if hopes may be dupes, fears may be liars.

As distinct from Eastman, I argued that under a planned economy political freedom is difficult but possible; that it is more difficult when the economy is completely planned than when it is not; and that there are other kinds of planned economy—*not whole-hog*—that are both more efficient than total collectivism and better institutional frameworks for democracy—*where there is a will to democracy*.

Because it is the crux of my position, I wish to restate this for emphasis: (1) Freedom under a totally planned society is difficult but not impossible: its potential dangers to democracy are so great, however, that it is the better part of wisdom to discard total planning as an ideal of social reform. (2) Full employment, the efficient use of natural resources, a decent standard of living for the entire population, equality of opportunity, which is the moral postulate of democracy, are even more difficult to achieve under a system of free enterprise (in any recognizable sense of the phrase) than is political democracy in a fully planned society. The cumulative consequences of the periodic failures of free enterprise create conditions of need, social and psychological insecurity which imperil the preservation of political democracy, too. (3) The best alternative available to us today is a partially planned economy, in which certain areas are planfully left to free enterprise, and in which every further step in socialization is tested by its probable consequences on the democratic life of the community.

Eastman does not consider this third alternative as economically feasible. Fortified by Hayek, he maintains that if we have *any* economic planning, it must be *total* planning, and if total planning, then slavery. The notion that there is a half-way house to planning seems utterly fantastic to him. "It seems a little like hoping a boa-constrictor will eat only half your cow." It is either all or nothing; either control by one powerful hand from one directing center over everything and everybody, or control by the impersonal mechanism of the free market, i.e., "free buying and selling, freedom of entry into all trades, free movement of prices, and no control of the quantities of the goods produced."

All this is straightforward enough. We know where we stand with an argument of this kind and we shall return to it. But suddenly Eastman abandons this "either-or" and declares he is not arguing against public ownership of specific enterprises. "The roads, post-office, schools, the national parks—nobody would dream of turning them over to private control." He then adds to this power-plants, street car lines, waterworks and other public utilities, and a whole series of T.V.A.'s.[1]

Does Eastman realize what he has done? He has himself neatly removed the theoretical props from under his own position. What has happened to the impersonal mechanism of the free market? He has abridged its sacred rights in a very important sector of our economy. All we need do is to add to this sector housing, oil, coal, railroads, copper, steel, and a few other gigantic combines, which obviously fall just as much in the category of public utilities as do power-plants, and we have something close to the program of the Socialist Party and the Social Democratic Federation. Doesn't Eastman realize that on the basis of the position he has taken over from Hayek, he has no right even to this limited socialization? Doesn't he realize that the argument he uses against the notion of democratic Socialism is the very same argument that Tories hurled against the T.V.A. and the use of government credit in subsidizing employment? Doesn't he realize that if he is for the unrestricted "free movement of prices," he cannot be in favor of government regulation of *any* prices in *any* field, including utilities, that he cannot even favor trade-union organization because it undoubtedly is a restricting influence on the free movement of prices? Doesn't he realize that he has set loose a whole nest of boa-constrictors?

By convicting Eastman of gross inconsistency, I am not seeking to score a debater's point against him. In fact, I applaud his good sense in abandoning Hayek as a guide. But theoretically Eastman is in a hopeless position, for although consistency is not an infallible sign of truth, inconsistency is a sign of confusion. The road back to Adam Smith is hard, but Eastman must summon up the courage to take it. Or else he must surrender the theoretical gospel, adapted from Hayek, which confronts us with the ultimatum: *no planning—or total planning.*

But what of Eastman's theoretical position in its pure form?—Can we return to a system of free enterprise, *not the ideal system which was always an economic fiction,* but to the historical situation of early capitalism before government began to intervene extensively in the economic process? I believe that such a return is not theoretically impossible but involves the compounding of so many improbabilities that it may be regarded as practically unrealizable. At any rate, it is much more difficult to return to the economic condition of the days of Adam Smith or Thomas Jefferson than to achieve democracy in a planned society. One of the reasons is that the capitalists themselves don't really

---

[1] Mr. Eastman eliminated reference to this in his revised version.

believe in the system of free enterprise as a method of guaranteeing political democracy or of serving the community. They accept it only insofar as it enables them to make profit.

Consequently, every entrepreneur accepts free enterprise as a system for *others* but not for himself if he has reason to fear that he will lose money by its operation or make less profit than he would if he combined forces with his competitors at the expense of the public. Adam Smith realized this when he said: "People of the same trade seldom meet together, even for merriment or diversion, but the conversation ends in a conspiracy against the public, or in some contrivance to raise prices." For good and sufficient economic reasons entrepreneurs reach out to make the state an instrument for achieving their economic ends. Usually the most powerful economic groups exercise the most powerful influence on the state.

For all the metaphysics of his labor theory of value, it seems to me that Marx possesses much more economic insight than Hayek, as reported by Eastman, into the development of capitalist production, the emergence of large-scale industry, the centralization of capital, financial control, and political power, the choking off of free competition, and the dwindling extent of capitalist expansion in its ever-renewed quest for maximum profit. It is in virtue of the "impersonal mechanism of the market economy" that in the United States, using the figures of 1935, one hundred of the largest manufacturing companies employed 20.7 percent of all manpower engaged in manufacturing and accounted for 32.4 percent of the value of all manufactured products. (These figures, which are a graphic symbol of the immanent process of capitalist development, are taken from *The Structure of the American Economy*, p. 102, published by the National Resources Committee, U. S. Government Printing Office, 1939.) Since 1935 these proportions have greatly increased.

If by a miracle we could set the historical clock back a hundred and fifty years or so, the inner workings of the system would swing its hands around once more to the present time of economic day. The only way to prevent it would be by a series of governmental interventions and restraints so thorough-going that we would have the very *statism* that Hayek and Eastman fear so much without the standard of living which modern large-scale industry makes possible. But we cannot return to the days of Adam Smith or even to those of Herbert Hoover. It would cost too much. *Where our intelligent choice lies is not in trying to contest an irreversible trend but in determining who the state shall be, how it shall intervene, and the extent to which planning in production shall go.*

Despite the great achievements of free enterprise, it fails to use natural and human resources efficiently. It is a wasteful social system—wasteful through its *Raubwirtschaft* of sources of raw material, wasteful through enforced idleness of men and machines and its concomitant effects, wasteful through failure to employ the best known technology. All this waste is irretrievable, unnecessary from a social point of view, and yet unavoidable in a profit economy.

Finally, to skip a score of other arguments, as free enterprise works out, it is incompatible with equality of opportunity; it tends to nullify the presuppositions of the democratic process by its maldistribution of wealth and power; it prevents the use of intelligence wherever it conflicts with profit. It does all the things which for the greater part of his life Max Eastman properly indicted it for doing. On grounds of security, utility, morality, art and ultimately of democracy, the system of free enterprise has less claim on our support than an intelligently planned, democratic form of Socialism.

Much more illuminating than Max Eastman's excursion into economic theory are his observations on the *political* problems of achieving a democratically planned society. Although I still find myself in theoretical disagreement with him, I recognize certain important insights which can constitute a basis of working practical agreement for all genuine democrats.

I said that industrial serfdom was introduced in Germany and Russia *after* political democracy was destroyed. Eastman counters with the assertion that this temporal succession is immaterial and that by its very nature a planned society *must* destroy democracy. But this is precisely the point at issue! He does not show that this is necessarily true even for a completely collectivized society; and he certainly fails to establish his claim for the modified type of collectivism I proposed as the economic base of democratic planning. Nonetheless, as I originally pointed out, the kind of democratic planning I proposed was nowhere in existence, and I undertook to sketch the non-economic factors (distinguishable but not separable from economic factors) which had a bearing upon the possibility of its realization.

It was in this connection that I stressed the significance of our present form of planned war-economy and degree of political democracy *in contrast* with the unplanned economy of the first World War and its political and cultural terror. Eastman does not contest the truth of the contrast; nor does he deny that consciousness of the evils of the past makes *some* difference to the present. He retorts that the facts in the case can be more easily explained by the existence of a greater national solidarity in World War II than in World War I. "A war tends to unite men's wills and make extreme coercion unnecessary. That union of wills was far more perfect in America in this war than in 1917–

1918." I am not sure that this is so in respect to the war against Germany. Isolationism is still a powerful even if dormant force. Why all the complaints about public apathy and complacency? England is even a clearer illustration of what I mean. The same pattern is observable there, too, although in not so extreme a form. There was a greater union of wills in 1914 than in 1939, when a considerable section of conservative British opinion was not unfriendly to Hitler. And yet there seems to be more freedom in England during this war than the last. However, I do not wish to stress the point since the evidence is very difficult to assess.

There is a much greater wisdom in Eastman's remark than appears on the surface. A popular war does tend to unify a nation and make different groups more willing to negotiate objective conflicts of interest. Nationalism serves the same purpose. It seems to me that the kind of political democracy that both Max Eastman and I want to preserve and extend depends upon capturing some of the enthusiasm and élan generated by war and nationalism and harnessing it to the democratic ideal. Unless the democratic faith to some extent becomes, in William James' phrase, the moral equivalent of war and nationalism, society will always remain in a state of incipient civil war.

Far from divorcing "the realities of economics" from the "ideals of democracy," I am maintaining that an unplanned class economy produces, as we have seen, such insecurity, want and hunger that it sharpens the conflict of interest to the breaking point. Those who suffer dismiss the ideals of democracy as irrelevant, while those who have power abandon them out of fear. On the other hand, a planned society *can* produce enough goods and services to banish the evils of unemployment and poverty—this Eastman does not deny. Once the basic conflicts generated by these evils are removed, the ideals of democracy, as a moral equivalent of war and nationalism, are more securely anchored in "economic realities." Democracy *and* planning make easier the resolution of other types of economic conflict by extending the area of *common* interest and providing the mechanism for peacefully compromising the economic conflicts that may never be common. If men do not care enough to preserve democracy in an economy of abundance, why does Eastman expect them to care enough to preserve it in an economy of scarcity and need—particularly in view of his admission that he "is not relying upon capitalist economy to guarantee political freedom"?

In my brief comments on how a planned Socialist society would function, I said that its aim would be "public welfare." Max Eastman makes merry over this. He calls on the shade of Karl Marx to witness how far I have sunk into Utopianism. "Public welfare," "public interest," "common good" are, he tells us, vapid and meaningless abstractions. The great Hayek has declared that these terms "have no sufficiently definite meaning to determine a particular course of action." "They serve only (*sic!*) 'to conceal the lack of agreement about specific ends.' "

This is extremely odd. If terms like "public welfare" and "public interest" have no definite meaning, then what sense does Max Eastman make of the passage in his essay—the most sensible passage in it— in which he proposes that instead of socializing the whole economy at once or even the major part of it, "we should expend [our mental energy] in a minutely specific examination of every particular proposal of 'socialization' to make sure that it genuinely promotes the *public interest,* makes private industry function better (as in the case of the T.V.A.), and protects it from strangulation by monopolies that are inevitable." (My italics.)

I do not want to linger over this example of crass contradiction. All the more so because, once more, it arises when Eastman abandons Hayek and follows his own good sense. The truth is, of course, that although terms like "public welfare," public interest" and "common good" are often used as indefinable symbols with purely emotive associations, they can be given definite meaning. *The truth is that no one who proposes anything to the community as reasonable or desirable can avoid using the terms "public welfare" or "public interests" or their synonyms.* If Eastman believes that Marx never employed the notion, he is altogether mistaken. The whole force of Marx's moral denunciation of the evils of capitalism depends upon his assumption that Socialism is a better form of organization to achieve the common interests of society. Indeed, Marx carries the notion of common interests too far, for in the classless society he assumes that there will be no further conflict of interests, that the state will lose its repressive functions and become only the administrative mechanism for establishing public welfare.

The analysis of the meaning of the phrase "public interest," like that of "justice" which it implies, is very difficult and I shall not attempt it here. I content myself with the observation that what is in the "public interest" can be determined only in respect to *specific* problems. If there is a threat of plague, what the public interest requires is easy to tell even if it involves the destruction of property and the segregation of persons. That is to say, the public interest may sometime override, where it cannot include, the private interest. Similarly, unemployment of those willing and able to work, poverty, ignorance are *against* the public interest. In ascertaining the public interest, in relation to a specific problem, all the private interests that are affected should be taken into account, and the values assumed or postulated in any decision should be stated clearly. These, too, can be challenged and criticized by the same process. The task is never finished because problems are perpetually arising anew.

In connection with his discovery that I have abandoned Marx, Eastman charges that (a) I do not indicate what social forces will bring about democratic Socialism, and (b) that I rely only on such vague things—so reminiscent of the Utopians—as "education" and "on the ability of 'man' to learn by experience" to keep planning democratic when it is introduced.

The first charge represents a fair challenge. The second is not altogether accurate.

(A) I have not yet abandoned hope in the American labor movement as a nucleus for a new political realignment. Next to the independent intellectual, the worker has most to lose in a totalitarian economy, *for in the absence of political democracy he cannot enjoy economic security*. It is possible, as the Canadian C.C.F. has shown, to develop a program for a planned society that will not frighten the farmers. They will have a hard row to hoe after the war and must in any event turn to the government to help them keep their economic independence. The youth and the professions are also potential sources of strength. They cannot be won under the slogans of free enterprise which, when the postwar boom has run its course, will appear as much of a mockery to them as in 1929–1932. The difficulty is not, as Eastman seems to believe, that social groups cannot be found to act as dynamic carriers of the ideals of democratic planning. The difficulty is to wrest them away from the strangling influences of totalitarian leadership. With a position such as Eastman's, we are consolidating the hold that the Kremlin's fifth column has on the groups and organizations in which it occupies strategic positions.

(B) "There could be no more complete drawing back from Marx to his predecessors," writes Eastman, "than this resting of the essential argument for democratic collectivism on man's ability to learn." But I never invoked man's ability to learn as an abstract force! What I said was that specific mechanisms could be devised to safeguard democratic processes. A safeguard does not prevent accidents, it diminishes their likelihood. I listed some of the devices which would make for plural forms of political control: decentralized and regional planning, wider political participation on all levels, independent trade unions, an independent judiciary, a vested right in a job for those willing and qualified to work, the use of "public" corporations and cooperatives that would not be "government" property, group, *not* state, ownership and control of all instruments of publication, and a sector of free enterprise justified by its service to the community. I added, to this, the reorganization of the educational system from top to bottom with the central curricular stress on democracy as a way of life, and the development of critical intelligence. Begin with these, and we increase our chances of preserving democracy!

In a certain sense, however, Eastman is right. I do stake my belief in the possibility of Socialism on man's ability to learn from experience provided he has the *opportunities* to acquire relevant information, and the *power* to act on it. *And it seems to me obvious that whoever surrenders this belief, must surrender the belief in the validity of the democratic ideal.* Democracy then becomes too good for creatures that are merely human.

There are passages in Max Eastman's essay which have implications that Max Eastman, the intrepid fighter for freedom, will be the first to repudiate. For example, he tells us that: "Power for the gang is an affirmative concept, liberty for mankind is, politically, a negative one. That is the gist of our dilemma in the sphere of politics." If this is true, we have a choice only between the fatality of dictatorship and the futility of *laissez faire* liberalism. The first spells outright totalitarianism; the second does nothing to remove the condition out of which the first grows. For if political liberty is only negative, then in the complex world of modern technology and large-scale industry, we cannot create institutional forms to protect individuals. We will lose to the gang. But this dilemma is defective. It can be turned by showing that political liberty is fundamentally a positive notion. Freedom to vote, to speak, to assemble, to worship, to criticize, to learn and teach, to work, to live, to organize—are all positive, and they depend upon the existence of positive conditions. We want freedom *from* interference not because we want to be left alone to do what we please but because we want freedom *for* these and similar activities. The rights of personality are rights *of* expression which are safeguarded by freedom *from* repression. In a world where, as individuals, we cannot achieve these rights, the state, like many other dangerous instruments, must be used to create the material conditions and opportunities without which all rights are empty. More simply put, the *equal opportunity* to develop personality freely, which I am confident is still part of Max Eastman's credo, cannot be provided by *laissez faire* economy but by the judicious intervention of the state—the democratic state.

But, argues Eastman, once you bring in the state and increase its power, you are lost, and democracy is lost. This he establishes by another dilemma. "You have no choice but to share that increased power with the Communists, for that is the meaning of democracy. If you organize to exclude the Communists, your organization is not democratic. If you admit them, they will soon be in totalitarian control." This whole position breathes a defeatism about democracy. Were the dilemma true, we would, of course, have to accept it. But it is not true. It confuses the political community with political organizations within the community. If by Communists you mean agents of a foreign power, then to exclude them from the democratic community is certainly not undemocratic. But whether agents of a foreign power or not, if they function within the democratic community, it does not follow that they will soon be in political control. That again depends on you. In a fair fight you can beat them every time. If they don't abide by democratic procedures, if they don't fight fair, they can be excluded with a good democratic conscience; if they do abide by democratic procedures, *you must take your chances—if you believe in democracy*.

You must take your chances. A program of democratic planning increases your chances of winning against the Communists in a world where planning is a necessary condition for economic security. At the race tracks they say: "You can't beat a horse with no horse." And I add, nor with a dead horse. Eastman is entering in the race a horse that died a long time ago.

What distresses me most in Eastman's morganatic marriage to the ghost of free enterprise is that it contributes to the fragmentation of the democratic front in American culture. Scattered in divergent social camps, without a common and coherent program, the democratic front does not exercise an influence commensurate with its potential intellectual strength and moral authority. It is necessary to find a way to bring members of the democratic front together.

Eastman wants to curb socialization in the interests of democracy. As he very well knows, many groups that today support this position, want to curb socialization in the interests of profit and their own vested power. From Eastman's point of view, these are wrong reasons. I propose, therefore, to take Eastman's own ground as a principle of decision and action. The older I grow, the more suspicious I become of wholesale solutions. Except in extraordinary circumstances, I envisage socialization, in the sense I have described it, as a piecemeal affair, as a next step in this sector of the economy and that. I am perfectly willing to make "a minutely specific examination of every particular proposal of 'socialization', to make sure that it genuinely promotes the public interest." . . . If it restricts political democracy, I pledge myself to oppose it. But the restriction must be shown to be specific and not derived from an *a priori* theory that socialization and democracy are by their very natures impossible.

29   The Nature and Sources of Fascism

THE PHRASE "social revolution" has no fixed meaning in current popular usage. Most writers who use it intend to suggest by it vast social changes whose character is indicated, if at all, only in the vaguest way. Hitler's remarkable military victories together with the reports of the death-defying enthusiasm of his soldiers led many people in 1940 to reevaluate Nazism as a profound social-revolutionary movement. The conclusion in some cases was that we should not underestimate its strength, its reservoir of human energy, or place any hope on the activities of underground groups within Germany. Others warned that because Hitlerism was a social-revolutionary movement, it could only be defeated by social-revolutionary movements within the remaining democracies which would parallel Hitlerism in all respects except in its ultimate ends and in the character of its leading elite. And here and there, particularly among not altogether orthodox Stalinist sympathizers, there were soft insinuations that since Nazism was a social-revolutionary movement, Hitler's victory would not be altogether calamitous. "After all, what if a few liberals and Jews are beaten!" Though these events and reactions may now seem in the dead past, the attitudes then expressed have a continuing relevance.

There is no illumination to be found in a loose use of terms. If the enthusiasm of Hitler's soldiery was a sign of a social-revolutionary movement, then any victorious army sweeping everything before it in an offensive on enemy soil is social-revolutionary. In the first months of the war of 1914 the German soldiers and populace were every whit as enthusiastic as they were in 1940. But no one regarded the 1914 war as an expression of revolutionary energies. On the other hand, even armies which are avowedly revolutionary are not enthusiastic in retreat or defeat. German military victory was the cause, not the effect, of Nazi enthusiasm. And what gave the Germans victory at the beginning was superior military leadership, strategy, and equipment. Morale is always a factor; its absence may be fatal, but its presence is rarely decisive except when two armies are approximately equal in other respects.

It may be argued that without its industrial coordination and planned economy, the German army would not have achieved its technical superiority. Undoubtedly. But a planned economy is not a sufficient condition for military success. Otherwise Russia would not have had such a difficult time of it in Finland. It cost the Soviet military colossus great losses to crack the Mannerheim Line. The important point, however, is this: if the existence of a planned economy in Germany was evidence of a social revolution, then Germany accomplished its social revolution *before* the War, and it is hard to understand why the war should have proved what everyone already knew.

It is sometimes said that Nazism was a social-revolutionary movement because, in consequence of the war it unleashed, the Western world will never be the same. Quite true, but this holds for any international war or even any major event. The world is never the same. Any one old enough to remember will admit that the United States was profoundly different in many respects after World War I, but it would be using language in arbitrary fashion to speak of these changes as constituting a social revolution.

What, then, is the ultimate significance of German Fascism? Nothing indicates so eloquently the sterility of Leninist theory as the view that fascism is the last phase of finance capitalism. This has been the dogma of all Leninist schools—Trotsky, Dutt, Guerin, etc. It assumes that the individual capitalist, who as a capitalist is interested *only* in profit, is willing to sacrifice himself for the interests of the capitalist class—in actuality, the interests of a few finance capitalists. Not only is this the sheerest mysticism, it is demonstrably false. Finance capitalists—insofar as any were left in Hitler's Germany—took their orders from the Nazi party and not vice versa. Nor is there any evidence that their counsel has greater weight in Nazi party circles than that of other social groups.

The difficulty with most discussions of the Nazi state is that they are carried on either with no clear conception of the meaning of the terms used or with traditional concepts drawn from the arsenal of orthodox Marxism, according to which a social revolution *must* be progressive and, in our age, in the interests of the working class and its allies. From the first position almost anything can be called a "social revolution," Fascist dictatorships, Popular Front governments, the New Deal, etc., since they indisputably do introduce "profound" social changes. From the second position, the possibility of any social revolution different from the type envisaged by the orthodox schema is ruled out *by definition*. The first position induces a kind of political *delirium tremens* in which social revolutions chase one another in a mad succession; the second results in stark blindness.

If we follow the customary usage of scientific historians, the term "social revolution" will designate (1) a change in property relations, (2) effected by a transfer of political power from one class to another. Once we define property functionally, i.e., as the right, enforced by state power, to exclude others from the use of goods and services, then it is strictly accurate to say that in Nazi Germany (as in Russia) the instruments of production were owned by the party bureaucracy. This bureaucracy includes individuals who may not hold membership in the party but who, strategically placed in the sectors of production, education, and the military arm, accept party orders and objectives. The ruling bureaucracy constitutes a social class with differential living conditions and a unifying world outlook. It excludes all other groups of the population from participation in working out controlling basic policies. In this sense, despite differences in paper decrees and constitutions, Fascism in its classic German form is just as much a social revolution as Bolshevism. Power has been transferred from the capitalists but *not* to the workers. As an independent force the workers could exercise more influence in a capitalist state than they can today under totalitarianism. More than ever before the state is the executive committee of one group of the population—the party functionaries, factory executives, military men, and administrators whose professional life consits of coordinating their rule with the help of a national mythology. This has been, or should have been, obvious even to ideological diehards since 1935. The war revealed nothing to modify this picture.

At the same time, however, Nazism like every other variety of Fascism is culturally a counter-revolutionary movement. Counter-revolutionary in respect to what? Counter-revolutionary to the cultural, political and social ideals of the French Revolution and, therefore, to the socialist movement.

Every one of the ideals of the French Revolution, with one possible exception, is anathema to the Fascist philosophy of life. All one need do to verify this is to run over the specific rights of men enunciated in the basic declarations of the French (and American) Revolution which were partially fulfilled in practice, and compare them with the Fascist German practices. The one possible exception is fanatical nationalism which did not emerge with the French Revolution but with Napoleon, who arrested even as he consolidated some of its gains.

Why, it may be asked, if Nazism is counter-revolutionary from the standpoint of the French Revolution is it therefore counter-revolutionary from the standpoint of the socialist movement? The answer would be commonplace were it not for the Leninist perversion of Marx. For the cultural and political *ideals* of the French Revolution, whose very letters were erased under the Vichy regime imposed by Hitler on a prostrate France, are an integral part of the socialist movement. The socialist critique of capitalism was directed to proving that the development of capitalist economy frustrated the realization of these ideals. The Nazi critique of capitalism was that it abode by these ideals even in their very imperfect forms. Hitler was well aware of this. "Democracy of the West today," he observed, "is the forerunner of Marxism which would be inconceivable without it."

It follows at once that every democrat and socialist must always be an irreconcilable opponent of Fascism, and that it is plain lunacy to expect socialism to be introduced by the back door after a Fascist victory over democratic capitalism. Those who said, "Who knows? Perhaps Hitler will for once unify Europe," forgot that to pacify and to unify are two different things. Even on his own philosophy, Hitler could "unify" Europe only by universalizing terror. A Nazi-planned economy for Europe, like Stalin's planned economy, would have given Hitler power of life and death over whole peoples and served as the most terrible instrument of cultural repression the world has ever witnessed.

Insofar, then, as Fascism wages war against existing democracies, it is an elementary duty of socialists not merely to join the fight against it but to lead in that fight. The specific situation from country to country naturally determines what form cooperation should take with other groups opposed to Fascism. It may be true that the most effective struggle against Fascism can be conducted only by a socialist or labor government. This is a wish or a hope rather than a fact. But in any event it is no reason for lagging in support of *any* government which is genuinely opposed to Fascism. It is foolish when we cannot have the best to choose the worst.

It was perfectly consistent in 1940 for sincere Stalinist and Trotskyist partisans of the Berlin-Moscow axis to hamstring labor and socialist support of the Western democracies in their war of defense against the Fascist cultural counter-revolution. For Bolshevism in their eyes has already accomplished a "social revolution"; and despite variations in detail, the German Fascists recapitulated the essential history of the Russian Revolution—the transfer of property in the basic instruments of production from the capitalist class to the party bureaucrats. In both countries this could only be done by a cultural counter-revolution against the liberating ideals of the French Revolution. Here again with some differences of an historical and traditional kind, the underlying pattern is the same. *Culturally,* Leninism must be regarded in the light of its development, as the first Fascist movement of the twentieth century.

Our conclusion then is that Fascism is economically a social revolution but politically and culturally a counter-revolution. The evidence for this conclusion does not depend upon World War II but upon the way Fascism functions at home.

30 Hitlerism: A Non-Metaphysical View

WITH THE EXCEPTION of the Russian Revolution, the triumph of National Socialism has been the most fateful socio-political event of the twentieth century. Its impact on contemporary life and culture is shown not only in the blows it has struck but also in the countermeasures taken to thwart its victory. Hitler left his mark on the world. It is hard to conceive of any future history in which either his name or his movement will be ignored. The origins of National Socialism and the causes of its rise to power will be of perennial interest.

Clarity about the causes of Nazi success is of practical as well as theoretical significance. A survey of the different proposals offered to safeguard the world from future outbreaks of Nazism will show that they are integrally bound up with varying theories of the causal factors responsible for Hitler's advent to power. How, indeed, can anyone present an intelligent program to insure us against the renewal of National Socialism without definite notions of what brought it about? A re-examination of the question is all the more urgent because voices have been raised both in Europe and America warning us that unless we learn certain positive lessons from Hitler about the power of faith, the hunger for wholeness and the meaning of existence, our struggle against him will have been but a prelude to further struggles against other Hitlers.

I

Konrad Heiden in his monumental study, *Der Führer,* has assembled and sifted all available materials on the life of Hitler from the time of his birth—not overlooking his ancestors—to the great purge in 1934 when he became undisputed master of the German people. There is nothing like this book in any language. Despite its apostrophes to fortune and the rather tortuous probings into Hitler's psyche when objective data run out, it includes all the facts that are known and almost all the theories that have been invented to fit them. Heiden tells us that in his own mind he organized his material to answer two questions: What sort of people constituted the leadership of the Nazi movement? And what sort of people were capable of submitting or yielding to that movement? The interplay of social, economic and political forces is considered in the analysis of the conditions under which the Nazis emerged and won their mass following. The result is a powerful and dramatic narrative in which we never lose sight of the fact that human beings make history, not merely statistics of production.

The question of the type of individual that constituted the Nazi leadership is, first of all, a question about Hitler himself. There is something curiously ambiguous and unsatisfying in the composite effect produced by Heiden's portrait of Hitler, the man, and Hitler, the political personality. Hitler, the man, is pictured as a weak and wretched mediocrity, a personal "nothing." As a political personality he is characterized as "one of the most tremendous phenomena of all world history." One and the same man cannot be both. In the light of Heiden's arresting data on Hitler's pre-political life as well as his political writings and activities, Hitler appears as a man of more than average intelligence and of extraordinary courage and tenacity. These are not enough to explain the origin of his fanatical belief in himself as a man with a mission. Although emotionally volatile to a point bordering on hysteria, there is no evidence of inner doubt and uncertainty. Nor is there any reason why a man should be torn by personal doubt who, at almost the very outset of his political career, was treated as an equal by Ludendorff, and received the personal homage and benediction of Houston Stuart Chamberlain— two of Germany's most eminent figures.

On the other hand, to justify Heiden's ascription of political genius to Hitler, and the comparisons of him to Moses and Napoleon, one would have to see him as a genuine "event-making man,"[1] a factor more decisive in the determination of events than anything else, not only indispensable to the victory of Nazism but as one whose political qualities turned the historical tide. Heiden makes no such claim for Hitler, and I do not believe that anyone can make out a convincing case for such a claim. Without Hitler, Nazism would certainly have taken another form. It would probably have been less anti-Semitic. But what Hitler stood for was represented by others as well. One social crisis after another, not his own creative activity, carried him closer to his goal. He

---

[1] I have defined the meaning of an "event-making man" at some length in my *Hero in History—a Study in Limitation and Possibility,* chap. ix.

lived to rejoice publicly that he had failed in his one great independent action in 1923. At the very last he *was given* power; he did not take it. His specific political contribution to his own ultimate victory lay in a fanatical intransigence against sharing power, a clear perception of the weaknesses of his enemies, both in the capitalistic and proletarian camps, and great tactical flexibility in propaganda. Hitler emphatically did not make the Nazi Revolution in the sense in which it can be established that the Russian Revolution was the handiwork of Lenin. It may be more persuasively argued that he was the chief architect of the ruin of Nazi Germany.

Much more successful than his characterization of Hitler is Heiden's description of the type that flocked to him and became his standard-bearers and lieutenants. Heiden calls them "the armed intellectuals," and sometimes "the armed Bohemians." This choice of words is extremely unfortunate. Its misleading connotations are not nullified by a footnote which explains that the reference is not to "intellectuals" in the English sense nor to a group characterized by "a common economic or material interest," but by a "common outlook." It is much more accurate to characterize these men as *declassed professionals*. This is not only closer to Heiden's actual account of their antecedents, but is more fruitful. For it points to the significant facts in the social and economic history of Germany from 1919 to 1933 that created this type. The declassed professionals were army officers without vocations or poorly paid ones, engineers and technicians without opportunities, academic youth without a future and an office salariat cast adrift on a tidal wave of bankruptcies. And from these groups Hitler recruited the most chauvinistic, lawless and needy. What they had in common was not a philosophical outlook on life but specifically what Heiden denies—"a common economic or material interest" in a guaranteed position, in material plunder and other perquisites of office and prestige. Heiden provides evidence for this in his fascinating treatment of Hitler's uneasy relations to his subordinates whose desires to cash in on his promises were not always politically opportune. Indeed, Hitler's failure to provide for a substantial portion of his lieutenants was the chief motive of their cry for that second revolution which was choked in blood.

The existence of this large group of declassed professionals was bound up with two features of German life, one of which Heiden handles in a brilliant and illuminating way, while the other he systematically underplays. The first is the existence of the skeletonized Reichswehr, which really constituted a permanent inner government in Germany; the second is the role of the German capitalists among the gravediggers of the Weimar Republic.

II

The most original feature of Heiden's analysis is his exposure of the intimate relationships between the Reichswehr and the Nazi Party. It would be an exaggeration to say that Hitler was a creature of the Reichswehr. The point is that the aim of both—the rearmament of Germany—was identical. Hitler may have been the stool-pigeon of the Reichswehr in the early days at Munich but we can be certain that he did not do it for the money. He always considered himself an army man, a simple soldier. But he remembered that Napoleon was one, too. No matter what Hitler thought, the Reichswehr was prepared to use him as it did many others. And the more he won out over his rivals, the more useful he was to it. The reduction of the German Army to 100,000 soldiers left almost that many more lower line officers unprovided for, and restricted the opportunities for advancement of those remaining in military service. Hitler's party and private armies offered not only a haven for officers at loose ends but also a hope, to those in and out of the Reichswehr, that he could furnish ready material for the army of tomorrow. The Reichswehr, and the nationalist officialdom which served it more faithfully than it did the Republic, were intrigued neither by Hitler's anti-capitalistic nor by his anti-Semitic agitation. Hitler himself, as a personality, was not to their liking; nor was the large contingent of homosexuals in his train. But all this was incidental to their search for a man and a movement that would clear the ground politically for open and complete rearmament. The secret rearmament had already begun. Hitler was only one of the cards held by the Reichswehr. It cooled to him when he figured in a wrong play but it never discarded him. At the end it played him to win. For all of Hitler's differences with the Reichswehr, Heiden proves that he never bucked it at any crucial point. If he did not hesitate to sacrifice his own party comrades at its dictation, it was because the dictation flowed from a military program and ambition to which both he and the Reichswehr had been committed for so many years.

Looking back over the years, nothing seems so pathetic as the illusion, nourished in liberal quarters in Germany and abroad, that the Reichswehr was an independent counterweight to the Nazis, and that at the last moment it would step in to prevent their taking power. It was confidently assumed that at the very least it would check Nazi excesses. Speculation about a rift between them was current even after Hitler became Chancellor, and continued down to the war. This is a tribute to the silent precision with which the Reichswehr went about its work—a work that began almost on the very day after the Treaty of Versailles was signed.

The offstage role of big business in the Nazi march to power is much more significant than Heiden indicates. It is not merely a question of the financial contributions of Kirdorff, Thyssen, and their circle when the Nazi organization faced losing its armed bands because it could not house and feed them. Nor is it a question of the use of industrial slush funds at a still earlier time to finance other terrorist groups besides those of Hitler. This support is important enough even if it be regarded as insurance that Hitler would abide by his distinction between productive German capital and "Jewish" finance capital. Big business, or heavy industry (metal, coal, steel), prepared the way for National Socialism, first by its virtual alliance with the Reichswehr, and second by its unremitting hostility to the Weimar Republic which culminated in attacks upon its shaky economic structure. The cardinal point in its political orientation was the restoration of German armaments. In its view this was demanded by the expansion of German economy. Rearmament would provide a great internal market for the goods and services that could not be used by a disarmed Germany. It would make possible the recovery of those regions, so rich in raw materials, that had been wrested from Germany by the Treaty of Versailles; and if diplomatic negotiations failed, it would enable German industry to win new markets in Europe as well as regain its colonies. Heavy industry dealt major blows against the economic structure of the Republic during the inflation period and after the crisis of 1929. It kept up a constant struggle to paralyze the social services whose costs were declared onerous. In the end it brought the consumption-goods industry, which had tried to play a different role, into its political orbit.

It is probably true that heavy industry did not have a clear picture of the internal regime which Hitler had in store for it. Like the generals, the industrialists did not fancy Hitler's demagogic rhetoric or the wild men in his entourage. But they believed that what held true in the past would remain true for the future: the politician proposes but the Reichswehr disposes. They did not anticipate that in the very process of restoring Germany's status as a world power Hitler would succeed in becoming master of the Reichswehr and of heavy industry, too.

III

If these were the organized groups which actively supported Hitler, what was the character of the groups which actively opposed him? Their story is almost as interesting and just as essential to an understanding of what happened in Germany. Very roughly, the opposition to Hitler may be classified as liberal-capitalist with support from the Catholic Center, Social-Democratic, and Communist. We must content ourselves with brief characterizations. On the whole, the liberal-capitalist group, representing consumption-goods industry, loyally supported the Weimar Republic. They were prepared to adopt a reconciliation policy with the Allies. As patriots they were not concerned so much with German rearmament, from which they had little to gain, as with general disarmament by Germany's enemies which would thus give Germany equal status with other nations. They had confidence that the Allied Powers would voluntarily ease the burden of reparation. In this they were right. But in their even greater confidence in the stability of capitalism, they were tragically wrong. In the end, although reluctant to see Hitler in power, they reconciled themselves to supporting him with the illusion that he would be tamed by the responsibilities of office.

The Socialists, who were the largest group in the German Republic, apprehended the danger of fascism rather belatedly. But they could not recover from the disastrous error of permitting German militarism to remain in existence. Nor could they recapture the golden opportunity to go forward with their program after the Kapp *putsch*. They, too, staked everything on the stability of an economic system whose decline was an axiom of their doctrinal faith. They were socialists who did not believe in socialism, and revolutionists who feared revolution almost as much as counterrevolution. They underestimated the agony which Hitler would impose on them and made no adequate preparation to meet it.

The Communists after 1923 were merely cat's-paws of Russian foreign policy. In the crucial years before Hitler's rise to power, they concentrated their energies in attacking the Social-Democrats as Social-Fascists, or "twins of fascism." The only united front actions they undertook were *with* the Nazis against the Weimar Republic. They carried their lunacy to such a point that as late as December 1933—after Hitler had destroyed both the Communist and Socialist Parties—their spokesmen declared Social-Fascism still the chief enemy of the working class. Had the Communists not been under foreign control, the necessity of saving their lives would have compelled them to unite with the Social-Democrats against Hitler. Civil war would have raged in Germany. At the worst, it could not have surpassed the horrors that followed. But it would probably have averted a world war.

By far the most important question posed by Heiden is why and how Hitler won mass-support, why and how he was able to retain and extend it? Or, put differently, what sort of people permitted themselves to be conquered by his political Satanism? Heiden's answer is a variant of a now fashionable view that explains Hitler's triumph as a consequence of the failure of moral, religious and metaphysical belief. "Hitler was able to enslave his own people because he seemed to give them something that even the traditional religions could not provide; the belief in a meaning to existence beyond the narrowest self-interest. The real degradation began when people realized they were in league with the Devil but felt that even the Devil was preferable to the emptiness of an existence which lacked a larger significance."

This answer is arbitrary and radically false. Every piece of certifiable evidence in Heiden's book refutes it. Far from giving people "a meaning beyond the narrowest self-existence," it would be truer to say that Hitler gave his supporters the means to existence, the jobs and security that insured "the narrowest self-existence" for which they craved in vain during the black years of 1929–1932.

Not the meaning of existence but security of existence is the key to Hitler's mass following. He gave this security first in the form of promises, and later in actuality by transforming the whole of Germany into a war economy. Examine the appeals Hitler addressed to the different strata of the population, the peasants, the shopkeepers, the unemployed, the war veterans, the youth, the unmarried women. To each he made solemn commitments that were quite specific and material. These commitments canceled one another, of course, but each group felt that those made to it would be honored. Besides, they were not encouraged to look too closely at the program but to brood about their pressing wants. And not even by these shrewd propaganda methods alone was Hitler able to win a majority of the population. Power was bestowed upon him, and he proceeded to consolidate it by three methods: wholesale terror, the creation of jobs, and totalitarian education. His metaphysics of race, which his "respectable" camp followers were wont to dismiss as peripheral, gave not more but less meaning to existence than the metaphysics of conservative nationalism, of the Catholic Center and of the Socialist left.

The problem to be met here is why Hitler was able to fool so many different groups with conflicting interests into supporting him. Their needs of course were acute. Like other demagogues he dangled promises of better conditions and jobs before their eyes, but he did so under conditions which they would not so readily have accepted had they been aware of them. The small tradesmen lost their fight against the department stores, the women were sent into factories, the peasants and workers became the servants of the State. Everybody, except the Jews and other victims of terror, could get jobs. But all the jobs were war-jobs. There is no evidence that except for the Reichswehr, the Nazi armed horde and the big industrialists, the German people were eager for war. It was not Hitler's rhetoric and propaganda they believed but his promises. However, the rhetoric and propaganda prevented them from seeing through the promises. They voiced their resentments and frustrations against the *status quo* as well as their desperate hopes for a better future. Whatever doubt they had could be stilled by the grandiose, unanalyzable abstractions of Hitler's rhetoric. The unanalyzable abstractions in Hitler's writings and speeches, and in those of Goebbels and Rosenberg, differed only in idiom from those of Mussolini. But they served a common function—to draw a veil over the facts and to make absurdities seem plausible.

In Germany, at the time, the decisive forces which limited the possibilities of historical development and narrowed the alternatives of effective political action, were material—in the main, economic. But the way people *thought* about things, their traditions and habits of interpretation, contributed to determining the choice between relevant historical alternatives. To the extent that the thought patterns of the German people, especially its opinion makers, were unscientific and metaphysical, any program that pretended to take their needs into account could be set before them as hallowed by the central myths of Nation, State and Race. Empirical, scientific thinking about values was denounced as an intrusion of vulgar materialism into the realm of the Spirit because it pitilessly revealed the profane facts concealed behind the symbols of the sacred. Hitler's *Mein Kampf* is replete with passages in which he stresses the importance of metaphysical ideas as the basis of any political faith capable of driving the masses into blind and fanatical action. These metaphysical ideas must not be given any definite or verifiable meaning, for in that case they would be open to criticism by reason and the confrontations of experience. They remain undefined, and therefore infinitely interpretable by those who believe what they wish to believe. But their still more important function is to enable the holders of power to insert into the undefined Ideas any concrete filling demanded by political exigency. No one can predict what will be read out of the Idea.

All this is strikingly confirmed by the use Hitler made of his metaphysics of Race. What is Aryan or non-Aryan was not determined by scientific definition but only by the Führer's intuition. That intuition on different occasions proclaimed the Finns, the Arabs, the Japanese, to be Aryans. Who was to deny it, and on what grounds? After the Jews could no longer serve as convenient scapegoats, Hitler interpreted the idea of Aryan to mean the natural born leaders who are to lead in perpetuity the inferior mass of *Germans*—yesterday's Aryans.

In conclusion. The problem of the causes of Hitlerism is an empirical question. The answer to it does not depend upon metaphysical or religious assumptions any more than answers to causal questions in other fields. The historical influence of metaphysical ideas is an empirical phenomenon, difficult but possible to evaluate. All the available evidence warrants the conclusion that the cause of Hitler's rise to power was the conjunction of capitalist decline in a defeated country, plus political errors of great magnitude in one camp and criminal astuteness in another. To the limited extent that ideas influenced mass behavior, Hitler exploited certain metaphysical, mystical tendencies which distort critical habits of thought.

Those who believe that a false religion or metaphysics is responsible for Hitler's enslavement of the German people are inclined to urge the re-education of Germany as the primary task of German postwar reconstruction. On the basis of the contrary analysis here presented, it follows that immunization from another plague of Nazism is conditional upon profound social and economic changes to be carried out by a democratic revolution which will give the masses security of existence without terror. Re-education will be necessary, but if it is to have any effect, it will have to be conducted by the Germans themselves after the long-postponed German revolution is made.

31 The Strategy of Political Warfare

THE DISTINCTION BETWEEN political warfare and other kinds of warfare is hard to draw clearly. This is recognized in the celebrated maxim of Von Clausewitz that war is the continuation of politics by other means. When war threatens, even when their cause is just, civilized men will seek to explore all possible means of achieving victory in the hope of forestalling the resort to military means.

No matter by what name we choose to characterize it the Western world, primarily the United States, was only too recently engaged in a limited war with the puppets of the Soviet Union on the battlefields of Korea. Deplorable as that situation was, we must remember how much worse all-out or total war would be. It is therefore morally necessary, even as we gird ourselves militarily, to exhaust every possibility of effective *political* warfare in defense of democratic survival.

Other considerations reinforce this conclusion. The gains of political warfare are cheaper and may be more lasting than military victory. During the last few years the Soviet regime has been employing political warfare against the West with tremendous success despite the evidence of its open aggressions in places as far apart as Berlin and Korea. We also know that even our limited use of political warfare during World Wars I and II paid off in appreciable dividends by winning adherents to our side and to some extent paralyzing the will to resist of some groups in the enemy camp.

The pattern of political warfare in our time must be of a fundamentally different character from that of previous times. For in the past it was waged against an enemy particularly inept in this kind of warfare. Too much was already known about conditions in Germany to permit the Nazis to use our own relative evils and imperfections as arguments

389

in behalf of their cause. But the Communists are not only master strategists in the technical arts of political warfare, they are aided by two powerful forces—a mythology about their ultimate goals and a profound ignorance in many countries about their internal regime.

Part of the success of the Communists' political warfare in the West for many years was due to the fact that they were actually waging a counter-revolutionary war against democracy with the use of revolutionary slogans and battle cries. This use of such standard words in the lexicon of moral idealism as "freedom," "peace," and "defense" of democratic rights was coldly calculated and goes back to the very beginnings of the Russian October Revolution. In a little-known speech of Stalin, delivered in 1924, this procedure was revealingly described in conjunction with the practice of masking an offensive action under the cry of "defense." In a passage which should be pondered by all the statesmen of the world, Stalin wrote:

> An original peculiarity of the revolutionary tactics of this period must be pointed out. This peculiarity consists therein that the revolution attempted to carry out every, or almost every step of its attack under the appearance of *defense*. There is no doubt that the refusal to permit the transfer of troops was a serious aggressive act of the revolution; nevertheless this attack was undertaken under the slogan of the *defense* of Petrograd against a possible attack of the external enemy. There is no doubt that the formation of the revolutionary military committee was a still more serious step in the attack against the Provisional Government; nevertheless it was carried out under the slogan of the organization of the Soviet control over the activities of the military staff. There is no doubt that the open going over of the garrison to the revolutionary military committee and the organization of the network of Soviet commissioners indicated the beginnig of the insurrection; nevertheless these steps were taken under the slogan of the *defense* of the Petrograd Soviets against possible attacks of the counter-revolution.

In passing it should be noticed that all Communist Parties are apt students of this lesson whenever they say that they believe in violence only "in defense" of democracy or when they justify invasion in the interests of "peace" or when they claim they are willing peacefully to take power provided no one attempts to resist their efforts to do so. Deplore it as one may, the truth is that the Communists have made headway with these and similar tactics.

What can the democracies oppose to it?

And here the beginning of political wisdom is the realization that as necessary as social reforms are to eliminate those evils in the Western world which Communist propaganda seizes on, such reforms are not sufficient. For social reform is an unending process and there are always relative evils, which if not evaluated in terms of the direction of the process can be inflated by hostile propaganda until they blot out the evidence of the genuine progress towards social justice which the democracies have made. After the Hitler regime came to power, neither social reform nor the growth of pacifist sentiment in other countries could stop its expansion: the same is true of the Soviet regime.

The democracies must take and keep the offensive in political warfare against the totalitarian regime of the Soviet Union. But the strategy and tactics of the offensive must be formulated differently for the different areas of conflict. These areas may be roughly delineated as the Soviet Union; the satellite countries; the nations of Western Europe; and not least our own country.

I

Why our own country? Certainly not because of the domestic strength of the Communist Party, but to prevent democratic resolution from faltering, isolationism from reviving, and the mood of appeasement from taking root—all of which are the goals of communist propaganda. Political warfare in our own country is nothing more than political education. What is required is comparatively easy, but not very much in evidence.

First, making available the sober truth about Communist theory and practice, in place of the flamboyant articles of a sensational character which end by immunizing readers to the genuine dangers of the extension of Communist power in the world.

Second, a continuous reminder that we *are* a democracy and that our public and private actions must live up to our professions within the limits of national security.

Third, avoidance of hysterical outcries that the unfortunate episodic violations of our democratic faith make our culture "just as bad" as Soviet culture.

A word of explanation about each of these is necessary.

Not all who denounce the Communist movement understand it. Those who see in it primarily a heresy, rather than a conspiracy, and lack intellectual tolerance, are likely to direct their fire against the critically loyal rather than the actually disloyal. And if they see in it a conspiracy on the old-fashioned order of the palace revolution or purely military insurrection, they may be inclined to let Europe alone until it comes to its senses. Some American statesmen have been heard to say that once European countries get an actual taste of Communist rule, they would get rid of it fast. The notion that a Communist regime can be dislodged as easily as an unpopular administration or a South American dictator ignores one of the basic features of Communist dictatorship. A Communist regime is more thoroughly totalitarian than any despotism in history in that every field of culture from chess to the circus, is reorganized and politicalized to serve the purposes of party dictatorship. Naiveté among Western statesmen after the war about how Communist regimes come to power, and keep power, contributed to the loss of Eastern Europe and China and weakened the defense of the West. Every American must understand that no Communist regime will ever permit itself to be turned out, no matter how great popular discontent grows, and that every Communist regime is a declared, fanatical, and unappeasable enemy of the democratic way of life.

But it is not only the Communist movement we must learn to understand but the meaning of democracy and the inalienable right of opposition, even of annoying opposition. Democracy is as democracy does. This means not only that heresies in public life should be tolerated but also measures taken to extend democratic rights into all fields in which questions of security are not vital. And this not merely to prevent the Communists from exploiting our shortcomings, but for the sake of our own integrity and morale. We should recall the figure of that indomitable French patriot, Georges Clemenceau, whose critical opposition to the French regime in the darkest days of World War I turned out to be essential to French victory.

As legitimate and necessary as criticism is, it becomes downright irresponsible to equate the lapses from our own ideals of freedom, which have always been temporary, with the complete absence of freedom for any opposition in the U.S.S.R. The critic who proclaims from the house tops that the United States is a fascist dictatorship or well on the way to becoming one—when the fact that he can say it is already disproof of his claim—is a fool or worse. He knows perfectly well he would be shot or exiled in the U.S.S.R. for even hinting at such a thing in private. He usually is a person who did *not* say we had surrendered to Fascism during the last war when the Japanese residents of the West Coast were forcibly relocated—an act infinitely worse than the thoughtless actions of cultural vigilantes and asinine officials which can be reversed overnight by court or legislative action. One well known critic in commenting on the Soviet purges of the arts reminds us that all officials everywhere, from Queen Victoria's day to our own, are opposed to modern art. This is quite true, but the difference, not unappreciable, between Philistinism and murder seemed to have escaped him.

No one in this world, nations or individuals, is blameless for its condition. But to infer from this that all are equally guilty is absurd.

Yet this is precisely the conclusion drawn by so many critics who see, in some ill-considered action by a legislature or by an individual overstepping the bounds of his authority, "the end of democracy" or proof that in fighting communism we have acquired the face or the soul of the enemy. When I was in Europe last, I was shown a clipping from a well known American magazine in which an eminent American professor of history, who should have known better, asserted that we were going through the worst period of political terror and hysteria in American history. No one who recalls the events which followed World War I in this country, not to speak of other episodes since the days of the Reconstruction, will fail to see in this description of the present state of America a fantastic exaggeration of the facts. But the Communist and influential portions of the non-Communist press were citing such exaggerated accounts by American writers with devastating effect. The evils of American life are real and should be the subject of sustained and vigorous criticism. But it is not necessary to lie about them to call public attention to them.

Proper political education should make for a self-imposed intellectual discipline and a sense of proportion in making comparisons between the West and the Iron Curtain countries. Those who are bewailing our national hysteria as a wave of terror comparable to what exists in the Iron Curtain countries should be asked to reflect on the instructive difference between American *procedures* toward the persons who plotted the open assassination of Mr. Truman and the procedures of the Soviet regime after alleged attempts on Stalin's life.

II

Political warfare in Western European countries is of the very first importance in fanning the will to resist aggression. General Eisenhower's trip abroad strengthened the resolution of government statesmen, but it is no secret that defeatism and especially neutralism, from which powerful currents of anti-Americanism flow, are still the dominant moods of the opinion makers. Current political warfare in Western Europe is largely based on a truth campaign about the United States. Although a certain amount of information about the United States is necessary for political purposes, the emphasis is mistaken. What is required—primarily, if not exclusively—is the dissemination of the truth, not so much about the United States as about the Soviet Union.

It is true that most West Europeans are ignorant of numerous details of American life, but they are well enough aware of the massive ground facts of our culture—our standard of living, our great public debates which disprove the nonsense of our being a police state, the existence of our free trade unions, our free press and schools, and our generosity to other peoples in distress.

The reasons Europeans resent us will not be affected by any new knowledge they acquire about the facts of American culture. For this resentment, among the intellectuals especially, derives from a sense of their enforced dependence upon us, their dislike of American tastes in almost all fields except the novels of violence, and above all from their fear that their countries may become the battlefield of the next war. This is coupled with the illusion born of ignorance and wish-thinking that if Communism triumphs in France or Italy or Belgium (or any other Western country) it will take a unique national form.

The logic of French neutralism is today not essentially different from the logic of French neutralism in 1939—only deeper. Having experienced a German occupation and deluding themselves that a Soviet one will be no different, many are resigned to the latter in preference to the costs of a victorious resistance. Because they are ignorant of the concrete facts of Soviet life and the transformative character of the terror of a Soviet occupation, the neutralists are the Pétainists of any future occupation if and when it comes. This ignorance of the real nature of life under Soviet communism is startling to anyone who has visited the countries of Western Europe (including England!). Although closer to the borders of the U.S.S.R., the various groups of the West European population know much less about Soviet life than do corresponding groups in the United States.

The French teachers are not acquainted with the facts about Soviet education; the Italian worker is ignorant of the role of the Soviet trade unions and the punitive provisions of the Soviet labor laws; the Belgian housewife has no conception of the rigors of Soviet family life in one room. Only in consequence of the Kravchenko and Rousset trials have some facts about the concentration camp universe in the U.S.S.R. percolated into the French press.

Were a truth campaign about the Soviet Union waged in Western Europe and carried into every city, street, and village square, the moral position of the mass Communist Parties of France and Italy would be strongly undermined because the latter have so strongly identified themselves with the U.S.S.R. Nor should this campaign neglect to underscore the motives of extreme Russian nationalism behind Soviet international professions.

As for other groups of the population, our political warfare cannot and need not induce them to love the United States. But it can bring home to them what they have to lose in the event that the Kremlin occupies Europe. And it is not hard to show that everyone has something to lose—even the Sicilian peasant whose lot cries out for improvement, an improvement which we should press, not only in his behalf but of all underprivileged groups elsewhere, more strongly than ever. Judging by their past actions, the leaders of the Kremlin from Stalin down are not above deporting a major part of the European population to the icy vastness of Siberia if they regarded it as necessary for their security.

The fear of war cannot be exorcised from the minds of West Europeans, but it is not difficult to make them understand that its likelihood is in inverse proportion to European strength and readiness to resist. This was established in Berlin at the time of the blockades. How successful this political warfare would be cannot be foretold in advance. But it is surely worth the cost of a half-dozen bombers to launch it.

III

In the satellite countries the main emphasis of our political warfare need not be the truth about the United States nor the truth about the Soviet Union. The truth about the United States is known since the days when we helped them achieve their independence. The truth about the Soviet Union they have learned on their own skins, so to speak. Every satellite country under the iron heel of the Kremlin is well aware of the character of the terror under which it lives. Political warfare in this sphere should pursue three tactically interrelated lines.

The first must be the continuous assurance to the peoples suffering under the Communist yoke that they are not alone in their struggles, that the West has not forgotten them nor the names of their taskmasters and official oppressors. The second must suggest ways of continuous opposition to communist rule. Without exposing themselves too soon or running suicidal risks, they can still give their masters no rest. The third, directed especially at the Communists among the satellite powers, should drive home the fact that their country is being systematically pillaged by the Soviet Union, their national interests betrayed, and their best traditions dishonored.

Refugees from behind the Iron Curtain report that the greatest danger to the cause of freedom in their countries is the feeling of hopelessness which sets in after years of struggles against the hydra-headed Communist machine. The risks of opposition are enormous not merely to oneself but to one's family. Few are heroic enough to sacrifice themselves willingly for a problematic liberation which, if it comes, may come after their time. Still fewer feel morally justified in exposing their dependents and relatives to the ruthless reprisals of the Soviet security forces. Yet it is precisely these groups which experience acute discouragement at every gesture of genuine appeasement made by the

West or at any rumor of American withdrawal from Europe that would rivet the chains of social and national peonage on them.

Means should be found by private citizens of the West, acting independently of their own governments, to establish regular contact with individuals who have an interest in things of the mind. For the free mind knows no national frontiers. The satellite regimes go to every length to preserve a blackout of news concerning independent thinking among its teachers and students lest other elements in the population be emboldened to overt opposition. But it should not be difficult to breach this blackout so that the entire nation becomes aware of the struggles being waged by its citizens against what is in effect a Soviet occupation. Until now no one encouraged these people to resist Communist despotism. They acted on their own. But they are actually our allies prepared to sell their lives dearly in behalf of the common Western cause. To ignore them is to abandon them; to help them only half-heartedly is to weaken our own side; to encourage them to resist and then to abandon them is criminal.[1]

Soviet domination of the satellite nations is marked by systematic looting of their resources. Strenuous efforts are made to conceal the facts from the inhabitants, but the tell-tale signs of shortages speak an eloquent lesson. There is evidence that recent recruits to the Communist Parties in these nations, as distinct from the much-purged Moscow-trained cadres, are still patriotic. Local piety, pride of language and national tradition cannot be uprooted overnight. The period between the two world wars witnessed the recrudescence of nationalism in small countries. For all these reasons the line of political propaganda in the satellite nations should emphasize the way in which the Soviet Union holds their economies captive. The new devices which aim at the Russification of these national cultures should be exposed. Particular attention might be given to the miserable role the representatives of the satellite countries play in the U.N. as messenger boys of the Soviet foreign office. The attempt not only to purge Masaryk's ideas but to wipe out all memories about him, from references in text books to postage stamps, cannot sit well with the Czechs. Soviet parallel activities in every other satellite country create deep resentment and bitterness which look for outlets of significant protest.

IV

All efforts of political warfare must be ultimately directed to weakening the Communist Party dictatorship in the Soviet Union. For it is the head and fount of Communist opposition and aggression throughout

---

[1] This was written several years before the Hungarian Revolution which took the West by surprise.

the world. The most massive concentration of the weapons of propaganda and education should therefore be trained on these tasks and their contents carefully appraised.

For technical reasons, resulting from the regime's self-imposed cordon against the West and the stringency of its internal controls, the vast masses of the Russian people cannot be reached by political warfare. Yet we know, in virtue of the measures the government takes against its own citizens, that there is a strong distrust of popular feeling in the Kremlin. Fear of the regime is strong among the people and hardly a family exists in many sections of the Soviet Union which has not lost some member to the dreaded secret police. Nonetheless, active opposition is practically nonexistent, except perhaps for sporadic outbursts in regions of minority culture like the Ukraine, because the regime, in a manner described in detail by former N.K.V.D. agents, organizes by ingenious devices its own potential political opposition in order better to destroy it.

It is also clear that nothing we can tell the Russian masses about their own lot will be news to them. They probably would be relieved to hear that the Kremlin's attempt to picture the United States in the role of a Fascist country ready to invade the U.S.S.R. with atom bombs is false—if they ever put stock in such canards to begin with. Among the many things we do *not* know about the Soviet Union is the extent to which the great masses of the people believe their own press. They know it is censored and absolutely controlled. But they have hardly any access to other sources of information because of controls on importation and because of the massive jamming of foreign radio broadcasts.

We do know that the political propaganda directed to the Soviet Union, and the little circulated *within* it, is received primarily by Communist Party officials and members in the multiform organizations in which they play the leading role. It is this fact which should determine the kind of political warfare we should wage in the U.S.S.R. In the improbable event that techniques can be found to reach the workers directly in their factories, the peasants on their collective farms, and the rank-and-file of the military services, the content of our political warfare will have to be altered. Until then we must recognize that in the nature of the case—a case in which only government agencies and officials have short-wave radios and in which the possession of all unauthorized literature, be it so much as a leaflet, is a serious political offense—it is primarily those whom the Kremlin entrusts with the dissemination of its own propaganda who receive ours.

By now it can be safely assumed that those whom the Kremlin uses as guardians of the nation's morale are doctrinal Communists or imagine themselves such. Many of them are probably frightened by, or dissatisfied with, the unpredictable twists and turns of the party line, but the formal mythology in terms of which these variations are justified remains constant. The nature of a mythology, especially where no opposition is permitted, is that those who are continually exposed to it and who themselves invoke it, end up by believing a considerable part of it or, what is practically the same thing, imagining that they believe it. Psychologically it is overwhelmingly likely that the major portion of the Kremlin's guardians of Soviet public morale and faith are not merely passive members of the Communist Party but give more than lip allegiance to the theories of Bolshevik-Leninism.

It is not for nothing that the Soviet regime is most ruthless with those who criticize it in the light of its own professed ideology. Madame Elinor Lipper, as well as other veterans of the concentration camps, confirms the impressions one derives from reading the Soviet press, that until a few years ago the worst of all offenses against the state was considered "counter-revolutionary Trotskyism"—a generic term for *any* kind of political nonconformity—real or alleged. Today it is one or another variety of Communist "revisionism."

The political strategy of our approach to those in the Soviet apparatus should be that the Communist chiefs in the Kremlin have betrayed all the principles of the October Revolution, wiped out its early progresive measures, liquidated the few remaining traces of democracy which existed in the first years, destroyed the rule of the Soviets as well as the inner life of the Party, abandoned the principle of self-determination of peoples, converted the trade unions, the schools, the press into agencies of the police, and substituted a sickening hero-worship of bureaucrats for the open criticisms of the party leadership which flourished at the outset of the Revolution.

To the extent that these men regard themselves as Marxists, we must contrast Marxist principles, especially where they promise freedom and speak about the dignity and independence of the worker, with current Soviet practices, and lay these practices squarely at the Kremlin's door. The theme song should be: what Marx (and even Lenin) proclaimed, the present leaders have betrayed. The story of Lenin's testament, the degradation of Lenin's general staff, the truth about the Moscow Trials, the Hitler-Stalin Pact, the roll call of the martyred, imprisoned, executed men of eminence in different fields—all this and similar material should pour in a constant stream over the present-day cultural and political Soviet elite.

Lenin's writings could be used with devastating effect even from the pre-October days. What would the ordinary Communist say if he heard the following—and was told that they were Lenin's words:

The Russian people are still the serfs of the officials. Without the permission of the officials the people cannot call meetings, they cannot print books or newspapers! Is this not serfdom? If meetings cannot be freely called or books freely printed, how can one obtain redress against the officials . . .

The Social Democrats demand that the people have complete freedom to move from place to place and to choose their occupations. What does this mean, *this freedom to move from place to place?* It means that the peasant must be free to go where he pleases, to move wherever he wants to, to choose for himself the village or town he prefers, without having to ask for permission. It means that passports must be abolished in Russia too (in foreign countries passports were abolished long ago), that no police officer must be allowed to stop any peasant from settling down or working wherever he pleases. The Russian peasant is still the serf of the officials to such an extent that he is not free to move to a town, or free to settle in a new district. The Minister issues orders that the governors should not allow *unauthorized* settlement! The governor knows better than the peasant what place is good for the peasant. The peasant is a child who does not move without authority. Is this not serfdom, I ask you?

Industrial serfdom is indeed, as Professor Oscar Lange pointed out years ago, before he threw his lot in with the Communists, the most scientific designation of the current Soviet social system.

Whatever one's view about the relation between socialism and freedom, the basic documents of socialism as well as the propagandistic speeches and writings of socialist leaders of the past appeal in most eloquent fashion to the human desire for freedom. It is these elements in the writings of Marx and Lenin that can be taken as texts without neglecting or ignoring similar appeals in the writings of libertarian spirits in the library of world literature. In this connection the basic humanistic message in the works of the Russian classics, for example, Pushkin and Tolstoy, which are still permitted to circulate, should be underscored and contrasted with the actual conditions of life under which the Russians live.

Appeals of this sort must not be pitched in a key of dialectical debate or carried on as if they were exegeses of sacred texts. They should seek to stir and twist the conscience of their listeners while they recall to them the inspiring lives of their freedom-loving progenitors. For all the Soviet talk about the "new man" its system has produced, the members of the Soviet elite were human beings before they became Marxists or Leninists or Stalinists. The inhumanity of the Kremlin's actions can easily be dramatized for them. Their official writings boast that they have inherited the legacy of freedom. They should be reminded of the principles of that heritage and how point by point they are being trampled underfoot in the daily life around them. And it goes without saying that the form in which these things are to be said should be simple and straightforward and reach directly for the heart of the listener and not merely his mind.

Every doubt under the existing regime is a heresy, and every heresy is unforgivable. Whether doubts actually arise or not as a result of this kind of political warfare is less sure than that, judging by the history and temperament of the Kremlin leadership, doubt will arise in their mind concerning the complete loyalty of the Soviet elite. Their suspicions are always preliminary to purges and continued purges. If successful, political warfare may keep the Soviet Union indefinitely in turmoil because suspicion grows on what it feeds. When guardians are set to watch the guardians, the latent seeds of civil war which every totalitarian system carries within itself find a favorable atmosphere for germination.

There are many individuals in the West who are quite adept in calling up the ghosts of Marx, Lenin, and a whole gallery of revolutionary figures from the past to plague the powers that sit on bayonets in the Kremlin. There is evidence that the most susceptible elements in the Soviet Union as in the satellite countries are to be found among the Party and non-Party youth.

Political warfare by itself of course is not everything. Events too have a language, and they may speak much louder than words. Good deeds, as the United States should have learned long ago, do not talk by themselves whether it be Lend-Lease, UNRRA, or the Marshall Plan. Bad deeds, however, do talk, even when the Communists fail to broadcast them, with a deafening volume.

Effective political warfare presupposes that the United States in deed, as well as word, wherever possible will support the cause of freedom, not reaction. If we take reactionaries to our bosom as allies we weaken our position in Western Europe in the democratic circles whose support should be our first concern. If we permit Czarist Russians, instead of democratic, liberal, and socialist Rusians in exile, to appear as our spokesmen, the Kremlin's rule in the Soviet Union will be reinforced. Even in relatively small matters what happens in this country as well as abroad creates conditions under which our political warfare may succeed or fail. Few who are not in intimate touch with Europe can understand what a setback the United States suffered when the seven Negroes, executed in Martinsville in a crime for which no white man ever paid the extreme penalty, were denied clemency during the very week when notorious Nazi criminals, guilty of a thousand worse crimes, had their sentences commuted.

It is not too late for American officials, and the American public who must back them up, to understand the importance of political warfare and the close relevance of our own domestic and foreign policies to that warfare. If the Kremlin can be defeated in political warfare before it undertakes military adventures, it will be a blessing not only to Americans but to all mankind and not least the Russian people.

32   Socialism and the Prospects of Liberation

WE HAVE TRAVELED a long way since 1950. At that time it seemed that despite the policy of containment pursued by the West, the Kremlin would seize the offensive in Western Europe and launch a war while the United States was pinned down in Asia countering the Communist North Korean, and later the Chinese, invasion of South Korea. Partly to prevent such a war, and partly in the hope that if such a war were forced on the West the people of the satellite world would rise against their oppressors, the slogan of "liberation" received gradual but equivocal support, equivocal because no government or leading statesman thought through what a policy of liberation—as distinct from a hope—really entailed.

The development of nuclear weapons by the Soviet Union made it apparent that liberation by means of war might very well mean liberation from existence. Although there is considerable evidence that the Soviet regime cannot be provoked into war, and, further, that whenever its leaders feel they can win by a sudden move that will at the same time forestall any devastating retaliation, they will discard their slogans of "peaceful coexistence"—nonetheless, the danger of war is sufficiently great, and the reaction to that danger so fearful, that it is the prime cause of the widespread moods of appeasement and neutralism periodically generated in recent years in Western Europe. Anyone frank enough to admit it knows that despite the evidence of Budapest and its aftermath, this mood is as strong as ever in Europe today.

No leading statesman of the West has ever preached or advocated a preventive war; and even the leaders of the Assembly of the Captive European Nations believe that a firm and consistent policy of liberation can be pursued by the free world *without* war. But if war is ruled out as as instrument of liberation, one cannot so easily rule out the possibility of liberation by revolution. Those who proclaimed that "There is a finality, for better or for worse, about what has now occurred in Eastern Europe"—and proclaimed this *before* Poznan, *before* the Polish October and the Hungarian November—were much too hasty in their judgment of finality. And unfortunately such a judgment itself had an enormous influence on the response to these events.

I am among those who believe that at the time of the Hungarian revolution a firm and direct intervention by the United Nations and the West in response to the appeal of the Nagy government would probably have led to the withdrawal of Soviet troops. The Kremlin will not be slow, we can be sure, to learn the lesson of Hungary. It is now clear that it will use force sufficient to suppress any popular revolt against a Soviet puppet regime, and that mere declarations of disapproval by the West will not keep the Russian tanks from moving in. A revolution under such circumstances can achieve heroism, martyrdom, but not victory. In the modern technological age, a practically unarmed nation cannot, without help from outside allies, stand against the massed might of tanks and other armor.

The only realistic perspective in the next historical period—short of a revolution or civil war within the Soviet Union itself—is, it seems to me, liberation by evolution. I mean by this the gradual transformation, within the ideological tradition of Marxism-Leninism, of the totalitarian system of Communism in satellite countries into a libertarian culture in which the strategic political and cultural freedoms of an open society are legally recognized and *in fact* realized.

I make no prediction that such a transformation will actually occur or when it will occur. That depends upon many factors outside the scope of this discussion. I assume only that such a transformation is desirable. I shall raise the question of whether such a transformation is possible; and, if possible, how, and especially which elements in the traditional Marxist ideology as well as in the current Communist theory and practice lend themselves to this development.

Of course, the ideology of Marxism and Leninism cannot so simply be assimilated to the ideal of human freedom. Yet anyone acquainted with the history of ideas knows that the same generic terms and doctrines have encompassed the widest variations in personality, belief and practice. Communism as a secular religion has often been compared with Christianity, and identified by Toynbee—mistakenly, I believe—with one of its sects. But how vast and full of incompatible elements is the spectrum of beliefs called "Christian." The development of Christianity is largely the history of radical changes, both in doctrine and in practice, by those who claimed to be doing no more than returning to the pure essence of the doctrine.

The evolution of Christian doctrine and organizational practice is a very complex theme. We owe the very fact that Christianity is— unlike its ancestral form, Judaism—a universal religion, to the first great revisionist, Paul. But for Paul, Christianity might have remained a Jewish sect with the complacent approval of Christ's immediate disciples. Paul's was the first organizational revolution in the history of Christianity and there have been many others. Even more impressive are the major *intellectual* readjustments Christianity made when confronted with different systems of belief; at the outset it almost invariably suspected and opposed such systems as heretical. But they were all assimilated, in time—some easily, others with difficulty. No matter how often the motto *semper idem* is proclaimed, the irreversible phenomena of social, scientific, and technological change enforce corresponding changes in organization, doctrine, dogma, and above all *behavior*. Those who say only the extrinsic trappings of faith change, overlook the fact that the distinction between intrinsic and extrinsic is a shifting one and that the way in which dogmas are *expressed* and *lived* determines their meaning.

What is true of religious movements is also true of other fields of human experience. Even in so recondite an aspect of intellectual history as pure philosophy, whose terms and meanings are presumed to be controlled by the immanent logic of texts, we find William of Ockham, the father of modern nominalism, claiming that he is doing nothing more than returning to the orthodoxy of Aristotle. Yet hardly anything has more powerfully undermined European Aristotelianism and contributed to the rise of modern science than has Ockham's criticism in the name of Aristotle of the doctrine of substantial forms.

Whether we consider the actual content of the slogan "the return to Christ" or "the return to Kant," the "return to Rome or Jerusalem" —we will find that these returns always mark an original departure in doctrine and movement, sometimes in opposition to the actual intentions of the innovators.

What is for present purposes more to the point, is that even Lenin's slogan "Back to Marx," which he borrowed from Rosa Luxemburg, marked a tremendous revision in what until then had been understood by Marxism. Lenin's extremely voluntaristic *What's to Be Done?*, although too simply characterized by some critics as spawned under Bakuninistic and Blanquist influence, was certainly not the Marxism of Kautsky and Plekhanov. What Lenin did to Marx in the name of Marxism, Stalin in lesser measure did to Lenin in the name of Leninism.

This raises the question of the extent to which it will be possible in the current atmosphere of ambiguous devaluation of Stalin to initiate in satellite countries even more far-reaching departures in Communist theory and practice by "returning" to Marx. I am not here assuming that what may be possible in the satellite countries can be mechanically extrapolated to developments within the Soviet Union. This is a different even if related question.

However we explain it, the historical spectacle of the European past shows us Christian fighting Christian in the name of "true" Christianity. It is perhaps hardly an exaggeration to say that had the West not come to the support of the chameleon Tito when he was threatened by Stalin, we might have seen Communist fighting Communist in the name of the principles of "true Communism." Our problem is: can we disintegrate or transform Communist parties in satellite countries by heretical reinterpretations of the meaning of Marx? It is the Communist *parties* we must influence, for the people are not Communist. Communist regimes lack even the popular support the Kremlin can command by posing as the defender of Russian nationalism, for nationalism in all the satellite countries is hostile to Communism.

Communist theory and practice hang together more closely than in other ideologies, but it is possible to exaggerate their monolithic unity. Although adherence to a set of doctrines or better, a set of formulas, is, and always has been, *de rigueur* for all Communist parties affiliated with the Kremlin, some variations were permitted in the road to power —especially if they proved successful and were not taken in defiance of the Kremlin's orders. Stalin explicitly condemned the American theory of exceptionalism, which simply asserted the banal proposition that each Communist party must take note of the distinctive peculiarities of its own political history and geography—primarily to replace one Communist faction by a more compliant one. Yet when the opportunity presented itself after the war, he heartily approved of the manner in which the Czech, Yugoslav and Chinese Communists seized power, even though in one case it involved making the peasantry, not the proletariat, the basis of the Communist movement (China), and in no case did it involve the use of Soviets in whose name the Communist Party seized power as it did in the Russian October Revolution.

When we turn from the consideration of "different roads to power" to "different roads to socialism" we find the variations in the practices of Communist states just as great, but enormously more significant.[1]

---

[1] See the illuminating survey by Peter Wiles, "Polycentric Communism," in *Soviet Survey* (May, 1957).

Even if we consider all these different roads to socialism as different ways of enslaving the human spirit—as at the present time they are—they may also be assessed as providing varying opportunities if not for immediate liberation at least for some extension of the areas of freedom.

Different roads to *power* are comparable to different roads leading to a city. The city is the same irrespective of the way we reach it. But different roads to socialism, about which the classics of Marxism really say little, may be compared to different ways of building a city. The different ways of building a city result in substantially different cities because the means used are not like the scaffolding torn away when the building is constructed but are like the bricks and mortar, the steel and glass which become intrinsic elements of the finished construction. The architectural metaphor pervades the entire literature of Marxism and Communism and for most purposes is defective and misleading since it cannot express the facts of historical process and reciprocity. But it serves admirably to drive home the logic of the means-end relation. If it is true that not pious words but means determine ends, then the adoption of different means of constructing socialism involves the very real likelihood of different *kinds* of socialism, unwelcome as this may be to the leaders of the Communist movement. In his remarkable speech to the Eighth Plenum of the Central Committee of the Polish Communist Party in October, 1956, Gomulka spoke of the construction of the best model of socialism and of improving the design of the model by using better spare parts. The metaphor is different but the point is the same. By the method of replacing spare parts with better ones, modern technology can make a standard Ford coupe go faster than a Cadillac.

Today, under the name of Communism and Marxism, we find considerable differences in the theory and practice of "socialistic society" in four different regions—the Soviet Union, China, Yugoslavia, and Poland. Some of these differences reflect, so to speak, the historical and geographical landscape and the accidents attendant upon origin. The differences in theory may turn out to be even more momentous because to the extent that theory is a guide to action—and it is often only a rationalization of action—differences in doctrine can lead to the intensification of differences in social, economic and cultural behavior. Thus, when Mao-tse Tung says that socialism is a garden in which many different theories can be permitted to grow, he has said something of which Khrushchev cannot approve without the danger of letting the "thaw" get out of hand. Even though, as seems likely, Mao-tse Tung will destroy as a poisonous weed any doctrine he does not like, his words may meanwhile inspire programs of liberalization in other countries—programs hesitant and tentative, to be sure, but still possible bases for further development. Even more significant, when Gomulka proclaims that "the best definition of the social contents inherent in the idea of socialism is contained in the definition that socialism is a social system which abolishes the exploitation and oppression of man by man," and that "what is immutable in socialism can be reduced to the abolition of the exploitation of man by man," these pronouncements, under present conditions, constitute a more radical revision of traditional Marxism-Leninism-Stalinism than do Titoism and Maoism. Its sweep is as radical as Ockham's intellectual transformation of Aristotle. For it follows at once from this conception of socialism that it is absent in the Soviet Union and the alleged people's democracies—since it is not difficult to show that their populations, as they very well know, are exploited and oppressed economically, culturally, and politically. It follows that even a Jeffersonian community of small landowners who till their own soil and one of individual craftsmen who own their instruments of production, do not employ others and hence cannot exploit their labor, would have to be called socialistic!

To be sure these formulations will be qualified, modified, withdrawn when some of their consequences are grasped. But there will be others that lend themselves equally well to critical indictment of existing practices as unsocialistic and contrary to the letter or spirit of Marxism.

The very conception of "different roads to socialism" gives rise naturally to the notion of "national Communism" so much feared by the Kremlin and therefore even by Tito and Gomulka. For "national Communism" is just as much a departure from the classic views of international communism as "national socialism" is from the socialism of the Communist Manifesto. And in a genuine sense the first expression of national Communism is to be found not in Titoism but in Stalinism, under which the concluding line of the Communist Manifesto was in practice made to read: "Workers of the World Unite—to Defend the Soviet Union."

The question I wish to raise is whether, in terms of the official ideology and in the light of incontestable realities, the totalitarian integument of Communist doctrine can be shattered by uncovering, developing and re-interpreting the rich legacy of ambiguities in the intellectual and social movement of Marxism. The existence of these ambiguities is obvious from the fact that both the Social Democrats and the Communists invoke the Marxist traditions which are actually far more ambiguous than even the Social Democrats imagine. The existence of these ambiguities is revealed in the accounts given by former ideological functionaries of Communist parties, such as Wolfgang Leonard, of the process by which their difficulties developed into cancerous doubts, and Stalin was gradually rejected in the name of Lenin, and Lenin finally rejected in the name of Marx. I am *not* raising the question of whether any profound institutional changes can take place by way of doctrine *alone,* for this seems to me very improbable. Economic and international political factors are usually more weighty. I am asking only whether *in the struggle* for freedom, any aspect of the Marxist tradition can be refashioned and sharpened into a serviceable weapon. Today in Poland there is an intense discussion of the basic meaning of Marxism, which may have such effects.

Let us look at some key Marxist concepts in this light.

There are two conceptions of property in Marx and the Marxist tradition, one of which provides the basis not only for the critique of capitalism but even more powerfully for a critique of what passes for socialist economy in all the satellite countries as well as the Soviet Union.

The first conception of property is substantial and legalistic. It defines property in terms of legal relations where the law is construed as a decree certifying *title* of ownership. The development of modern economy in the West has limited the usefulness of this concept by separating title from actual economic power. The second conception of property in Marx is functional and sociological. It is bound up with the Marxist ethical critique of capitalism. According to this conception, property is a form of power—the power not so much to use or abuse instruments, goods and services (since this is always limited) as the power *to exclude* others from using them. That is why property *in* things may be power *over* the lives of human beings if they need access to these things to continue life. Wherever property in land and instruments of production gives power to exclude individuals from the land and from access to instruments of production, it gives a very real power over the personal lives of these individuals.

Without reference to the institutional, social and political framework of a community, one cannot tell whether the substantial legal *title* to the property of anything is any more than a *promise,* not so much even of income—for income may all be taxed away—as only of non-transferability. That is why the British Labour Party believes it can move toward socialism *within* the framework of existing legal relations, without expropriation. Conversely, even *after* expropriation, where legal title to property has been abolished, the continued *de facto* power to deny access to others to goods and services, and especially access to the means of livelihood, in effect gives those who wield this power most of the traditional rights of ownership under classical capitalism. This cuts right to the heart of the fiction that collectivized or nationalized industry, since it is no *one* man's individual property, *eo ipso* automatically spells the end of exploitation. Under any system of socialization, where the institutional framework makes it possible for workers to be systematically denied access to the means of production, to the means of their livelihood, to speak of the workers' ownership of the productive plant, to say it belongs to them is a mockery.

Nor is it any different when we hear it said that the property in question is *state* property. For this merely pushes the question further back. To whom does the state belong or who controls the state? If a group is excluded from effective political participation, what sense does it make to say that the state belongs to that group? In the Nazi political economy, for example, those who had legal *title* to the instruments of production, once stripped of powers of control in their own industries, after being deprived of political power, were reduced to the status of operatives of the German state, which really meant the ruling hierarchy of the Nazi Party. At most they received a return on their investment, but the size, frequency, and above all, the reinvestment of that return depended on the Nazi high command. They could not close down their factories if they were unprofitable: they could not hire or fire at will. In effect these industries belonged to the Nazi Party. They were *party* property.

The same situation obtains in the Soviet Union and in most of the satellite countries—only more so. The juridical change in proprietorship transferred title from capitalists and landlords to the collectivity. But the collectivity is a legal fiction whose actual content, according to sound Marxist principles, depends upon how it is actually organized, how it functions, and the different roles played by different groups in the actual processes of production. Since almost from the very beginning, the Communist Commissars had absolute power to deny access to farm or factory to any peasant or worker, to decide what should be saved, spent and how, and to determine the conditions and rewards of work, and everything else connected with the use of the industrial plant, natural resources, etc., and since this power was in no way responsible to those whom its decisions so fatefully affected, in effect—and again according to legitimate Marxist categories—the instruments of production belonged to the Communist Party hierarchy, giving it all the traditional privileges of ownership except the right to buy and sell and the right of testamentary disposition. Under such a setup, workers can be and have been exploited more intensively, i.e., more surplus value sweated out of them, than under other forms of legal ownership since the early days of the Industrial Revolution.

Despite the semantic outrage of referring to the Soviet Union or any other Communist economy as a "workers' state" and to the productive plant as "state property," the facts were really not in dispute. When Lenin brutally proclaimed to the Eleventh Congress of the Russian Communist Party, in 1922, "We are the state," he might as well have said: "We are the owners of the economy." Insofar as Marxism is a critique of the economies of exploitation, it can be used more legitimately and with greater devastation in present-day Communist countries than in most of the present-day democratic capitalistic countries of the West.

In general, modern economic developments have made the contrast between capitalism and socialism, as economic systems, very difficult to draw in practice. To the extent to which it is an issue, the question reduces itself to *more* or *less,* not to either/or. The ever-increasing intervention of the welfare states of the West in economic affairs, the planning in many sectors of the economy, progressive taxation which reaches beyond 90 per cent at certain levels in the United States, the alienation of ownership from management in large industry described in the epoch-making study of Berle and Means, the growth and power of free trade unionism, the establishment of minimum wages and multiple forms of social insurance, the movement toward co-determination in industry and a guaranteed annual wage—all these indicate the degree to which the picture of classical capitalism as drawn by Marx has been altered. On the other hand, in the so-called socialist economies we find large deviations from classic socialist ideas— enormous differences in income, reliance upon strategic centers for private enterprise not only in agriculture but in industry, too (China), the influence of the international markets and sometimes the domestic market on prices, and a tendency toward economic decentralization.

It is obvious when we look at the economies which are called socialist in countries like the U.S.S.R., China, Yugoslavia, Czechoslovakia and Poland that there are considerable differences in *practice.* I wish to suggest that when we examine Marxist *theory* we can detect even greater potential differences in meaning—a complex of ambiguities which manifest, or can be given, either a democratic or totalitarian variant. Because Marxism is primarily a critique of capitalism, it provides no specific directives but only general guides as to how to build socialism. These guides are more social, political and moral than economic in nature, because Marx assumed that the processes of accumulation would have progressed to a point where there would be no problem of having to construct capital goods industries. The ambiguities in Marxism are aggravated by the bolshevik success in refuting (or revising) Marx in their attempt to lay the foundation of socialist economy *by political* means in industrially backward areas—something presumably ruled out by historical materialism. The most fervent

"Marxists" today are those who have actually refuted Marx while excoriating the revisionists of Marx.

There is no historical necessity in the way in which socialism is to be built, otherwise we could not speak of different paths to socialism. No matter what the objective economic conditions, other factors enter into the situation. Among them an important—I do not say decisive—factor may be the way in which traditional Marxist principles are interpreted and developed. The direction in which "socialist" economy and society will develop may depend, for example, in some countries upon how the principle of "workers' control," stressed in pre-revolutionary terms by both syndicalists and Marxists alike, is understood. Let us look more closely at this concept.

There has always been an ambiguity about the nature and function of "workers' control" in socalist theory. The Utopian theory of Marxism, according to which some day the state will disappear, made the organs of workers' control on the level of the factory, the administrative unit of society which would function without coercion by the voluntary cooperation of an historically new species of man. For purposes of revolutionary struggle, "workers' control" was stressed as a means of heightening the pitch of a revolutionary situation, breaking the resistance of the class enemy, and getting production going again. All tendencies within the socialist movement declared themselves *for* workers' control but few seemed clear about what it meant and those who were clear were not always in agreement with one another. Some held that workers' control was a kind of industrial democracy which would *supplement* political democracy, others that it would *replace* political democracy. Some thought it meant only a consultation *with* the workers by management, others that it meant participation by the workers with powers of co-decision *in* management. These differences polarized around the generic views that workers' control was something exercised *for* the workers by a political group monopolizing power or, on the other hand, that it was something exercised *by* the workers themselves, following whatever leadership they chose.

In the early days of Bolshevism, on the eve of taking power and shortly thereafter, the Communists stressed in the most emphatic way the desirability of workers' control in every factory. In the beginning there was hardly any difference between the Communist and anarcho-syndicalist views of how a socialist society would function. In countries in which anarcho-syndicalist traditions were strong, Communists actually seized the factories and tried to run them even before they destroyed the existing political power. Before long, however, the control of the Communist Party asserted itself so forcibly that the phrase "workers' control" became a transparent piece of terminological hypocrisy. Lenin himself led the fight against "the workers' opposition," a group in the Communist Party which took the earlier agitational and propaganda slogans seriously, as an anarcho-syndicalist deviation.

The Yugoslav Communists who speak today of "workers' control" imply that Stalin revised Lenin's position on the question while *they* are following the Leninist pattern. This is a misleading over-simplification. It results from confusing decentralization of industry and planning, which permits greater autonomy to the individual plant, and which the Yugoslavs *have* carried out, with independent workers' control in the decentralized plants, a control which the Yugoslavs only *promise.* And if they follow Lenin, they will never deliver on their promises. For even in the most liberal period of Russian economic life, Lenin insisted that in the interests of rapid construction of large-scale industry "it is absolutely essential that all authority in the factories should be in the hands of the management."

We need not stop to point out that management in the so-called capitalist countries has much less power over workers than management in socialist societies, while trade unions in the former in actual practice enjoy far more control than workers' councils in theory. Lenin recognized the limited role of the trade unions in correcting "the excesses and blunders resulting from the bureaucratic distortions of the state apparatus," and this stand was of tremendous importance in that it provided a justification of the right of the workers to strike in the so-called "workers' state"—to strike in all state enterprises. That this right was hedged in by all sorts of restrictions and qualifications, that it was more honored in the breach than in the observance, does not detract from its significance and its use as a rallying cry in the present and future. It was this truncated right which was lost under Stalin and in all Stalinist regimes. It was a grievous loss, for the abolition of the right to strike means in effect the existence of a system of forced labor with all its multiform kinds of exploitation and aggression.

In Yugoslavia today a very limited kind of workers' control through workers' councils operates in conjunction with a largely decentralized industry planned to meet the market needs of local regions. This system came into existence more because of economic necessity than because of political virtue. And however limited the control, Soviet critical reaction has not been less severe. What is interesting is the theoretical justification of these institutional deviations from the Soviet pattern expressed by Kardelj and other Yugoslav Communists in grandiose ideological terms.

Kardelj, in his speech of December 7, 1956, before the Yugoslav People's Assembly, frankly accepts the theory of exceptionalism, but he claims Yugoslavia to be exceptional in being most faithful to the conceptions of Marx and Lenin. The development of socialist industry, he asserts, must take place concomitantly with a progressive democratization of all social relations. "Human beings should not in a socialist system become the slaves of a state machine in the name of any higher interests whatsoever." To achieve independence from the state machine, the social and economic position of the worker must be secured by strengthening the democratic control of the workers in the factories and in their communities. Only in this way can the state wither away in Marxist fashion instead of becoming an all-devouring Frankenstein monster.

Kardelj makes some interesting distinctions, for example, between "socialized property"—what is produced in a factory whose workers decide what is to be produced—and "state property" which is administered by organs of government beyond the influence of workers. There is a further distinction between "socialized property" and the workers' own "individual property." There is a dialectical relationship, according to Kardelj, "a unity of opposition," between the socialized property of the worker and his own individual property which if disrupted either transforms the worker into a slave of a state capitalist system or leads to the abolition of social ownership of the instruments of production.

For Kardelj, the key issue is to avoid the bureaucratization of socialism. This is inevitable, according to him, unless there is "active, direct and increasing participation of the producers in the direction of state and industry." Those who like the Russian Soviet apologists interpret this as undermining the dictatorship of the proletariat are indifferent, he says, to the fact that "the dictatorship which they characterize as 'proletarian' can be anything else in the world except proletarian, precisely because it is not filled with a democratic content."

Here again, I am not concerned with the motivation of this theoretical departure from Stalinism, the extent to which it is actually embodied in Yugoslavian practice, and the political uses to which it is put. Tito, for example, although professing to blame the Hungarian Stalinists for refusing to follow the lead of the Hungarian workers, inconsistently supports the Russian suppression of their councils. Similarly Khrushchev, after blowing off about the Yugoslav deviation during his visit to Czechoslovakia, sings softly after his meeting with Tito in Rumania. Considerations of *Staatsräson* obviously determine the official reactions. But ideas, although not independent, once launched upon the world may develop a life and an influence of their own. It is the *direction* of the Yugoslav heresy which is important—not only its nationalism, its claim that all Communist states are equal in dignity in a common cause, but its emphasis upon a conception of workers' democracy which might turn out, once material conditions are favorable to it, to be an ideological hydrogen bomb.

It is not necessary to claim that this conception of decentralized workers' control is economically viable or that the democratic elements it embodies cannot be introduced in other ways. Obviously, a system which aims at a maximum of efficiency cannot permit any really great independence to the economic decisions of the workers' councils. But maximum efficiency need *not* be the highest desideratum of a socialist society or any society. Further, bureaucracy without any semblance of workers' control or participation may be inefficient too—perhaps more inefficient than a relatively anarchic, non-bureaucratic system. Human beings normally appraise an economy by other than strictly economic norms.

The most significant thing about the ideological position of the Yugoslav regime is that, if it is taken seriously, it spells the end of the political monopoly of the Communist Party. In actual fact, there is less workers' control in Yugoslavia than in Poland, where even Gomulka views the workers' councils suspiciously. One of the reasons is that the Communist Party in Yugoslavia is more monolithic, less democratic, and closer to the Stalinist model than the Polish party. Workers' control, to the modest extent that it actually exists in Yugoslavia, was not a spontaneous demand made by the workers themselves, as in Poland and most conspicuously in Hungary, but was carried through under the tutelage and control of the Yugoslav Communist Party.

A "workers' control" which is in turn controlled by a party faction with the secret police behind it collapses of itself—it dies of boredom and disinterest, like the Russian soviets and local trade unions. Some semblance of power, no matter how fearfully guarded by the party watchdogs, must be given to the workers. This power in time either grows on what it feeds or becomes atrophied. It is the natural form through which, where it exists, opposition can be "legitimately" channeled.

That Kardelj, for all his lack of clarity, his inconsistencies and backtracking, is on the right road, from the point of view of intensifying the struggle between the democratic and totalitarian potentials of socialism, is evidenced in part by the character of the embittered reply made to him by A. Rumjanzew in the Moscow *Kommunist*. Rumjanzew recognizes that in effect Kardelj is charging that the Soviet Union is a new form of class state in which, although the legal title of ownership has been transferred to the workers and peasants, the latter are in fact being exploited by the state apparatus, its functionaries and pensioners, and that consequently the class struggle is still being waged in the alleged socialist society, not between non-existent capitalists and landlords, on the one hand, and the toiling masses, on the other hand, but between the latter and the new class of Communist officials, managers and their retainers. Rumjanzew attempts to toss this off with a laugh as a *reductio ad absurdum* too ridiculous to require refutation—and then attempts one anyhow. If the workers by definition own the instruments of production, he asks, how can they be said to exploit themselves? He is oblivious to the possibility that there may be something wrong with his definition, and that to resort to it in the face of the glaring facts of political and economic inequality is merely to fall back on a question-begging definition.

Gomulka's discussion of the function of the workers' councils is something else. He sees their development as one of the three main elements in the Polish road to socialism. In his speech before the Ninth Plenum of the Party Central Committee, Gomulka outlines seven chief tasks of the workers' councils which if taken literally would make them masters of the factories and, therefore, of all of industry. He warns against conceiving the councils "as organs of political power" but at the same time is fearful lest the political leadership of the Communist Party fractions be displaced. He wants workers' councils to be autonomous and at the same time seeks, in vain it seems to me, to limit their functions to purely industrial issues. Because of the nature of the Polish economy, he is undoubtedly sensible in cautioning the workers' councils against a too near-sighted and too decentralized view of the needs of production. But if they are actually given the right to make mistakes in these matters, they are being given very real powers indeed. And he is quite forthright in acknowledging the right of the workers to strike, although he does not regard this as the best way of rectifying grievances.

Gomulka has ambiguous feelings about increasing the power of the workers' councils as well as that of the people's councils because of his fear that they may work free of the influence of the Communist Party, whose leading position he regards as essential to the building of socialism. As if aware that all the elements which define the Polish road to socialism, if given their head, may carry Poland out of the Kremlin's orbit, as if to reassure the uneasy Russians, he delivers even stronger attacks against those he calls revisionists, and who really are democratic socialists of Western vintage, than against the Stalinist dogmatists and conservatives. Gomulka taxes the revisionists with believing that socialism can be built without any class struggle. The accuracy of this characterization I regard as very questionable. The difficulty is to know what kind of class struggle can be waged after the capitalists and great landholders disappear. Struggles still go on, but if they are class struggles they are of the kind that Kardelj describes—between the toilers, the workers and peasants, and the state and party officialdom. More accurate is Gomulka's charge against the revisionists that they are opposed to the dictatorship of the Communist Party. This *is* true. But it is also true of Marx.

As everyone knows, "the dictatorship of the proletariat" as interpreted by Lenin and Stalin is substantially the dictatorship of the Communist Party *over* the proletariat and all other social groups. That this represented a radical departure from the meaning Marx gave to the rarely used phrase in his writings can scarcely be doubted. Marx and Engels pointed to the Paris Commune as illustrating what they meant by "the dictatorship of the proletariat." The Commune was one in which several different political groups or parties participated, and in which the followers of Marx were a tiny minority. In the *Communist Manifesto,* Marx had said that Communists "do not constitute themselves a special party over and above other working-class parties."

The "dictatorship of the proletariat" in the corpus of Marx's writings is not in the first instance a political concept but a social one. The opposite of the phrase is the "dictatorship of the bourgeoisie." Since, according to Marxist theory, a "dictatorship of the bourgeoisie" is compatible with many political forms ranging from monarchy, Bonapartism and other expressions of dictatorship through an entire spectrum of parliamentary democracies, it is clear that the economic and social content of the dictatorship of the proletariat, in theory at least, is compatible with the existence of one or more political parties and with political structures ranging from dictatorship to democracy.

Socialism declares itself opposed to *all* forms of exploitation and oppression, to any kind of class society in which coercion, open or veiled, is present. Marxism recognizes, however, that every dictatorship, even when it is considered progressive with respect to expanding the forces of production, is a form of oppression. If one takes Marx literally, the elimination of all coercion from human relations, the complete withering away of the state, is a Utopian ideal—but pragmatically it can be interpreted as an ideal of diminishing coercion and exploitation in human society.

If one reads Marx in the light of modern sociology, one understands that classes will continue to exist, class struggles will continue to be fought, even though the role of classes will differ when different social relationships are introduced. A strike under socialism is a struggle even though some terminological purist may balk at calling it an expression of class struggle. In either case, or on either interpretation, there is an imminent dynamic toward greater democracy in the Marxist ideal, toward a permanent revolution against whatever series of evils the social process generates. This tendency is accentuated by the heritage of

Utopian and anarchistic socialism which Marxism accepted despite its scorn of it.

Marxism is a philosophically primitive system but it never identified the social system of the future with the end or process of history itself in the way in which Hegel identified the Absolute Idea or the Way of God with the Prussian state. Because Communism is a disease of idealism, if only it does not harden into the fanaticism which makes a fetish of the instrument—the instrument of the Communist Party—it may prove to be susceptible to the virus of political liberalism, so long as some center of democracy remains outside the Communist world.

Historically, in the Soviet Union the Bolsheviks took power with the Left Social Revolutionists as a cover. They permitted other socialist parties to exist for a time in a tortured way. On paper, but only on paper, bourgeois parties could exist. On occasion, in order to bring home the distinction between the dictatorship as a social and economic instrument and dictatorship as a political weapon, Lenin maintained that it is "quite conceivable that the dictatorship of the proletariat may suppress the bourgeoisie at every step without disenfranchising the bourgeoisie . . . while it is essential to suppress the bourgeoisies as an [economic] class, it is not essential to deprive them of their suffrage and equality."

What this meant with respect to bourgeois parties, and later all other parties, is that if they agreed not to oppose the program of the Communist Party in any way whatsoever after the latter seized power, they would be permitted to exist, although it is not clear what the point of their political existence would be. With respect to other working-class or socialist parties, Bolshevik fanaticism led to the same result. For the Bolsheviks believed that any serious disagreement with the Communist Party by *definition* had counter-revolutionary objective consequences, which led to the sardonic observation of one of their leaders in the twenties: "Of course the Bolsheviks believe in the existence of several working-class parties—one party in power, the others in jail."

The Communist regimes in the Soviet Union, Yugoslavia and some of the satellites are unabashed one-party dictatorships. In China, Poland, Czechoslovakia and East Germany the Communist Party rules with the device of phony coalition parties. The existence of these parties is in part the price the Communists pay for their hypocritical pretenses to democracy, but under a favorable conjunction of circumstances, especially in the satellite countries, where aspirations to national independence are strong, conditions may compel them to pay a higher and higher price in granting political independence to these other parties. In some countries, as in Hungary today, such ostensibly non-Communist parties would be betraying their people by giving some protective national coloration to Russian puppets like Kadar. In Poland, where the situation is in flux, another tactic may be required.

In this connection, of course, Gomulka's regime is unique. Since he is trying to do the impossible, to keep the dictatorship of the Communist Party and to encourage the independence of the Peasant Party, Gomulka must fail. But he and those who support him can fail in two ways—fail in encouraging other political parties or fail in being good Bolsheviks. In the view of democracy, the latter failure is of course preferable. When Gomulko proclaims, "It is a poor idea to maintain that only Communists can build socialism, that only peoples holding materialistic social views can do so," he should certainly be applauded, and even more so when he characterizes socialism in ethical terms as "the system of social justice."

When with this conception of socialism he urges "competition between our Party and the Peasant Party as well as between all those in favor of strengthening the socialist system" he has taken a longer stride away from the Leninist and Stalinist conception of the political dictatorship of the minority Communist Party than he is aware of. When he also calls for the revitalization of the Sjem, its assumption of greater legislative tasks, and control over the work of the government and state organs, when he proclaims that "In my opinion Sjem control over the executive organs of state power should be exercised by an institution subordinated directly to the Sjem and not to the government as has been the case up to now," who can fail to hear with his inner ear, despite the uncertain words and reluctant tone, the voice of parliamentary democracy? That voice is muffled and fearful, to be sure, lest it be overheard by the Kremlin, interpreted as an abandonment both of socialism and the Warsaw Pact, and serve as a pretext for Soviet invasion.

All Gomulka need say explicitly to promise the restoration of political democracy as we understand it, is that in the legally recognized competition among political parties to achieve the best system of social justice, all proposals can be put forth, *even* proposals to abandon socialism. It would be unreasonable to expect him to go as far as this at once, especially if socialism is defined as "social justice"—since this makes everybody a socialist. In the end, a democratic society must go this far, but the task today is to win victory for the right to propose different roads to socialism *within* Poland. In such a situation the Communist Party, or any other, would have to win its leadership, and not claim it merely in virtue of the fact of dictatorship.

As if he were reading the minds of his listeners, Gomulka assures his fellow Communists that "we shall not allow anyone to use the processes of democratization to undermine socialism." Now, how does anyone go about "undermining" socialism if one really believes in, and employs, the processes of democratization? Actually, Gomulka's fear is not so much that democracy will undermine socialism as that it will undermine the Kremlin's patience. Capitalism is largely an anachronism, anyway, in countries that have existed for a decade under Communist rule. Even in a country like England, the Conservatives accepted a good deal of the socialized sector of industry because of the social costs involved in returning it to private hands.

It is safe to predict that Gomulka will recall his words if the Kremlin's frown deepens. But he cannot recall their effect. Some variant of his words will be repeated again and again in the future.

Many of the moves away from total or extreme collectivization and the more conspicuous forms of party terrorism in Communist countries are motivated today by considerations of political strategy. They may be reversed overnight. Nonetheless they are all points of ideological and institutional infection in the Communist body politic. If these heretical germs get into the Marxist blood stream, they may produce fevers in the short time and languors in the long time resulting in profound organic changes in the system.

Recent events behind the Iron Curtain have shown that socialist humanism, despite its exaggerated claims to novelty, has a greater continuity with traditional forms of Western humanism than both its official spokesmen and its hostile Western critics imagined. The new Soviet men, the new Communist men with new criteria of the true, the good, and the beautiful, of whom Stalin boasted and whom the West feared, are a myth. Despite the principle of *"partinost"* or partisanship in dialectical materialism, Communist intellectuals, whether scientists or historians, know the difference between truth and lies, facts and fiction. They have not succumbed to the totalitarian psychoses described by Orwell in his *1984;* and if they rewrite the past at the behest of Big Brother or of a Committee of Big Brothers, they know what they are doing. If they confess to imaginary and impossible crimes, it is not because of the sacrificial mysticism attributed by Koestler to Rubashov but because of the beatings, the broken ribs and other violent methods admitted by Khrushchev at the Twentieth Congress to be the standard techniques of examination.

Things can never be the same again after the fumbling attempt of Stalin's accomplices to de-Stalinize, after the Polish declaration of independence, after the heroic spectacle of the Hungarian nation in arms against the Russian occupation. Even without war and foreign intervention, even without violent revolution, the intellectual elite of all Communist countries will produce in each generation, and in every social group or class, critical spirits nurtured on the ideals of freedom expressed in the classics of Marxism as well as in those of the humanist tradition, well aware of the discrepancies between Soviet promise and performance, and of the Communists' betrayal of almost all the liberating ideals which inspired the socialist movement. Their presence, whether articulate or eloquently silent, will constitute a permanent opposition to cultural and political tyranny. What is required above all else is to make these critical spirits, whether or not any one of them is a potential Djilas, Kolokowski, or Ignotus, aware of the fact that their predicaments, their problems, their struggles and their sufferings are known beyond the borders of their own countries.

The pace of democratic change in Communist countries cannot be predicted, but we know that since the false internationalism of the Soviet Union has been shown to be only an expression of Russian imperialism, every critic, every dissident, will conceive his struggle for greater liberalization in social and political life as a struggle for national liberation. In a free Europe, nationalism may be transcended but only when the legitimate claims of patriotism expressed as piety for the sources of one's being and tradition, have been recognized. The Kremlin cannot seriously extend the right to genuine national self-determination to its satellites without starting a chain reaction whose consequences will take these countries still further out of the orbit of Communism.

Given the history of the twentieth century, once a "thaw" sets in in any aspect of culture in a totalitarian society, it has a tendency to extend not only into neighboring cultural fields but to take political form as well. The chagrin and rage of the Soviet Communist leaders at the Hungarian and Polish intellectuals is due to their relization that the heretical cultural ideas of these men will prove in the long run *politically* infectious. The logic of the situation is such that every concession made to artists, writers, or scientists carries with it consequences that call for further concessions, which when denied put into question the sincerity and genuineness of the first concession. History often shows that changes are more rapid when things begin to get a bit better. Despair paralyzes the will to action, especially risky action; hope inspires it. We can be sure that the slight taste of the freedoms which the peoples of the satellite countries have been given, after being deprived of them for almost a decade, will generate an enormous appetite for more—and perhaps this hunger will spread to the Soviet Union itself.

33 A Foreign Policy for Freedom and Survival

AMERICAN FOREIGN POLICY has been in a state of crisis ever since the end of World War II. The crises have been partly of this country's own making. It has made error upon error, all based on a failure to understand the nature of the Communist threat. It sacrificed essential political principles in the military struggle against Nazi totalitarianism. It demobilized its troops in Europe too soon. It failed to use its monopoly of atomic power to effect world disarmament and international control of nuclear weapons. It withdrew American troops from Korea, practically inviting Communist aggression. It fought the Korean War against the Chinese under self-imposed limitations. It liquidated the war short of victory when the Communist Chinese were in retreat. It stood idly by when Soviet troops slaughtered the Hungarian freedom-fighters, who were actually the allies of the West.

Whatever these tragic errors, and however disastrous their consequences, it seems indisputable that they have all flowed from the American desire for peace in a divided world. The simple truth is that the United States, and the concert of powers of which it is a part, has accepted the principle of peaceful coexistence and faithfully tried to live by it. This is to its eternal credit. Yet, despite the concessions, the meetings, the restraints, the United States today, together with its uncertain and uneasy allies, is relatively weaker vis-à-vis the Communist world than it was ten years ago. This is evidenced not only by the development of Soviet intercontinental weapons and the Soviet technological strength symbolized by the sputniks but by the expansion of Communist power in Asia and Africa, and the increase of neutralist and pacifist sentiment throughout the world.

Even those who disagree with this reading of the past and present must admit that American foreign policy, with the exception of the Marshall Plan and some other aid programs, has been largely a matter of improvisation, of reaction to moves taken on the initiative of the Communist world. The United States has never really taken the psychological or political offensive. It has always contented itself with defending the *status quo* even when the *status quo* was changing. Its policy of containment did not contain and its policy of liberation did not liberate. The rhetoric of the Democratic and Republican Administrations has differed, but the strategic principles of United States foreign policy from Roosevelt to Eisenhower seem to me to have been essentially the same (and equally mistaken) with respect to the Soviet Union, alternating between weakness and bluster.

The most crucial mistakes can be easily stated. The first was the underestimation of the significance of Communist ideology as a determinant of Soviet behavior. This ideology accounts for the implacable hostility, the incessant war of nerves, war of words, and, wherever it seemed safe, war of weapons waged by the Kremlin against the free world. This ideology explains the fact that the Communist slogan of "peaceful coexistence" is a deception masking the myriad campaigns of infiltration and propaganda by which Moscow seeks to undermine free cultures.

The second mistake was the failure to understand that, despite this unappeasable fanaticism, the Soviet Union really did not desire a general war—that, although it moved in wherever there was a vacuum of power or an opportunity to create mischief, it moved out wherever there was a danger of its being completely embroiled. Its belief that the processes of history were on its side, the evidence of disunion and weakness in the free world, the uncertainties of survival in any all-out struggle against the West reinforced its fear of a general conflict. This meant (and it should have been clear from Soviet history from the beginning) that the Communist leadership, short of a direct attack upon its territories, *cannot be provoked into war.* After all, Japanese and Soviet armies fought on the banks of the Amur, Hitler challenged the Soviet Union for years with naked threats without a general war being unleashed. Stalin's quarrel with Tito began with the latter's demand that Stalin help him take Trieste; Stalin refused because of his fear that this would result in world war.

Bolshevism is the greatest movement of secular fanaticism in human history. The only thing that can tame a secular fanaticism is a fear of failure, of defeat in the only world it knows. Unless it is certain of victory, or unless it fears certain defeat, it will not venture everything upon a war in which, although it may defeat the enemy, it cannot itself survive.

Of course, there are those who maintain that Bolshevism has changed its spots, that the internal terror of the Soviet regime has eased, and that, just as Stalin revised Lenin for the worse, Khrushchev is revising Stalin for the better. Even if Khrushchev's policies really did represent a return to Leninism, this would hardly be a cause for rejoicing. For Leninism in international affairs was even more intransigent than Stalinism, which originally was the ideology of socialism-in-one-country. Lenin placed greater emphasis on the extension of Bolshevik power throughout the world than on its retention in the Soviet system.

There have been changes in the Soviet Union since Stalin died. The reign of internal terror has somewhat moderated, purges are fewer and not so bloody—these domestic effects of the transition from Stalin to Khrushchev are not to be denied. Khrushchev's speech at the Twentieth Party Congress has had irreversible consequences. All this, nonetheless, leaves the monolithic structure of political power within the Soviet Union unaffected. More important, it has led to no basic reorientation in Soviet foreign policy. The propaganda of the big lie has been continued. The techniques of infiltration and penetration in non-Communist countries have been intensified. Soviet power has moved into the Middle East and rattled atomic weapons at England and France for purposes of diplomatic blackmail. By his cunning in Poland and ruthless brutality in Hungary, Khrushchev has shown himself a worthy successor of Stalin, who trained him and raised him to power.

Whatever changes in American foreign policy are indicated, they do not follow from any changes in the basic Soviet strategy for world conquest by subversion and aggression.

I wish to defend a course for American foreign policy in Europe which will not be popular with either the defenders or most critics of our foreign policy. It is not the position of the British Labor party, of the German Social Democratic party, of George Kennan's Reith lectures, but it is in the same quarter of the compass. This policy is designed to preserve peace, defend the free world, and roll back the Iron Curtain in Europe to the prewar borders, if possible, of the Soviet Union.

The most explosive area in Europe today is Central Europe—Germany and the Soviet satellite states. It is the most explosive area because the last two years have shown that the overwhelming majority of the population in these countries is anti-Communist, that even the Communist parties in most of the satellite countries are probably more nationalist than Communist, and that, to the extent they are Communist, they would, if they could, seek political independence of the Kremlin. If the Red Army were withdrawn from East Germany and Eastern Europe today, these countries in all probability would soon, without any intervention from the West, rewin their political freedom.

If, however, the Soviet Army remains astride their lands, then the free nations of the world are in the intolerable moral position of either having to encourage the people of these countries to accept their bonds of tyranny or standing idly by and seeing them slaughtered, as in Hungary. In effect, we become the unwitting allies of the Kremlin in holding down the countries of Eastern Europe—at the very time when the Eastern European satellites have become an *economic* liability to the Soviet Union, and at a time when, since Hungary, they are a *moral* liability to the Soviet Union. (The myth that Soviet troops are in Central and Eastern Europe at the invitation of the peoples of those countries is now in everyone's eyes a blood-stained fiction. And for the moment the Soviet Union seems to have more appetizing fish to fry in Asia and Africa.)

The present time seems to provide appropriate opportunity to help liberate Eastern Europe from the threat of the Red Army. It is obvious that we cannot do this unless we offer a *quid pro quo* to the Kremlin, a concession which would test the sincerity of its professions for a settlement before the entire world.

It seems to me therefore that the NATO nations should offer publicly a phased withdrawal of their military forces from West Germany on condition that Soviet troops withdraw from East Germany and Eastern Europe and that the Soviet Government assent to unification of Germany by free elections. Further, this offer should be coupled with a proposal to keep Germany and Eastern Europe militarily neutral.

The advantages of establishing this neutralized area are many. First, the satellite powers would liberate themselves from Soviet rule. Second, the spectacle of this development may accelerate the processes of democratization—at least, the processes of dissent and dissatisfaction—within the Soviet Union itself. Third, under the umbrella of a Western guarantee of its neutrality, the resources of Central Europe could be diverted in large measure to raising its standard of living and reinforcing, by the contrast in living conditions and cultural freedom, the discontent in the Soviet Union. Fourth, if the neutralization is effective in this area of the world it could be extended to other areas—perhaps the Middle East, perhaps the Far East.

There are, of course, certain dangers in this plan for the neutralization of East and Central Europe.

How can we trust the Kremlin to live up to its pledge in view of the long history of its violation of its pledged word? In the event that Communist regimes are overthrown in the satellite countries, what is to prevent the Soviet Army from marching in and violating the neutrality of these countries? To the last question, I reply by asking another: What is to prevent the Kremlin, in the event that a satellite regime changes its character *now,* from acting in the same way as it did in Hungary? Nothing that *we* are pledged to do.

Once neutralization is agreed upon, these countries should be entrusted with sufficient weapons, conventional and perhaps nuclear, to prevent the Kremlin from over-running them without some opposition. I make a distinction between neutralization and demilitarization. More important, I believe that the NATO countries should publicly declare in advance that a violation of the neutrality of these nations would be a *casus belli.* To be sure, the history of Korea is instructive on this point; undoubtedly, Dean Acheson's bitter criticism of George Kennan is the result of his memory of the Korean incident, in which, after the American troops marched out, North Korean Communists marched in. But I am confident that, had the Kremlin been convinced that we would resist aggression in Korea and resist it by taking the struggle beyond Korean borders, there would have been no Korean invasion. Had not Mr. Acheson declared that Korea was outside the interests of American policy, there would have been no Korean War.

As Henry Kissinger and others have pointed out, uncertainty in these matters represents the greatest danger of all to peace. It is questionable whether even a psychotic like Hitler would have moved when he did had he been convinced that it meant war with England and the United States as well. After he was permitted his triumphs at Munich and at Prague, Hitler complained that he was "tricked" into war, since he had every reason to believe that, if England would not fight to preserve the Czech borders, she certainly would not fight to preserve the integrity of the Polish frontiers.

A second danger of neutralization is that the Kremlin might move to recapture control of the satellite countries not by outright aggression but by subversion or by a coup. This seems to be not a very formidable threat. Internal subversive movements can be handled by domestic military forces with conventional weapons if they are sufficiently alert to the possibilities.

A third danger of neutralization is that the West, and particularly the United States, might not risk the destruction of its cities and its very survival in order to defend Poland or East Germany. This is a very real danger, strong enough in my eyes to make the withdrawal of all American troops from Europe (as Kennan proposes) far too premature. To some extent, the problem can be met by using measures of graduated deterrence ranging from conventional weapons to tactical atomic weapons. Retaliation would be a function of the kind of weapons the enemy himself used. We would say to the Kremlin, in the words of Denis Healey: "If you move, we will hit you so hard that it will hurt you more to keep on fighting than you can possibly gain by persisting in aggression."

No one knows whether the use of tactical atomic weapons can be limited and the use of the ultimate weapons with thermonuclear warheads avoided. During the last war, despite all the prewar Cassandras, poison gas was not used because of the certainty that it would be employed by the other side in retaliation. The same might be true for hydrogen bombs in the next war. Nonetheless, it seems to me to be true that the ultimate weapon can be a deterrent only if the Kremlin believes it will be used. *This means that the ultimate weapon of the West is not the hydrogen bomb or any other super-weapon but the passion for freedom and the willingness to die for it if necessary.* Once the Kremlin is convinced that we will use this weapon to prevent it from subjugating the world to its will, we will have the best assurance of peace. Once the Kremlin believes that this willingness to fight for freedom at all costs is absent, that it has been eroded by neutralist fear and pacifist wishful thinking, it will blackmail the free countries of the world into capitulation and succeed where Hitler failed.

Shortly after the first atomic bomb was exploded, Elmer Davis responded to the call for one world with the retort: "No world is better than some worlds." It is possible to panic the West by a picture of the universal holocaust a nuclear world war would bring, to panic the West to a point where survival on any terms seems preferable to the risks of resistance. The pages of history show that moral integrity in extreme situations is often the highest political wisdom. The struggle against totalitarianism is not only a political struggle but also a moral one, which limits the extent to which we can carry appeasement. If Hitler had commanded the weapon resources of the Soviet Union, would we have yielded to one Munich after another until the world was one vast concentration camp? I hardly think so. Those who are prepared to sacrifice freedom for peace and for mere life will find after such sacrifice no genuine peace and a life unfit for man. Paradoxical as it may sound, life itself is not a value. What gives life value is not its mere existence but its quality. Whoever proclaims that life is worth living under any circumstances has already written for himself an epitaph of infamy. For there is no principle or human being he will not betray; there is no indignity he will not suffer or compound.

Sometimes those who should know better seem to ignore this. Bertrand Russell recently declared in an interview with Joseph Alsop that, if the Communists could not be induced to agree to reasonable proposals for controlled nuclear disarmament, he would be in favor of unilateral disarmament even if this meant Communist domination of the entire world. Although he stated this view as only his own, the fact that he made it public is tantamount to an advocacy of a policy sure to be widely interpreted both in the West and in the Kremlin as one of complete capitulation to Communist intransigence.

It is with a feeling of great personal sadness that I observe Bertrand Russell urge that, to avoid the risk of war, we in effect haul down the colors of freedom and moral decency to save mankind for Communist rule. After all, we cannot be certain that, if we have to defend ourselves by nuclear weapons, they will inevitably destroy the entire human race; nor can we be certain that the terror of Communism will not endure or be followed by something worse. "Oh! what a noble mind is here o'erthrown!" The man who in *The Free Man's Worship* was prepared to defy the very cosmos and "the trampling march of unconscious power," in order to sustain the ideals of human freedom come what may, now sinks on unwilling but still bended knees before Khrushchev at the thought of the danger of universal destruction.

Bertrand Russell's career as a counselor to mankind, here as in some of his observations about the United States as a police state, proves that all the mathematical logic in the world is not a substitute for common sense. In so many words, he says: "I am for controlled nuclear disarmament, but, if the Communists cannot be induced to agree to it, then I am for unilateral disarmament even if it means the horrors of Communist domination." When they listen to sentiments like this, why *should* the Soviets consent to controlled nuclear disarmament? All they need do is wait and the world will be given to them on a platter to do with as they will. Why *should* they compromise? Not knowing whether they will survive *our* resolution to fight if necessary for freedom, they may be tempted to accept reasonable proposals. But words like Russell's tell them that all they need do is sit tight, make threats and wait for us to come crawling to them disarmed. It is like saying to a ruffian or burglar: "You let me alone and I'll let you alone, but if you insist on not letting me alone you can have your way with me. If you find my lock too difficult to force, be patient and I shall remove it." This is almost a provocation to the burglar to make the most extreme demands and reject any reasonable settlement. Russell's words express a dubious political morality and a bad strategy. They bring about the very intransigence among the Communists which he uses as the justification for capitulation.

We do not, however, need to strike an heroic stance in shaping a viable foreign policy. Intelligence must be our guide. If we can keep the free world from falling into the trap set by the Kremlin and preserve peace by increasing the power and readiness of the free world, we can then rely upon the processes of education, the force of example, the contagion of free ideas, the cultural osmosis of the great traditions of the West gradually to soften, to liberalize, to round off the edges of the totalitarian regimes of the world until their own peoples rally their energies to overthrow their oppressors and establish one free world republic.

I conclude that our foreign policy in Western Europe must be based on a proposal for cautious, vigilant military withdrawal—not political disengagement, for European affairs are our affairs—in order to win more elbow room for free culture in Eastern Europe.

In Asia and Africa, our task is more difficult and complex. The emphasis on economic aid on the order of a new Marshall Plan is good as far as it goes. But more important than economic aid is the effective use of it. The foreign-aid program, if it is spread universally, is too thin. Waste is enormous. What we must do here is concentrate on massive aid to some key countries or develop some public projects in which adjacent countries can join.

All the economic aid in the world will not win us friends and allies unless the United States regains for itself its reputation as an anti-imperialist power. Here we have followed French policy and sometimes British policy with disastrous consequences. The policy of France in Indo-China and now in North Africa, the adventure of Suez, the repressions in Cyprus have alienated large sections of the uncommitted peoples of the earth from the cause of the free world. They have made it difficult for us to put Soviet Russia on the spot as the chief colonial power in the world. From the North Sea to the Pacific Ocean, from the Arctic to Turkestan, the Communists have imposed their rule by force on a score of non-Russian peoples. But instead of the Soviet Union being the target of Asian-African scorn, it is the United States, because of our allies' sins of commission and omission, which is widely regarded as imperialistic.

I do not underestimate the difficulties of a coalition of powers, but, as the strongest member of the NATO group, we are called upon to give leadership. Our greatest mistake is that we followed the lead of France and Britain too long. It is alleged that our abrupt reversal on the Aswan Dam, which led to fateful developments in Egypt, was taken at the request of Great Britain—which didn't prevent our British friends from criticizing the action after its consequences were clear. We would be more respected by our allies if we took a strong stand against colonialism and made bold and imaginative proposals to counteract Communism politically, diplomatically and economically. Many people scoff at the idea of a war of propaganda despite the fact that the Kremlim has been winning the cold war mostly by its propaganda. The war of weapons is much more likely to break out when we lose the war of words and the war of ideas. And it is our *ideas,* the common ideas of the free world, the heritage of the Atlantic democracies and their allies, which can inspire a continuing offensive against Communism all along the line. To us, much more important than a cultural exchange of technicians, metallurgists and farmers with the Soviet Union should be an exchange of philosophers, historians, literary critics, economists and sociologists. We can open our gates safely to thousands of Soviet students and teachers, no matter how indoctrinated they are, provided they permit thousands of our students and teachers to study and travel in the Soviet Union.

It is often said that democracies cannot successfully wage cold wars. They are not geared for it. They are too self-critical. And the factions of normal political life sometimes regard each other with more hostility than the enemy at the gate. All this is true. But a democracy also possesses the virtues of its defects. Once it is informed, its voluntary discipline can accomplish more than columns that are dragooned into goosesteps. It is tougher in crisis than its totalitarian enemies, but this will not avail for victory or even for survival unless it follows the lead of intelligence.

APPENDICES

A. A Reply by Bertrand Russell

Dr. Sidney Hook's article, "A Foreign Policy for Freedom and Survival" contains much with which I am in agreement—more, I think, than Dr. Hook realizes. Before embarking upon controversial matters, I will emphasize the extent of agreement by repeating a statement, the first three paragraphs of which were originally made to the American Nobel Anniversary Committee and subsequently published, with the addition of the last paragraph, in many countries on both sides of the Iron Curtain:

"Negotiations between East and West with a view to finding ways of peaceful coexistence are urgently desirable. Certain principles should govern such negotiations: (1) Any agreement arrived at should as a whole be not advantageous to either party; (2) it should be such as to diminish causes of friction; (3) it should be such as to diminish the danger of a more or less inadvertent outbreak of nuclear warfare.

"The procedure I should wish to see adopted would be, first, a meeting at the highest level between the governments of the U.S. and the U.S.S.R., not intended to reach binding agreements but to explore the possibility of a compromise which both powers would accept. The negotiations involved should be secret until the possibility of such compromise had been established. If such a compromise seems feasible, it should be recommended by both parties to the other powers of NATO and the Warsaw Pact.

"If an agreement is to be successful in averting the risk of nuclear warfare, it must provide for the destruction of nuclear weapons and the cessation of their manufacture under the guarantee of inspection by an agreed neutral authority. It must also provide for the removal of all alien troops from agreed territory including, as minimum, East and West Germany, Czechoslovakia, Poland and Hungary—Germany not to remain in NATO or the above satellites in the Warsaw Pact. The countries in Eastern and Western Europe must be free to adopt whatever form of government and whatever economic system they may prefer.

"I have been dealing with measures that are imminently necessary if the risk of a great war is to be diminished. But in the long run the only solution which will make the world safe is the establishment of a World Government with a monopoly of the major weapons of war. The world is not yet ready for such an institution, but it may be hoped that experience will gradually convince men of its necessity."

It will be seen that this statement is very similar to the first part of Dr. Hook's article. Where he and I disagree is as to the advisability of an ultimate resort to nuclear war if the Communist powers cannot be contained by anything less. Both Dr. Hook and I are concerned with possibilities which we respectively think improbable. Dr. Hook maintains that, even if his policy led to the extinction of human life, it would still be better than a Communist victory. I maintain, on the contrary, that a Communist victory would not be so great a disaster as the extinction of human life. He admits that his policy *might* lead to the one disaster, though he does not think that it would. I admit that the policy which I advocate *might* lead to the other disaster, though I, again, do not think that it would do so. We are agreed that both these extreme consequences are somewhat hypothetical, and we are also agreed that both of them would be disasters. We differ only as to which of them would be the greater disaster.

Before arguing this question in impersonal terms, there are some observations of a more personal kind that may help to clear the ground. Those who oppose the policy which I advocate insinuate that it is inspired by personal cowardice. A moment's reflection would show them that such a supposition is absurd. Neither universal Communist domination nor the extinction of the human race is likely to occur before I die a natural death. I do not, therefore, have to consider whether I should most fear my nuclear disintegration or my slow torture in an Arctic labor camp. At my age, views as to the not immediate future are necessarily impersonal.

Another thing which is insinuated is that I am surreptitiously favorable to Communism. One might as well accuse Dr. Hook of wishing to see the human race exterminated. Obviously, he does not wish the one and I do not wish the other. We both admit that both would be disasters. We differ only, I repeat, as to which would be the greater disaster.

I cannot but deplore the passage in which Dr. Hook laments my supposed moral downfall. It is not by such arguments that difficult issues can be decided. He does not seem aware that it would be easy to make a retort in kind and to accuse him of being a super-Caligula. But argumentation in this vein is an obstacle to rationality. I shall, therefore, abstain from it, and I wish that he would do likewise.

I come now to an impersonal consideration of the issue. There are here two quite distinct matters to be discussed: First, what is the likelihood that the policy which I advocate would lead to the universal domination of Communism? And, second, if it did, would this be worse than the ending of human life? It is the second question that I wish to examine, since the first involves difficult political and psychological considerations as to which differences of opinion will inevitably persist.

Dr. Hook asserts that "Bolshevism is the greatest movement of secular fanaticism in human history." I will not dispute this, but is there not also fanaticism in the attitude of Dr. Hook and of the powerful men who agree with him? Human history abounds in great disasters. One civilization after another has been swept away by hordes of barbarians. The Minoan-Mycenaean civilization was destroyed by savage warriors whose descendants, after a few centuries, became the Greeks whom we still revere. When the Mohammedans swept over the greater part of the Eastern Roman Empire, it seemed to Christian contemporaries that the civilization of the regions which they conquered was being destroyed, and yet, before long, it was the Arabs who mainly preserved the heritage of antiquity. Genghis Khan was quite as bad as Stalin at his worst, but his grandson Kublai Khan was a highly civilized monarch under whom Chinese culture flourished.

The men who think as Dr. Hook does are being un-historical and are displaying a myopic vision to which future centuries are invisible. A victory of Communism might be as disastrous as the barbarian destruction of the Roman Empire, but there is no reason to think that it would be more disastrous than that event. While the human race survives, humaneness, love of liberty, and a civilized way of life will, sooner or later, prove irresistibly attractive. The progress of mankind has always been a matter of ups and downs. The downs have always seemed final to contemporaries, and the ups have always given rise to unfounded optimism. Western Europe in the year 1000 gave no promise of the renaissance that began some centuries later. The human spirit throughout Western Christendom was as narrowly imprisoned as it was in Russia under Stalin. Any person who supposes that the evils of Communism, if it achieved a supremacy, would last forever is allowing himself to be so limited by the heat of present controversies as to be unable to see their similarity to equally virulent controversies in the past or to realize that a dark age, if it is upon us, like the dark ages of the past will not last forever.

Dr. Hook says quite truly that life, in itself, is not of value. It gives, however, the only possibility of any value. I cannot applaud the arrogance of those who say: "If the next century or so is to be such as I (if I were alive) would find unpleasant, I shall decide that not only this period but all future time shall be destitute of life." Nor can I wholly admire the kind of "courage" which is advocated by Dr. Hook and others who think like him, which has, in large part, a vicarious character somewhat detracting from its nobility. I have nothing to say against the man who commits suicide rather than live under a regime which he thinks evil, but I do not feel much approval of the man who condemns everybody else to death because he himself does not find life worth living.

I have tried to keep this discussion on a rational rather than an emotional plane, but I cannot resist giving expression to my final judgment, which is that to risk the end of human life because we regard Communism as evil is fanatical, defeatist and pusillanimous in the highest possible degree.

B. A Rejoinder to Bertrand Russell

It is a debater's stratagem, unworthy of Bertrand Russell's great gifts, to assert that I called his personal courage into question in criticizing the policy he advocates as one of surrender to Communism. It was his political judgment I criticized, not his character. Indeed, despite his praiseworthy declaration that arguments in the impersonal mode will best clarify our disagreements, it is he who descends to the use of personal epithets. I shall not follow him. I ask only that he stop pretending that anyone is charging him with cowardice or that any politically literate person believes he favors Communism. He no more favors Communism than the democratic Western statesmen who appeased Hitler out of fear of war favored Fascism. Nonetheless they were the assisting architects of the ruin of millions.

The issues between us are two. The first Russell wholly avoids, even though it is my main point and by far of greater political weight. Russell has declared to the entire world that, if the Soviet Union refuses to accept reasonable proposals for international disarmament, the West should disarm unilaterally—even at the cost of the universal reign of Communist terror. I criticized this view as helping to produce the very situation in which we may have to choose between capitulation to Communist tyranny or war.

I find bewildering Russell's claim that the four paragraphs he cites in his rejoinder are "very similar" to the first part of my article. These paragraphs are worth precisely nothing when coupled with his present advice. They flatly contradict it. The first principle he recommends to govern negotiations between East and West is: "Any agreement arrived at should as a whole be not advantageous to either party." Excellent! Then he broadcasts to the world: If the Kremlin refuses to make such an agreement, the West should disarm unilaterally. Why, then, should the Kremlin enter into any such agreement or abide by it if it does? Russell's position today constitutes positive encouragement to the Communist leaders to be unreasonable and thus inherit the world without a struggle.

Let us not deceive ourselves: It is obvious that the leaders of the Soviet Union are keeping a sensitive watch on the pulse of public opinion in Western countries. It is not for nothing that the man whom they called "the running dog of imperialism," and who still despises their tyranny, is now built up in their controlled press as the "true friend of peace." Throughout the world, Communists are infiltrating into the pacifist movement whose non-pacific demonstrations they often spark. I am convinced that the growth of pacifist and neutralist sentiment in the West was at least partly responsible for the Soviet Union's withdrawal from the sessions of the UN Disarmament Commission, where reasonable proposals along the lines of Russell's paragraphs could be considered; its hardening attitude along the political front; its repudiation of the Geneva agreement on Germany; its recent UN veto of the proposal for Arctic inspection. Such actions may also be based on the hope that a position like Russell's will undermine the West's resolution to resist aggression.

Arguments from history are rarely decisive, but I think it is fairly well established that the appeasement of Hitler—not only Munich but the mood that nothing could be worse than war—encouraged Hitler in his aggression. I go further. Even if in my heart I agreed with Russell (as I do not) that in the ultimate event, capitulation to Communism was a lesser evil than the risks of war, I should regard it as a piece of unmitigated political foolishness to proclaim it. We live in a contingent world. What we do, even sometimes what we say, counts. Especially important are the policies we advocate. For, to the extent that they influence human action, they influence future events. Russell's proposal is tantamount to playing with all cards face up against a shrewd and ruthless gambler with a hidden hand. When the stakes are human freedom, it is irresponsible to play a game which invites the Kremlin to bluff us into submission with threats of atomic blackmail. The Soviets are just as vulnerable to us as we are to them.

The Soviet leaders belong to the human race, too. For them, survival is an even more important value than for many in the West. That is why I am convinced that ultimately they are more likely to consent to reasonable proposals for a peaceful settlement once they are persuaded that we will fight rather than surrender, than if they are persuaded by Russell and others that we will surrender rather than fight. *This* is the crucial point which Russell has completely ignored.

Santayana somewhere defines a fanatic as one who, having forgotten his goal, redoubles his efforts. Among my goals are freedom *and* peace. That is why I believe that all nations should freely choose their economic and political systems. That is why I have never advocated a preventive war for the sake of peace, as Russell did in 1948, when the West had a monopoly of atomic power. He was wrong then in urging that the Soviet Union be forced, by atomic bombs if necessary, to yield to a world government. (Many A-bombs could have the effect of a few H-bombs.) He is wrong now in urging capitulation on the West because the Soviet Union has the hydrogen bomb. He went too far in one direction; he now goes too far in the other, as if he were atoning for his early extremism. In both cases, he underestimated the political and psychological elements in the situation and overestimated the technological ones.

I do not see why a policy which seeks to confine the fanaticism of Bolshevism by taming it with the fear of failure should be called fanatical. As well say that a man who believes in tolerance and is therefore intolerant of those who manifest intolerance is himself intolerant. On the contrary, assuming belief to be a habit of action, a person who is tolerant of a show of intolerance does not really believe in tolerance. If the West follows the foreign policy I have advocated, it will not have to choose between capitulation to Communism or war. This is the choice Russell's proposal forces us into. It seems to me today that the probability of Communism destroying human liberty everywhere is considerably greater than the probability, if it comes to war, of human life being destroyed everywhere—particularly if we keep up scientific inquiry into defense.

After all, just a few short years ago, Russell declared that the destruction of the whole of Europe was not too great a price to pay in order that "Communism be wiped out." There were some who regarded this position as "fanatical, defeatist and pusillanimous," since such a war if prolonged might have had a disastrous effect on the human race. It may be that today, if the scientists of the free world rally to the cause of freedom's defense and not to the cause of Russell and unilateral Western disarmament, discoveries will be made which will counteract some of the lethal after-effects of weapons. In that case, even if the Kremlin forces a war on the West, it may be repelled without the destruction of all human life or even the whole of Western Europe. It is an error to assume that a balance of armaments or even an armaments race inevitably makes for war. Else we would never be at peace. Unpreparedness also may lead to war. There is a risk, of course. The important thing, therefore, is to see to it that the potential aggressor never is certain that he can win. But this is precisely what Russell's policy prevents us from doing.

Suppose now we were confronted with the limiting case: choice between the horror of Communism for some hundreds of years and the end of human life. Here every lover of freedom and of life is on uncertain and tragic ground. One cannot be sure that at the decisive moment the situation will look the same. Yet every compassionate person, including Russell, feels that there is a limit in suffering and ignominy beyond which the whole human enterprise comes into moral question. The problem is where to draw the limit. At present, I cannot, like Russell, find grounds in history for reconciling myself to the first of the above alternatives. Some of my reasons are:

(1) In the past, the triumphs of barbarism were local, not universal. Today, a Communist world would be a tightly knit despotism of fear without sanctuaries, without interstices to hide, without possibilities for anonymity.

(2) In the past, tyrants ruled with a primitive technology. The possession today of refined scientific techniques increases immeasurably the extent and intensity of terror ruthless men can impose on those they rule. A Communist world could easily become a scientific Gehenna—something incomparably worse than the destruction of the Roman Empire by the barbarians.

(3) I cannot regard the achievement which in the past has sometimes followed the triumph of cruel tyrants as worth the price in torture and agony that preceded it. To me, the splendor and glory of the Court of Kublai Khan were not worth even one of the many pyramids of human skulls his grandfather, Genghis Khan, heaped up in carving out his empire. And a few years ago I believe Bertrand Russell would have agreed with me. If the

triumph of Hitler were a necessary condition for a new renaissance, what anti-Fascist would be willing to pay the price?

(4) It is not at all unlikely that factional struggle will break out again either at the Communist center or periphery among the political gangsters who rule the Communist world. In such an event, thermonuclear weapons of even more destructive power than those we know may be used to end men's miserable lives, and all the additional agony and terror would have been in vain.

(5) It is no arrogance on my part to propose to the generation of the free that they follow a policy of resistance rather than of surrender, any more than it is arrogant for Russell to propose surrender rather than resistance. But perhaps he means it is arrogant for any generation of men to make a decision which will prevent the future generations of the yet unborn to have their chance and make their choice. I must confess that I have some difficulty with this notion of obligation, as if it implied there were millions of souls extending into eternity waiting to be born. I do not share this theology. If there are such souls, they may perhaps become embodied elsewhere.

Communists have always argued that it is justified to bury several generations, if necessary, in order to fertilize the soil of history for a glorious future to be enjoyed by the still unborn. In some respects, Russell's argument is similar except that, as an opponent of Communism, he puts the glory much further into the future. Cosmic optimism, however, seems no more credible to me than historical optimism.

Morally, those who are unborn cannot reproach us for denying them the bliss of birth in a Communist world but those who already exist, our children and grandchildren, may curse us for turning them over to the jailors of a Communist 1984 in which, brainwashed and degraded, they are not even free to die until their masters give them leave. There are more horrors in the Communist heaven or hell than Russell seems aware of.

There is an air of unreality about this phase of the discussion. It is improbable that Englishmen who refused to knuckle under to Hitler and his V-2 bombs will seriously consider doing so to Khrushchev and his more powerful bombs. If they did, the United States and Canada would still remain staunchly opposed to Communist tyranny. The discussion seems fanciful, almost bizarre, because only if we accept Russell's position or one similar to it will the enemies of freedom be emboldened to confront us with the momentous *choice* of total surrender or total war. Human life may be destroyed by accident or by the maniacal whim of a dictator, against which there is no safeguard—even by surrender. But, if it is destroyed by war, it will be because our foolishness will tempt the enemy to forget his mortality.

In conclusion, I wish to repeat that nothing I have written is intended in any way as a personal reflection on Bertrand Russell, a man and philosopher whom I have usually admired even when I have strongly disagreed with him. I impugn only his political intelligence in this grave crisis of human freedom. I lament the fact that he has capped a lifetime of gallant opposition to despotism with the unsound recommendation that we unconditionally surrender to the cruelest tyranny in human history.

C. A Counter-Reply by Bertrand Russell

My discussion with Sidney Hook in your pages has not given a clear picture of what my position is. I do not blame Dr. Hook for this. I have been led into a purely academic issue as if it were one of practical politics. Everybody knows that neither the United States nor the U.S.S.R. will disarm unilaterally. The question of whether either would be wise to do so is, therefore, no more than an exercise in theoretical ethics. Speaking practically, and not theoretically, what I advocate is that methods should be sought of, first, lessening the East-West tension and then, negotiating agreements on vexed questions on the basis of giving no net advantage to either side. Such negotiations, if they are to be satisfactory, must include the mutual renunciation of nuclear weapons with an adequate system of inspection.

It is true that I advocate practically, and not only theoretically, the abandonment of the H-bomb by Britain and the prevention of the spread of H-bombs to powers other than the United States and the U.S.S.R. I do not consider that unilateral renunciation of British H-bombs would have any measurable effect upon the balance of power, and I do consider that the acquisition of H-bombs by many powers will greatly increase the danger of a nuclear war. This makes the question of British renunciation of H-bombs quite distinct from that of general unilateral disarmament by one of the two camps.

The question at issue between Dr. Hook and myself arises only if all attempts at negotiation fail. Dr. Hook speaks as though I wished the United States Government to announce that it is prepared to give way at all points and suggests that I have no such wish as regards the Soviet Government. I think this question is quite unreal since, whatever might be the part of ideal wisdom, it is certain that neither side will surrender completely to the other. However, since the question is considered important, I will do my best to restate my opinion more unmistakably.

To eliminate emotional factors, I shall speak of two power blocs, A and B, leaving it completely undetermined which of them is Communist and which anti-Communist. The argument proceeds on the hypothesis that, if there is a war between the two blocs, the human race will be exterminated. It further supposes a situation in which one of the two blocs is so fanatical that it prefers the ending of mankind to a rational compromise. In such a situation, I think that the less fanatical bloc, if it had the welfare of mankind in view, would prefer concession to warfare. I should say this equally to both sides.

There are those in both camps who think that the extermination of the human race would be a smaller evil than the victory of the "enemy." I regard this view, whether held by A or by B, as insane. Dr. Hook and some of Mr. Khrushchev's supporters agree when it is held by one side, but not when it is held by the other. The opinion which I have expressed that it would be better to yield than to indulge in a nuclear war is addressed to both parties equally, and I do not think it likely to have any more influence on the one side than on the other.

The argument that you cannot negotiate successfully if you announce in advance that, if pressed, you will yield, is entirely valid. If I were the government of either A or B, I should make no such announcement. But this has no bearing on the purely academic question of what it would be wise to do if the completely desperate situation arose. I must, however, once more insist that the view in favor of avoiding nuclear warfare even at great cost is one which applies to both sides equally and which, as far as I can judge, is no more likely to be adopted by one side than the other. It is entirely unjust to regard the opinions that I have expressed as more useful to the one side than to the other.

So much for defense. I pass now to attack.

Dr. Hook begins his rejoinder by a lofty rejection of personalities to which, his readers are led to suppose, I was the first to descend. He relies upon their forgetting his crocodile tears expressed in his lament, "Oh! what a noble mind is here o'er-thrown!" I am compelled to think that criticisms of him are "personalities," whereas criticisms of me are impersonal declarations of Truth.

Throughout his article, he gives his readers to understand that it is only to the West that I proclaim the view that submission would be better than nuclear war. In fact, I proclaim this to both sides equally, and my advocacy of this view has been published as widely in Communist countries as in the United States. He will retort: "Bah! You don't suppose the Communists will listen to you." I reply: "Pshaw! I don't suppose that America will listen to me either."

He points out that "the leaders of the Soviet Union are keeping a sensitive watch on the pulse of public opinion in Western countries." Of course they are; and of course the West keeps an equal watch on opinion in Communist countries. He supposes that my advocacy of peace, though it may have some influence in the West, can have none in the East. This is contrary to all the evidence I have been able to obtain. I do not attribute any very great influence to my efforts to diminish East-West tension, but I have reason to think that this influence has been quite as great in the East as in the West.

Dr. Hook says: "If the West follows the foreign policy I have advocated, it will not have to choose between capitulation to Communism or war." This is at least equally true of the foreign policy which I advocate. I do not believe that either side wants a nuclear war, and I think a modicum of sanity on both sides will prevent it. The question at issue between Dr. Hook and me would arise only if one side lacked this modicum of sanity.

Dr. Hook's reasons for supposing that, if Communism conquered the world, its bad features would persist indefinitely are, to my mind, completely untenable. The worst features of Communism have been developed under the influence of fear and would almost certainly grow less if fear were removed. He points out that "in the past, tyrants ruled with a primitive technology." But it was no less effective for being primitive. He alludes to Genghis Khan's pyramids of heads, which were just as thorough-going as Auschwitz. It is an example of his slippery methods of controversy when he says that "the splendor and glory of the court of Kublai Khan were not worth even one of the many pyramids of human skulls his grandfather, Genghis Khan, heaped up." I had never maintained that they were. What I had said was that they gave reason for hope that a bad regime might improve—which is a very different thing.

Another example of his dubious controversial methods is his argument that we owe no obligation to generations that, if his policy is followed, will never be born. He says, "I do not share this theology." There is, as he perfectly well knows, and knows that I know, no question of theology involved. The question involved is whether it is likely to be worth-while that future generations should exist. It is not a question of "rights," since obviously the nonexistent have no "rights." But I am sure Dr. Hook, in his calmer moments, will admit that "rights" are not a fundamental ethical conception.

Dr. Hook is guilty of curious inconsistencies which are an indication of his fanaticism. He says: "Communists have always argued that it is justified to bury several generations, if necessary, in order to fertilize the soil of history for a glorious future to be enjoyed by the still unborn." His own position is that it is justified to bury not several generations but *all* future generations, not in order that they may enjoy a glorious future, but in order that they may have no future at all. This is an immeasurable exaggeration of the very fault for which he criticizes the Communists.

I should like to correct a misunderstanding promoted, I think, by a report of an interview in which only a small part of my thought was expressed. I think that, with wise statesmanship on the part of the West, it will not be at all difficult to avoid both nuclear war and surrender. What I advocate in practice, and not as the outcome of an artificial logical dilemma, is a conclusion of agreements between East and West admitting the inevitability of co-existence and the disastrous futility of war. I wish both sides to realize that war cannot achieve anything that either side desires, and that, in consequence, points in dispute can only be settled by negotiation.

Dr. Hook is in the habit of proclaiming that he values freedom. On this point, however, he deceives himself. He does not think that those who prefer life under Communism to death should be free to choose the alternative that they prefer. Not only the inhabitants of Communist nations but the inhabitants of all the uncommitted nations, are denied by him the most elementary freedom, which is freedom to choose survival. The view that No World is better than a Communist World, or that No World is better than a Capitalist World, is one that is difficult to refute by abstract arguments, but I think that those who hold it should question their right to impose their opinion upon those who do not hold it by the infliction of the death penalty upon all of them. This is an extreme form of religious persecution, going far beyond anything that has been advocated in previous human history.

D. A Counter-Rejoinder to Bertrand Russell

The attentive reader will have observed that Bertrand Russell has retreated from the position he took in his interview with Joseph Alsop. This was the occasion of my original criticism. He was not talking into the wind. His words were reported all over the world. They came with an impact of brutal intellectual and political shock in democratic countries. Nonetheless, although the wire services were always available to him, he neither retracted nor qualified what he said until this discussion began. Nor, as is obvious from his tone, has he welcomed the opportunity to clarify his stand.

Normally I should have been content to leave his reply unanswered. It is in effect an admission that it was politically foolish to have declared that, in the event the Kremlin refuses to negotiate on reasonable terms, the West should disarm unilaterally "even if it means the horrors of Communist domination." The issues, however, are so momentous and Russell's recent views about them have already done so much harm to the free world, that I feel I must continue the discussion. Perhaps if I eschew poetry (the line from Hamlet was directed only at his political judgment) and irony (the reference to theology!), he will understand me better even if he agrees with me less.

First of all, it is disingenuous for Russell now to maintain he was not advising the West, including the U. S. Government, to disarm unilaterally and risk the triumph of Communism, and that he was merely engaging "in no more than an exercise in theoretical ethics." The very language of his interview with Alsop, as well as his first reply to me in *The New Leader* (5/26/58) shows how false this is. In the former he proposed "unilateral disarmament" if the Kremlin continued to be unreasonable. What has this got to do with theoretical ethics? In the latter he stated that there are two matters at issue: "First, what is the likelihood that the policy I [Russell] advocate would lead to the universal domination of Communism?" He refused to discuss it but admitted it involves "political and psychological considerations." These, indeed, are of the very essence. The matter at issue is certainly not one merely of theoretical ethics.

Even if it were, Russell would still be wrong. Whatever does he imagine "theoretical ethics" to be? All theoretical ethics has an indirect bearing on practical life and conduct. For it is concerned not only with the nature of the right and the good but with *what* actions are right and *what* things are good and which should be preferred when they conflict. Russell would be the first to point out that the theoretical ethics of certain groups—*e.g.*, which teach that if it is impossible to save the life of both pregnant mother and child, the mother should be sacrificed—sometimes has important and fateful bearings upon practice. Similarly is there any doubt that belief in Russell's "theoretical" proposition, that capitulation and the risk of Communist domination with all its barbarity should be preferred to war and the risk to human survival, *tends* to undermine the will to resist Communist aggression? Russell is so absolutely convinced of the validity of his proposition in theoretical ethics that he believes that only the insane can disagree with him. Why, then, does he not accept the responsibility for its practical effects?

Second, Russell asserts that "The question at issue between Dr. Hook and myself arises only if all attempts at negotiation [between the West and the U.S.S.R.] fail." He is wrong again. The primary issue between us is whether Russell's position will contribute to the failure of those negotiations and whether mine will contribute to their success. Russell's belated second thoughts indicate that he, too, now believes it was not practically wise to declare what he did in his interview. The inferences I and others drew from his interview were perfectly legitimate. Further thought, I hope, will convince him that the Kremlin is less likely to risk aggression if it believes the West will resist to the end than if it is persuaded that Russell's proposition in "theoretical ethics" will guide the West's action. Only if Russell admits this are our remaining differences minor.

In this connection, I wish to challenge the truth of Russell's contention that he offered his "ideal wisdom" to both sides impartially. He has emphatically *not* addressed the Communists and advised them that, if the West refused to be reasonable in its negotiations, the Kremlin should unilaterally disarm even if it meant the triumph of the free world. What has been published in Communist countries and the neutralist world on *this* particular choice has been only his advice to the West, as expressed in his Alsop interview, with no corresponding specific advice to the Communists. As I read the evidence, Russell's recent efforts to diminish East-West tensions have helped disarm psychologically only the West and strengthened the position of the Communist world as well as the resolution of the Kremlin to pursue its present tack. Some of the atomic scientists of West Germany have cited his position as justifying their abandonment of defense research in nuclear weapons. Russell should know that the absence of a free press and of any possibility of freely expressed dissent makes it impossible for him to have any appreciable influence in the Communist world the Kremlin is not willing to let him have. He refers to public opinion in the Soviet Union on which "the West keeps an equal watch." There is no public opinion in the Soviet Union except the opinion of the Kremlin.

That Russell can believe that his influence has been "quite as great in the East as in the West" is simple wishful thinking. Without intending it, he has made more difficult the tasks of the Western governments which fear that the Kremlin desires renunciation of all atomic weapons, even of defense, so that it can overwhelm the free world with seas of Soviet and Chinese soldiery. Without intending it, he has made easier the campaign of propagandistic deception by Communist regimes which play off, whenever they can, politically naive men of intellectual distinction, as well as mindless millionaires like Cyrus Eaton, against the policy of the West. That policy has been weak but it has been genuinely peaceful.

This is ignored in the Olympian intellectual posture taken by Russell toward the hypothetical case of the two power blocs. It is a fundamental mistake to treat the problem as if it merely involved abstract mathematical relationships between two anonymous blocs, instead of the *historical* relations between the Communist bloc and the Western bloc only one of which threatens the peace of the world. The foreign policy of the West, and of the United States in particular, has been deficient in many respects and I have been among its unremitting critics. But all we need do is to call the roll of aggression in East-West relations—Eastern Europe, Czechoslovakia, the blockade of West Berlin, Korea, Hungary—to determine who threatens whom. It is unrealistic in the extreme therefore to draw a simple equation between two power blocs in the abstract if we wish to predict their behavior or propose a reasonable policy.

Third, Russell's illustration of the two power blocs supposes, as he says, that one of them is fanatically insane. This removes it still further from any relevance to the present situation. The rulers of the Kremlin are not insane. They are determined men with nerves of steel, wonderful actors of surpassing skill in duping the politically unwary. "Agreements are like piecrusts, made to be broken" is one of their maxims. But they have never taken an aggressive move until they thought that victory was surely in their grasp. Their basic doctrine, their operational code and their historical behavior all confirm this. To be sure, they are ruthless and fanatical and can play a waiting game. Their cat-and-mouse gambit toward Tito shows they will never stop trying to destroy the slightest deviator. Just because they are sane, however, they must never be encouraged to think that the West will not resist. Despite his intent and present disavowal, this is precisely what Russell's "ideal wisdom" encourages them to think. The greater the number of people in the West who accept and proclaim this piece of "ideal wisdom," the greater grows the danger of appeasement and war. I do not fear Khrushchev's insanity but his shrewdness, made all the more formidable by the foolishness of those who underestimate it.

I come now to Russell's "ideal wisdom"—the "purely academic issue" he believes has no practical consequences. Russell's wisdom comes into play, he repeatedly reminds us, only if one side lacks "a modicum of sanity." If the Communists attack, shall we resist and probably go down fighting, or shall we surrender?

In my rejoinder I said: "Here every lover of freedom and of life is on uncertain and tragic ground. One cannot be sure that at the decisive moment the situation will look the same [as now]." I believe I am open to argument on the point, but at present I am not persuaded that a choice of resistance, even if it threatens the probable destruction of the human race, is morally worse than a surrender to those who lack, on Russell's own supposition, even a modicum of sanity. Indeed, if they lack a modicum of sanity I fear all the more the tortures and cruelties they can impose on the living generations—the only ones who count—in weighting the scales of joy and pain, dignity and human degradation whose balance determines basic moral judgment.

Russell impugns my sanity because I do not agree with him. But surely *in principle* everyone can imagine a situation in which to prefer the non-existence of mankind to its continued torture would be to choose a lesser evil. For example, if as a result of some mutational change, a universal and incurable ailment caused men to die in slow agony, would it be wrong to prefer a world without man? I vaguely recall a conversation with Russell or a passage from his writing in which he expressed the view that a world without human beings sometimes seemed preferable to him than one in which bloodthirsty sadists ruled. Such preferences, like my own, may be irrational. I am not so fanatical as to have closed my mind on the subject.

It is at this point that Russell brings in the hope of the future and reminds us that the agony of present generations may be followed by improvement. "Genghis Khan," he wrote, "was quite as bad as Stalin at his worst, but his grandson Kublai Khan was a highly civilized monarch under whom Chinese culture flourished."

In my criticism I did not contest the possibility of improvement. I denied, *what is essential to Russell's argument,* that it was necessarily worth the price. To which Russell retorts with indignation: "[Hook] says that 'the splendor and glory of the court of Kublai Khan were not worth even one of the many pyramids of human skulls his grandfather, Genghis Khan, heaped up.' I had never maintained they were. What I said was that they gave reason for hope that a bad regime might improve—which is a very different thing."

Of course, it is a very different thing. But Russell misses my point which is that it is not enough to sustain his position. For unless it is believed that these possible improvements are worth the price paid in suffering and submission to Genghis Khan, there would be no justification for choosing to endure his tyranny rather than ending human history. It is not enough for Russell to believe that no dark age lasts forever, that after Communism triumphs for some hundreds of years, there may be improvements.

He must also believe that the anticipation of these possible improvements is worth *to the living* the agony and, to use his own words, "the horrors of Communist domination." Otherwise his recommendation makes no sense, even as a proposition in theoretical ethics!

This argument is solid and straightforward: if Russell finds it "slippery," it is only because of the burden of the position he is defending. I am puzzled to explain Russell's failure to see that in order to justify submission to Moscow, he cannot stop short with believing that there may be improvements in the distant future but must also believe that the expectation of these improvements is worth the cruelties and indignities which will follow submission in the present. (*Mutatis mutandis,* the same logic holds in relation to Genghis and Kublai Khan.) I suspect his lapse at this point flows from a natural and creditable reluctance to drain the cup of appeasement to its bitter dregs.

Russell may retort (1) that in time Communism may be followed by much greater glories than those of the court of Kublai Khan, and that *these* glories are worth the price of submission to Moscow; and (2) that, as he actually says, "the worst features of Communism have been developed under the influence of fear and would almost certainly grow less if fear were removed."

Let us consider the second point first. If the worst features of Communism have developed under the influence of fear of the outside world, how account for the fact in the early years, when seven invading armies stood on Soviet soil, political and cultural terror was not as widespread or severe as when the Soviet Union was subsequently free of invaders and at peace? The entire history of Communist Russia (and China!) makes Russell's generalization dubious. Cruelty and arbitrariness are indigenous to the very system of totalitarian Communism, and the fear in the hearts of the Soviet rulers is not so much of the free world as of their own oppressed people. Further, Russell ignores my argument that it is likely that future Titos and Maos and Stalins will war on each other and use the existence of differences in Communist states as pretexts for their organized cruelties. I grant that some things may grow better, but I am not sanguine that the worst features of Communism will grow less, or sufficiently less to justify Russell's recommendation to surrender to universal torture rather than to resist. Perhaps under Communism, in time, greater glories will develop than those of the court of Kublai Khan. But the probability is just as great that greater infamies will also develop.

Russell taxes me with inconsistency where there is none. I criticized the Communist view which cruelly sacrifices existing generations for a glorious future to be enjoyed by the still unborn. To which Russell retorts: "His own position is that it is justified to bury not several generations but *all* future generations, not in order that they may enjoy a glorious future but in order that they may not have any future at all. This is an immeasurable exaggeration of the very fault for which he criticizes the Communists."

This contains a serious misstatement and another logical lapse. The misstatement conceals the fact that I justify my choice of resistance rather than of surrender *only in terms of the experiences of the existing generations,* not future generations. And the ground of my choice is not that existing generations will escape any future but that they will escape a future of torture and infamy which Russell admits will be theirs if they submit to "the horrors of Communism." The error in logic arises from Russell's failure to note that, since on my argument there are no future generations whose desires need be considered, I cannot sensibly be criticized for trying to bury them. I have not returned to the ontology of Plato and the early Russell. My argument is addressed only to the present generations. *They* must make the choice—only *their* desires, wishes, fears and hopes count. This is as far away as anyone can get from the Communist position, Russell to the contrary notwithstanding.

Even more misleading is Russell's statement that I am denying to those who prefer life under Communism, whether in Communist and neutralist countries, freedom to choose the alternative they prefer. I have no quarrel with those who live in Communist countries—only with their dictators who seek to impose the yoke of bondage on other peoples. To say that because I urge resistance to aggression I do not believe in freedom for those who wish to live under Communism, is as absurd as to charge Russell, because he urged resistance to Hitler, with not believing that those who preferred a peaceful life under Fascism should be free to make their choice. Hitler was morally responsible for the fate of the victims of the resistance against him. The rulers of the Kremlin are morally responsible for the consequences of the resistance to their aggression.

Russell's argument would make every rebel in history who believed in resistance to injustice a fanatic who wanted to deprive others of their freedom of choice. Of course, it is the barest tautology that if two choices are mutually exclusive, where one is taken the other cannot be. By the same token, should not those who prefer to *resist* aggression be free to choose the alternative *they* prefer? Russell's choice excludes theirs as much as theirs excludes his.

It is from this tautology that Russell derives the remarkable conclusion that I am guilty of "an extreme form of religious persecution" because, forsooth, resistance to the Kremlin will deprive those who want to live under Communism of their chance to do so. This is a surprising comment from one who, like the rest of us, supported a war against Fascism in which the victims of Allied air raids were deprived of "their freedom to choose survival." Was this "religious persecution"? Was Russell guilty of "religious persecution" in advocating a preventive war against Russia and declaring that the destruction of the whole of Western Europe was not too great a price to pay in order that Communism be wiped out? Would he not have deprived the victims of their freedom to choose survival?

Russell, of course, does not believe in religious persecution. Nor do I. That he can make the charge betrays the atrophy of his sense of proportion.

In my article "A Foreign Policy for Freedom and Survival," I advocated a policy of military disengagement in Central Europe and other troubled areas of the world under certain guarantees. Although I believe we were remiss in not making proper political use of the atom bomb when we enjoyed its monopoly, I have never advocated an aggressive or preventive war. "If we can keep the free world," I wrote, "from falling into the trap set by the Kremlin and preserve peace by increasing its power and readiness, we can then rely upon the processes of education, the force of example, the contagion of free ideas, the gradual osmosis of the great traditions of the West gradually to soften, to liberalize, to round off the edges of the totalitarian regimes of the world until their own people rally their energies to overthrow their oppressors and establish the democratic governments necessary to establish one free world republic."

I am convinced that most of the people behind the Iron Curtain deplore the position taken by Russell in his interview with Alsop and which Russell himself has now modified. Despite this, and his earlier statement that he agrees much more with my article than I think, I am under no illusion that, with all his hedging and tacking, Russell's position on foreign policy is like mine. Granted the need for continuous effort to negotiate a reasonable settlement with the Kremlin, the troublesome questions arise when we ask: If the Communists seize West Berlin, should the free world resist? Or if

West Germany is invaded? Or the rest of Western Europe? Or England? As distinct from Russell, I believe the free world should declare it will resist wherever the Communist world resorts to force, and to declare it in such a way that the Kremlin has no doubts it *will* resist. There will then be no war.

No man can win freedom and peace unless he conquers his fear of death. No nation can preserve its freedom unless it is willing to risk destruction in its defense. To do otherwise is to break faith with those who died to keep it free.

The free society from Pericles to the present has survived because it has valued some things more than survival, because its vision of human excellence, dignity and joy has made some kinds of life unworthy of man. Bertrand Russell is one of the great moulders of the traditions of the free society. In disagreeing with him strongly on a matter of policy, we nonetheless honor the values and visions he has served during a long life and which he has taught us to cherish.

(*Reprinted with permission of the Editor of* The New Leader, *from the issues of April 27, May 26, and July 7, 1958.*)

34 The Intellectual in America

IT IS HARD to define an "intellectual." Although ideally all intellectuals should be intelligent, not only are many intelligent people not "intellectuals," which is as it should be, but unfortunately all too many "intellectuals" seem to lack intelligence.

The "intellectual" is, to borrow a phrase from W. E. Johnson, most comprehensively and least controversially defined as a member of what used to be called "the intelligentsia." He is a person professionally concerned with general ideas and values—their nature, application, and criticism. A politician may be an intellectual if he is more than a machine boss or a disciplined member of a political caucus; in that case he borders on being a statesman. There are obviously few such in America at present, but there is some reason to hope that as the years go by their numbers will increase. All literary men, novelists, poets, dramatists, essayists, editors, and critics are intellectuals by virtue of their calling, some of them obviously only by courtesy judging by their concern with ideas. Teachers, scholars and other denizens of the academy whose writings have more than narrow vocational interest are also intellectuals.

As the rate and quality of literacy grows and as appreciation develops for the simple truth that intelligence is a *sine qua non* for survival in the modern world, we can expect the intellectuals to be held in higher esteem in America. Directly and indirectly it is likely that they will exert more influence on the centers of power even if they cannot share the responsibility for the exercise of that power save as they appraise and criticize it.

The "intellectual" is the natural guardian of quality in the life of mind and the natural critic of shoddy. He is the partisan of the ideal.

That is why, if he is faithful to his calling in the imperfect world and culture in which he lives, he cannot become the poet-laureate of the *status quo*.

Today, as in the decade when Fascism was the chief danger, he must be active on two fronts: against the powerful threat that would destroy, root and branch, the free society which makes his vocation possible, and against the multiple evils within the free society that compromise its ethos and undermine the integrity of free men. This was a common-place when Hitler was knocking at the doors of Western civilization. It required no soul-searching agonies to understand that one could oppose *both* the racial genocide the Nazis practiced and our own racial segregation. This could be done without making an absurd equation between the two, without assuming either a posture of Olympian neutrality towards both or a position of hostility towards both as evils of equal magnitude between which there could be no reasonable order of emphasis or priority. The truth is that the struggle against Hitlerism made more poignant to Americans realization of their own failings and what they owed to those who had been excluded from the democratic community. The defeat of Hitlerism was a signal for a great advance towards political and social equality for all minorities.

What was grasped without difficulty when Fascism challenged the survival of free institutions has become a complex and thorny problem to not a few intellectuals today in face of the challenge of Communist totalitarianism. They are acutely aware of the inequities and vulgarities of American culture which they judge not historically but from the standpoint of a European elite to whom the United States is nothing but "a semi-barbarian superstate of the periphery." So the Greeks might have regarded the Romans. Yet the legacy of Greece was saved for the world not by the Greeks, unable to unite in a genuine common-wealth, not by those elevated spirits who condemned equally the bar-barians of the East and West, but by the Romans who stood firm against the autocracy of Asiatic Byzantinism. Corresponding to "the new fail-ure of nerve" a decade or two ago, one can observe among intellectuals of our decade "a failure of political intelligence."

I cannot understand why American intellectuals should be apologetic about the fact that they are limited in their effective historical choice between endorsing a system of total terror and *critically* supporting our own imperfect democratic culture with all its promises and dangers. For after all within our culture they are not *compelled* to choose whereas in the Soviet world neutrality or even silence is treason. Surely, this should count for something even with those who, although de-pendent upon the protective security of our relatively free culture for their neutralism and cultivation of purity, regard its struggle for survival as a vulgar battle of ideologies. Nor is it clear to me why an appreciation of the values of American life is incompatible with vigorous criticism of its many deficiencies and with determined efforts to enhance both its chances of survival and the quality of its cultural experience by more enlightened domestic and foreign policies. And if there are any seers or prophets among us, let them make their visions known!

The political and moral issues of our time are no different for the intellectual classes, the writers, artists and scholars, than they are for the working classes who recognize that even under the dislocations of our mixed economy, they enjoy more bread and freedom than the working classes anywhere else in the world. If anything, one expects the intellectuals to see even more clearly that the relative autonomy of their craft is threatened by Soviet totalitarianism more completely than by any other social system in history.

I must also confess to some perplexity in understanding laments about the "alienation" of the creative artist in American culture if this means that he faces more obstacles to doing significant work or finding an appreciative audience than was the case fifty or a hundred years ago. Surely, compared with his forebears, he can have no complaint on the score of creature comforts, which he certainly deserves no less than other human beings. The notion circulated in some quarters that university life is the Golgotha of the intellectual spirit is absurd. It seems to me that the creative life in America suffers more from mediocrity than from frustration. Equally bewildering is the view that mass culture or the popular arts constitute a profound menace to the position of American intellectuals. Certainly those who love cream more than their work may drown in it. The only sense I can find in the violent garrulities of Ortega y Gasset is that the mass "kind of man" who threatens the individual, is the man who lurks inside of anyone who fears to be himself. That mass "kind of man" in one form or another has always existed. And he sometimes is present in the man who strives and strains to be different as distinct from one who genuinely feels and thinks differently from his fellows.

There are all kinds of alienations in the world and one can get startling effects by confusing them. Hegel understood by self-alienation the process of dialectical development by which the individual consciousness progresses from innocence to maturity, from the simplicity of bare perception to the richly funded comprehension of a complexly interrelated system. Remove the mystification about the Absolute Self, drop the consolatory, religious overtones about the meaningfulness of the Whole, and what we get in the language of a barbarous literary psychology is an account of the travail of spiritual growth in any culture—not only for the artist but for every human being.

Marx's notion of self-alienation is historically circumscribed and has much less sweep than Hegel's. It applies primarily to the worker who is compelled to labor at something which neither expresses nor sustains his own needs and interests as a person. The unalienated man for Marx is the creative man. He is anyone who, under an inner compulsion, is doing significant work wrestling with a problem or striving to articulate a vision. The artist for Marx is the unalienated man par excellence to the extent that he does not produce *merely* a commodity. Remove the Utopianism of believing that all work in an industrial society can make a call on man's creative capacities, and of imagining that everybody, once a market economy disappears, will be able to do creative work, and what Marx is really saying is not obscure. The more truly human a society is, the more will it arrange its institutions to afford opportunities for creative fulfillment through uncoerced work. Man humanizes himself through work, which in association with others, is the source of speech. Man is dehumanized by *forced* work. There are some echoes of Rousseauistic myth in this and by a strange un-Marxian lapse Marx refers to a society in which there is no forced labor as a more natural society. From this point of view, the workers attending a conveyor belt, feeding a machine, endlessly filing orders or names are far more alienated than those intellectuals who have chosen their vocations and enjoy some freedom in setting their own goals or selecting their tasks.

There is a third conception of alienation popular with some sociologists and Bohemians which is applied to the artist who breaks with the conventions or norms of his family, society, or class. He is pitied and sometimes pities himself because he has no market or patron or reputation on the assumption that this is a necessary consequence of his non-comformity despite the fact that other non-conformists created their own audience and following and feel unalienated in the Marxian sense even when hostile critics ignore or rage against them. This is the most popular conception of the alienated artist in America and the shallowest. Why it is so popular I do not know unless it be that many individuals mistake the indifference of the world or their private creative agonies—which may very well be due to lack of creative capacity or to an ambition altogether incommensurate with their talents—for unerring signs of election to an alienated elite. But all a free culture can do is to provide opportunities for revolt: it cannot guarantee professional success.

No one knows the secret of significant creativity. We do know it cannot be mass produced and that it cannot emerge under conditions of extreme privation. But since the material lot of American artists has improved considerably in the last few decades and since the cultural atmosphere in America is much more receptive to the notion of total dedication to a creative calling—the son's announcement that he refuses to enter business or a profession but wants to be a writer, artist or musician no longer causes a family crisis—I must confess I do not know why the American arts are more anemic than the arts abroad *if* they are. And I suspect that no one else knows. Certainly, American work in science, scholarship and medicine does not lag behind European achievements. The hypothesis that mass culture and the popular arts—the Hollywood trap!—threaten the emergence of a significant culture of vitality and integrity because they constitute a perpetual invitation to a sell-out seems very far-fetched. Unless one is an incurable snob (I am old enough to remember intense discussions by otherwise intelligent people as to whether the cinema is an art), the forms of mass culture and the popular arts should serve as a challenge to do something with them. There are "sell-outs" of course but there are two parties to every "sell-out." The writer who "sells out" to Hollywood or the slicks cannot absolve himself of responsibility on the ground that he wouldn't be able to live as plushily as if he did. Why should he? I shall be accused of saying that I am sentencing artists and writers to starvation. But if scholars can live Renan's life of "genteel poverty" and do important work so can those who don't go to Hollywood.

Finally, I see no specific virtue in the attitude of conformity or non-conformity. The important thing is that it should be voluntary, rooted in considered judgment, an authentic expression of some value or insight for which the individual is prepared to risk something. 'Conformity' or 'non-conformity' are relational terms. Before evaluating them I should like to know *to and with what* a person is conforming or not conforming and *how*. Under the Weimar Republic, Stefan George, Spengler and Hitler were non-conformists: under the Czarist regime Dostoevsky in his most fruitful years was a conformist. To the greatest of men the terms 'conformist' or 'non-conformist' have singularly little relevance—Shakespeare, Milton, Goethe, Plato, Aristotle, Kant, or Dewey.

Particularly inexplicable to me is the broad question of whether the American intellectual should continue the tradition of critical non-conformism. The social function of the American intellectual is to think, and to act in such a way that the results of his thinking are brought to bear upon the great issues of our time. The cardinal attribute of the life of thought—its proper virtue—is the capacity to discriminate, to make relevant distinctions. He is no more un-American when he is intelligently critical of the United States than he is chauvinistic when he is intelligently appreciative. Many American intellectuals are unaware of the extent to which the social climate and objective possibilities for a democratic welfare state have improved in the last twenty years. Some still think of socialism as a good in itself. Having made a religion of a form of economy, they are incapable of learning from experience. They comfort themselves with a superior terminological intransigence in the belief that their sincerity atones for their stupidity. Their opposite numbers now regard socialism as an evil in itself. Socialism is no longer a form of economy for them, but the principle of welfare or social control itself. Like the most orthodox of Marxists they believe that any economy uniquely entails one political way of life. Fortunately, more and more intellectuals are beginning to understand what they could have learned from John Dewey long ago, that democratic process is more important than any predetermined program, and that persons and values are the test of adequate social relations not conversely.

Outside their own immediate craft too many intellectuals are irresponsible, especially in politics. They don't know enough, don't think enough, and are the creatures of fashion. It is sufficient for the majority to believe anything, for them to oppose it. They are too conscious of "public relations." Some are exhibitionists who are always washing their hands in public, Mary Magdalenes making a cult of purity. The lowest form of intellectual life is led by left bank American expatriates who curry favor with Sartrian neutralists by giving them the lowdown on the cultural "reign of terror" (sic!) in America.

Most American intellectuals still do not understand the theory, practice, and tactics of the Communist movement. Because McCarthy made wild and irresponsible charges, too many are inclined to dismiss the Communist danger in its total global impact as relatively unimportant. American intellectuals were more frightened of Franco in 1936 and of Hitler in 1933 than they are of Krushchev today. In 1933 and 1936 they did *not* say that, after all, there were few Fascists in America, fewer Fascists than there ever were of Communists since 1919. As country after country has come under the Soviet knife, concern in the colleges, in literary circles, even scientific quarters has *not* increased. The term "anti-Communist" has not got the same overtones as "anti-Fascist." It is not enough to say that McCarthy and reactionary demagogues have ruined the term "anti-Communist." Why didn't the Communists ruin the term "anti-Fascist"? They were just as vehement in their anti-Fascism as McCarthy was in his anti-Communism and even more irresponsible, because they called men like John Dewey and Norman Thomas "Fascists."

The task of the intellectual is still to lead an intellectual life, to criticize what needs to be criticized in America, without forgetting for a moment the total threat which Communism poses to the life of the free mind. Our own vigilantes and reactionaries are much more like witches and straw scarecrows than are the paid and unpaid agents of the Kremlin who constitute the membership of the Communist Parties in all countries. They can be cleared out of the way by a little courage and a sense of humor. They have nuisance value especially because of their effects abroad.

We face grim years ahead. The democratic West will require the critical support, the dedicated energy and above all, the intelligence, of its intellectuals if it is to survive as a free culture. With the possible exception of the technical arts and their theoretical ancillaries, great creative visions, conforming or non-conforming, can today flourish only in the soil of a free culture. It was not always so. But modern totalitarianism is not the same as ancient absolutisms.

Let the neutralists of the world remember. In the West non-conformists, no matter how alienated, can always win a hearing, even if they do not win a place in the Academy or earn the Order of Merit. In the land of Purges and Brainwashing, the only thing a non-conformist can earn is a bullet in the neck. This is the historical premise of our age whose recognition is binding on all humanists whether they are democratic socialists or civil libertarian conservatives or members of the alienated avant-garde.

INDEX